10651337

THE
BASEBALL
READER

THE BASEBALL READER

Favorites from
**THE FIRESIDE BOOKS
OF BASEBALL**

Edited
by Charles Einstein

BONANZA BOOKS
New York

Major portions of this work originally appeared in *The Fireside Book of Baseball, The Second Fireside Book of Baseball,* and *The Third Fireside Book of Baseball.*

Copyright © MCMLVI, MCMLVIII, MCMLXVIII, MCMLXXX by Charles Einstein
Copyright © renewed 1984, 1986 by Charles Einstein
All rights reserved.

This 1989 edition is published by Bonanza Books,
distributed by Crown Publishers, Inc., 225 Park Avenue South,
New York, New York 10003, by arrangement with Charles Einstein.

Printed and Bound in the United States of America

Library of Congress Cataloging-in-Publication Data

The Baseball reader.

   1. Baseball.   2. Baseball stories.   I. Einstein,
Charles.
GV873.B28   1989   796.357   88-30418
ISBN 0-517-67577-3
h g f e d c b a

Designed by C. Linda Dingler

Grateful acknowledgment is made to the following for permission to reprint previously published material:

The American Mercury Magazine (P.O. Box 73523, Houston, TX): For "The Hell It Don't Curve" by Joseph F. Drury, Jr. Copyright 1953 by American Mercury Magazine, Inc.

Arthur Bugs Baer, Jr.: For "The Crambury Tiger" by Arthur "Bugs" Baer. Copyright 1942 by the Crowell-Collier Publishing Company.

A. S. Barnes & Company: For "Slide, Kelly, Slide" from *Sports Tales and Anecdotes* by Frank G. Menke. Copyright 1953 by Frank G. Menke.

Brandt & Brandt Literary Agents, Inc.: For "Mumford's Pasture Lot" from *Grandfather Stories* by Samuel Hopkins Adams. Copyright © 1955 by Samuel Hopkins Adams.

Heywood Hale Broun: For "1923: New York Yankees 4, New York Giants 2" by Heywood C. Broun. Originally published in New York *World.*

Chicago Sun Times: for "The 1934 All-Star Game" by Carl Hubbell as told to John P. Carmichael; "1938: Chicago Cubs 6, Pittsburgh Pirates 5" by Gabby Hartnett as told to Hal Totten; "1934: St. Louis Cardinals 11, Detroit Tigers 0" by Frankie F. Frisch as told to Ken Smith. Reprinted with permission from Field Enterprises Inc.

The Chronicle Publishing Company: "The Sporting Way" by Stanton Delaplane from *The San Francisco Chronicle.*

Mrs. Bob Considine: For "Mr. Mack" by Bob Considine from *Life* Magazine, July 26, 1948. Copyright 1948 by Time, Inc.

Richard Donovan: For "The Fabulous Satchel Paige" from *Collier's.* Copyright 1953 by the Crowell-Collier Publishing Company.

(continued)

Farrar, Straus & Giroux, Inc.: For "braves 10, giants 9" from *Raising Demons* by Shirley Jackson. Copyright © 1953, 1954, 1956, 1957 by Shirley Jackson.

Estate of Paul Fisher: For "The Spitter" by Paul Fisher. Copyright 1950 by Paul William Fisher.

Fox Chase Agency: For excerpt from *Bang the Drum Slowly* by Mark Harris. Copyright © 1956 by Mark Harris.

Harper & Row, Publishers, Inc.: For an excerpt from *You Can't Go Home Again* by Thomas Wolfe. Copyright 1940 by Maxwell Perkins as Executor; renewed 1968 by Paul Gitlin.

Indiana University Press: For "Polo Grounds" from *Collected Poems of Rolfe Humphries.* Copyright © 1956 by Indiana University Press.

International Creative Management: For a selection from *Papa Hemingway* by A. E. Hotchner. Copyright © 1955, 1959, 1966 by A. E. Hotchner.

Alfred A. Knopf, Inc.: For an excerpt from *The American Language, Supplement Two* by H. L. Mencken. Copyright 1948 by Alfred A. Knopf, Inc.; and for "Hub Fans Bid Kid Adieu," Copyright © 1960 by John Updike. From *Assorted Prose* by John Updike. Originally appeared in *The New Yorker.*

Ann Landers and Field Newspaper Syndicate for "We Can't Afford a Lawyer."

Lippincott & Crowell, Publishers: For an excerpt from *Baseball Has Done It* by Jackie Robinson, edited by Charles Dexter. Copyright © 1964 by Jack R. Robinson and Charles Dexter; and for an excerpt from *For 2¢ Plain* by Harry Golden. Copyright © 1959 by Harry Golden.

Little, Brown and Company: For an excerpt from *God's Country and Mine* by Jacques Barzun. Copyright 1954 by Jacques Barzun; and for "Line-up for Yesterday: An ABC of Baseball Immortals" from *Versus* by Ogden Nash. Copyright 1949 by Ogden Nash.

Lopez Publications: For "The Rocky Road of Pistol Pete" by W. C. Heinz. Copyright © 1958 by Fawcett Publications Inc.; and for "Ty Cobb's Wild, Ten-Month Fight to Live" by Al Stump. Originally published in *True* Magazine.

The Sterling Lord Agency, Inc.: For an excerpt from *A Day in the Bleachers* by Arnold Hano. Copyright © 1955 by Arnold Hano.

Scott Meredith Literary Agency, Inc., on behalf of the Estate of P. G. Wodehouse: For "The Pitcher and the Plutocrat" by P. G. Wodehouse. Published in *Collier's* Magazine, 1910.

MVP Sports, Inc. (and Furman Bisher on behalf of the Estate of Rudy York) for "A Letter to My Son" by Rudy York as told to Furman Bisher; (and Don Hoak and Myron Cope) for "The Day I Batted Against Castro" by Don Hoak and Myron Cope. Copyright 1953 by Macfadden Publications, Inc.; (and Bob Feller) for "How I Throw the Slider" by Bob Feller. Copyright 1953 by Macfadden Publications, Inc.; (and the Estate of John Lardner) for "The Unbelievable Babe Herman" by John Lardner. Copyright 1949 by Macfadden Publications, Inc.; (and Edward J. Acton, Inc., and Ed Linn) for "The Kid's Last Game" by Ed Linn. Copyright © 1961 by Macfadden-Bartell Corporation. All reprinted from *Sport Magazine.*

New Directions Publishing Corp.: For "The Origin of Baseball" from *Collected Poems* by Kenneth Patchen. Copyright 1942 by Kenneth Patchen.

New York Daily News: For "Brooklyn Dodgers 3, New York Yankees 2" by Dick Young from *New York Daily News,* 1947.

The New York Public Library: For "Excelsior Baseball Club By-Laws" #9, 10, 11, 13, & 14.

The New York Times Company: For "1924: Washington Senators 4, New York Giants 3" by M. W. Corum; "1926: St. Louis Cardinals 3, New York Yankees 2" by James R. Harrison; (May 3, 1939) "2,130" by James P. Dawson; "1941: New York Yankees 4, Cleveland Indians 3" by John Drebinger; "1977: Reggie: How Far Did That Last Homer Go?" by Dave Anderson. Reprinted from *The New York Times.* Copyright 1924, 1926, 1939, 1941, 1977 by The New York Times Company.

Harold Ober Associates, Inc.: For an excerpt from *Hello Towns* by Sherwood Anderson. Copyright 1929 by Sherwood Anderson. Published by Horace Liveright 1929. Reprinted by permission of the Harold Ober Associates, Inc.

Random House, Inc.: For an excerpt from *Portnoy's Complaint* by Philip Roth. Copyright © 1967, 1968, 1969 by Philip Roth.

San Francisco Examiner: For "Casey at the Bat" by Ernest L. Thayer.

Charles Scribner's Sons: For "Alibi Ike" from *How to Write Short Stories* by Ring Lardner. Copyright 1915 by Curtis Publishing Company; renewal copyright 1943 by Ellis A. Lardner.

Vin Scully and the Los Angeles Dodgers: For "1965, Los Angeles Dodgers 1, Chicago Cubs 0," simultaneous broadcast of the Sandy Koufax perfect game.

Simon & Schuster, a Division of Gulf & Western Corp.: For "Game Six, Game Six" from *Five Seasons* by Roger Angell. Copyright © 1972, 1973, 1974, 1975 by Roger Angell. First published in *The New Yorker.*

Red Smith: For "1951: New York Giants 5, Brooklyn Dodgers 4." Copyright 1951 by The New York Herald Tribune Inc.

Sports Illustrated: For "Mr. Rickey and The Game" by Gerald Holland. Copyright © 1955 by Time Inc.

Mrs. James Thurber: For "You Could Look It Up" from *My World—and Welcome to It* by James Thurber, published by Harcourt Brace Jovanovich. Copyright 1942 by James Thurber, renewed 1970 by Helen W. Thurber and Rosemary T. Sauers. Originally published in *The Saturday Evening Post.*

Vanguard Press, Inc.: For an excerpt from *Father and Son* by James T. Farrell. Copyright 1940, renewed 1967 by James T. Farrell.

Viking Penguin, Inc.: For "Hometown Piece for Messrs. Alston and Reese" from *The Complete Poems of Marianne Moore.* Copyright © 1956 by Marianne Moore; and for "They're Afraid to Come Out" from *Can't Anybody Here Play This Game?* by Jimmy Breslin. Copyright © 1963 by James Breslin.

The Washington Post: For "1956: New York Yankees 2, Brooklyn Dodgers 0" by Shirley Povich. Copyright © 1956 by The Washington Post.

Contents

Introduction

At New York in 1977, Reggie hit three home runs in a game to win the World Series. At St. Louis, half a century earlier, the Babe hit three home runs in a game to win the World Series. At Mudville, another half century before that, again the air was shattered by the force of slugger's blow. Minor problem there: Casey failed to connect. But all three men shared the same reputation, and all three—Reggie and the Babe and the mighty Casey—prowl the pages of this book, direct witness to baseball's unique and magnificent disregard for the passage of time.

It was that selfsame factor that animated the "Fireside Library"— *The Fireside Book of Baseball,* published in 1956; *The Second Fireside Book of Baseball,* published in 1958; and *The Third Fireside Book of Baseball,* published in 1968—which gained gratifying audience and acclaim. One appraisal among others said the three Fireside books might well be "baseball literature's greatest monument." That's the good news. The bad news is that production costs of the seventies forced the books out of print; and in the remarkably short period of time since, they have acquired genuine collector's-item status, the boxed sets being today unobtainable almost at any price. As editor of the Firesides, I found myself put in mind of Abraham Lincoln's story of the miscreant who was tarred, feathered, and ridden out of town on a rail. "If it wasn't for the honor of the thing," the man said, "I'd just as soon walk."

But a new opportunity arose. It was the idea to publish a single volume that would be essentially a compendium drawn from all three Fireside books, an abundant sampling of their contents: the great moments, the great stars, the great writers. (It is no accident that time and again, those three elements coincide. As William Styron has noted, great writing "comes up" to great subjects, and it is the American experience that baseball has attracted more great writing than all other sports combined.) There would of course be some updating in this new book, just as was found in the second and third Fireside books: the hero of *Portnoy's Complaint,* playing center field on a psychiatrist's couch, didn't achieve publication till after the third Fireside, so you won't find him there. But you will find him here, in expression of yet one more great American writer's not-so-secret love affair with baseball. So welcome now also Philip Roth to these pages.

Yet even the updating is almost incidental. Baseball not only ignores the passage of time, it literally defies it. Not even television has affected it in any meaningful way. "You can't put a diamond in a box," Tom Boswell observed, and indeed not even the commercial breaks have dented the structure of this game; coming as they do when the teams change sides or a pitcher is replaced, they simply occupy what have always been the natural breaks in the action. True, television has given us Howard Cosell, who during the 1979 World Series treated viewers repeatedly to his mystifying dictum that a pitch was a "called ball." But such reporting has always been part of the game. One account I have seen from years past says, "In the fifth inning the Red Sox pulled a triple play with nobody out." According to another vintage story of another game, "Two runners scored on the play, one of them all the way from second." Is the ability to confuse therefore an integral part of the game itself? You bet your sweet boopie it is. If you have reservations on that score, turn to the page in this book where Casey Stengel commences his testimony before the august Subcommittee on Antitrust and Monopoly of the Committee of the Judiciary of the United States Senate. After that, I can only suggest, school is out. And if also in these pages you find Fidel Castro on the pitcher's mound, bear with that too. Several major league teams were seriously scouting him.

It falls that way. One of the entries in this book is exactly 19 words long. Another runs somewhere around 16,000 words, maybe more. The format is the Fireside format, with the selections printed in alphabetical order by author, without regard for category or chronology (what respect does baseball have for either of those?), although I do supply, where the need is indicated, a few prefatory words in those directions.

One of the two moving forces that brought this book, *The Baseball Reader,* into existence was, of course, the success of the Fireside books, and that is why, even with updating here and there, the original format still obtains. The other force constituted the thought that over and above the commercial success of the Firesides, this one would be just as much fun to read and reread. And maybe that would be because this book, like the Firesides, reflects baseball most precisely in the way it takes its occasional walk on the wild side. If you are looking for Ring Lardner's "Alibi Ike," the most famous baseball story ever written, you'll find it here. But you'll also find Paul Fisher's never-published story "The Spitter." If you want Bobby Thomson's "homer heard round the world," you've got it. But you'll also find a player named L'n'h's'r, who is known to have played in place of Ty Cobb—except there is no record of L'n'h's'r's real name and, as Bugs Baer points out, his wife probably doesn't believe him to this day.

A final note. One piece which appeared in *The Third Fireside Book of Baseball,* and which is reproduced again here in these pages, drew the only two negative reader responses over the course of all three Fireside books. That piece is Vin Scully's radio account of the last half of the ninth inning of Sandy Koufax's perfect game against the Cubs. Both objections went to the same point, accusing me of having edited the thing with an eye toward improving its grammar. No broadcaster, the letter writers said, could conceivably speak that brilliantly *ad lib.* The letter writers are right: such presentation is improbable in the extreme. But the truth is that Scully's account, as you will find it here, is taken verbatim from the untouched tape recording of his broadcast.

So as editor, I did no editing, and that too is what went on here. The game is in these pages. Nobody has to edit it. It doesn't have a clock on it. The scoring is done by the team that doesn't have the ball. Former U.S. Senator Eugene McCarthy of Minnesota pointed out that indeed baseball is "forever resilient." That is true, and most of all it means something else that is equally true: baseball comes with the springtime.

Charles Einstein

THE
BASEBALL
READER

SOMEBODY should have thought to ask Franklin P. Adams, ace panelist in the halcyon radio days of "Information Please," to name three poems in which three proper names appear in a single line. I can think of four. One is "Wynken, Blinken and Nod." The other three are baseball poems, and Mr. Adams wrote one of them himself. Tom Meany said that the following, which appeared in the *New York Globe* in 1908, "has retained a baseball immortality which is without precedent."

Baseball's Sad Lexicon

FRANKLIN P. ADAMS

These are the saddest of possible words,
  Tinker-to-Evers-to-Chance.
Trio of Bear Cubs fleeter than birds,
  Tinker-to-Evers-to-Chance.
Ruthlessly pricking our gonfalon bubble,
Making a Giant hit into a double,
Words that are weighty with nothing but
    trouble.
  Tinker-to-Evers-to-Chance.

Baseball in
Mumford's Pasture Lot

SAMUEL HOPKINS ADAMS

A SMART SINGLE RIG drew up to the hitching post of No. 52 South Union Street as we three boys approached. Out of it stepped a short, red-faced, dapper man who secured his horse and then addressed us.

"Does Mr. Myron Adams live here?"

"Yes, sir," John said.

"We're just going in to see him," Sireno added. "He's our grandfather."

"Well, you can wait," the stranger said. "I've got private business with him."

"If you're trying to sell him a colored enlargement of a photograph . . ." John began but got no further.

"I ain't," the caller interrupted. "My name is Phillips and I represent the Rochester Baseball Club."

"There isn't any," I said glumly.

It was cause for humiliation to every right-thinking inhabitant of the city, young and old, that in the spring of the baseball-mad year of 1879, Rochester was represented by no professional team whatever.

"There will be if I can sell fifty of these here tickets, good for the whole season and only ten dollars," Mr. Phillips said. "D'you think he'll pony up? How's he on baseball?"

"He wouldn't know a Dollar Dead from a Young America if it hit him in the snoot," Reno answered. The Dollar Dead was the standard amateur ball, the Young America the twenty-five-cent junior favorite.

"I'll have a crack at him anyway," Mr. Phillips decided. He vanished into the cottage, and in a few minutes we heard Grandfather, in his deep and resonant voice, putting an end to the interview. "What?" he cried. "Money? To witness what should be a *gentleman's* pastime? Nonsense! Fustian! Good day to you!"

The crestfallen visitor came out, silently climbed into his buggy, and drove away. We went in to pay our duty call.

A week later, the three of us ran upon Mr. Phillips again, this time in Livingston Park, and heard from him tidings of great joy. In spite of Grandfather's recalcitrance, Rochester was to have its team. Mr. Asa T. Soule, the patent-medicine magnate, had just come forward with an offer to finance a club out of his private pocket, provided it should bear the name of Hop Bitters, the cure-all he manufactured.

The news spread fast and, as the opening of the season drew near, Rochester glowed with restored pride. In its first game the new club swamped an amateur nine, fourteen to six.

Next, an exhibition game was scheduled against Rochester's ancient and bitter rival, the Buffalos, who were in the National League and therefore supposedly a cut above us. It was to be the event of the year, and the admission was fifty cents. John, being ten years old and our senior member, put the painful question to Reno and me.

"Where are we going to get half a dollar apiece?"

"Grandpa Adams," I suggested doubtfully.

"In your mind, baby mine!" Reno said, using the most emphatic negation of the time.

"What other chance have we got?" I asked. Nobody had an answer. Fifty cents was unthinkably hard for a small boy to come by in those days. Grandfather was our only hope.

In preparation for the desperate attempt upon his purse, we all three devoted the next week or so to attending him with great assiduity. We mowed his lawn. We weeded the vegetable patch. We suffered errands gladly. When but two days remained before the game, we decided the time had come. We washed our hands and brushed our hair, and since none of us coveted the honor of putting the momentous question, I plucked three timothy heads for the purpose of drawing lots.

"Shortest straw pulls the skunk's tail," I said. This was formula; no disrespect was intended.

John drew the short one, and, led by him, we went to face our grandfather. John opened cautiously, speaking of the importance of the coming event to Rochester and the Hop Bitters Club. "You know, Grandpa, our team's named for the medicine," he said brightly.

The old gentleman glanced at the mantel, where stood a dark-amber bottle containing the spirituous and inspiriting "Invalid's Friend & Hope."

"Why, yes," he said. "A superior restorative. Very comforting to the system," a sentiment shared by thousands of the old gentleman's fellow teetotalers.

"It's a dandy ball team," Reno gloated.

"I assume that you refer to its costume?" Grandfather said coldly. He did not countenance slang on our lips.

"Yes, sir," Reno agreed hastily. "You ought to see their uniforms."

"I am willing to believe that they present a macaroni appearance," the old gentleman said. "But what is the precise connection between this remedy and the projected contest?"

"Mr. Soule is giving the money for the club," John explained.

"Mr. Asa T. Soule? I was not aware that he had sportive proclivities."

"Oh, he's not really a sporting man," John hastened to disclaim. "No, sir! He—he's quite religious. Why, he won't have a player on his team who ever played on Sunday."

I saw that Grandfather, a strict Sabbatarian, was impressed. "They've got a rule against Sunday games in the National League," I said, opportunely recalling an item in the *Democrat & Chronicle.*

"Baseball is a very Christian game, sir," John added.

"I daresay, I daresay," the old gentleman conceded. "But it is not, by all accounts, what it was in my day. When I first came here, the Rochester Baseball Club met four afternoons a week. We had fifty members. That was in 1827."

"I play first base on the Livonia Young Eagles," Reno said eagerly. "Where did you play, sir?"

"In Mumford's pasture lot, off Lake Avenue."

"Reno means what position, Grandpa," I explained.

"Batter, for choice," said the old gentleman.

"You couldn't bat all the time," Reno demurred.

"No," Grandfather said. "But I preferred to. I frequently hit the ball over the fence."

"When your side was in the field, where did you play?" John asked.

"Wherever I thought the ball most likely to be batted, naturally," the alumnus of Mumford's pasture lot replied, manifestly annoyed at the stupidity of the question.

"That's a funny kind of a game," Reno muttered.

"I see nothing humorous in it," Grandfather retorted. "The cream of Rochester's Third Ward ruffleshirts participated in the pastime."

"Lots of the nicest boys in town go to baseball games now," I said hopefully.

"Well, well." Our grandfather's deep accents were benevolent. "I see no reason why you should not attend. You are old enough to go by yourselves, I suppose."

"It isn't that exactly, Grandpa," John said. "You see, sir—"

"It costs money to get in," Reno blurted.

"So I was informed by the person with the inflamed nose," said Grandfather dryly.

"Only fifty cents," John said with admirable casualness; then he added, "We thought, sir, that perhaps you would like to come along with us and see how they play it now, just for once."

There was a breathless pause. Then Grandfather said, "Fetch me the emergency cashbox from the desk."

Hardly able to believe our ears, we fell over one another to obey.

During the next forty-eight hours, John, Reno and I debated long and seriously as to whether we should brief Grandfather on modern baseball, which he was about to see for the first time. All of us were, of course, experts, although we had never seen a professional game. We knew the rules and the etiquette of the diamond and could have passed perfect examinations on the quality and record of every wearer of a Hop Bitters uniform. Reno and I were for giving Grandfather the benefit of our erudition, but John outargued us. Older generations, he pointed out, did not take kindly to instruction from younger.

"He'd just tell us that he played the game before we were born," he said.

On the great day, Grandfather and the three of us arrived early at Hop Bitters Park and found good places in the fifth row directly back of the plate. Before our enchanted eyes there stretched the greensward of the diamond bounded by the base paths. It was close-cut, but the outfield was practically in a state of nature, its grass waving gently in the breeze. We had heard that the Buffalo manager had entered a protest against the outfield's unmown state, complaining that he had not brought his players all the way to Rochester to have them turned out to pasture.

The stand filled up promptly. There must have been as many as three hundred people present, mostly of the prosperous classes. Mr. Mudge, the undertaker, and Mr. Whittlesey, the Assistant Postmaster, took seats in front of us and were presently joined by Mr. Toogood, the

Troup Street livery-stable man. Two clerks from Glenny's China Empo-
rium crowded past us, while on the aisle side the manager of Reynolds
Arcade took his place, accompanied by Professor Cook, the principal and
terror of No. 3 School. Back of us sat a red-necked, hoarse-voiced canal-
man. Mr. Mudge addressed our grandfather.

"A pleasure and a surprise to see you here, Mr. Adams."

"The young must have their day," Grandfather replied amiably.
"Maxima debetur puero reverentia, you know."

"Yes, sir; I don't doubt it for a minute," the liveryman said earnestly.
"I hear those Buffalos are tough."

"We can lick 'em," I said loyally.

"Rochester boasted a superior club in my day, also," Grandfather
said.

"Did you play on it, Mr. Adams?" inquired Professor Cook.

"I did, sir, for two seasons."

"I assume that the game as then played differs from the present
form."

"You are justified in your assumption, sir," said Grandfather, who
then entered upon an informative discourse regarding the baseball of
1827.

The play at Mumford's pasture lot, he set forth, was open to all fifty
active members of the club. The pitchers, who were ex officio the captains, chose up sides. Twelve to a team was considered a convenient
number, but there might be as many as fifteen. A full turnout of members
would sometimes put three teams in the field. Mr. Mudge expressed the
belief that this must result in overcrowding. Where did they all play?

Pitcher, catcher and baseman, Grandfather said, remained in their
positions. The basemen stood touching their bases with at least one foot
until the ball was hit. The remainder of the out team formed a mobile
defense, each man stationing himself where he foresaw the best opportunity of making catches. Mr. Toogood wished to know what the third team
did while two were in the field. It waited, the veteran explained. At the
close of each inning, when three batters had been put out—whether on
flies, fouls, or by being touched or hit with the ball—the runs were totted
up and the side with the lower score was supplanted by the third team.
This continued until the hour agreed upon for stopping, which was usually sunset. Then the team with the largest total was adjudged the winner.

"Sounds like three-old-cat gone crazy," Reno muttered in my ear.

Further elucidation of the baseball of Grandfather's day was cut
short by a shout of "Here they come!" as, amidst loyal clamor, the
home team strode forth in neat gray uniforms, the name of the spon-
soring nostrum scarlet across their breasts. They were a terrifically
masculine lot, with bulging muscles and heavy whiskers. Eagerly we
boys identified our special heroes, having often trailed them through

the streets to the ball-park entrance. "That's Meyerle, the first base," John said. "He can jump six feet in the air and catch the ball with his left hand."

"The little, dumpy one is Burke," said Mr. Toogood. "He's shortstop. You oughta see him handle daisy-cutters! Oh, my!"

"McGunnigle, our right fielder, batted pretty near three hundred with Buffalo last year," Mr. Mudge told Grandfather proudly.

"Three hundred runs?" Grandfather asked with evident skepticism.

The reply was drowned by the loudest shout of all. "There he comes! Tinker! Tinker!" A hundred voices chorused, "What's the matter with Tinker!" and three hundred antiphonal howls responded, "HE'S ALL RIGHT!"

The canaller leaned over and spoke confidentially in Grandfather's ear. "You watch that fellow Tinker, Mister. If a high fly goes out to left field, he'll git under it and do the prettiest back flip ever you seen before he catches it. You wouldn't see nothing like that in the League. Used to be a circus man."

"I shall make it a point to observe him," Grandfather said.

Out came the enemy at a carefree trot. They were even more muscular-looking than our heroes and sported whiskers at least as luxuriant. They lined up near the plate, faced the stand, and saluted the crowd grimly, fingers to the peaks of their green caps. We boys joined lustily in the chorus of opprobrious hoots that was the response. A man in street clothes appeared and took a stand a yard behind the catcher, who stood five yards back of the plate.

"On which side does that person play?" Grandfather asked.

"He doesn't play," Mr. Mudge answered. "He's the umpire. He makes the decisions."

"In our game, we had no need of such intervention," Grandfather said. "If a point of dispute arose, the captains consulted and came to a composition."

"Suppose they disagreed?" Professor Cook suggested.

"Then, sir, they skied a copper for heads or tails and abode by arbitrament of the coin, like gentlemen and Corinthians," Grandfather replied. He turned his attention to the scene below. "Why is the tall man throwing the ball at the short man?" he inquired.

"That's our pitcher, Critchley, soopling his arm up," Mr. Toogood said.

Grandfather frowned. "That is *throwing,* not pitching," he said. "He should keep his arm down."

"He's only got to keep it as low as his waist," Reno said.

The old gentleman shook his head obstinately. "Knuckles should be below the knee, not the waist. A highly improper procedure."

The Hop Bitters team had now taken their positions and were standing, crouched forward, hands upon knees, in the classic posture. A burly

Buffalo player stalked to the plate, rang his bat upon it, and described threatening arcs in the air.

"High ball," he barked at the umpire.

The umpire shouted to the pitcher, "The batsman calls for a high ball."

Grandfather addressed the universe. "What in Tophet is this?"

We boys were glad to enlighten him. "He wants a pitch between his shoulder and his belt," John said.

"If he'd called for a low ball, it'd have to be between his belt and his knee," Reno added.

"Do you mean to say that he can choose where the pitch is to come?" Grandfather asked incredulously.

"Yes, sir. And if it doesn't come there, it's a ball, and if he gets eight balls, he can take his base," I said.

"I should admire to bat in such circumstances," said Grandfather.

"Maybe it wouldn't be so easy," Reno said. "Critchley's got a jim-dandy curve."

"Curve?" asked the old gentleman. "What may that be?"

"Outcurve or incurve," Reno told him. "It starts like this, then it goes like this or like this—sorta bends in the air—and whiff! One strike!"

"Bends in the air!" An indulgent smile appeared on Grandfather's visage. "These young folk will accept any absurdity," he said to Professor Cook.

"Some do hold it to be an optical illusion," the principal said diplomatically.

"Certainly," Grandfather said. "Anything else would be contrary to the laws of God and nature. Let me hear no more of such fahdoodle," he concluded sternly, turning his back upon Reno.

The first inning was uneventful, as were the second and third. Pitcher Critchley's optical illusions and those of the opposing pitcher were uniformly and dully successful. Grandfather fidgeted and commented sharply upon the torpor of the proceedings.

"Lackadaisy-dido!" he said. "Why does not someone hit the ball?"

"A couple of goose eggs is nothing, Grandpa," John said. "Just let our team once get a start and you'll see."

The last of the fourth inning supplied a momentary stir. A high foul came down just in front of us, and the Buffalo catcher raced after it. The ball slithered from his outstretched fingers. We boys shrieked with delight. He glared at us and Grandfather addressed him kindly.

"Young man, that was ill-judged. You would have been well advised to wait and take it on the first bounce."

We held our collective breaths, but the wrath died out of the up-turned face.

"Look, Mister," the catcher said, earnestly argumentative, "that ball was a twister. How'd I know where it would bound?"

The canaller back of us raised a jeering voice. "Butterfingers! Whyncha catch it in your cap?"

"You can't catch a ball in your cap any more," John said to the canaller. "It's in this year's rules."

"Back to the berm, fathead!" the catcher added.

The umpire walked up, lifting an authoritative hand. "No conversation between players and spectators," he snapped, and the game was resumed.

Later, there was a considerable delay when a foul sailed over the fence. Both teams went outside to search for the ball, and Grandfather took the occasion to expatiate upon the superiority of the old-time game.

"Our Saturdays," he said, "were very gala affairs. Ladies frequently attended and refreshments were served."

"Did you have uniforms, Grandpa?" I asked.

"Uniforms? We had no need of them. We removed our broadcoats, hitched our braces, and were prepared."

John said, "Our nine has militia caps with brass buttons."

"Fabricius Reynolds played catcher in a canaller's tall castor," Grandfather recalled. "It was of silky beaver, gray, with a picture of the *Myron Holley* passing through Lock Twenty-three painted on the front. Very bunkum."

"I've got a fifteen-cent Willow Wand with 'Home Run' on it in red letters," Reno said proudly.

"Hamlet Scrantom's bat was of polished black walnut with his initials on a silver plate," the old gentleman went on. "He was a notorious batsman."

The quest for the lost ball was eventually abandoned, Mr. Soule reluctantly tossed out a new one, the umpire called "Play ball, gents!" and the dull succession of runless innings continued. Then, in the opening half of the sixth, with two Buffalos out and two on base, a break came. A towering fly to left field brought a yelp of anticipatory delight from the admirers of the accomplished Tinker. Fleet of foot, he got beneath the ball while it was still high in air. His back flip was a model of grace and exactitude. Down came the ball into his cupped and ready hands—and broke through. Amid howls of dismay, he chased it, scooped it up, and threw it home. It went four feet above the catcher's reach, and the Buffalo runners galloped merrily in.

"Boggle-de-botch!" Grandfather exclaimed.

John plucked at his sleeve. "I want to go home," he said brokenly.

"Do not show yourself such a milksop," the old gentleman said. "How far is our own club behind?"

"Three runs," John groaned.

"And there's another," I added, almost in tears, as the Buffalo shortstop sent the ball over the left-field fence.

"Pooh!" said Grandfather. "Four runs is not an insuperable advantage. Why, I once saw Hamlet Scrantom bat in more than that at one stroke."

We stared at him. "How could he, Grandpa?" John asked. "Even if there were three men on base—"

"There were. I was one of them."

"—that would be only four runs."

"Seven, in this instance," the old gentleman said cheerfully. "Hamlet knocked the ball into a sumac thicket, and we continued to run the bases until it was found and returned."

From then on, the Hop Bitters were a sad spectacle. They stumbled and bumbled in the field, and at bat, as the embittered Reno said, they couldn't have hit a rotten punkin with the thill of a four-horse bob. On their side, the enemy fell upon Pitcher Critchley's offerings with dire effect. They dropped short flies over the basemen's heads. They slashed swift daisy-cutters through the impotent infield. They whacked out two-baggers and three-baggers with the nonchalance of assured victory. Grandfather assayed the situation.

"The Buffalos appear to have the faculty of placing their strokes where the Rochesters are not," he said sagely, a comment later paralleled by Willie Keeler's classic recipe, "Hit 'em where they ain't."

We boys and the Rochester rooters around us became silent with gloom. Only Grandfather maintained any show of interest in the proceedings. He produced a notebook from the pocket of his ceremonial Prince Albert coat and, during what was left of the game, wrote in it busily. We were too depressed even to be curious. It was a relief when the agony ended, with a pop fly to the pitcher.

"Three out, all out," the umpire announced. "The score is Buffalos eleven, Hop Bitters nothing. A game will be played in this park . . ."

But we had no heart in us to listen.

We went back to Grandfather's cottage, and over a consolatory pitcher of raspberry shrub in the sitting room he delivered his verdict.

"The game is not without merit," he said thoughtfully, "but I believe it to be susceptible of improvement."

Surprisingly, the Hop Bitters nine beat both Worcester and Washington in the following fortnight. On the strength of their improvement, a return game with Buffalo was scheduled for August, and we boys resumed what Grandfather would have called our "officiousness" at Union Street; we were sedulous in offers to mow, to weed, to fetch and carry. On the last Saturday in July, when a less important game, with Syracuse, was on the card, we found the front door locked and our stepgrandmother out back, tending her hollyhocks.

"Where's Grandpa?" I asked.

"You'd never guess," the old lady said with a twinkle.

"Gone canalling," John surmised.

"Mr. Adams is attending the baseball game, if you please," his wife said, "and no more thought of the fifty cents expense than if it was so many peppercorns. This is the second time since he took you boys. I do believe he has ideas."

Grandfather did, indeed, have ideas. We learned of them later. The notes made while the Buffalos were swamping the wretched Hop Bitters were the groundwork of a comprehensive plan which turned up among his papers after his death. It was a design for the betterment of baseball and was addressed to Mr. Soule, the Hop Bitters Baseball Club and the Citizens of Rochester, New York. A prologue, which still seems to me to have its points, introduced it.

The purport and intent of the game of baseball, as I apprehend, is to afford healthful exercise to the participants and harmless entertainment to the spectators. In its present apathetic and supine form it fulfills neither desideratum. A scant dozen runs for an afternoon's effort is a paltry result, indeed. I have seen twice that number achieved in a single inning when the game was in its prime. I therefore have the honor, sir, to lay before you a prospectus for the rejuvenescence of the pastime and its reclamation from the slough of inertia and monotony wherein it is engulfed as practiced in your ball park.

The plan provided for an extra shortstop between first and second bases and two additional outfielders to take care of long flies. But the really revolutionary proposal dealt with the pitching. The expert of Mumford's pasture lot approved of one innovation he had witnessed, the right of the batter to call his ball. But this did not go far enough. Grandfather's rule proscribed the pitcher from "any motion or pretense delusive of or intended to delude the eye of the batter."

"Such practice," he wrote, "savors of chicanery and is subversive of true, Corinthian sportsmanship." So much for curves!

Whether Mr. Soule ever received the memorial I don't know. Certainly he did not act upon it. A Rochester team took the field in the following spring with the usual complement of nine players and Grandfather never went to another ball game.

--------------------- SPOT REPORTING ---------------------

AT ONE POINT during the 1977 season, Reggie Jackson was quoted as having made a remark that disparaged his Yankee teammate Thurman Munson. "Munson, naturally, was outraged," Dave Anderson of *The New York Times* would later recall. "Then the Jackson-Martin feud was there on a Saturday-afternoon televised game for the nation to see. Martin benched Jackson in mid-inning for allegedly loafing on a looper that became a double. They almost had a fight in the dugout. Not long after that, Reggie suggested we have a drink after a game.

"'I need somebody to talk to,'" he said.

"We went out for a drink again a few weeks later. At the time, both conversations were off the record. But when I got home, I made notes on what Reggie had talked about. I've learned that, sooner or later, what is said off the record often becomes on the record. And if that happened in this situation, I wanted the quotes to be accurate. The night he emerged as the World Series hero, I asked him if, in order to put his accomplishment in perspective, I could now write what he told me when he was discouraged. He agreed."

What resulted was the following remarkable account, made even more poignant today by the death of Munson in the crash of his small plane in 1979.

1977: Reggie

DAVE ANDERSON

NEARLY THREE HOURS after his three home runs had won the World Series for the Yankees and redemption for himself, Reggie Jackson, like almost everyone else, appeared in awe of what he had accomplished. "There's a part of me I don't know," he was saying softly at his locker. "There's the ballplayer in me who responds to all that pressure. I'm not sure I hit three home runs but the ballplayer in me did."

And above all his complex parts, Reggie Jackson is a ballplayer. When he took nearly $3 million from the Yankees, most people scoffed that he wasn't worth it. He even agreed he wasn't worth it. But he's worth it now. No matter what he does from now on is a bonus. What he did Tuesday night put Reggie Jackson up there with Muhammad Ali winning back the heavyweight title in Zaire, up there with Joe Namath and the Jets winning Super Bowl III, up there with Tom Seaver and the Mets winning the 1969 World Series, but to appreciate how the "part of me I don't know" put Reggie Jackson up there, it is necessary to remember how another part, his sensitive ego, put Reggie Jackson down so that he might ascend.

"I got to get dressed," he was saying now. "I told some people I'd meet them at Seventy-sixth and Third."

In that same East Side area, at a sidewalk table at Arthur's Court in July, he was sipping white wine and saying, "I'm still the straw that stirs the drink. Not Munson, not nobody else on this club."

All the other Yankees had dressed and departed Tuesday night except for Thurman Munson, who was on his way out now.

"Hey, coon," called the catcher, grinning. "Nice goin', coon."

Reggie Jackson laughed and hurried over and hugged the captain.

"I'm goin' down to that party here in the ballpark," Thurman Munson said, grinning again. "Just white people but they'll let you in. Come on down."

"I'll be there," Reggie Jackson said. "Wait for me."

"I got to make myself go to the ballpark," he said in July. "I don't want to go."

"You'll change your mind," somebody told him.

"I don't want to change. I've closed my mind. Remember the thing in Boston," he said, referring to his dugout confrontation with Billy Martin in Fenway Park, *"the next day we had a meeting in Gabe Paul's suite and Billy challenged me. He stood over me and said, 'I'll make you fight me, boy.' But there was no way I was going to fight him. I'm two hundred and fifteen pounds, he's almost fifty years old. I win the fight, but I lose."*

In the manager's office half an hour earlier, Reggie Jackson and Billy Martin had finished a TV interview together when the slugger overheard the manager talking about punching somebody.

"Anybody fights you, Skip," Reggie Jackson said, "he's got to fight both of us."

"And anybody who fights you," Billy Martin said, "got to fight the both of us."

"We can't win this way," he said in July. "The Red Sox can hammer. We got nobody who can hammer except me. I should be batting third or clean-up, not sixth. I always hit third or clean-up."

"How far did that last homer go?" the clean-up hitter asked.

"I figured it to be about four hundred and fifty feet," a sportswriter said.

"Make it four hundred and seventy-five, it sounds better," the clean-up hitter said, laughing. "I hit that one off a knuckler, the first two off fast balls. The general consensus on how to pitch to me is hard and in. On the first one, I knew [Burt] Hooton would pitch me there, but I had an inkling I'd hit one. As soon as they brought in [Elia] Sosa, I got on the phone to Stick [Gene Michael, the Yankee scout] upstairs and asked him about Sosa, because Sosa popped me up with a fast ball in spring training. Stick told me he throws hard stuff—fast ball, slider, good curve. I hit another fast ball. I hit the second one even better than I hit the third, the one off [Charley] Hough's knuckler. Brooks Robinson taught me how to hit a knuckler. Just time the ball."

"Hough said that knuckler didn't move much," somebody said.

"It didn't," Reggie Jackson said, "until I got hold of it."

"I should've signed with the Padres," he said in July. "I'd be happy there. Or with the Dodgers."

"Did you hear," Reggie Jackson was told, "what Steve Garvey said —that after your third homer, he applauded in his glove?"

"What a great player Steve Garvey is, what a great man," Reggie Jackson said. "He's the best all-around human being in baseball. My one regret about not playing with the Dodgers is not being around Steve Garvey, but I got a security blanket here, Fran Healy [the Yankees' bullpen catcher]. Before the game he told me I was swinging the bat good."

"I don't need baseball," he said in July, "I'm a businessman. That means as much to me as baseball. I don't need cheers."

"When you hit the third one," a visitor was saying now, "George Steinbrenner had tears in his eyes."

"Get my bat, Nick, please," Reggie Jackson told a clubhouse man. "I started using this bat Saturday after I broke one in Friday's game. Look at the wide grain. The older the tree, the wider the grain, the harder the wood. I think I'll give this bat to George, he'll appreciate it."

"George," somebody said, "ought to put a marker out there halfway up the bleachers where that third homer landed."

"That'd be something, Babe Ruth, Lou Gehrig, Joe DiMaggio, Mickey Mantle and Reggie Jackson. Somehow I don't fit."

"You know what Bobby Vinton sings, 'Color Me Gone,' that's me," he said in July. *"Color me gone. I want to hit .300, thirty homers, fifty doubles, drive in ninety runs, be the most valuable player in the World Series, get to win the World Series, and then go. Color me gone."*

Thurman Munson reappeared. "Hey, nigger, you're too slow, that party's over but I'll see you next year," the captain said, sticking out his hand. "I'll see you next year wherever I might be."

"You'll be back," Reggie Jackson said.

"Not me," said Thurman Munson, who has talked of demanding to be traded to the Cleveland Indians. "But you know who stuck up for you, nigger, you know who stuck up for you when you needed it."

"I know," Reggie Jackson said. "But you'll be here next year. We'll all be here."

IT IS difficult to categorize this small vignette, which is from *Hello Towns,* a collection of editorials that Sherwood Anderson wrote for two Virginia weeklies. The following is from an editorial that, according to Anderson's biographer James Schevill, concerned a visit Anderson made to a photographer who secretly wanted to be a professional baseball player.

From *Small Town Note*

SHERWOOD ANDERSON

HE DID NOT know I was coming. . . . The man was in his house alone and had become in fancy a ball player. I saw what happened through a window. The man was squatting, with his hands on his knees, in the living room of his house. He had become a shortstop and was all alert. I dare say someone like Babe Ruth was at bat. When the man had gone to the cities to see the professionals play he had noted how the infielders kept talking to each other.

"Now, Ed. Careful now, Ed. Watch him, Ed!" I heard the photographer cry. He spoke sharply to the pitcher. "Get it over the plate, Bill!" he cried.

It was evident the batter had made a hit. I saw him dash across the room for second base. He had knocked over a chair on the way, but he did not care. He had made the play.

I saw him receive the ball and throw to first. There was an intent look in his eyes. Would the ball get to first ahead of the runner? It did. "Ah," I heard him sigh with relief.

It goes without saying that I went away and returned on the next day to see him about taking the photographs we wanted.

——————— HISTORY ———————

THE SIXTH GAME of the 1975 World Series. Roger Angell, the master of the art, begins his account of that game by saying that even to describe it is to diminish it—and were it anyone but Angell at the typewriter, he'd have quite a point.

Television deserves its due here too. Not only did it deliver the sights of that game to uncounted millions, it brought its viewers the shot of Carlton Fisk's body English the moment after his game-winning home run in the 12th inning—something no one actually at Fenway Park was likely to have noticed.

1975:
Boston Red Sox 7,
Cincinnati Reds 6

ROGER ANGELL

GAME SIX, GAME SIX . . . what can we say of it without seeming to diminish it by recapitulation or dull it with detail? Those of us who were there will remember it, surely, as long as we have any baseball memory, and those who wanted to be there and were not will be sorry always. Crispin Crispian: for Red Sox fans, this was Agincourt. The game also went out to sixty-two million television viewers, a good many millions of whom missed their bedtime. Three days of heavy rains had postponed things; the outfield grass was a lush, Amazon green, but there was a clear sky at last and a welcoming moon—a giant autumn squash that rose above the right-field Fenway bleachers during batting practice.

In silhouette, the game suggests a well-packed but dangerously overloaded canoe—with the high bulge of the Red Sox' three first-inning runs in the bow, then the much bulkier hump of six Cincinnati runs amidships, then the counterbalancing three Boston runs astern, and then, *way* aft, one more shape. But this picture needs colors: Fred Lynn clapping his hands once, quickly and happily, as his three-run opening shot flies over the Boston bullpen and into the bleachers . . . Luis Tiant fanning Perez with a curve and the Low-Flying Plane, then dispatching Foster with a Fall Off the Fence. Luis does not have his fastball, however. . . .

Pete Rose singles in the third. Perez singles in the fourth—his first real contact off Tiant in three games. Rose, up again in the fifth, with a man on base, fights off Tiant for seven pitches, then singles hard to center. Ken Griffey triples off the wall, exactly at the seam of the left-field and center-field angles; Fred Lynn, leaping up for the ball and missing it, falls backward into the wall and comes down heavily. He lies there, inert, in a terrible, awkwardly twisted position, and for an instant all of us think that he has been killed. He is up at last, though, and even stays in the lineup, but the noise and joy are gone out of the crowd, and the game is turned around. Tiant, tired and old and, in the end, bereft even

of mannerisms, is rocked again and again—eight hits in three innings—
and Johnson removes him, far too late, after Geronimo's first-pitch home
run in the eighth has run the score to 6–3 for the visitors.

By now, I had begun to think sadly of distant friends of mine—
faithful lifelong Red Sox fans all over New England, all over the East,
whom I could almost see sitting silently at home and slowly shaking their
heads as winter began to fall on them out of their sets. I scarcely noticed
when Lynn led off the eighth with a single and Petrocelli walked. Sparky
Anderson, flicking levers like a master back-hoe operator, now called in
Eastwick, his sixth pitcher of the night, who fanned Evans and retired
Burleson on a fly. Bernie Carbo, pinch-hitting, looked wholly over-
matched against Eastwick, flailing at one inside fastball like someone
fighting off a wasp with a croquet mallet. One more fastball arrived, high
and over the middle of the plate, and Carbo smashed it in a gigantic,
flattened parabola into the center-field bleachers, tying the game. Everyone out there—and everyone in the stands, too, I suppose—leaped to his
feet and waved both arms exultantly, and the bleachers looked like the
dark surface of a lake lashed with a sudden night squall.

The Sox, it will be recalled, nearly won it right away, when they
loaded the bases in the ninth with none out, but an ill-advised dash home
by Denny Doyle after a fly, and a cool, perfect peg to the plate by George
Foster, snipped the chance. The balance of the game now swung back,
as it so often does when opportunities are wasted. Drago pitched out of
a jam in the tenth, but he flicked Pete Rose's uniform with a pitch to start
the eleventh. Griffey bunted, and Fisk snatched up the ball and, risking
all, fired to second for the force on Rose. Morgan was next, and I had very
little hope left. He struck a drive on a quick, deadly rising line—you could
still hear the loud *whock!* in the stands as the white blur went out over
the infield—and for a moment I thought the ball would land ten or fifteen
rows back in the right-field bleachers. But it wasn't hit quite that hard
—it was traveling too fast, and there was no sail to it—and Dwight Evans,
sprinting backward and watching the flight of it over his shoulder, made
a last-second, half-staggering turn to his left, almost facing away from the
plate at the end, and pulled the ball in over his head at the fence. The
great catch made for two outs in the end, for Griffey had never stopped
running and was easily doubled off first.

And so the swing of things was won back again. Carlton Fisk, leading
off the bottom of the twelfth against Pat Darcy, the eighth Reds pitcher of
the night—it was well into morning now, in fact—socked the second pitch
up and out, farther and farther into the darkness above the lights, and
when it came down at last, reilluminated, it struck the topmost, innermost
edge of the screen inside the yellow left-field foul pole and glanced
sharply down and bounced on the grass: a fair ball, fair all the way. I was
watching the ball, of course, so I missed what everyone on television saw—
Fisk waving wildly, weaving and writhing and gyrating along the first-

base line, as he wished the ball fair, *forced* it fair with his entire body. He circled the bases in triumph, in sudden company with several hundred fans, and jumped on home plate with both feet, and John Kiley, the Fenway Park organist, played Handel's "Hallelujah Chorus," *fortissimo,* and then followed with other appropriately exuberant classical selections, and for the second time that evening I suddenly remembered all my old absent and distant Sox-affiliated friends (and all the other Red Sox fans, all over New England), and I thought of them—in Brookline, Mass., and Brooklin, Maine; in Beverly Farms and Mashpee and Presque Isle and North Conway and Damariscotta; in Pomfret, Connecticut, and Pomfret, Vermont; in Wayland and Providence and Revere and Nashua, and in both the Concords and all five Manchesters; and in Raymond, New Hampshire (where Carlton Fisk lives), and Bellows Falls, Vermont (where Carlton Fisk was *born*), and I saw all of them dancing and shouting and kissing and leaping about like the fans at Fenway—jumping up and down in their bedrooms and kitchens and living rooms, and in bars and trailers, and even in some boats here and there, I suppose, and on back-country roads (a lone driver getting the news over the radio and blowing his horn over and over, and finally pulling up and getting out and leaping up and down on the cold macadam, yelling into the night), and all of them, for once at least, utterly joyful and believing in that joy—alight with it.

It should be added, of course, that very much the same sort of celebration probably took place the following night in the midlands towns and vicinities of the Reds' supporters—in Otterbein and Scioto; in Frankfort, Sardinia, and Summer Shade; in Zanesville and Louisville and Akron and French Lick and Loveland. I am not enough of a social geographer to know if the faith of the Red Sox fan is deeper or hardier than that of a Reds rooter (although I secretly believe that it may be, because of his longer and more bitter disappointments down the years). What I do know is that this belonging and caring is what our games are all about; this is what we come for. It is foolish and childish, on the face of it, to affiliate ourselves with anything so insignificant and patently contrived and commercially exploitative as a professional sports team, and the amused superiority and icy scorn that the non-fan directs at the sports nut (I know this look—I know it by heart) is understandable and almost unanswerable. Almost. What is left out of this calculation, it seems to me, is the business of caring—caring deeply and passionately, really *caring*—which is a capacity or an emotion that has almost gone out of our lives. And so it seems possible that we have come to a time when it no longer matters so much what the caring is about, how frail or foolish is the object of that concern, as long as the feeling itself can be saved. Naïveté—the infantile and ignoble joy that sends a grown man or woman to dancing and shouting with joy in the. middle of the night over the haphazardous flight of a distant ball—seems a small price to pay for such a gift.

THIS QUATRAIN is supposed to have appeared in print in this country in 1774.

Baseball

ANONYMOUS

The ball once struck off,
Away flies the boy
To the next destined post
And then home with joy.

HA! You don't think there *is* such a thing as fact-fiction? Read.

The fact part, as far as I can tell, includes the dilemma of L'n'h's'r, cf, in the funniest box score of all time. The Cobb incident *did* happen and Detroit, playing with a pickup team in order to retain its franchise, *did* lose to the A's 24 to 2. As for the rest . . . well, meet Mr. Baer.

The Crambury Tiger

ARTHUR "BUGS" BAER

SURE, The trouble was over a girl. What isn't?

Tink was too good-looking for his own good before there were movies. He had the tickets to make the big leagues but he was as lazy as a fed cat. Tink could pitch at times.

Nippers had the general appearance of an accident looking for a lawyer and he had a profile you could saw lumber with. He couldn't field good enough to stop a water wheel in a dry spell. But he sure shook that pepper-box around the infield.

Playing semipro baseball in the summer was a softer touch than face powder. We got around like ringworms and if we weren't bums we would certainly do until bums came along.

I called myself a semipro although it might have been closer to three eighths. Too much beer in Bustleton is what stopped me in addition to

18

other habits that would have tightened the hide on a bloodhound's jowls. John McGraw once sent a scout to look me over but he decided I was too much of a grandstand player when I wasn't throwing them into the bleachers.

At the bat I couldn't hit all the leather in the world if I owned all the lumber. But both Tink and Nippers could throw their weight around at the plate. I was so round-shouldered I had to have my coats made twice as long in the back as in the front. I guess I played in more places than sunbeams in a forest. I wound up as the only left-handed shortstop in semipro baseball, but I finished better than Tink.

Fast as Nippers got a girl in the small towns Tink would take her away from him. But once he gave Nippers a girl, and it was just too bad.

It was all the fault of Ty Cobb. And a bit over like a baker's dozen.

Now, I know that Ty never heard of us cow-pasture punks who used a fence post for a bat and slid into a lot of things that weren't second base. But when he came up from Georgia to the Detroits he was gamer than a dentist pulling his own teeth and could take it like a carpet on the line. But he was as touchy as fingerprint powder and would climb a mountain to take a punch at an echo.

Ty fought everybody on the Detroits until the other Tigers realize that all he wants to do is win baseball games. Then they get in back of him as solid as wet sand and Detroit cops the berries in 1907, '08 and '09—and almost repeats in '10 and '11. But they go very bad in the spring of '12 and Cobb is sorer than ingrown hairs on a porcupine.

There's no living with Ty when he's in that mood, so when a grandstand manager in New York named Lucas or Lookis or something like that gives him the Bronx roll call from the dollar seats, Ty climbs into the stands and hands him a dry shave with his knuckles. The other Yankee fans choose up sides and Cobb is elected Queen of the May on the sixteenth of that month as I remember. The Yanks' fans were sure going to town on Ty's transportation system when the entire Detroits barge into the stands and rescue him with their baseball bats. When the cops pull everybody loose from their pet holds it turns out that the fellow Cobb popped has no fingers on his right hand.

Well, Ty didn't know that and Lucas or Lookis has certainly used some pretty rough talk. That doesn't stop Ban Johnson from giving Cobb the indefinite works with the option of making it permanent.

The entire Detroits club their mad money in a lump and send Ban a testimonial telegram: "Feeling that Mr. Cobb is being done an injustice by your action in suspending him, we the undersigned refuse to play in another game until such action is adjusted to our satisfaction. We want him reinstated or there will be no game. If players cannot have protection we must protect ourselves." (Signed) Sam Crawford, Jim Delahanty, Davey Jones, Oscar Stanage, Oscar Vitt, George Moriarity, Jack Onslow,

Ed Willett, Bill Burns, Covington, Paddy Bauman, Louden, George Mullin and all the others.

That makes it serious for the Detroit owners if they don't put a team in the field on Saturday, May 18, 1912, in Philly where their next game is. Owner Navin can lose his franchise and can be plastered with a five-grand fine.

Manager Hughey Jennings comes to Philly at the Aldine Hotel and gives out word that he is in the market for a brand-new Detroit team and no reasonable offer will be refused. Any ballplayer who can stop a grapefruit from rolling uphill or hit a bull in the pants with a bass fiddle has got a chance of going direct from the semipros to the Detroits and no questions asked.

Tink, Nippers and me are booked to play for Millville in southern Jersey the next day but we light out for the Aldine Hotel in time to run into a parade of seven hundred semipros all anxious to fill Ty Cobb's shoes. A baseball writer named Isaminger on the *North American* said that seven hundred was about the right number. The seven hundred of us semipros walk single-file past Jennings and he taps the ones he wants on the shoulder with a pool cue like we were buttons on a wire over a billiard table. He runs us fifty or no count and that's his team for tomorrow.

Out of that fifty he will pick nine players who will get fifty smackers each. Then he will pick a couple more for emergency who will get twenty-five just for sitting on the bench. That was almost a full season's salary for a semipro in Philly. Tink and me are among the fifty but Nippers can't score with the pool cue even though he has a piece of chalk in his vest pocket.

That all gets into the papers and the Georgia folks get behind Cobb. A congressman named William Schley Howard made a speech about it in Washington and sent Ty a wire as follows: "As Georgians we commend your action in resenting uncalled-for insult in New York. We hope for complete exoneration and reinstatement in clean sport of baseball. Congratulations to you as a leader and fighter of your profession."

Howard signed the telegram and it was seconded by a famous senator from Georgia named Hoke Smith. Howard also tagged Senator Bacon's name to it. One more signature and Gordon McKay of the *Inquirer* said it would have been an amendment to the Constitution. Cobb got thousands of wires and letters and the Wall Street brokers got up a petition for him that I guess they could use themselves now.

Cobb spent that Friday night in conference with his fellow Detroits and they sent a telegram or two. The White Sox were playing the Red Sox in Boston, so Ty wired Harry Lord of the Chicagos and Smokey Joe Wood of the Bostons asking if they would join a protective association of players with short tempers. That was thirty years

ago and Lord and Wood are still giving the matter their serious attention. Us ballplayers stick together like a wishbone in a pulling contest.

Philly is giving the strike of the Detroits a lot of publicity because
their Athletics look like sure pennant winners even though the Red Sox
finally cop and Washington winds up second. So, even if Nippers doesn't
make the grade he decides to cut Millville and watch us play for the
Detroits. When you're a semipro, your schedule is as loose as a skeleton
on roller skates. The three of us light out for the A's park Saturday
morning at eight o'clock. We swiped a bottle of milk and a loaf of bread
off a porch and ate it under a bridge.

At ten, Jennings drives up with his trunks and bats. He has picked
fifty ballplayers on suspicion and he wants to see if we are guilty or not.
He also has two faithful Detroits with him named Sugden and McGuire
and I'll tell you about them. They are so old they can sleep in a swamp
without mosquito netting. At the present time Jennings was using them
for coaches and scouts but he announces McGuire will catch anything
that comes near him, and Sugden will play first base for everything
except fast grounders and overthrows. Jennings elects himself captain,
manager, coach and utility. I know my baseball and I remember Sugden
was with Baltimore in 1889 and here it is 1912. He was a fatigued old
gent who should have spent his summers pointing out sea shells for his
grandkids to pick up.

There was a McGuire with Washington in 1892 when Washington
was in the National League. I think he bobbed around a lot and finally
tried umpiring but he had spots before his eyes and gives a batter his base
on four of them.

That leaves seven positions for Jennings to fill and Tink and me are
out. But we make the bench for twenty-five smackers and that suits us.
He picks a semipro named Travers to pitch and a good lightweight
fighter Billy McHarg for third. There are also a couple of old-timers from
Georgetown University and a few more sand lotters who can field all
right but can't hit their weight on a diet.

The fellow who got the toughest break was the semipro picked
to play Ty Cobb's spot in center. His monicker was too wide for the
printers and it came out in the Sunday papers this way, "L'n'h's'r."
Today nobody knows whether his name was Loopenhouser or Lagen-
hassinger and I bet his wife still calls him a liar when he says he once
played on the Detroits.

Anyway, the fans didn't ask for their money back when they saw a
lot of bums in Tigers' clothing. Here's the way the game came out in the
box scores:

DETROIT

	AB	H	O	A	E
McGarr, 2b	4	0	3	0	1
McHarg, 3b	1	0	2	0	0
Irwin, 3b, c	3	2	1	2	1
Travers, p	3	0	7	0	1
McGarvey, lf	3	0	1	0	3
L'n'h's'r, cf	4	0	1	0	0
Sugden, 1b	3	1	2	1	1
McGuire, c	2	1	3	1	2
Smith, 3b	1	0	1	0	0
Meaney, ss	2	0	3	0	1
Ward, rf	2	0	0	0	0
x Jennings	1	0	0	0	0
Totals	29	4	24	4	10

x Batted for exercise.

ATHLETICS

	AB	H	O	A	E
Maggert, lf	4	3	0	0	0
Strunk, cf	6	4	0	0	0
Collins, rb	6	5	0	1	0
Baker, 3b	5	2	0	0	0
Murphy, rf	3	2	1	0	0
McInnis, 1b	6	3	7	0	0
Barry, ss	4	2	3	1	1
Lapp, c	4	1	16	1	0
Coombs, p	1	0	0	1	0
Brown, p	3	2	0	2	0
Pennock, p	1	1	0	1	0
Totals	43	25	27	7	1

									RUNS	HITS	ERRORS
DETROIT	0	0	0	0	2	0	0	0	0	2	4	10
ATHLETICS	3	0	3	0	8	4	4	2	x	24	25	1

SUMMARY OF THE GAME

RUNS, Sugden, McGuire, Maggert 2, Strunk 3, Collins 4, Baker 3, Murphy 4, McInnis 2, Barry 2, Lapp, Brown 2, Pennock.

TWO-BASE HITS, Maggert, Strunk, Barry, Pennock.

THREE-BASE HITS, Strunk, Baker, Murphy, Irwin 2, Brown, Maggert.
SACRIFICE HIT, Lapp.
SACRIFICE FLY, Barry.
STOLEN BASES, Collins 4, Baker, Murphy, McInnis 2, McGarvey.
STRUCK OUT, By Coombs 3, by Brown 5, by Pennock 7, by Travers 1.
DOUBLE PLAY, McGarvey and Smith.
LEFT ON BASES, Detroit 4, Athletics 4.
FIRST BASE ON ERRORS, Athletics 2.
BASES ON BALLS, Coombs 1, Pennock 1, Travers 7.
TIME OF GAME, One hour and forty minutes.
UMPIRES, Dineen and Perrine.

Outside of shooing Sugden and McGuire around the bases for old times' sake the A's bore down all the way like guards putting a strait jacket on the star pupil in a laughing academy. Eddie Collins did more yelling than Solomon's thousand wives catching him out with another dame. Eddie hustled all the way like a long-haired rabbit in a prairie fire. This was a regular baseball contest and it held the Detroit franchise. I still feel sorry for L'n'h's'r, who blew his big chance like a pyromaniac sneezing on his last match. It was just as well that I never got into the game because I raised a pompadour of goose pimples on the bench.

Jennings saved the bacon for Navin but when Ban Johnson got the result of the game between the A's and the Pick-Ups and heard that four apostrophes were playing center field for Cobb he called himself out on that one strike.

For the first time in his life Ban copped a plea and let Cobb off with a ten-day suspension. The regular Detroits played again and got their uniforms back from the semipros. All except the one shirt that Tink wore home under his coat. It belonged to Ty.

Tink wore the Detroit shirt next Monday morning out on the sand lots in the park and word went around that he was one of the striking Detroits who refused to go back. There's a Glassboro scout there and when he hears that, he gets hotter than a one-cycle engine. He offers Tink fifteen dollars a game but Tink is stringing a couple of towns along and finally nails twenty bobbins for himself for Crambury on Decoration Day. I went with the deal and got eight dollars for playing shortstop.

Tink won for Crambury by his pitching and batting and actually lived up to the Detroit "D" on his shirt. The visiting team couldn't holler about it because they were padded like an idiot's cell themselves. The Crambury fans and the local girls thought he was the top berries and there was one pretty little girl who went for him big.

Going home on the train that night Tink told me her name was Jennie and her father was a motorman. Well, that's society for Tink. He pitches four Saturdays straight for Crambury and wins against Big Timber, Tacony, Southwark and Upper Darby. But for some reason he switches to Pennsylvania towns in August even though Crambury is offering him up to thirty-five dollars a game. I'm still playing short for short dough and I see Jennie each Saturday afternoon looking for Tink. She asked me about him and I said he had sprained his arm and gone back home to Philly. She doesn't even know his last name.

Well, the biggest day in semipro baseball in Jersey and Pennsylvania is Labor Day. Crambury is going to play its big rival North Chester for the weedbending championship and it wants Tink. But Tink is going to Bound Brook for less money and I know why. I tell the Crambury manager I can get a pretty good man named Nippers but he says the local folks want a big leaguer and I tell him that maybe I can get one. He says he will pay forty for a leaguer and raise me from eight to ten. I tell Nippers about it and he tells Tink he will split the forty with him if he will lend Nippers his Cobb shirt for Labor Day.

That's twenty more in the bag for Tink and he grabs it. When I tell the Crambury manager that I have another Detroit pitcher who walked out with Cobb and didn't go back he snaps it up.

Nippers touched up the big D on his chest with black ink until it stood out like a frog's eyes. On Labor Day he looked like a leaguer and pitched all the way like one coming down to the ninth. North Chester is leading one to nothing mostly because they have a ringer from the Tri-State who can pitch and bat. He smacks a homer in the first half of the ninth and is a little winded, so he hits a Crambury in the ribs, passes one, and they move up on an infield out. The next bird is a soft touch and it brings Nippers up with two on, two out and a single needed to cop.

It gets down to three and two on Nippers and it's closer than beds in a charity ward. Nippers is waving his bat at the big Tri-Stater, who winds up and is about to let it go when he sees he is pitching to two men at the plate. The other fellow is a middle-aged gent and he is packing a shotgun, which is aimed at Nippers. The Crambury manager claims a balk but the umpire disallows because nobody can outpitch a shotgun. The fellow with the gun then explains himself.

"I've lived in this town for sixty years," he said, "and the population has been exactly six hundred and thirty-two from 1852 to 1912. The reason for that is every time somebody is born somebody leaves town."

Well, Nippers wants to know what that has to do with him. The old boy said, "My daughter told me to look for a fellow with a Detroit D on his shirt," so I know now it's the motorman speaking, "and you're going to marry her."

Well, we plead with the old man to let the game go on and settle the matter in a legal way. But he swings the gun around to the umpire and says, "Pridemore, you're the Justice of the Peace and you're going to marry my daughter with this Detroit fellow." He calls out, "Jennie," and Jennie walks out of the crowd with her head down and a handkerchief stuffed in her mouth to hold her sobs back. She never once looks up during the ceremony, not even when the Crambury runner on third tries to steal home when Pridemore is asking, "Do you take this man for your lawful wedded husband?"

He goes back when the shotgun swings his way for Jennie's daddy knows his baseball. Then the ceremony is over and Jennie looks up and sees it isn't Tink and she faints. She's married to Ty Cobb's shirt all because Lucas or Lookis or something had to shoot his face off. Pridemore makes a wave of his hand that declares the couple married and starts the game again.

The fans go back to their places, everybody on the field gets set, the runners take a big lead and the Tri-Stater winds up and lets her go.

Nippers takes a toe hold on some loose dust and swings. Well, the happy bridegroom misses it farther than a dunce getting Constantinople in a spelling bee.

Nippers is now in a fine spot. He is struck out and married on a wide outshoot.

Jennie's daddy has brought her around okay and he also collects Nippers and they go down the road looking like Daniel Boone moving his family farther west. I get myself invited to the wedding supper and the motorman isn't a bad sort of apple-knocker if you let him have his way. I tell Nippers that I will take the Detroit shirt back to Tink, but I advise him to keep the whole forty buttons for himself for he has earned it. Nippers keeps the shirt.

Let me tell you something about Ty's shirt. It must be magic because the bird who wears it acts like a leaguer. It is better for nailing a job in a small town than an average of 99.9 in a civil service quiz for letter carriers. Nippers has a couple more pitching jobs that fall and wins both. He gets sixty-five dollars for the last game of the season. Along about February at the end of winter I hear the population of Crambury has finally hopped to six hundred and thirty-three. Also that Nippers is offered a trial with a Hoss and Buggy League in Carolina.

Down there he meets Tink, fights him for the shirt and hammers him to a blister. They meet a second time that season and Nippers breaks the blister. The man wearing Cobb's shirt gets to think he is Ty and when the war busts loose in 1917, Nippers enlists and wins a whole flock of decorations.

He goes over the top in his Detroit shirt and eighty-seven Germans surrender to him because they think a new nation has declared war on the Kaiser.

When he got home to Crambury, Jennie and number six hundred and thirty-three are waiting for him. He starts in pitching again and he gets offers from the Three-Eye, the International and the South Atlantic leagues. But he refuses to play in any town that doesn't fit his shirt.

And, Believe It or the Marching Chinese, before the 1919 season is half over, the population of Crambury is one less than its average for sixty years, for Jennie and six hundred and thirty-three have packed up and gone west with Nippers, who is a fine husband and loving father, but once he gets out there on that baseball field, is meaner than the man who invented uphill.

And he gives Ty Cobb his shirt back. For Nippers now has a Detroit shirt of his own.

GENERAL

FRENCH-BORN Jacques Barzun, the distinguished historian, puts it very simply: "Whoever wants to know the heart and mind of America had better learn baseball."

From *God's Country and Mine*

JACQUES BARZUN

PEOPLE WHO CARE less for gentility manage things better. They don't bother to leave the arid city but spend their surplus there on pastimes they can enjoy without feeling cramped. They follow boxing and wrestling, burlesque and vaudeville (when available), professional football and hockey. Above all, they thrill in unison with their fellow men the country over by watching baseball. The gods decree a heavyweight match only once in a while and a national election only every four years, but there is a World Series with every revolution of the earth around the sun. And in between, what varied pleasure long drawn out!

Whoever wants to know the heart and mind of America had better learn baseball, the rules and realities of the game—and do it by watching first some high-school or small-town teams. The big-league games are too fast for the beginner and the newspapers don't help. To read them with profit you have to know a language that comes easy only after philosophy has taught you to judge practice. Here is scholarship that takes effort on the part of the outsider, but it is so bred into the native that it never becomes a dreary round of technicalities. The wonderful purging of the passions that we all experienced in the fall of '51, the despair groaned out over the fate of the Dodgers, from whom the league pennant was snatched at the last minute, give us some idea of what Greek tragedy was like. Baseball *is* Greek in being national, heroic, and broken up in the rivalries of city-states.

And that it fitly expresses the powers of the nation's mind and body is a merit separate from the glory of being the most active, agile, varied, articulate, and brainy of all group games. It is of and for our century. Tennis belongs to the individualistic past—a hero, or at most a pair of friends or lovers, against the world. The idea of baseball is a team, an outfit, a section, a gang, a union, a cell, a commando—in short, a twentieth-century setup of opposite numbers.

Baseball takes its mystic nine and scatters them wide. A kind of individualism thereby returns, but it is limited—eternal vigilance is the price of victory. Just because they're far apart the outfield can't dream or play she-loves-me-not with daisies. The infield is like a steel net held in the hands of the catcher. He is the psychologist and historian for the staff—or else his signals will give the opposition hits. The value of his headpiece is shown by the ironmongery worn to protect it. The pitcher, on the other hand, is the wayward man of genius, whom others will direct. They will expect nothing from him but virtuosity. He is surrounded no doubt by mere talent, unless one excepts that transplanted acrobat, the shortstop. What a brilliant invention is his role despite its exposure to ludicrous lapses! One man to each base and then the free lance, the trouble-shooter, the movable feast for the eyes, whose motion animates the whole foreground.

The rules keep pace with this imaginative creation so rich in allusions to real life. How excellent, for instance, that a foul tip muffed by the catcher gives the batter another chance. It is the recognition of Chance that knows no argument. But on the other hand, how just that the third strike must not be dropped. This points to the fact that near the end of any struggle, life asks for more than is needful in order to clinch success. A victory has to be won, not snatched. We find also our American innocence in calling "World Series" the annual games between the winners in each big league. The world doesn't know or care and couldn't compete if it wanted to, but since it's us children having fun, why, the world is our stage. I said baseball was Greek. Is there not a poetic symbol in the new meaning—our meaning—of "Ruth hits Homer"?

Once the crack of the bat has sent the ball skimmering toward second, between the infielder's legs, six men converge or distend their defense to keep the runner from advancing along the prescribed path. The ball is not the center of interest as in those vulgar predatory games like football, basketball, or polo. Man running is the force to be contained. His getting to first or second base starts a capitalization dreadful to think of: every hit pushes him on. Bases full and a homer make four runs, while the defenders, helpless without the magic power of the ball lying over the fence, cry out their anguish and dig up the sod with their spikes.

But fate is controlled by the rules. Opportunity swings from one side to the other because innings alternate quickly, keep up spirit in the players, interest in the beholders. So does the profusion of different acts to be performed—pitching, throwing, catching, batting, running, stealing, sliding, signaling. Hits are similarly varied. Flies, Texas Leaguers, grounders, baseline fouls—praise God the human neck is a universal joint! And there is no set pace. Under the hot sun, the minutes creep as a deliberate pitcher tries his drops and curves for three strikes called, or conversely walks a threatening batter. But the batter is not invariably a tailor's dummy. In a hundredth of a second there may be a hissing rocket down right field, a cloud of dust over first base—the bleachers all a-yell —a double play, and the other side up to bat.

Accuracy and speed, the practiced eye and hefty arm, the mind to take in and readjust to the unexpected, the possession of more than one talent and the willingness to work in harness without special orders— these are the American virtues that shine in baseball. There has never been a good player who was dumb. Beef and bulk and mere endurance count for little, judgment and daring for much. Baseball is among group games played with a ball what fencing is to games of combat. But being spread out, baseball has something sociable and friendly about it that I especially love. It is graphic and choreographic. The ball is not shuttling in a confined space, as in tennis. Nor does baseball go to the other extreme of solitary whanging and counting stopped on the brink of pointlessness, like golf. Baseball is a kind of collective chess with arms and legs in full play under sunlight.

The team is elegance itself in its striped knee breeches and loose shirts, colored stockings and peaked caps. Except for brief moments of sliding, you can see them all in one eyeful, unlike the muddy hecatombs of football. To watch a football game is to be in prolonged neurotic doubt as to what you're seeing. It's more like an emergency happening at a distance than a game. I don't wonder the spectators take to drink. Who has ever seen a baseball fan drinking within the meaning of the act? He wants all his senses sharp and clear, his eyesight above all. He gulps down soda pop, which is a harmless way of replenishing his energy by the ingestion of sugar diluted in water and colored pink.

Happy the man in the bleachers. He is enjoying the spectacle that the gods on Olympus contrived only with difficulty when they sent Helen to Troy and picked their teams. And the gods missed the fun of doing this by catching a bat near the narrow end and measuring hand over hand for first pick. In Troy, New York, the game scheduled for 2 P.M. will break no bones, yet it will be a real fight between Southpaw Dick and Red Larsen. For those whom civilized play doesn't fully satisfy, there will be provided a scapegoat in a blue suit—the umpire, yell-proof and even-handed as justice, which he demonstrates with outstretched arms when calling "Safe!"

And the next day in the paper: learned comment, statistical summaries, and the verbal imagery of meta-euphoric experts. In the face of so much joy, one can only ask, Were you there when Dogface Joe parked the pellet beyond the pale?

HISTORY

THERE WAS the temptation to label this one science fiction on account of its being a chapter from Jimmy Breslin's astonishing book *Can't Anybody Here Play This Game?* Incredible to relate, though, every word of it is true. The subject, it goes without saying, is the New York Mets in their first year under Casey Stengel.

"They're Afraid to Come Out"

JIMMY BRESLIN

THE SECOND HALF of the season for the New York Mets was, generally speaking, a catastrophe. The second half of the season consisted of the months of July, August, and September, although some of the more responsible players on the team insisted it never really happened. Whatever it was, it left an indelible impression on many of those connected with the club.

In Rochester, New York, during the winter, Casey Stengel sat in the lobby of the Sheraton Hotel, and, in the middle of one of his highly specialized lobby seminars, he stopped and shook his head.

"Everybody here keeps saying how good I'm looking," he said. "Well, maybe I do. But they should see me inside. I look terrible inside."

And in Tilden, Nebraska, one afternoon, Richie Ashburn called a Philadelphia advertising agency to tell them that he would certainly like to retire from baseball and take their offer to announce the Philadelphia Phillies games.

"Weren't you making more with the Mets?" he was asked.

"Yes, quite a bit more."

"Why did you quit, then?"

"Well," he said.

He meant he was taking a big cut in pay for the privilege of not having to go through another year with the Mets.

From a non-Met viewpoint, however, the last part of the 1962 season was something else. It was not rough. It was, instead, the finest thing to happen to the sport of baseball since Abe Attell helped save the game by deciding that, seeing as long as it made people so mad, he was not going to become involved with anyone who was trying to fix World Series games.

You see, in the last fifteen years baseball has needed help. This is becoming a tired, predictable game. It is overexposed on television. It is played too slowly to maintain a hold on this fast-moving era. And, probably worst of all, it has become so commercialized, and the people in it loaded with so many gimmicks, that it all reminds you of the front window of a cheap department store. For money, a baseball player will go to the end of the world to embarrass himself. One word from Madison Avenue, the world center for poor taste, and a ballplayer will rub some hog-suet compound into his hair and say it isn't greaseless. Or he will make a toy-company commercial that should be jammed by the FCC. Or, most sickening of all, for a check of $500 or so he will show up at any dinner of any organization this side of the Murder, Inc., Old-Timers Association and sign autographs for the kids, mutter some sort of speech, then disappear out the side door with the waitress from the cocktail lounge. All of it is demeaning at best, and in the long run harmful to the game. Other athletes from other sports go in for this too, and they have the same quick-buck air about them, but since baseball is the biggest sport it is the one in which this sort of thing is most prevalent. And most sickening. The idea of a ballplayer taking money to go out and promote his own business is, at best, disgraceful.

And, in the playing of the game itself, baseball acts as if we are still in a depression and nobody has any place to go. There is the manager's strategy. With nominal maneuvering, a major-league manager can halt a game for ten minutes while changing pitchers. Baseball still thinks this is 1934. Only this is 1963 and people are working and have money and move around and spend it. The entire character of leisure time has changed drastically. Since 1945 everything has changed with it except baseball, and that is baseball's trouble right now.

But last season the New York Mets came to the rescue. Dressed in their striped uniforms, with blue lettering and orange piping, they put fun into life. It was hell to play for them, but for anybody who watched them it was great. This was what you wanted out of life. This was Bert Lahr in *The Wizard of Oz* or the Marx Brothers in *Room Service.* The Mets tried to play baseball, and the players trying to do it were serious. But the whole thing came out as great comedy, and it was the tonic the sport needed. People did not follow the Mets. They loved the Mets.

Absolutely anything the Mets did last season, from a viewer's position, was great. They were great during the season. And even in the long winter layoff they didn't let anybody down. In January, for example, the Mets called up their three best pitchers from the minor leagues. They were Larry Bearnath, who won 2 and lost 13 at Syracuse; Tom Belcher, 1 and 12 at Syracuse; and Grover Powell, who was 4 and 12 between

Syracuse and the Auburn, New York, club. The three had a combined record of thirty-seven losses and only seven wins.

"I saw all their old pitchers," cab driver Martin Goldstein, hack license 437-265, assured us one afternoon. "But I can't wait to see Stengel bring one of these new ones out of the bullpen."

It will be hard to top the final half of last season, however. All of it went along the lines of the night game the Mets played against the Reds at Crosley Field on August 10, although dates are of no consequence here because things were substantially the same each day or night the team took the field.

In the third inning of this particular contest, Frank Robinson of the Reds led off with a double down the left-field line off Al Jackson, the Mets' pitcher. Wally Post then grounded out, Robinson holding second. Robinson then stole third. The batter, Don Pavletich, walked. There was now one out, men on first and third. The Mets' infield came up a step or so. The hope was for a sharply hit ground ball which could be converted into a double play or a play at home plate to prevent the run from scoring.

Jackson pitched to Hank Foiles, the Reds' catcher. Pitched beautifully, too. Al's curve was coming in low, the kind of pitch that winds up being hit on the ground. Which is exactly what Foiles did. He hit a sharp one-hopper toward first. Throneberry made a great stop. Then he straightened up and looked around. He found that the ball had been hit so sharply that it gave him all the time he needed to make an inning-ending double play any way he wanted.

Here was Pavletich running toward second. He wasn't halfway there. Throneberry could throw to second for one out, then take the return throw and get the batter. That would be easy. Foiles was still scrambling away from the batter's box. There was another play Marv could make too. He could step on first and then throw to second. Only then they would have to tag Pavletich out at second. That could be dangerous, for Robinson might score in the meantime. But you still had plenty of time. When you have time you rarely make errors. Marvin stood alongside first base, the ball firmly held in his glove, and thought it out. Then he made his decision.

He threw to the plate. His throw arrived just after Robinson slid across with a run.

There were now runners on first and second with one out. Pitcher Jackson seemed to sway a little on the mound. Then he threw four balls to Vada Pinson, and that loaded the bases.

Don Blasingame stepped in to hit. By now, Jackson had talked himself into trying again. He stretched, then came in with that good low curve once more. Blasingame slapped a hard ground ball straight at Rod Kanehl at second base. It was a certain double-play ball. Kanehl, in his exuberance, neglected to field the ball. It kicked off his leg, and another run scored. The bases were still loaded.

Jackson now has forced the Reds to hit into two certain double plays. For his efforts, he has two runs against him on the scoreboard, still only one man out, the bases loaded, and a wonderful little touch of Southern vernacular dripping from his lips.

Jim Maloney, the Cincinnati pitcher, stepped in. The count ran to three and two on him. Then, for some reason, the Cincinnati base runners broke with the pitch. With two out, this is normal. But there was only one out here, and there is a slight suspicion somebody on the Reds was so mixed up by now he thought there were two out and he had the runners going. At any rate, Jackson came right back with that low curve, and Maloney went for it and here came another grounder straight at Kanehl. This time Rod wasn't going to make any mistakes. He kept his head down, scooped up the ball, and flipped it to second with the same motion. It was a fine move for starting a double play. Except Blasingame, running from first with the pitch, was now standing on second. He was safe. So was everybody else. During the maneuvering, the third Red run of the inning came across.

Jackson held out his glove for the ball, scuffed the dirt, then looked down for the sign so he could pitch to the next hitter. Don't ever say Al Jackson is not a well-trained pitcher. People come out of West Point and go on to become big generals and they don't have this kind of discipline. And when Leo Cardenas got in to hit, Jackson came right back with that curve ball and he got Cardenas to go for it and hit into the dirt.

The ball went right at Charley Neal at shortstop. The temptation was to go for the inning-ending double play, short-to-second-to-first. It looked easy. But you were not going to get Charley Neal into a sucker game like this. No, sir. Charley straightened up and fired the ball to first base to get one out. The fourth run of the inning came across.

When this happened, Richie Ashburn, out in right field, turned around and looked up at one of the light towers. In his time Ashburn had seen many things. Granny Hamner in a clutch: he always moved the runner up a base. Joe DiMaggio going after a fly ball: he covered half an outfield and never seemed to do anything hard enough to work up a sweat. Jackie Robinson bothering a pitcher: he would brazen the guy into a mistake. He had, Richie felt, seen just about everything. Except this.

"I don't know what's going on, but I know I've never seen it before," Ashburn mumbled.

Then he turned around and watched as Jackson finally got the third out and headed for the bench with the all-time record for making batters hit into consecutive double plays that did not work. As he got to the dugout, Stengel thought kind things about him.

"If I let this man go out there again, he may never be the same," Casey said. He ordered Ray Daviault to come in and pitch the fourth inning. This he neglected to tell Jackson. So when the Mets made their third out, Al picked up his glove and went out to the mound. He was in the middle of a warm-up pitch when the public-address announcer proclaimed, "Now pitching for New York, Number 35, Ray Daviault."

Jackson stopped dead.

"Everybody here crazy," he announced.

It went pretty much like this from the first day of July until the last day of the season, in September. Only a true hero could win a game for the Mets. Jackson, who was to wind up losing twenty, began to trust nobody. When he won a game, he won it by pitching a shutout. Even then, he was never too sure until he was back in the dressing room.

There was a night game in St. Louis that showed this. Jackson had a 1–0 lead as the ninth inning began. Ken Boyer was the first Cardinal hitter. Boyer hit sharply down the third-base line. Felix Mantilla went the wrong way for the ball, and it went through into left field. The Met's left fielder was Joe Christopher. Casey Stengel had put him into the game for defensive purposes. Christopher advanced on the ball, then touched it several times before finally holding on to it. Boyer had pulled up at second by the time Christopher was able to make the throw.

With one pitch the Mets had not only allowed the first man up to reach base, but they also had allowed him to advance into scoring position. Jackson, however, did not fold. He bent his back a little more and got the next two hitters. Then Red Schoendienst came up to pinch-hit. He is old, this Schoendienst, and maybe he has never been the same since being hit with tuberculosis a couple of years ago. But he is still Red Schoendienst, and in a spot like this he is dangerous. Jackson worked carefully on him. He got Red to go for an outside curve. Red hit a high pop foul alongside first. It was an easy third out. The fans started moving toward the exits. The Mets' outfielders started to come in for their showers. The bullpen crews reached for their gloves. Everybody moved but Jackson. He had been around too long. He was staying where he was until the result was official.

Throneberry circled under the pop fly. First, he moved in a little circle. Then he began to move in a bigger circle. With a great last-moment stab, Marvelous Marv got his glove on the ball. The ball hit the thumb part of Marv's glove and bounded away. Jackson then walked Schoendienst.

The next hitter was Bob Whitfield. He slammed a pitch right back at the mound. Now pitchers are not out there to make heroes of themselves. In self-defense they'll stop a batted ball. But only for that reason. Generally they like it much better if the ball goes past them and is handled by an infielder. That's what infielders are for. But this case was different. Jackson knew all about his infielders. He knew all about his outfielders too. He caught one glimpse of the ball as it buzzed toward his shoetops. Then Al Jackson went down for it. The thing could have hopped up and broken his jaw just as easily as not. It didn't matter to Jackson. He knew the only way he could win was to risk his life. With a loud slap, Jackson stopped the ball. Then he came up and threw to Throneberry at first. Marvin held on to the throw. The game, for a wonder, was over.

It was things like this that made an indelible impression upon a nineteen-year-old boy from Stockton, California, named Robert Garibaldi. Last July, Garibaldi, a sophomore at Santa Clara, was the most sought-after pitching prospect to come along in many years. He was a left-hander, and the bidding was up to $125,000 for his signature on a contract.

The Mets had sent Red Ruffing, the old Yankee pitching ace, to look over the kid for them. Ruffing's report was short and impressive: "Has big-league speed. Has big-league control. Ready right now."

On July 3 the Mets were in San Francisco. By the end of the fourth inning they were trailing by a tidy 10–1. Out of the dugout came Stengel. He ran up the right-field line and disappeared through a door leading to the clubhouse. Many people were speculating that Casey had decided he couldn't take any more. They were wrong. Stengel most certainly could take more. In fact, Casey Stengel at this point thought he could do anything. He had just heard that the Giants were going to sign Garibaldi the next day. So he had made a hurried date with George Weiss to drive to Stockton, sixty miles away, and try to charm Garibaldi into going for a Mets contract.

Charm the lad he did.

"He was wonderful," Garibaldi says. "It was great meeting him. I'd read about him all my life."

Stengel and Weiss sat down in the boy's living room and talked for two hours with him. They got down to money. The Giants reportedly had offered $130,000. The Mets certainly would top that, Weiss assured the boy. The boy said thank you, but there was no money in the world that could make it worth his while to pitch for the Mets. He signed with the Giants the next day.

This statement seemed borne out a week or so later when the Mets were in Milwaukee. The ace of their bullpen, Craig Anderson, who was in the midst of losing sixteen games in a row, needed a rest. For a relief pitcher Stengel called upon Wilmer (Vinegar Bend) Mizell. This one came on to walk the first three batters to face him in the seventh. Then he decided to effect pinpoint control and he served up a pitch that Joe Adcock hit six miles for a grand-slam home run. Out came Vinegar Bend. Stengel waved to the bullpen for somebody else. Nobody came.

"They're afraid to come out," everybody said.

For a Mets pitcher there were only two possibilities every time he took the mound. Either he was going to be hit for some of the longest home runs in baseball history, or he was going to have to stand around and watch his teammates make those astonishing plays.

Sometimes it was a combination of everything. There was one bright

Sunday in July in Cincinnati when the Mets lost two games. Not easily, either. It all began the day before, when Roger Craig, with the class of a real professional, had walked over to Stengel and volunteered for relief pitching in the doubleheader. Stengel nodded. It touches an old guy like this when a pitcher volunteers to work between starts. So in the ninth inning of the first game, with the score tied 3–3, Casey took Craig up on his offer. Roger came in from the bullpen, and immediately Cincinnati sent up Marty Keogh as a pinch hitter. Craig threw him one pitch. Keogh did not swing. Craig threw another pitch. Keogh swung. He hit the ball eight miles and the Reds won, 4–3.

"They get beat on favors now," everybody said.

Craig, however, was only part of the day's show. During the course of the eighteen innings the Mets managed to set some sort of an all-time record by getting four runners thrown out at home plate. In the first game Choo Choo Coleman was out trying to score from second on a single to left. In the second game Stengel jauntily ordered a double steal in the second inning. Cannizzaro was on first and Kanehl on third. Cannizzaro broke for second and drew a throw. Kanehl raced for the plate. The Cincinnati shortstop, Cardenas, cut off the throw, fired home, and that took care of Kanehl. In the fourth inning Elio Chacon, on first, put his head down and tried to go all the way around when Jerry Lynch, the Reds' left fielder, messed up a single. Chacon never saw Vada Pinson, the fine center fielder, come over for the ball. He should have, because Pinson, as he demonstrated here, throws quite well. He cut down Chacon at home by six yards. Finally, in the fifth inning, with Jim Hickman on third and breaking for the plate with the swing, Kanehl hit the ball hard. And squarely at third. Hickman was out by a mile at the plate.

In pitching for the Mets, then, it was best to take no chances. Don't volunteer, don't rely on getting any runs, no matter how many teammates get on base. The password was: beware. And the one who seemed to know this better than anyone was Ralph Branca. He had nothing to do with the team officially. His job was talking on a pre- and post-game program for a radio station. But by being around the Mets he understood that anything could happen. So on July 14, when the Mets held an Old Timers' Day and Branca was out in the bullpen, he did not merely sit on a bench and look at the crowd. He stayed loose. He also stayed determined.

The moment Bobby Thomson came up to bat, here was showman Leo Durocher waving to the bullpen for Branca to come in and pitch. Ralph walked in, just as he had come in that day in 1951. Thomson greeted him with a smile. Everybody else out on the field lolled around and made jokes about the situation.

Branca did not say any jokes. And a small thought crossed his mind: Stick the first pitch right in his ear. He dismissed it.

He then wound up and nearly broke his arm off throwing his best curve at Thomson. He threw a couple more of them, and Bobby, fooled by one, barely lifted an easy fly to center field.

Following this, the Mets took the field to play the Dodgers. In the stands to watch them were such as Zack Wheat and Carl Hubbell and Frank Frisch. At the end of five and a half innings the Mets were slightly behind. They were behind by 17–0, and that night Frankie Frisch sat in his house in New Rochelle and he told the neighbors, "I don't have to go out of this house again as long as I live. I've seen everything."

This view was being echoed on 52nd Street in New York, where the man named Toots Shor runs his restaurant and bar. He is generally considered to be the town's number-one sports fan, and around his circular bar he is known, simply, as The Best Customer.

"I have a son," Toots announced over brandy, "and I make him watch the Mets. I want him to know life. You watch the Mets, you think of being busted out with the guy from the Morris Plan calling up every ten minutes. It's a history lesson. He'll understand the depression when they teach it to him in school."

He shook his head. "That Frank Thomas is one helluva guy, you know. But he makes a throw against the Cardinals. He's on third base and he makes a throw to first. He makes the wildest wild throw in baseball history. It goes 125 feet over the first baseman's head. Nobody ever done a thing like that. Well, what the hell, there never was a club like this."

Anderson is a case in point here. His sixteenth loss was memorable. It left him two short of the all-time National League record, and only a step or two short of asking to be farmed out to an institution. The date was September 8, and the Mets were in Houston for a day-night doubleheader. They were leading, 3–2, in the ninth inning of the day game when Bob Lillis of Houston singled. Johnny Temple bunted down the first-base line. Marvin Throneberry approached the ball thoughtfully. Marvelous Marv's estimate was that the ball would roll foul. He was wrong. He then picked it up and threw to first, too late to get the runner. Stengel waved to the bullpen for help. Here came Anderson. Craig was in great form. He worked on Joe Amalfitano and got him to hit into a double play. Then he walked Norman Larker. This brought up Bob Aspromonte. He hit a sinking liner to left field. Frank Thomas broke for the ball. Then he charged the ball. Then he dove for the ball. He did not make the catch. Temple rounded third and scored the tying run. Larker, the runner from first, rounded second and began to go for third. Thomas grabbed the ball, stood up, and looked at Larker. It was going to be a close play at third. But Thomas was taking no chances. He was not going to let anybody reach second base. So he fired to second. There was nobody there. Aspromonte, the hitter, had remained at first. Kanehl and Neal, the Met's keystone combination, as the announcers call it, were widely scattered over the area. Thomas's throw roared past second untouched by human hands. Larker reached third, made the turn, and headed for home.

Throneberry made a remarkable save on the throw. He knew exactly what was going on. Larker was heading home with the winning run. A good throw would cut Larker down. Throneberry wanted to make that good throw. So he aimed at the plate. He took aim as if his life depended on this throw. He also took so much time aiming his throw that Larker simply slid across the plate with the winning run.

Jay Hook was another pitcher who found the Mets trying. On August 6, a hot Monday night at Los Angeles, Jay allowed the Dodgers five hits. He did not walk a man. But in the sixth inning of a 1–1 game Maury Wills of the Dodgers dragged a bunt past the mound and beat it out. He then stole second. This infuriated Chris Cannizzaro, who was catching Hook. Chris crouched down and looked out at second. Willis was taking his usual long lead off the base. Chris planted his feet and got ready to make a comeback. He was going to pick Willis off. On the first pitch, Chris threw to second. Threw hard. If there is one thing he can do, it is throw a baseball hard. He threw this one so hard that the only reason Wills had to hold at third and not score was that Jim Hickman, the Mets center fielder, caught the ball on the fly. Willie Davis then hit a ground ball, and Wills came across with what was to be the winning run.

Hook also had the privilege of pitching when the Mets lost their hundredth game of the year. This was late in August at Philadelphia. Jay went ten innings before losing to the Phillies, 3–2. He lost the game primarily on a ground ball to Charley Neal at short. Don Demeter hit the ball. Neal picked it up and made a bad throw to first. It pulled Throneberry off the bag. Marv had to come up the line and into foul territory to stay with the throw. He grabbed it. Then he went to tag Demeter. His feet slipped and he fell on his face.

This was Throneberry's best kind of play. And because of this, people sitting behind first base at the Polo Grounds soon began to show up with T-shirts which read VRAM (MARV spelled backwards) on them. And they took up a great chant: "Cranberry, strawberry, we love Throneberry."

This was the Marvin Throneberry Fan Club. At the peak of the season over a hundred letters a day were arriving at Marvin's locker at the Polo Grounds.

"The hell of it all is, I'm really a good fielder," Throneberry kept insisting.

This was something Ralph Houk gladly backed up one evening during the summer, in Washington. Houk, who manages the Yankees, sat in the bus taking his team to the ball park and he chewed on a cigar and talked about Marvelous Marv.

"I can't understand what's happening to that Throneberry," he said. "I had him three years at Denver. He's not that bad a ballplayer at all. Why, he opened the season with the Yankees one year there [1958].

Skowron was hurt, I guess. Marv never made plays like they say he makes now. I guarantee you he never did. If he ever played that way for me, I'd of killed him with my bare hands."

The year Marvelous Marv had in 1962 just happened, then. Nobody had any indication he knew how to play baseball this way. He just arrived from Baltimore one day in May and replaced an ailing Gil Hodges at first. After that, things began to happen. They kept happening too, and by August 18 he was an institution.

On that night the Mets' management held a special day in honor of Stan Musial. But the fans, proudly wearing their VRAM T-shirts and shouting their cheer, showed much more affection for Throneberry. Musial? He was fine. Great guy, magnificent baseball player. A perfectionist. Only who the hell needed him? The mob yelled for Marvelous Marv.

"I hated to take the play away from Stan on his big day here," Marv apologized after the game.

Throneberry is a balding, likable fellow who has been known to buy a writer a drink, something unheard of in a ballplayer. He is anything but a clown. He simply came into the 1962 season accident-prone, and he barely got out alive. Nothing went right at any time. There was even one night, late in the season, when there was supposed to be some sort of a small party in his honor at a little Italian restaurant called the Grotto on the West Side. Somebody mixed things up, and 125 people showed up instead of an expected 30. The lone chef, hired to work this small party on a usually dead Sunday night, took one look at the mob and pulled off his hat.

"Small-a party, huh?" he said. "Well, you take this small-a party to the Automat. 'Cause that's where I'm going to have my dinner on the way home."

The place got so jammed that there was no room for Marvelous Marv when he arrived. After trying to get in, he finally gave up and went across the street from his party and had dinner in another place.

The strange thing about the Mets is that, for all their great comedy on the field, they had no real characters off the field. This was a team of twenty-five nice young men who came to the big leagues to play baseball. The fact they played it rather strangely was, obviously, out of their control. The only player on the club who might be counted as unusual is Frank Thomas. His only quirk is that he wants to be an airline hostess. Yet here again you are dealing with a basically serious matter, because Thomas is a damn good airline stewardess.

"He's awful neat," Miss Barbara Mueller of United Airlines noted one day. "He does everything the way the regulations say you should. Outside of this girl Jane, who handles first class on our New York to San Francisco champagne flight, I think that Frank Thomas is the best stewardess on United Airlines."

Once the Mets are airborne, going to or from a game, Thomas jumps out of his seat, strides up the aisle to the kitchenette, and takes over the running of the plane. Trays slide in and out, coffee is poured, and he starts moving rapidly up and down the aisle, serving meals. He is very particular about it too. One night, en route to Houston by plane, Thomas started serving the back of the plane first. He thrust a tray under the nose of Barney Kremenko, the sportswriter, and a couple of partners he had gotten into a pinochle game. The partners were not good at pinochle. Thus Mr. Kremenko preferred to have nothing break up his game.

"We're not ready now," Barney said. "We'll eat later."

"All right," Thomas announced. "But that means you eat last, and I don't want to hear any squawks about it."

Offended, Thomas stormed off. Any housewife can understand how he felt. Here he had a whole meal prepared, and it was being turned down.

Presently Kremenko's game broke up. He hailed the regular stewardess and asked her to bring a tray, which she did. Thomas found out about this some minutes later. His eyes flashed.

"You cheated," he told Kremenko. "I told you to wait your turn, and you cheated. That's the last time you're going to pull that."

Otherwise, to travel or live with this club was to be with a normal group of young men in the major leagues. In fact, as Ashburn observes, the Mets were the only losing club he can recall on which there was no dissension.

"Any losing team I've ever been on," Richie says, "had several things going on. One, the players gave up. Or they hated the manager. Or they had no team spirit. Or the fans turned into wolves. But there was none of this with the Mets. Nobody stopped trying. The manager was absolutely great, nobody grumbled about being with the club, and the fans we had, well, there haven't been fans like this in baseball history. So we lose 120 games and there isn't a gripe on the club. It was remarkable. You know, I can remember guys being mad even on a big winner."

By this he meant a rather famous episode in more recent baseball history. On the last day of the 1950 season Ashburn's Phillies held a one-game lead over the Brooklyn Dodgers. At Ebbets Field, in the ninth inning, the score was tied, 1–1, with none out and Dodgers on first and second. The highly dangerous Duke Snider was at bat against Robin Roberts of the Phillies. Ashburn was in center field. If anything happened and the runner on second, Cal Abrams, scored, the Dodgers would tie for the pennant and go into a playoff heavily favored.

At shortstop for the Phillies was Granny Hamner. When they played it with money on the table, Hamner was one of the real big ones. It has been a while since he has been around, and maybe some people forget him, but when they talk about big men in the clutch Granny Hamner should always be mentioned. On this afternoon, with Abrams edging off second, Hamner flashed the pick-off sign to Stan Lopata, the Phillies' catcher. With Snider, a left-handed batter, up, Hamner was playing over toward second. For the pick-off throw, he would duck in behind Abrams and take the throw. Oh, they wouldn't get Abrams. That would be too much to ask for. The idea was to keep him as close to the bag as possible. If Snider bunted, they could try for Abrams at third. If he hit away and the ball went into the outfield, there still would be a chance to get Abrams at the plate.

Lopata called for a pitch-out. In center, Ashburn moved in. He would back up second in case of a bad throw. Hamner began to edge toward second. Abrams had not picked up the action yet. On the mound, Roberts nodded he had the sign. He started to go into his stretch. Then he threw. He threw a fast ball right down the pipe. Hamner's mouth fell open. Snider rapped it on a line up the middle, over second, and into center field. Abrams started running. Dirt flew from his spikes as he tore around third. From the stands came one great roar: *"Abie, you should run fast."*

But in the middle of this huge mistake, here was Ashburn. He had raced in to back up second base. And as he came in, the ball landed right at his feet. By now, Richie was only a short distance on the outfield grass behind second. He picked up the ball and threw to the plate. And suddenly all of Brooklyn realized what was happening. Halfway down the line, Abrams was beaten. A wail rang out over Brooklyn as Lopata tagged out Abrams. Roberts, whose bacon had been saved, proceeded to get out of the inning unscathed.

In the tenth inning Dick Sisler hit a home run into the left-field seats and the Phillies won the pennant. But after the game Hamner didn't want to talk to anybody. Particularly Roberts. He wanted to kill Roberts.

"I need a drink," he kept saying. "Alone."

The Mets never had even a faint tinge of this. This was a nice, placid, thoughtful team. There was one Sunday night, coming back to New York from Chicago, when Solly Hemus, the coach, and a couple of the players sat in the lounge part of the plane, and the talk was the same as you would hear anyplace around the major leagues. Except they soon got to talking about throwing knockdown pitches at Willie Mays.

"The pitch right after you throw at him, that's the time to watch him," Joe Pignatano, one of the catchers, said. "He's ready then. He's mad."

"Knock him down twice in a row, then," a tall kid said.

"Do you mean knockdown pitches bother Mays?" they were asked.

"Bother him?" one of the players said. "He's scared to death. If he wasn't so scared of being hit with a ball, he'd hit .600."

"You go up to him before the game," one of them said, "and you tell him, 'Willie, sometime today. Sometime today I'm going to stick it right in your ear.' He'll be standing around the batting cage and he gives you this: 'Go ahead, man, throw at me all you want. It don't bother me, man.' But that's talk. I know it bothers him."

They sat and discussed handling Mays with these pitches. It was excellent talk, and it would have made a great impression on the listener except for one thing. It was a red-covered scorebook, and a flip through the pages showed little items like this:

May 26: Mays hits two home runs against the Mets. *May 27:* Willie gets four hits against the Mets. *June 1:* A home run. *June 2:* Another homer. *June 3:* Still another homer. *July 4:* Willie hits two homers and has seven runs batted in.

I closed the book. "You're right," I told one of the players. "Mays is a yellow dog."

Why a discussion of this type should come up at all is a question. If there is one matter which irked Stengel over the season, it was the refusal of his pitchers to throw tight pitches and move the batter back. Against the Mets, all hitters practically stepped on the plate and remained there until they had either hit the ball out of sight or reached base through an error.

Stengel, in one of the finest talks on baseball anybody has ever heard, made much of this one night.

"All these pitchers we have," he said, "I see them with their lovely wives and their lovely children. Oh, grand children. So they go out there to pitch, and here is the batter. Ohhh, he digs right in there and he swings that bat and he has a wonderful toehold. And our pitchers, they say they won't throw at him. They say you have to think of the lovely wife and children the batter has. Well, some of these pitchers of mine ought to think about their own children. That batter up there doesn't care about them. He's in there to take the food right off the table from the pitcher's children. These fellows of mine, they better start thinking of their own lovely children and move that batter back off of the plate a little."

It was excellent thinking. However, every time you bring it up, you also think of the game against the Reds on August 12, and it shows, as well as anything, the way the Mets, advice or no advice, played baseball all year.

Before the game a home-run-hitting contest was held. Wally Post of the Reds had five pitches thrown to him. He pulled four of them over the left-field wall to win the contest. Now in a contest such as this the batter tells the man pitching to him just where to put the ball. Then it is thrown at three-quarter speed. In Post's case he wanted it a little bit over belt high and a little bit on the outside.

As each contestant comes up, opposing pitchers normally watch closely from the dugout. Whatever pitch the home-run hitter calls for is the one never to give him in a game.

Later in the day, in the eighth inning with two on and the Reds ahead, 5–4, Post was sent up as a pinch-hitter. On the mound for the Mets was Kenneth MacKenzie, who is a graduate of Yale University. Don't ever let anybody tell you that a guy can get into Yale just because he has money behind him. It takes more than that. Those kids that go to Yale have to be very good spellers. So MacKenzie is no dunce. This is a bright boy.

He threw a pitch a little bit over belt high and a little bit outside to Post. Wally hit it exactly three miles over the left-field fence.

—————————————— SPOT REPORTING ——————————————

THE OPENING sentence of the following account, which appeared in the old *New York World,* is probably the most famous in baseball journalism, and the piece itself won several prizes and has been exhibited as a model lead.

1923:
New York Yankees 4,
New York Giants 2

HEYWOOD BROUN

THE RUTH is mighty and shall prevail. He did yesterday. Babe made two home runs and the Yankees won from the Giants at the Polo Grounds by a score of 4 to 2. This evens up the World Series with one game for each contender.

It was the first game the Yankees won from the Giants since October 10, 1921, and it ended a string of eight successive victories for the latter, with one tie thrown in.

Victory came to the American League champions through a change of tactics. Miller Huggins could hardly fail to have observed Wednesday that terrible things were almost certain to happen to his men if they paused any place along the line from first to home.

In order to prevent blunders in base running he wisely decided to eliminate it. The batter who hits a ball into the stands cannot possibly be caught napping off any base.

The Yankees prevented Kelly, Frisch and the rest from performing tricks in black magic by consistently hammering the ball out of the park or into sections of the stand where only amateurs were seated.

Through simplicity itself, the system worked like a charm. Three of the Yankees' four runs were the product of homers, and this was enough for the winning total. Aaron Ward was Ruth's assistant, Irish Meusel of the Giants also made a home run, but yesterday's show belonged to Ruth.

For the first time since coming to New York, Babe achieved his full brilliance in a World Series game. Before this he has varied between pretty good and simply awful, but yesterday he was magnificent.

Just before the game John McGraw remarked:

"Why shouldn't we pitch to Ruth? I've said before and I'll say again, we pitch to better hitters than Ruth in the National League."

Ere the sun had set on McGraw's rash and presumptuous words, the Babe had flashed across the sky fiery portents which should have been sufficient to strike terror and conviction into the hearts of all infidels. But John McGraw clung to his heresy with a courage worthy of a better cause.

In the fourth inning Ruth drove the ball completely out of the premises. McQuillan was pitching at the time, and the count was two balls and one strike. The strike was a fast ball shoulder-high, at which Ruth had lunged with almost comic ferocity and ineptitude.

Snyder peeked at the bench to get a signal from McGraw. Catching for the Giants must be a terrific strain on the neck muscles, for apparently it is etiquette to take the signals from the bench manager furtively. The catcher is supposed to pretend he is merely glancing around to see if the girl in the red hat is anywhere in the grandstand, although all the time his eyes are intent on McGraw.

Of course the nature of the code is secret, but this time McGraw scratched his nose to indicate: "Try another of those shoulder-high fast ones on the Big Bum and let's see if we can't make him break his back again."

But Babe didn't break his back, for he had something solid to check his terrific swing. The ball started climbing from the moment it left the plate. It was a pop fly with a brand new gland and, although it flew high, it also flew far.

When last seen the ball was crossing the roof of the stand in deep right field at an altitude of 315 feet. We wonder whether new baseballs conversing in the original package ever remark: "Join Ruth and see the world."

In the fifth Ruth was up again and by this time McQuillan had left the park utterly and Jack Bentley was pitching. The count crept up to two strikes and two balls. Snyder sneaked a look at the little logician deep in the dugout. McGraw blinked twice, pulled up his trousers and thrust the forefinger of his right hand into his left eye. Snyder knew that he meant: "Try the Big Bozo on a slow curve around his knees and don't forget to throw to first if you happen to drop the third strike."

Snyder called for the delivery as directed and Ruth half-topped a line drive over the wall of the lower stand in right field. With that drive the Babe tied a record. Benny Kauff and Duffy Lewis are the only other players who ever made two home runs in a single World Series game.

But was McGraw convinced and did he rush out of the dugout and kneel before Ruth with a cry of "Maestro" as the Babe crossed the plate? He did not. He nibbled at not a single word he has ever uttered in disparagement of the prowess of the Yankee slugger. In the ninth Ruth came to bat with two out and a runner on second base. By every consideration of prudent tactics an intentional pass seemed indicated.

Snyder jerked his head around and observed that McGraw was blowing his nose. The Giant catcher was puzzled, for that was a signal he had never learned. By a process of pure reasoning he attempted to figure out just what it was that his chief was trying to convey to him.

"Maybe he means if we pitch to Ruth we'll blow the game," thought Snyder, but he looked toward the bench again just to make sure.

Now McGraw intended no signal at all when he blew his nose. That was not tactics but only a head cold. On the second glance Snyder observed that the little Napoleon gritted his teeth. Then he proceeded to spell out with the first three fingers of his right hand: "The Old Guard dies, but never surrenders." That was a signal Snyder recognized, although it never had passed between him and his manager before.

McGraw was saying: "Pitch to the Big Bum if he hammers every ball in the park into the North River."

And so, at Snyder's request, Bentley did pitch to Ruth and the Babe drove the ball deep into right center; so deep that Casey Stengel could feel the hot breath of the bleacherites on his back as the ball came down and he caught it. If that drive had been just a shade to the right it would have been a third home run for Ruth. As it was, the Babe had a great day, with two home runs, a terrific long fly and two bases on balls.

Neither pass was intentional. For that McGraw should receive due credit. His game deserves to be recorded along with the man who said, "Lay on, Macduff," "Sink the ship, Master Ginner, split her in twain," and "I'll fight it out on this line if it takes all summer." For John McGraw also went down eyes front and his thumb on his nose.

Some of the sportsmanship of the afternoon was not so admirable. In the sixth inning Pep Young prevented a Yankee double play by diving at the legs of Ward, who was just about to throw to first after a force-out. Tack Hardwick never took out an opposing back more neatly. Half the spectators booed Young and the other half applauded him.

It did not seem to us that there was any very good reason for booing Young, since the tradition of professional baseball always has been agreeably free of chivalry. The rule is, "Do anything you can get away with."

But Young never should have been permitted to get away with interference. The runner on first ought to have been declared out. In coming down to second Young had complete rights to the baseline and the bag, but those rights should not have permitted him the privilege of diving all the way across the bag to tackle Ward around the ankles.

It was a most palpably incompetent decision by Hart, the National League umpire on second base. Fortunately the blunder had no effect on the game, since the next Giant batter hit into a double play in which the Giant rushline was unable to reach Ward in time to do anything about it.

Ruth crushed to earth shall rise again. Herb Pennock, the assistant hero of the afternoon, did the same thing. In the fourth inning, Jack Bentley toppled the slim Yankee left-hander into a crumpled heap by hitting him in the back with a fast ball. Pennock went down with a groan which could be heard even in the dollar seats. All the players gathered around him as he writhed, and what with sympathy and some judicious massage, he was up again within three or four minutes, and his pitching efficiency seemed to be in no wise impaired. It was, of course, wholly an accident, as the kidney punch is barred in baseball.

Entirely aside from his injury, Pennock looked none too stalwart. He is a meager athlete who winds up with great deliberation, as if fearful about what the opposing batter will do with the ball. And it was mostly slow curves that he fed to the Giants, but they did nothing much in crucial moments. Every now and then Pennock switched to a fast one, and the change of pace had McGraw's men baffled throughout.

Just once Pennock was in grave danger. It looked as if his three-run lead might be swept away in the sixth inning. Groh, Frisch and Young, the three Giants to face him at that point, all singled solidly. It seemed the part of wisdom to remove Pennock immediately after Young's single had scored Groh. Here Huggins was shrewd. He guessed wisely and stuck to Pennock.

Irish Meusel forced Young, and it would have been a double play but for Young's interference with Ward's throw. Cunningham, who followed, did hit into a double play, Scott to Ward to Pipp. The Giant's rally thus was limited to one run.

Their other score came in the second inning, when Irish Meusel drove a home run into the upper tier of the left field stands. It was a long wallop and served to tie the score at that stage of the game, as Aaron Ward had made a home run for the Yankees in the first half of the inning. Ward's homer was less lusty, but went in the same general direction.

In the fourth the Yankees broke the tie. Ruth began it with his over-the-fence smash, and another run came across on a single by Pipp, Schang's hit to right—which Young fumbled long enough to let Pipp reach third—and Scott's clean line hit to center. This is said to be Scott's last year as a regular and he seems intent on making a good exit, for, in addition to fielding spryly, he made two singles.

The defensive star of the afternoon was Joe Dugan, third baseman of the Yankees. He specialized on bunts. McQuillan caught him flat-footed with an unexpected tap, but he threw it on the dead run in time to get his man at first.

Again he made a great play against Kelly, first batter up in the last half of the ninth. Kelly just nicked the ball with a vicious swing and the result was a treacherous spinning grounder that rolled only halfway down to third. Dugan had to run and throw in conjunction this time, too, but he got his man.

For the Giants, Frisch, Young and Meusel batted hard, and Jack Bentley pitched well after relieving McQuillan in the fourth. He was hit fairly hard and he was a trifle wild, but the only run scored against him was Ruth's homer in the fifth.

As for the local color, the only bit we saw was around the neck of a spectator in a large white hat. The big handkerchief, which was spread completely over the gentleman's chest, was green and yellow, with purple spots. The rooter said his name was Tom Mix, but offered no other explanation.

PROFILE

BOB CONSIDINE'S is one of the great journalistic names of our times. The following article appeared in *Life* magazine for July 29, 1948, and I wanted to include it here for what may be paradoxical reasons—it is a piece topical to that particular time, when the Philadelphia Athletics were still in Philadelphia; yet its subject represents all that is ageless and permanent in baseball. Needless to say, Mr. Considine was writing about the late Connie Mack. The last sentence of this article is one of particular poignancy in view of Mack's death within what was relatively so brief a period following the departure of the A's from Philadelphia.

Mr. Mack

BOB CONSIDINE

CORNELIUS MCGILLICUDDY, who was given the enduring alias of Connie Mack by an unsung newspaperman in 1884—because his full name could not fit in the small space of a newspaper box score—must be one of the oldest truly active businessmen in the U.S.

As president-treasurer-manager of the Philadelphia Athletics baseball club he works seven days a week 365 days a year and pays himself a salary comparable to that of the President of the U.S. But Mr. Mack, as his countless associates, friends and acquaintances call him religiously and with a certain awe, is not a rich man. He has, among other responsibilities, 15 great-grandchildren and a small army of personal pensioners dependent on his earning capacity. In 1946 he reported an income of $79,000, which made him perhaps the highest-paid 84-year-old employee in the country, but he was unable to buy the Buick he had on order. Minor stockholders in the Athletics, which Mister Mack has managed since 1901, chipped in, bought him the car and provided a chauffeur—one of the rare concessions made to Mr. Mack's incredible age.

Mister Mack, who will be 86 years old next December, might almost ask for patent rights to the game of baseball if he had not signed away such claims by lending himself to the pretty fable that the sport was the handiwork of the late General Abner Doubleday. He did much to fashion its rules, pioneered in developing the torturous art of catching, was a major manipulator in the rape of the National League at the turn of the century (which produced the American League and made big-league baseball big) and he introduced the modern style of pitching.

This occurred one day in Waterbury, Conn. when Mister Mack, crouching fifteen feet behind home plate and catching the ball on its first bounce with the aid of a fingerless kid glove, decided that there must be a better way for his pitcher to deliver the ball. He felt it was essentially unfair for his thrower to hop, skip and run through his cramped little 6×4 pitching box and to throw underhanded to a batter who not only was given seven balls and four strikes but could also demand that the ball be delivered to him at a favored height. So he walked out to the marked-off box in which his hurler stood and said, "Try throwing the ball overhand."

The man looked up at him as if he had gone mad, but followed his advice. The ball shot over the plate at a lively clip and the batter—as startled as a batter of today might be if Bob Feller suddenly delivered a through-the-legs pitch—missed it vaguely. It took the fans three more pitches to realize that Waterbury was being cruelly had. Then they rose and made as if to come out on the field and attack the pitcher.

But Connie reached him first. "Don't listen to those fellows," he ordered. "Just pitch your own game." The man did, and his daring new delivery produced a considerable vogue; so considerable, in fact, that the pitcher's box was moved back from 45 feet to its present 60 feet 6 inches from the plate. And pitchers have been throwing like that ever since.

Mack was one of the first catchers to move up to a position just behind the batter and catch the ball before it bounced. His proximity to the batters of that dimly distant era stimulated in him the devil which is part of his kindly nature. It occurred to him that if he was that close to a man who was bent upon bringing ruin to him and the Mack team he might as well trip him or "tip" his bat—to interfere with his swing— or in other ways militate against the man's getting a hit.

"Don't ever say I was a great catchaw," he told this reporter recently. "But," he added with a bit of glitter in his slightly watery blue eyes, "I was kinda tricky. We got away with a lot back in the days when we played with only one umpire. The only time I ever really got caught was by an old ballplayer named Weaver. I must have been with Washington. Anyway, this Weaver—a fine fellow—he got angry with me after I had tipped his bat a few times, and he used to say that he'd get even with me.

"Well, Mr. Constantine, he did. By gosh, the next time he had two strikes on him he just stepped back from the plate and instead of swinging at the ball he brought his bat down on my wrists. I dropped like a shot. Let me tell you it hurt.

"But I figured out a way to get back at him. I waited until our last game of the year against Weaver's team, and Weaver's last time at bat, and when he had two strikes on him I tipped his bat again, just to show him I could still do it."

Except that each passing decade gives him more and more the appearance of a stately and well-plucked gobbler, Mister Mack has not changed much in the last fifty years. He was born in East Brookfield, Massachusetts, either just before or just after the midnight which separated December 22, 1862, from December 23, 1862. His brother Mike, who lived to be ninety by sticking steadfastly to a daily glass of whisky (Connie gave up his own modest drinking and golf when he was seventy-six), liked to cackle that Mister Mack, who preferred the December 23 date, was a pretty smart fellow but just didn't know what day he was born on. Mike always said he saw the birth on December 22.

Whatever the date, the son of Michael McGillicuddy—who was at that moment fighting against the South with the Massachusetts Regiment —was christened Cornelius. At the end of the Civil War, Michael McGillicuddy returned to his job in an East Brookfield cotton mill, and when Cornelius was nine years old he also got a job there, working summers. He was given an hour for lunch but never used more than fifteen minutes of it to eat. The remaining forty-five were given to games involving a bat and ball, variously called one o'cat, four o'cat, roundball and baseball.

When he was fifteen Connie presented himself to the keeper of a general store in his neighborhood and asked to be measured. He blanched a bit when the man announced that he stood 6 feet 1. This confirmed his secret fear that there was something freakish about him. He began suffering claustrophobia at his cramped little desk in the local public school, and so, shortly after his sixteenth birthday, he abruptly quit. There was no furor in the McGillicuddy family. His schooling seemed adequate for the job he had in mind—that of a general hand in the Green and Twitchell shoe factory in East Brookfield.

Connie could pay more attention to his baseball now and by 1882 was the regular catcher on East Brookfield's best ball club. In 1883 his imagination was irrevocably fired by the appearance in East Brookfield for an exhibition game of the Worcester team, then in the National League. Later that year Cap Anson brought his mustached and mighty Chicago Colts to East Brookfield and Connie rubbed shoulders with these gods from another world and knew that nothing must stop him from trying to be one with them.

Early in March 1884 Connie received a telegram prompted by his East Brookfield battery mate, Billy Hogan, who had plunged onward to the comparatively lofty position of pitcher for the Meriden club of the Connecticut League. The telegram offered him a job with the club. Connie went straight to his foreman and told him he was quitting. "You'd better stay," said the foreman, a man named Morris (he is still alive today, at 100). "No, Saturday night's my last night in the boot shop," Connie insisted, a statement which he sometimes now regrets having made. "I hope Mr. Morris didn't think I was rude," he mused not long ago, as if he had been mulling it over for sixty-four years.

There was still the matter of proving to the manager of the Meriden club that he was able as well as willing. This Connie did in a game against Yale in which he handled his pitcher so well that the man struck out twenty-one Yales, including a vigorous young New Haven star named Amos Alonzo Stagg, who was later to make something of a name for himself in football. The lanky young catcher from East Brookfield was promptly offered $60 a month, held out and got $80, and became so popular with Meriden fans that at the close of the season they presented him with a gold watch.

Mister Mack was to become an almost starchy upholder of baseball ethics in the generations to come. But the game was unhampered by niceties in the '80s. With no twinge of conscience he deserted his loving fans in 1885 and jumped to the Hartford team of the same league because the Hartford management offered him $125 a month. By 1886 he was earning $200 a month, and in September of that year he and four other members of the club were sold to Washington of the National League for $3,500. It was a heady burst of good fortune, but Mister Mack was not dazzled out of his wits. He insisted on being paid $800 to catch the final month of the season at Washington. He also got a contract for $2,750 for the 1887 season and once again was so well received in a town whose ball park's grandstands then seated 1,800 (and whose White House incumbent was Grover Cleveland) that the fans presented him with a silver tea set.

Two years later, happily married to his childhood sweetheart, Margaret Hogan, and father of a growing family, Mister Mack jumped his job with Washington to join the ill-started Brotherhood, a league which the players themselves hoped to operate as a co-op in opposition to the entrenched National. He jumped for the same salary as was paid to him by the Washington team and became so warmly attached to the prospects of the new organization—especially those of his new club, Buffalo

—that he invested all the money he had saved and all that he could borrow. The league folded after its first year and with it went everything the little family possessed. The gaunt young man of the house hooked on to the Pittsburgh Pirates in '91, however, and was well on his way to becoming the National League's outstanding catcher in '93 when his left ankle was fractured in a game with Boston. His uselessness as a player, plus his keen baseball mind, prompted the Pittsburgh owners to appoint Connie manager of the club at the end of the 1894 season.

Mister Mack was 32 and considered, in those days, rather elderly for a freshman manager. But the owners, perhaps tolerant of his years, maintained their patience. When the Pirates finished sixth in 1896, however, he was discharged.

The man who was to be hailed forty-seven years later as perhaps the best manager in the American League was saved from complete obscurity by Ban Johnson, president of the Western League. Johnson, a ruthless dreamer who lived and died believing that baseball was perfected in order to serve him as a gigantic chess board on which to move his living pieces, lifted Mister Mack out of reluctant retirement and set him up as manager and one-fourth owner of the Milwaukee club. Johnson changed the name of his league to the American in 1900 and laid plans to invade the big time monopolized by the National. He ordered his friend Charles Comiskey, owner of the St. Paul franchise, to move his club to Chicago. He set up other clubs in Cleveland and Buffalo, and took over Detroit and Kansas City. He dispatched Mister Mack to Philadelphia one cold December day in 1900 to raise money for a ball park and to find a club which could successfully compete with the well-established Phillies.

Mister Mack found the needed money in the pocket of a dour and crusty baseball manufacturer named Ben Shibe, who spent enough of it to build a small park at 29th and Columbia Avenue, named Columbia Park. With $500 of a bankroll supplied by a willing but naïve Clevelander named Somers, Mister Mack persuaded the Phillies' greater star, Nap Lajoie, to jump to the new Philadelphia club. Then he talked another Phillies star, Lave Cross, into switching his allegiance. He also kept his eyes open for young men who showed promise. One of the young players he found before the curtain went up on American League baseball history in Philadelphia was a pitcher at Gettysburg College named Eddie Plank, who was later to enter baseball's Hall of Fame.

John McGraw, sharp-tongued critic of every club except his New York Giants, inadvertently gave the new Philadelphia American League team its nickname. Asked by a reporter to comment on the new club, Muggsy barked, "Looks like the American League's got a white elephant on its hands in Philadelphia." Mack read the interview and placidly selected the name "White Elephants" for his club. They finished fourth in 1901 and were on their way to winning the pennant in 1902 when the

Supreme Court of Pennsylvania ruled that Mister Mack could no longer use Lajoie and other appropriated stars. He was forced to break up his team and the experts immediately wrote off the chances of the club— which had by now been given the additional nickname of Athletics.

But Mister Mack was not defeated. He remembered an eccentric southpaw named Rube Waddell who had played in the Western League and whose major ambition in life was to become a bartender. He found Waddell pitching in a California league and had him shipped East. With the Rube's help the Athletics, or A's, won the pennant, their first of nine under Mister Mack, who also has the appalling record of finishing last in his league sixteen times.

From that time through the season of 1914 Mister Mack won five pennants and three World Series and produced in 1911 one of the two or three greatest ball clubs of all time, a team whose infield was made up of Stuffy McInnis at first, Eddie Collins at second, Jack Barry at short and Frank (Home Run) Baker at third. It was given the greatest plaudit that could be contrived in the minds of the sports writers of that unin- flated day. They called it "the $100,000 infield."

When the Athletics lost the 1914 series to the somewhat talentless Braves, Mister Mack smashed the club like an expensive china vase. His players had cupped attentive ears to the offers of the newly created Federal League, a rival to the American League which Mister Mack had so successfully built up, and several of them did make the jump. With this and a general housecleaning, the greatest reversal of fortunes in the history of any city's club got under way. His 1914 team had outdistanced its competitors by winning 99 games and losing 53. The 1915 relics won only 43 games and lost 109. The 1916 A's won 36 and lost 117. They finished eighth for seven consecutive seasons.

After a decade in the environs of the cellar Mister Mack came up again. By astute outbidding of his rivals he assembled a superb combina- tion of ballplayers. With this crew, built around Al Simmons, now his rough and adoring third-base coach, Lefty Grove, who was to win more than 300 games, Jimmy Foxx, Mickey Cochrane, George Earnshaw, Jimmy Dykes and others, the A's jumped from fifth in 1924 to second in 1925, and when the great Yankees declined after 1928 forged on to win the pennants of 1929, 1930 and 1931.

Mister Mack sometimes gets a little sentimental about that club. Recalling it recently, he remembered the seventh inning of the fourth game of the 1929 Series against the Cubs. The Cubs were leading 8 to 0.

"It was my intention at that stage of the game to send in substitutes for all the regulars at the start of the eighth inning," he said. "But when we came to bat in the seventh some odd things began happening. Al Simmons, the first man up for us, hit a home run which landed on the roof of the left-field stands, fair by just inches. If it had been foul—well, that doesn't matter now.

"Foxx then singled. So did Bing Miller. Dykes singled. It was his fourth straight hit of the day and I got the feeling that we had something special on the fire. Dykes's single scored Foxx, and now Joe Boley singled, scoring Miller. Burns batted for Rommel and flied out to English for the first out. But Bishop singled, scoring Dykes. The score was now 8 to 4.

"Joe McCarthy, a fine manager, took out Charles Root, his pitcher, and put in Artie Nehf. Mule Haas then hit a long fly to center which Hack Wilson lost and it went for a home run, making the score 8 to 7 in favor of the Cubs. When Cochrane walked, Joe McCarthy, a fine manager, replaced Nehf with Sheriff Blake. But Simmons singled to left, Foxx singled to center scoring Cochrane with the tying run. Big Malone started pitching then. He hit Miller with a pitched ball. Dykes then doubled for his fifth hit, scoring Simmons and Foxx with the ninth and tenth runs of the inning, and Burns and Boley—they struck out.

"You know, Mr. Constantine," said Mister Mack with a slight cough, "there was talk that I danced with joy during that big inning. It's not true. I just sat there, and when we won the game I walked off with hardly a word to the boys. It doesn't help any to appear to be too pleased before such an important series is won. Such an attitude might lead to overconfidence, and that's fatal."

These wondrous years of the A's lasted until 1933. Financially they represented a high tide in the fortunes of the ball club. With the possible exception of the New York Yankees, the Athletics had the fattest payroll in any league. Shibe Park had been renovated and with that and other expenses the club's overhead mounted. By 1933 the crash, which had already cut Philadelphia's ability to support a high-class ball team, hit Mister Mack: his club was $500,000 in debt. Simmons, Haas and Dykes had been sold to the White Sox for $150,000. Now, pressed to the limit by financial stringency, Mister Mack sold Grove, Foxx, Bishop and Rube Walberg, leaving himself with only tattered remnants of his former starring team. When the massacre was over he was told that if he dared come out of the dugout and show himself in the opening-day ceremonies of 1934 he would be booed as no man in the history of the city had ever been blasted. In face of the threat Mister Mack stalked gingerly off his barren bench on opening day and walked, head up, to the centerfield flagpole. The old man dared them to howl him down, and no one took the challenge. Suddenly a whole city seemed to agree with him that he had been forced to sell in order to survive.

From 1934 through 1947 Mister Mack's hapless teams never finished in the first division. But by late 1940 Mister Mack, who had bought out the shares of John Shibe, owned 58 per cent of the stock in the A's. He was now the Mr. Chips of baseball. The fans delighted in his gentle whimsy. There was the story of the Philadelphia cab driver, apparently new to the town because he did not recognize his passenger, who carried Mack to the North Philadelphia Station one night. The old gentleman, lost in thought, mechanically paid the sum recorded on the meter, picked up his bag and wandered off.

"Hey, pop," the driver snarled, "what about a tip?"

Connie stopped, lost in thought. "A tip?" he asked in a voice that sometimes spurts up an octave.

"Yeah, pop, a tip. How about one?"

"Certainly," Connie answered. "Don't bet on the A's."

By June of 1947 any outside observer might have been forgiven for assuming that Mister Mack's long career in baseball was drawing to a rather weary close. He had assembled a club of nobodies whose strength he estimated at the start of the season by telling Art Morrow of the Philadelphia *Inquirer,* "We can promise our patrons good baseball and nothing more." But to everyone's surprise he began getting excellent pitching from the likes of Phil Marchildon, who still bore the scars of his months of captivity by the Germans; Dick Fowler, a young man seemingly crushed by family troubles; Bill McCahan, whose uncle had played in the outfield for Mister Mack in 1905 (McCahan went on to pitch a no-hitter for him before the season was over); Joe Coleman, given to Connie by his friend, the late Brother Gilbert (who had discovered an incipient young tailor named George Herman Ruth at St. Mary's Industrial School in Baltimore 33 years before); Bob Savage, first big leaguer wounded in World War II, and a 20-year-old Pennsylvania Dutchman named Carl Scheib who had been pestering him for a job for the previous five years. He shaped these earnest young men around a resurrected second-rater named Bill Dietrich, who had been in and out of the league since 1930, and the A's began winning games.

Mister Mack decided about seventy years ago that pitching is 75 per cent of a team's worth, and nothing in the interim has changed his mind. By the end of the 1947 season he had added one or two other willing young hands, including the staff's only southpaw, Lou Brissie, a big courageous fellow who must play with a clumsy plastic guard over his shell-riddled left leg, part of which he left in Italy. He built a new infield around a revitalized veteran shortstop named Eddie Joost, put Hank Majeski, a Yankee castoff, on third base and unveiled an excellent young infielder in Ferris Fain, for whom he was subsequently offered a reported $100,000 by the Yanks. He inspired a phlegmatic young Czech named Elmer Valo with the energies of a human dynamo and breathed new life into a Detroit outfielder named Barney McCosky. In the other outfield position he placed Sam Chapman, a muscular former All-American gridman. The A's made a race of it and looked better than their fifth-place finish would indicate.

Mister Mack began to live all over again and the undercurrent of sincere wishes that he retire melted away. This year, more than ever, he is the grand old man of baseball, and though most of the seasoned observers feel that it would be too good to be true if Mister Mack in his fantastic antiquity came home in front, players, managers and owners throughout the league like to say that if they themselves cannot win the banner they want the old man to cop it.

Prosperity has returned to the Athletics. The 1947 spurt attracted 900,000 paid admissions to Shibe Park and the A's drew a million customers on the road, sharing the money those outlanders deposited at the box offices. This year the Athletics, contenders from the opening gong, will draw more than a million clients at home—the biggest attendance in the tremendous history of the team—and perhaps a million and a half on the road, though they have one of the smallest payrolls in either big league.

The highest-paid men on the team—Marchildon and Joost—make $17,500 a year or less, and the sweatful young Valo probably does not make more than $8,500. Mister Mack just does not believe in the kind of salaries paid by the rich owners of the Yankees, Red Sox, Indians and Tigers. Nor does he believe in paying a lot of money and trying to buy a ready-made winner. Except for the cost of helping half a dozen of his players through their colleges—Mister Mack's first advice to any teenager who wants to play for him is, "You'd better let me send you to school first"—he paid only $20,000 for his present pitching staff.

But seldom in the history of baseball has there been a closer affinity between labor and management than there is with the 1948 Athletics—otherwise a typically soulless baseball corporation. Mister Mack is a fabulously beloved figure, as such love is measured in baseball. There is no cow-eyed infatuation for him among his players. That would be asking too much of the average big-leaguer, who is fundamentally a mercenary. But the warmth of the player for Mister Mack is readily apparent. "I love that old guy," one said recently, "but what a shrewd old goat he is!"

Except for a new and sometimes alarming trembling of his classic scorecard, with which he wigwags signals to his boys from his vantage point in the dugout, Mister Mack has shown few outward indications this year of the suffocating excitement that is in him. He still wears the high, starched collars that have been his trade-mark for half a century; when the style went out in Teddy Roosevelt's day, Mister Mack persuaded the firm to keep making them for him. His 150 pounds are smoothed out tautly over his 6-foot 1-inch frame. The story that his strongest exclamation is "Fudge!" is as hardy a fairy tale as the never-dying report that Babe Ruth was an orphan. A historic outburst of his temper will always be remembered in the dugouts of America: his chronically gripping pitching ace, Lefty Grove, trudged into the dugout one day after Mister Mack had pulled him out of a game, threw down his glove in disgust, and growled, "Nuts!" Mister Mack stood up quickly and walked over to him. He pushed his face close to Grove's. "And nuts to you, too!" he shouted, then marched back to his place in his spindly way and sat down.

To Mister Mack this 1948 club is something special, and in his comparatively rare bursts of loquaciousness he likes to say it is his favorite

team because it is his fightingest. It could be, too. By the July 4 turning
point of the season, when it was only half a game out of first place, it had
won seventeen of its games by one-run margins; had snapped back to win
after the Red Sox had annihilated it in an early July game with a fourteen-
run rally in one inning, and had otherwise paid dividends on his enormous affection. At the end of July the A's were still only half a game
behind the Red Sox.

In his excitement these days Mister Mack sometimes makes plainly
discernible mistakes in simple strategy, and if these cost him a game he
is distraught as he goes home after a contest. He is beginning to shake
like a great angular twig whenever the team loses, and he finds it hard
to sleep those nights until he has reviewed each move of the game in his
mind. When he signals for an obviously wrong move these days Al Simmons turns his back a bit sadly on the old man, as if he did not detect
the signal, and calls for the right move. But this never fools Mister Mack.
When Al comes back to the bench at the end of the inning Mister Mack
usually speaks up.

"You used better judgment than I did, Al," he will say quietly, and
then go about his timeless task of wagging his scorecard at his fielders.

It is not good taste on the Philadelphia bench to second-guess Mister
Mack openly, but it has been done even in this year of dizzying success.
Not long ago he ordered his leading run-producer, Majeski, to lay down
a bunt. One man was out at the time and the A's were behind. Majeski
reluctantly did as he was bidden and sacrificed the runner to second. But
the next hitter popped up futilely and Majeski said with warm sincerity,
"That was lousy baseball, Mister Mack."

Mister Mack thought for a time and said, "You're right, Mr. Majeski!"

Mister Mack calls a lot of his players "Mister." In his relations with
them he reveals many other niceties which another manager might
scorn as a show of weakness. If one of his pitchers works himself out of
a tight hole, or a player makes a timely hit or a fine defensive play, Mister
Mack often will stand up as the player returns. He will shake hands with
him and say with voice-cracking warmth, "Thank you," then sit down
and go on with the business of running the game.

The A's bench is perhaps the quietest in baseball. Remarkably few
obscenities are heard and the razzing of the other team is always kept
above the belt. When a newcomer violates one of the unwritten laws of
bench conduct he soon learns that he has blundered. Bobo Newsom, a
garrulous soul who loves Mister Mack with a vociferous affection, showed
up at Philadelphia a few years ago in the course of his endless march
through the majors. "Hello, Connie!" he roared at their first meeting. Just
before the start of his second game with the A's, Bo was called upon by
six rather grim young A's. "We call him Mister Mack, see?" their spokesman growled. So did Bobo after that.

Mister Mack is handed a new scorecard before every game, and in warm weather a fresh bath towel is placed behind his back by any of a half dozen roughly adoring coaches, clubhouse attendants, players and the like. He makes impatient sounds like "stop babying me" when minor homages are being paid to him, but it is the belief of those very close to him that the old man would feel hurt if he were not thus pampered. Certainly what he gets in this line is precious little compared to the still enormous physical energies he alone must expend each day.

The old gentleman seldom sees his players after a game, unless one has made some catastrophic blunder. But, perhaps once a month, he does pop into the locker room, usually to have a concerned word with a coach or his son. Now and then it is a simple ceremonial call. Not long ago, pleased with the way in which his hard-working young team had just won another, Mister Mack poked in his head, patted his long, knuckly hands together in polite applause, looking around the room as he did. "This is for you," he said with quiet warmth.

Mister Mack doesn't go in for that newfangled nonsense of a telephone line running between the A's dugout at Shibe Park and the bull pen at the far end of the field. To call in a relief pitcher he uses a system that went out of style in most other big-league ball parks years ago. To get in Joe Coleman from the distant reaches of the pen Mister Mack orders a coach to stand out in front of the dugout—in view of the pen—and to pantomine a man shoveling coal. If the call is for Carl Scheib, the coach stands up and beats his fists against the nearest wall. Consulting briefly with himself, the bull-pen coach interprets this act as "man pounding on Shibe Park—Shibe—Scheib." But only a group well versed in the gentle wanderings of Mister Mack's mind could piece together his signal which calls in Dick Fowler. He orders the coach to stand out in front and make a stooping motion as if he were picking flowers. Mister Mack is extremely fond of Fowler and with unfailing courtliness always addresses him as "Mr. Flowers."

Mister Mack has possibly had more personal friends than any American now alive, for he has outlived several crops of them and is still enormously popular. A devout Catholic who never misses a Sunday Mass or a holyday of obligation, Mister Mack seems to attract waves of sports-minded priests at each stop along the big-league circuit. Considering the wideness of his circle of friends and those who feel friendly toward him, Mister Mack's memory is phenomenal. At Connie Mack Day in Meriden in 1947 an old fellow was helped to the microphone at home plate and recalled, "Con, you remember when we played against each other right here in '83? And remember I got a hit in the ninth and knocked in a run?"

Mister Mack took the microphone. "I certainly do!" he exclaimed, then added, "And I also remember that we won the game, 2 to 1."

Off and on since 1915 there have been reports that Mister Mack was ready to retire. He did quit once, without public knowledge. It happened a few years ago when he decided to hire Al Horwits, former Philadelphia baseball writer, as publicity man for the team. To show his sons, who hold various executive offices in the organization, that he was open-minded about the appointment he submitted it to them for approval. Two of them voted against Horwits and Mister Mack waxed indignant. "You have my resignation," he told his glum sons, and stalked out of his office. His retirement lasted for as long as it took the boys to run after him, telling him that on more sober thought they had decided that Horwits was just about the finest public-relations man obtainable—which he is. Mister Mack cocked his head like a reflective crane for a moment and relented.

The old gentleman has no thought of retiring, not even if by some dazzling and dramatic accident he wins the 1948 pennant to crown gloriously his sixty-fourth year in professional baseball. He has gone beyond the stage when a man can lay down his chores of his own volition. The sheer weight of his experience precludes a decision to call it a day. "People ask me if I'm tired of baseball," he said not long ago. "I can only give one answer. There is nothing in baseball I dislike. I'll stay in the game as long as my mind is clear. When I reach the stage when I don't know my business, or trade a .300 hitter for a .200 hitter, then you'll know I'm unfit."

But to his closest associates—his boys, his wife, his traveling secretary and chief minority stockholder, Benjamin Shibe Macfarland, and one or two others—the old man willingly gives the true reason why he'll never quit of his own accord.

"If I did," he says, and his old eyes mist up as he looks around helplessly, "I'd die in two weeks."

WITH MANY who are surely better qualified to judge, I believe this is one of the best baseball pieces ever written.

1924:
Washington Senators 4,
New York Giants 3

BILL CORUM

DREAMS came true in the twelfth—Washington's dream and Walter Johnson's—and when the red September sun dropped down behind the dome of the Capitol the Senators were the baseball champions of the world.

Washington waited twenty-five years for a World Series, but when it came it was the greatest one in history, and the king of pitchers waited eighteen years for the sweetest victory of his career.

For just long enough to beat the Giants, 4 to 3, in the seventh and deciding game the Old Master was the Johnson of old, the Kansas Cyclone, sweeping the proud champions of the National League down to their bitterest defeat.

"The team that won't be beaten, can't be beaten." Today that team was Washington. But the Giants did not deserve to lose. Chance and fate turned against the gray-clad team from the banks of the Hudson, but they went down fighting in the only way they knew and New York may still be proud of them.

Fate made a mark after the name of John McGraw in the eighth and closed the book. It was in that inning the Little Napoleon of the Diamond met his Waterloo. With the dogged, never-say-die Senators an all but beaten team and victory hovering over the Giants' bench, Bucky Harris hit a lucky bounding single over the head of young Lindstrom which scored two runs, tied the count and stemmed the tide that a moment before had been sweeping his team to defeat. It was not a hard hit, nor a clean one, but it counted and the Giants never quite recovered from it.

When the Senators took the field it was behind the broad shoulders of Walter Johnson, and this time their hero did not fail them. In danger in every one of the four innings that he worked, he rose superbly to every emergency. In each succeeding crisis he became a little more the master, a little more the terrible blond Swede of baseball fable. Twice he struck out Long George Kelly when the game hung by a thread so fine that thousands in the tense, silent throng turned their heads away with every pitch.

Somewhere, perhaps, in that little patch of sunlight that was filtering through the shadowy stands and down in front of the pitcher's mound the once mightiest arm of all was finding the strength to do the thing that twice before had balked it. In those four innings the grand old man struck out five batters, and when his need was direst he was best. Twice he turned McGraw's team back with two runners waiting to score and two other times with one.

In the very first inning that Johnson pitched, Frisch, the second batter to face him, tripled and then stayed on third to fret and fume while the calm Kansan passed Young intentionally, struck out Kelly and then made Meusel roll to the third baseman for the final out.

Again in the tenth, Wilson, first to face him, drew a pass, stayed on first while Jackson fanned and then died in a double play, Johnson to Bluege to Judge.

But it was in the eleventh that Johnson reached his greatest heights. Here it was that McGraw made his most desperate bid for victory. He sent the crippled Heinie Groh up with his bottle bat to hit for McQuillan when the inning began, and Heinie delivered a difficult single to right. Southworth scurried down to first to run for Groh, and no sooner was he there than Lindstrom moved him on to second with a perfect sacrifice bunt. The winning run was on second, there was only one out and Frankie Frisch was at bat.

Here was a situation to make any pitcher quail. That is, any pitcher but Walter Johnson. Frisch was captain of his team, but not of his fate, as it turned out; that was in the big, broad palm of the man he was facing. Up and down went that right arm. There was a prayer on every pitch, but there was something else on them, too. Frisch will tell you that. He swung three times, missed three times and sat down.

But the danger was not over yet. Young and Kelly were still to come. Young came, and went to first on four pitched balls. Kelly came, and went to first on three strikes, but the rest of the Giants went with him, and the Senators came in to bat. Long George had paid dearly for that home run he hit off Johnson last Saturday. He knows now why they call Walter the Old Master.

Once more in the twelfth the Giants put the Big Train in the hole at the start when Irish Meusel singled to right, but this time the lower end of the batting order was up and Wilson fanned, Jackson grounded to Bluege and Gowdy flied to Goslin.

Johnson not only saved the game with his arm, he also helped to win it with his bat. In the tenth he nearly turned the trick all alone. He drove a mighty fly to deep left center, but it lacked a few feet of being long enough for a home run, which would have turned a great game into an epic.

Wilson was under the ball and Sir Walter was out, but not down. He came back in that fierce and final rally in the twelfth. With Miller out on a grounder to Frisch, Gowdy made a $50,000 muff of a foul pop off Muddy Ruel's bat when he stumbled over his mask and let the ball get away from him. It was baseball history repeating itself. McGraw and Christy Mathewson lost the 1912 championship when Fred Snodgrass dropped a fly ball in the tenth.

Granted this reprieve, little Muddy from the Big Muddy hammered a double over third base and Washington's first baseball championship was in the making. Johnson jabbed a hard grounder at Jackson and Travis made the second error of a bad afternoon. Ruel wisely clung to second while Jackson scrambled for the ball.

With first and second occupied, Earl McNeely hit another hopper over Lindstrom that was a twin brother to Harris' hit of the eighth except that it was a little harder and, therefore, a more legitimate hit. As the ball rolled into left Ruel, running as he had never run before, rounded third and charged toward the plate. Meusel, galloping from deep left, picked up the ball, but didn't even throw it. It would have been the proper gesture, but neither one of the Meusel boys are given to gestures.

Irish knew, as did the joy-mad crowd, that the game was over. He kept running on in toward the plate with the ball in his hands. The rest of the Giants stood motionless and stunned and in the next instant the crowd swirled over the field and blotted out the quiet men in gray and leaping ones in white.

Many in the roaring throng that came piling on the field like college boys after the victory of their football team thought that it was Pep Young who carried off the ball that beat the Giants. With two out and two on, in the Senators' half of the eleventh, and Bluege, a dead left-field hitter at bat, McGraw had shifted Young and Meusel to get the faster man into left, but they went back to their regular positions in the twelfth.

This jockeying about of players was typical of the entire game, for it was a battle of wits as well as bats and balls. Manager Harris tried to cross his veteran rival on the New York bench even before the game started. He announced that he would pitch Curley Ogden, a right-hander, and actually sent him to the mound, although he planned to have him pitch to only one batter. The idea was to induce McGraw to name the line-up he had been using against right-handers and then to send Mogridge, a southpaw, to the mound.

The New York manager could, of course, shift his team to meet the change, but if he did he could not change back again if Mogridge was knocked out and Marberry, another right-hander, sent in. In other words, Terry's being named in the line-up actually put him in the game and he could not be withdrawn and then sent back.

Ogden struck out Lindstrom and then started walking toward the

Washington bench, but Harris showed himself to be a shrewd leader by calling him back and having him pitch to Frisch also. If Ogden was going to have a great day—and that would have been wholly possible in the face of his record—Bucky wanted to take advantage of it. He worked the same trick in Detroit near the end of the American League race, and successfully, but against the canny McGraw he derived no great benefit from it.

McGraw allowed Terry to stay in until the pinch in the sixth, when he substituted Meusel. Harris met the change by waving in Marberry to replace Mogridge, but Meusel hit the Texas right-hander for a fly that traveled long and far to right and Young scored with the tying run. So while there was no very decisive and far-reaching effect from the strategy one way or the other, what little there was came to McGraw.

Just prior to this, and in the same inning, McGraw had introduced a bit of strategy on his own part which had far more effect on the game. With Young on first, Kelly at bat and Mogridge patently nervous, McGraw called for the hit and run, with the count three balls and one strike on Kelly. The obvious play, of course, would have been to let Kelly take the next one in the hope that it would be a fourth ball. But McGraw seldom does the obvious thing. He figured that Mogridge would try for the heart of the plate, and that was just what Mogridge did. Kelly singled over second and Young easily reached third. It was from that point that he counted on Meusel's fly, and it was smart baseball that had put him there.

From the eighth on both teams were threatening each time they came to bat and any one of a hundred things might have changed the result completely.

"It might have been" were sure to be the saddest words, no matter which team lost. Many a Washington fan who had more gray hairs in his head tonight than he had this morning could testify to the chances that the Giants had and missed. Time after time any kind of a hit or any kind of a play but the one which was forthcoming would have settled the issue for good and all. When the break came finally, it came to Washington. Washington had waited for it, watched for it, and deserved it, but all the heroes did not wear spotless white.

There was Virgil Barnes of Centerville, Kan., for instance. Virgil proved that while all the great pitchers may come from his state they do not all come to Washington. For seven and two-thirds innings Barnes was a master pitcher. Until Harris hit a long fly, which just did drop over the temporary bleachers wall for a home run in the fourth, the Senators had not got a single ball past the Giant infield. Only three batters faced Barnes in each of the first three innings, four in the fourth, three in the fifth and three in the sixth, and four in the seventh again, making only twenty-three batters to face him in seven innings.

In those seven frames he yielded only three hits, a homer and fluky single by Harris and a single by Goslin. Even in the eighth, when he was taken out, he did not break completely, but he faltered, and that was enough to let the Senators break through and cause his downfall. That blow of Harris', which a high bound and the sun in Lindstrom's eyes helped to make a hit, was the one that ruined him. Until then he had furnished the most brilliant bit of pitching seen in the series. Besides Barnes, there were Frisch, Kelly and Wilson, all three of whom made sparkling plays in the field and timely hits at bat.

But to the victor belong the spoils. When future generations are told about this game they will not hear about Barnes, or Frisch, or Kelly, or even about Harris or McNeely. But the boy with his first glove and ball crowding up to his father's knee, will beg:

"Tell me about Walter Johnson."

HISTORY

A Letter to Edward B. Talcott

JAMES WHYTE DAVIS

Mr. Edward B. Talcott:

My good friend,

Referring to our lately conversation on Baseball I now comply with your request to write you a letter on the subject then proposed by me and which you so readily and kindly offered to take charge of, after my death, namely, to procure subscriptions to place a Headstone on my grave.

My wish is that Baseball players be invited to subscribe Ten Cents each and no matter how small a sum is collected, it will be sufficient to place an oak board with an inscription on my resting place, but whatever it may be, I would like it as durable as possible without any ornamentation—simply something that "he who runs may read."

The Knickerbocker Baseball Club was formed in 1845. I joined in Sept. 1850. At that time it was the only organized club in the United States. I was a member for thirty years and the only one claiming so long a membership. My excellent friend Mr. Samuel H. Kissam being next in duration of membership, and who would gladly assist you in your undertaking.

The cognomens of "Father of Baseball," "Poor old Davis" and "Too Late," as applied to me, are well known to the Baseball fraternity.

All relations and immediate friends are well informed that I desire to be buried in my baseball suit, and wrapped in the original flag of the old Knickerbockers 1845, now festooned over my bureau and for the past eighteen years and interred with the least possible cost.

I suggest the following inscription in wood or stone:

Wrapped in the Original Flag
of the
Knickerbocker Base Ball Club of N.Y.
Here Lies the Body of
JAMES WHYTE DAVIS
a member for thirty years
He was not "Too Late"
Reaching the "Home Plate"
Born March 2, 1826
Died

I should be pleased to show you my Glass Case containing the trophies of my Silver Wedding with the Old Knickerbockers in 1875 and which I intend to bequeath to you, should you so desire as a mark of appreciation of the kindly act which you have undertaken to perform. Kindly acknowledge receipt of this.

And I am Yours sincerely and thankfully,

James Whyte Davis

———————————— SPOT REPORTING ————————————

DATELINE Detroit . . . May 2, 1939 . . .

2,130

JAMES P. DAWSON

LOU GEHRIG'S matchless record of uninterrupted play in American League championship games, stretched over fifteen years and through 2,130 straight contests, came to an end today.

The mighty iron man, who at his peak hit 49 home runs in a single season five years ago, took himself out of action before the Yanks marched on Briggs Stadium for their first game against the Tigers this year.

With the consent of Manager Joe McCarthy, Gehrig removed himself because he, better than anybody else perhaps, recognized his competitive decline and was frankly aware of the fact he was doing the

Yankees no good defensively or on the attack. He last played Sunday in New York against the Senators.

When Gehrig will start another game is undetermined. He will not be used as a pinch hitter. The present plan is to keep him on the bench. He may swing into action in the hot weather, which should have a beneficial effect upon his tired muscles.

Meanwhile Ellsworth (Babe) Dahlgren, until today baseball's greatest figure of frustration, will continue at first base. Dahlgren had been awaiting the summons for three years.

It was coincidental that Gehrig's string was broken almost in the presence of the man he succeeded as Yankee first baseman. At that time Wally Pipp, now a business man of Grand Rapids, Mich., was benched by the late Miller Huggins to make room for the strapping youth fresh from the Hartford Eastern League club to which the Yankees had farmed him for two seasons, following his departure from Columbia University. Pipp was in the lobby of the Book Cadillac Hotel at noon when the withdrawal of Gehrig was effected.

"I don't feel equal to getting back in there," Pipp said on June 2, 1925, the day Lou replaced him at first. Lou had started his phenomenal streak the day before as a pinch hitter for Peewee Wanninger, then the Yankee shortstop.

The latest momentous development in baseball was not unexpected. There had been signs for the past two years that Gehrig was slowing up. Even when a sick man, however, he gamely stuck to his chores, not particularly in pursuit of his all-time record of consecutive play but out of a driving desire to help the Yankees, always his first consideration.

What Lou had thought was lumbago last year when he suffered pains in the back that more than once forced his early withdrawal from games was diagnosed later as a gall bladder condition for which Gehrig underwent treatment all last winter.

The signs of his approaching fade-out were unmistakable this spring at St. Petersburg, Fla., yet the announcement from Manager McCarthy was something of a shock. It came at the end of a conference Gehrig arranged immediately after McCarthy's arrival by plane from his native Buffalo.

"Lou just told me he felt it would be best for the club if he took himself out of the lineup," McCarthy said. "I asked him if he really felt that way. He told me he was serious. He feels blue. He is dejected.

"I told him it would be as he wished. Like everybody else I'm sorry to see it happen. I told him not to worry. Maybe the warm weather will bring him around.

"He's been a great ballplayer. Fellows like him come along once in a hundred years. I told him that. More than that, he's been a vital part of the Yankee club since he started with it. He's always been a perfect gentleman, a credit to baseball.

"We'll miss him. You can't escape that fact. But I think he's doing the proper thing."

Gehrig, visibly affected, explained his decision frankly.

"I decided last Sunday night on this move," said Lou. "I haven't been a bit of good to the team since the season started. It would not be fair to the boys, to Joe or to the baseball public for me to try going on. In fact, it would not be fair to myself.

"It's tough to see your mates on base, have a chance to win a ball game, and not be able to do anything about it. McCarthy has been swell about it all the time. He'd let me go until the cows came home, he is that considerate of my feelings, but I knew in Sunday's game that I should get out of there.

"I went up there four times with men on base. Once there were two there. A hit would have won the game for the Yankees, but I missed, leaving five stranded. Maybe a rest will do me some good. Maybe it won't. Who knows? Who can tell? I'm just hoping."

Gehrig's withdrawal from today's game does not necessarily mean the end of his playing career, although that seems not far distant. When the day comes Gehrig can sit back and enjoy the fortune he has accumulated as a ballplayer. He is estimated to have saved $200,000 from his earnings, which touched a high in 1938, when he collected $39,000 as his Yankee salary.

When Gehrig performed his duties as Yankee captain today, appearing at the plate to give the batting order, announcement was made through the amplifiers of his voluntary withdrawal. A deafening cheer resounded as Lou walked to the dugout, doffed his cap and disappeared in a corner of the bench.

Open expressions of regret came from the Yankees and the Tigers. Lefty Vernon Gomez expressed the Yankees' feelings when he said:

"It's tough to see this thing happen, even though you know it must come to us all. Lou's a great guy and he's always been a great baseball figure. I hope he'll be back in there."

Hank Greenberg, who might have been playing first for the Yanks instead of the Tigers but for Gehrig, said, "Lou's doing the right thing. He's got to use his head now instead of his legs. Maybe that Yankee dynasty is beginning to crumble."

Everett Scott, the shortstop who held the record of 1,307 consecutive games until Gehrig broke it, ended his streak on May 6, 1925, while he was a member of the Yankees. Scott began his string, once considered unapproachable, with the Red Sox. By a strange coincidence, Scott gave way to Wanninger, the player for whom Gehrig batted to start his great record.

With only one run batted in this year and a batting average of .143 representing four singles in twenty-eight times at bat, Lou has fallen far below his record achievements of previous seasons, during five of which he led the league in runs driven home.

HISTORY

The Sporting Way

STANTON DELAPLANE

WE DON'T GET much sports in this department. I can't get in the depths of despair when outfielder McTootsieroll pulls a muscle.

I have a neck myself that baffles medical science. But nobody writes about it. I just put on a felt collar and take an aspirin.

Even so, it seems to be baseball season. So, to press.

The most important thing about baseball is the hot dog. There are several stories about its origin. You can't tell the players without a program; and you can't tell the true story of hot dogs without a lie detector.

One story goes like this:

"Charles Feltman brought the frankfurter from his native Bavaria in 1871 and featured it at his famous Coney Island restaurant, introducing the hot dog to the U.S."

Here's another:

"It was at the St. Louis Louisiana Exposition in 1904. A concessionaire loaned white gloves to his patrons so they could hold the piping-hot wieners.

"He found many people didn't return the gloves. So he turned to his brother, a baker, and had a bun made to fit the sausage. Thus inventing the hot dog."

This should add to your enjoyment of the national pastime invented by Abner Doubleday.

A little history spread on the chin along with the mustard.

I used to get background on the hot dog from Mr. Irving Hoffman, the New York historian.

Mr. Hoffman was press agent for Coney Island hot dogs. His stationery carried the message: "When a man bites a dog, that's news."

Once the King of England visited the U.S. President Franklin D. Roosevelt gave him a hot dog. Shown in all the photos.

The President announced that it was "a genuine Coney Island red hot."

The King and the hot dog (he said it was excellent) became famous. Down in Trinidad, a calypso singer wrote a song about it:

The King take de hot dog in his hahnd
Ahnd he face hot dog, mahn to mahn.

People talked about it all over the U.S. For it showed that English royalty was not stiff as a stick. Just give them a good old American hot dog, and they were just like you and me.

Hoffman retired shortly after. For you cannot go on topping yourself on work like that.

I don't know where the story of St. Louis and the white gloves comes from.

The story that Feltman brought the hot dog to Coney Island comes from the archives of the august *National Geographic.* (Though I wonder if this wasn't planted by Hoffman, too.)

I favor this version. When I was a baseball fan, hanging on the exploits of "Shoeless Joe" Jackson and worrying about "Red" Faber's arm, hot dogs were sold as "Coney Island red hots."

They contained mustard AND chopped pickle—which is the mark of the genuine article, beloved of the King of England.

That is my contact with the sporting world—the hot dog. Oh, once I tried to be a sportswriter. I wrote, "Snively hit a home run."

The sports editor was aghast. He said, "He wafted the spheroid over the pickets! Can't you write English?"

I had to admit I couldn't. Not sports English. So they put me back on pistol-packing mamas, talking dogs and club luncheons. I made a living out of it.

RICHARD DONOVAN'S profile of Satchel Paige appeared in *Collier's* in 1953, when Paige was with the St. Louis Browns, and the reader will want to take this time element into consideration. You may also observe that this is the longest piece in the book. That is because it is too good to cut.

The Fabulous Satchel Paige

RICHARD DONOVAN

MR. SATCHEL PAIGE, the lank and languid patriarch, raconteur and relief pitching star of the St. Louis Browns, fairly vibrated with dignity and satisfaction as he strolled around the St. Louis railroad station one recent evening. To begin with, his physical tone was splendid—no stomach gas, store teeth resting easy, plenty of whip in his pitching arm. More important, he was in a powerful moral position.

Because of an error in reading his watch, Mr. Paige had arrived almost an hour early for the train that was to take the Browns to Chicago for a series of games with the White Sox. Never before in nearly thirty years of baseball had Paige, called by many of history's greatest pitchers the greatest pitcher who ever lived, been early for a train or anything else. It gave him an uneasy, but exceedingly righteous, feeling.

As he strolled past the baggage stand, a police officer tapped his shoulder. "What's your name?" he asked, dispensing with preliminaries.

"Leroy Paige," said Paige, surprised.

"How old are you?"

Satchel pondered; it was a question he had heard many times before.

"Well, now," he said guardedly, "people says different things. I'd judge between thirty and seventy."

"Is that so?" said the policeman, his eyes narrowing. "Just get into town?"

"Oh, I'm in and out, in and out."

"What're you out of lately?" asked the officer.

"California," said Paige, referring to his recent participation in the Browns' spring training.

"And what were you doing in California?"

"Playing," sighed Paige.

The officer was reaching for his handcuffs when Browns catcher Les Moss arrived on the scene. "What's he done?" asked Moss.

"We're looking for a murder suspect," the officer replied triumphantly, "and I think we've got him."

"How old is this suspect?"

"Twenty-two," said the cop.

Moss grinned, and Paige swelled visibly. "Twenty-two!" the pitcher exulted. "You hear that?"

People, as Paige truthfully said, say different things about his age, but not for twenty years or more had anyone suggested that the count might be less than twenty-five. In fact, the usually forgetful Paige knew (to his sorrow, for it had cost him a $500 wager to find out) that he had been firing his hard one in the Negro Southern Association at least as early as 1926—or five years before the officer's murder suspect was born.

Apprised of these facts, the policeman retired. But from that night to the present, Paige, whose true age undoubtedly lies somewhere between forty-five and fifty-three, has belabored his teammates with accounts of the adventure. "Twenty-two," the youthful-looking Paige says on these occasions, casting up his eyes. "That's what the polices thought I was. Imagine."

Lately, however, it has been noticed that Paige's delight at being mistaken for a youth by the officer has vied with uneasiness at not being recognized by the man. "He probably thought I was passed on," he has been heard to grumble. There are many fans in the country who actually believe Paige is passed, and that irritates him. Even more aggravating are those who stubbornly accuse him of impersonating himself.

Paige recently was asked to make a round of bars in Harlem with two reporters who introduced him to patrons and recorded their reactions. Twelve of the twenty-three people approached told him to his face that he was too young to be the original Satchel. From this experience alone, it is clear that, somewhere along the line, that rarest of human conditions has crept up on Mr. Paige. He has become a legend.

That is an exasperating situation for Paige, who, before the 1953 season was a week old, had helped save three games for the Browns and who last year was probably the most valuable relief hurler in the American League (12 wins, 10 games saved, 10 losses).

Judging by his early-season performance, his fifth year in the majors may be his best.

"I'm making no predictions," his manager, Marty Marion, commented recently, "but I wouldn't be surprised if Satch crowded the 20-game-win mark this year."

Legend aside, the Browns rate Paige mostly in terms of present performance. His side positions of morale builder, historian and minstrel may have made him the most popular player on the club. But more important is his earned-run average, which was 3.07 last year—good enough to lead the Browns' regulars.

Not that the legend isn't useful. Paige is still one of the half-dozen great draws in baseball. Thousands of fans who first got wind of him in the mid-twenties now crowd parks in uneasy fascination, for who knows when he may come apart before their horrified eyes, like the one-hoss shay? It is a moving sight to see the old gentleman rise from his special canopied contour chair in the bull pen and creep out to the mound with his interminable, haste-makes-waste walk. It is even more moving to see him strike out highly advertised sluggers when he finally gets there.

Any sight of Mr. Paige is arresting, in fact. Rising six feet three and a quarter inches above size 12s, on semi-invisible legs, with scarcely 180 pounds strung between foot and crown, he sometimes seems more shadow than substance. His face mystifies many fans who peer at it to discover the secrets of time. Head on, it seems to belong to a cheerful man about thirty. From another angle, it looks melancholy and old, as though Paige had walked too long in a world made up exclusively of pickpockets. From a third angle, it seems a frontispiece for the great book of experience, with expressions of wisdom, restrained violence, cunning and easy humor crossing it in slow succession.

"We seen some sights, it and I," says Paige of his face.

Inside Paige, conditions are even more confusing. He faces batters, crowds, TV cameras or whatever, with the regal calm of a Watusi chieftain; yet his nervous stomach shows signs of long and severe emotional tension. He is a congenital AWOL, missing appointments, practice and, on a couple of occasions, games without much excuse ("My feet told me it was gonna rain," he explained after failing to show for a Red Sox game). He is one of the last surviving totally unregimented souls. Contracts box him in; off-field demands on his time make him jumpy; long stays in one place give him nervous stomach. With ballplayers, he is the soul of ease and friendliness; with reporters, people after him for public appearances, promoters of one kind and another, he is wary, abrupt or sullen.

When it is recalled that he had to pitch out most of his best years on cow pastures because of big baseball's color line, and that every time he pitched he was expected to win or else, Paige's more antic attitudes are easy to understand. Now that he's up there, it is also understandable that he should feel opposed to being called a legend. Legends are tricky. On this point, however, Paige should feel entirely at ease. For underneath all the mythology lies a fact. Paige threw, and occasionally he still throws, what was probably the fastest ball ever to leave the hand of man. That is the main and enduring reason for his having been raised to the supernatural.

There are other good reasons, of course. Although records of his career are lost, forgotten or twisted by generations of sports writers, it is reasonably certain that he pitched twenty-two years of organized sand-lot, semipro or Negro League ball (about one and a half lifetimes for the average pitcher) before he ever ascended to the majors, and he has been in that high company almost five years. Although he may be the oldest man on record to perform regularly in the big leagues, last year he was invited to play in the All-Star game. Year upon year, he has pitched summer (over most of the United States and Canada) and winter (in

California and Central and South America), and has pulled in more customers than Babe Ruth.

When historians meet, the matter of Paige's performance over the years is often the subject of mettlesome debate. It seems certain that Paige has worked a record total of at least 2,500 ball games in his life, often pitching 125 games a year, frequently working five to seven days a week without rest. He has won around 2,000 of those games, it is estimated, including some 250 shutouts and 45 no-hitters. In one month in 1935, he pitched 29 days in a row against smart hitters with but one loss; in four winter seasons (1932 to 1936), often playing against the best of the Negro leaguers and various off-season combinations of major-league all-stars, he lost but four games.

For some twenty years Paige was booked as a solo star, wearing a uniform with "Satchel" across the shirt, and playing with any team that could dig up $500 to $2,000 for three innings of his work. His travel average was 30,000 miles per year, and his earnings, in some years, $35,000. He was advertised as "Satchel Paige, World's Greatest Pitcher, Guaranteed to Strike Out the First Nine Men." Either he performed as advertised or he took side streets back to his hotel.

The Browns, who now have the legend as well as the man under contract, sometimes aren't sure whether it is a disadvantage or a benefit. On the disadvantage side, Paige's presence often tends to make opposing teams gun for early scores. Whenever the Yankees start to take the Browns too lightly, for example, Yankee manager Casey Stengel begins to pace up and down in front of the bench, pointing toward Paige warming up, and intoning: "Get the runs now! Father Time is coming!"

On the benefit side, rookie hitters, their little heads stuffed with stories of Paige's fast ball, are often retired flailing when they get nothing but floaters, slow curves and bloopers from the old gentleman. Many seasoned hitters are even more delightful to Paige because they are convinced he has lost his blinding speed and are laying for the soft one. These fellows seem perpetually outraged when the ball, delivered with the same motion Paige uses for his cute stuff, blazes across the sound barrier.

Once last season, Walt Dropo, Detroit's giant first baseman, swung embarrassingly wide of two Paige pitches, lost his head and loudly accused him of showboating. For reply, Paige threw a vicious fast ball.

Dropo swung so hard that he whirled around, ending in an odd, stooped position with the seat of his pants pointing toward the stands.

"My, my," clucked Paige, reproachfully. "Talk about showboatin'."

The anxious desire of most hitters, old and new, to drive him from the mound is regarded by Paige with fatherly amusement. Hitters have been trying it for approximately thirty years. As his legend grew, he became an individual target, like an old Western gun fighter whose reputation had gone out before him. Every hot-eyed bush kid, burning for immortality around the feed store, was fired up to knock him off as he rode through.

"Bangin' around the way I was, playing for guarantees on one team after another that I never heard of, in towns I never seen before, with players I didn't know and never saw again, I got lonesome," says Paige. "People didn't come to see the ball game. They came to see me strike out everybody, all the time. Occasionally I didn't."

One such breakdown took place in Union Springs, Alabama, one steaming Sunday in 1939. Paige had ridden all night in a bus, and had holed up at a hotel for a few hours' sleep before game time. He overslept, but it made little difference since the game was a social occasion and it was considered gross to arrive much before the third inning.

When Paige appeared, red-eyed and dragged out, in the middle of the fourth, the folks were just settling themselves, waving to friends, talking, sweating, looking everywhere but at the field.

"Then," says Paige, "I went in and it got quiet."

He went to work as usual and retired the first five men in order. Then, with the nonchalance of a seasoned barnstormer, he turned and waved the outfielders off the field. The crowd rose with a roar.

"I laughed to see it," Paige says. "I was still laughing when a little, no-account-looking fella come up, took that big, greasy swing and put my fast ball where my left fielder formerly was."

Paige sighed heavily at the memory. "The polices escorted me from the place as the little man crossed home," he said. "Without my guarantee."

Country boys were not the only ones seized with intimations of immortality after hitting Paige. In 1935, Joe DiMaggio, who was to go up to the Yankees the next year, got a single off Satchel and immediately lost all doubts about how he would fare in the majors.

Paige has forgotten this game, along with a couple of thousand others, but Oakland, California sports writers have not. At the time, DiMaggio was playing around the Bay Area with an off-season team of major-league all-stars. Yankee scouts, who wished to see how their new find reacted to serious fire, finally got hold of Paige, who was taking the sun in Los Angeles. Paige was willing, after hearing about the guarantee, and started north with his team, composed entirely of Ebel Brooks, catcher for the New York Black Yankees of the Negro National League.

In Oakland, Paige found three local semipro players, filled out the roster with high-school boys and gazed solemnly at the terrifying lineup of major-league talent. Then he proceeded with the business of the day, which was to fan fifteen, allow three hits in ten innings and lose the game, two to one, when his youths, possibly rendered hysterical by the reputation of the opposition, threw to the winds the three balls that came their way. With a man on third in the tenth inning, DiMaggio, who had struck out twice and fouled out once in his previous official times at bat, finally hit a hopper which Paige lost in the shadows of dusk. One ex-Yankee scout remembers sending a telegram east: DIMAGGIO ALL WE HOPED HE'D BE. HIT SATCH ONE FOR FOUR.

Paige, whose memories of names, dates and faces tend to blend in the haze of time, is always interested to learn of such past feats from archivists in the various towns he visits. But he is essentially a forward-looking man, besides being a seasoned raconteur, sage, wit and student of the human race.

As a guest of the Second International Gerontological Congress, held in St. Louis in 1951, Paige was almost as interested in the gerontologists as they were in him. The doctors had gathered to report on their studies of the effects of age upon the human body. "They heard there was a man ninety years old playing major-league baseball in the United States," says Paige, "so, naturally, we had to meet."

The doctors interested Paige because he had the impression that only one of them spoke English. "They was all from Venice [Vienna]," he explains. Everything about Paige interested the doctors—his legs, which resemble golf-club shafts, his great feet, his stringy chest and neck muscles. When they got to his right arm, there was acclaim and astonishment.

"Most of you could be between thirty-five and fifty-five," translated the English-speaking doctor, tensely, "but your arm—" the doctor hesitated—"your arm doesn't seem to be a day over nineteen."

"I just explained to the gentlemen," Paige says, "that the bones running up from my wrist, the fibius, which is the upper bone, and the tiberon, which is the lower bone, was bent out, making more room for my throwing muscles to move around in there. I attributed most of my long life, and so on and so forth, to them two bones. The gentlemen was amazed to hear about that."

The doctors did not examine Paige's head, which is a pity, for there is enough in it to go around the average infield. He is a mountain of information on hunting dogs, expensive cars, jazz, Central American dictators, quartet singing, cameras, Kansas City real estate, Missouri River catfish, Indian maidens, stomach powders, mules and other matters. Whenever the Browns gather in a railroad club car, Paige is generally in the middle, spreading light on such matters as the futility of spring training under men like Rogers (Rajah) Hornsby, the Browns' manager the first part of last season.

"With Mr. Hawnsby, it's all runnin'," Paige told some listeners recently. "Now, I don't generally run at all, except for the showers, because of the harmful effects. I believe in training by rising gently up and down from the bench. But old Mahjong had me flyin' around, shakin' my legs and carryin' on until I very near passed. Now, what did all that do for my arm?"

Despite his sharp observance of many things, Paige's coaches complain that he does not look closely enough at the faces of the men batting against him. According to St. Louis sports announcer Bud Blattner, for example, switch-hitter Mickey Mantle hit a left-hand home run off Paige his first time up in one Yankee-Browns contest last year, then changed over and batted right-handed from there on. All the rest of the game, Paige kept asking: "Where is that boy done me the injury?"

Chicago first baseman Ferris Fain has an explanation for the confusion Mantle created. "Paige always seems to be looking at my knees. I think he recognizes batters by their stance."

Besides his difficulty in identifying his opponents, Paige is said to suffer from a couple of delusions—that he is swift on the base paths and that he is a powerful hitter. Paige runs like an unjointed turkey, except when covering a bunt, at which time he runs like a jointed turkey. (When last checked, his major-league fielding average was 1,000.) As for his hits, he bunches them. He got five hits in 1952, three fifths of them in one 17-inning game against the Senators. Paige came on in the eleventh with the score 2–2 and, besides holding Washington hitless for five and two-thirds innings, got three singles, the last of which drove Joe DeMaestri home with the winning run. In gratitude and astonishment, owner Bill Veeck bought him a new suit.

Paige's uncertainty about names, while confusing to his audiences, rarely bothers him; he invents reasonable approximations of the original handles. Sitting in the trophy room of one of his two large brick houses in Kansas City a while ago, he recalled the tension Mark Griffin (Clark Griffith, owner of the Senators) must have felt in that 17-inning game. Reminiscence took him back a piece and he called up some of the great pitchers he had known. Bob Rapid (Feller) and ol' Homer Bean (Dizzy Dean) were among the best, he said. His memories of Grover (Big Train) Cleveland (a composite of Grover Cleveland Alexander and Walter Johnson) were vague, but he was positive about the hurling characteristics of Tom Lemons (Cleveland's Bob Lemon) and The Actor (ex-Brownie Gene Bearden of Chicago, who has been in two movies).

Hitters loom larger in Paige's mind, naturally. Josh Gibson, late home-run king of the Negro leagues, is the best batsman he ever faced, he says, with Detroit's Charley Gehringer next, and Larry Doby, Cleveland's stylish and cultivated outfielder, third. DiMaggio, with whom Paige never had much trouble, is also well remembered, probably as a social gesture. So is Boston's Ted Williams, now of the U. S. Marines.

Now that Paige is getting on toward evening, reporters are constantly prying into him for treasures of the past. Paige is discomfited by this curiosity, for he claims to be only forty-five and the questions hint at retirement.

"Who's gonna straighten out 2,500 ball games in my head?" he inquired indignantly a few weeks ago. "How many cow pastures you played on, Satchel? they wanta know. How many bus rides you took?

Who put the spike scars on your shinbone? Why is your feet flat? Who was it offered you $50 to pitch a triple-header that time?" Satchel screwed up his face, which indicated that the concentration was giving him indigestion. "Man," he said, "the past is a long and twisty road."

Leroy Robert Paige started down the road during the Teddy Roosevelt administration from a small frame house in the Negro section of Mobile, Alabama. His father was a gardener. His mother, Tula Paige, who is now eighty-three and for whom Satchel bought a house in Mobile recently, said he was the sixth of eight children when questioned by Bill Veeck a while ago. She also put his birth year at 1903.

"What mama knows when her little child was bawn?" Paige said patiently when he got this news. "My draft card says 1906. I say 1908. Take your pick."

Food and living room were permanent problems for the family, but for Leroy, who was almost six feet tall at age twelve, the big problems apparently lay on the outside. One problem—where to find money to buy baseball equipment—he solved by becoming a redcap at a Mobile railroad station. After a couple of days' labor, the headwork for which he is now revered manifested itself and he rigged a "totin' device" of sticks and ropes on which he could hang as many as ten bags for one trip. Staggering along one day, looking like a tree of satchels, he caught the eye of someone who gave him the name he has carried down the road.

The predatory warfare between Mobile's boy gangs was a much bigger problem for Paige. Several times he was beaten; just as often, he participated in the gang-beating of others. He rarely went to school. Reasoning that continuous battle against odds was the staff of life, he turned sniper, breaking windows and lumping heads with deadly, accurate rocks from his hand. The truant officer became a weekly caller; the police called, too, with complaints from parents of winged children. Finally, a juvenile judge sentenced him to the Alabama Reform School for Boys, at Mount Meigs. He was approximately twelve when he went in, sixteen when he got out.

"One thing they told me in the reform school," Paige says, "they told me that all that wild-a'-loose feelin' I put in rock throwin', I ought to put in throwin' baseballs. Well, I listened to that. Many men have watched my fast ball all these years without thinkin' what put that mean little hop on it. That's the wild-a'-loose."

Paige was six feet three inches tall and weighted 140 pounds when he rejoined society; he was reedy, solemn and taciturn in conversation but highly expressive on the mound. His mother kept him home nights but most afternoons he spent in sand-lot games, one of which happened to be witnessed by a Pullman porter in from Chattanooga. This man spoke to Alex Herman, owner of the Chattanooga Black Lookouts, and forthwith Mr. Herman appeared at the Paige house with offers. Mrs. Paige, who smelled sin in the footloose baseball life, refused to let Satchel go until Herman promised to watch him like a father and send his $50-a-month salary home. Full of reform-school warnings and memories at seventeen years of age, Satchel took the next train into the outer world.

When he appeared on the Lookouts' field for the first time, the legend-to-be was an arresting sight. His uniform flapped about him, his neck, arms and legs indicated severe emaciation, spikes had to be nailed to his street shoes until some size-12, triple-A baseball shoes could be found, his walk was labored, he cranked up like the Tin Woodman of Oz and he appeared to be speechless. Looking at him, veteran players expressed the gravest fears for owner Herman's judgment. The first man to face him in a practice session held his bat in one hand, for charity's sake.

Then Satchel threw his fast ball.

That evening, as the newly established most valuable player on the Lookouts, he was invited to dinner by several veterans. But he informed them that he had to eat at Mr. Herman's house and go to bed at nine-thirty.

When the team went on the road, Herman's watchfulness trebled. Crowds were wild about Satchel, female eyes followed him relentlessly, and scented notes, addressed to Mr. Paige, appeared at every hotel desk. This was heady stuff to Mrs. Paige's child; sometimes, after Herman had locked him in his hotel room, Paige felt the strain was too much for flesh to bear. In the warm Southern dusk, Satchel, gazing down from high hotel windows, could see the older players talking to the girls down below. When he chanced to hear soft voices inquiring as to the whereabouts of the tall pitcher, there were times he felt he'd have to jump.

Although Alex Herman delivered Satchel to his mother, as was, at the end of his first season, it was obvious that this arrangement could not go on. By the time he was twenty-one, Satchel Paige was a seasoned traveler and an apprentice philosopher, to say the least. He had run through two roadsters. He had sat in with Louis Armstrong and his band ("I played my own chords on the Spanish guitar"); he had had ham and whisky with ol' Jelly Roll Morton at a wake in Memphis ("I didn't know the dead man but Jelly thought he'd want me to be there"); he had gone across the river from New Orleans to have his palm read by the seers of Algiers, who found a short life line; he had been a running story in the Negro press, and from Savannah to Abilene and Mobile to St. Joe, he had heard of dozens of young ladies he had never seen who were letting it be known that they might shortly become Mrs. Paige.

"It was an education," Paige recalls now. "I was tired all the time."

As he put on a little more meat, Paige's fast ball got faster. This phenomenon has been explained by Biz Mackey, a memorable catcher for the Baltimore Elite Giants, of the late Negro National League.

"A lot of pitchers have a fast ball," says Mackey, "but a very, very few—Feller, Grove, Johnson, a couple of others besides Satchel—have had that little extra juice that makes the difference between the good and the great man. When it's that fast, it will hop a little at the end of the line. Beyond that, it tends to disappear.

"Yes, disappear. I've heard about Satchel throwing pitches that wasn't hit but that never showed up in the catcher's mitt, nevertheless. They say the catcher, the umpire and the bat boys looked all over for that ball, but it was gone. Now how do you account for that?"

Word of such disappearances got around the Negro leagues quickly, it seems, for competition for Satchel's services was intense. Since clubs issued loosely worded agreements in lieu of contracts, players could switch to the highest bidder.

Paige, a man of sound fiscal policies except in the savings department, jumped often, playing for such teams as the Birmingham Black Barons, the Nashville Elite Giants and the New Orleans Black Pelicans. But always he had in mind the goal of most Negro players of the time, Gus Greenlee's Pittsburgh Crawfords, a team that at one time might have won pennants in either major league. For the late Mr. Greenlee, who once managed light heavy-weight champion John Henry Lewis, Paige was also a goal. In 1930, he sent Satchel an offhand note: "The Crawfords might possibly be interested in having you pitch for them next season." Paige replied: "I might possibly be interested in pitching for the Crawfords sometime."

When Paige joined Pittsburgh in 1931, his receiver was Josh Gibson, a better-than-average catcher, and one of the great right-hand hitters. With the Paige-Gibson battery in action, the Crawfords could afford to be big.

At one time, for example, they were playing an exhibition game against a champion team from the U.S. Marine Corps. In the last of the ninth with the Marines up, two out, and the score 12 to 0 in favor of the Crawfords, Satchel and Gibson had a worried consultation.

"The United States Marines have got to have at least one run," said Paige.

Back behind the plate, Gibson asked who was the captain of the Marine team. It was the man at bat. "You're gonna be the hero," Gibson said.

Thereupon, Satchel pitched one so fat the surprised Marine chopped it into the ground a few feet in front of home. Gibson grabbed it and threw it thirty feet over the first baseman's head. While the Marine rounded the bases and dug for the plate, the astonished right fielder retrieved the ball and threw it home for the putout. The ball hit Gibson's chest protector and bounded high in the air. "I had a feeling you were gonna be the hero," Gibson informed the Marine captain later.

With the Crawfords, Satchel's pitching bag grew. He threw overhand, sidearm and underhand; he served up the "two-hump blooper," a queer-acting slow ball; "the barber," an upshoot that grazed the batter's chin; "Little Tom," a medium fast ball; "Long Tom," *the* fast ball, and the "hesitation pitch," a bewildering delivery in which Paige stops in mid-throw before following through.

Paige's reputation, by this time, had traveled afar. Toward the end of the 1931 season, he got a pleasing offer from a Señor Linares, owner of the Santa Clara, Cuba club, to play winter ball. He accepted with every expectation of adding to his education. He did.

As a pitcher in the United States, Paige had been expected to win most of the time, but it was also realized that he might lose someday. In Cuba, this realization never came to the fans. When he got behind in a game, a terrible hush settled over the barefoot señors in the low, rudely constructed stands; if he got further behind, he could see the sun glinting on machetes all around him. And then there was the language barrier. While Satchel toiled, his teammates would hop around, chattering in Spanish.

"Speak English, brothers!" Paige would cry helplessly. "I is with you!"

After twenty-four straight wins for the Santa Clara club, Paige finally did lose.

"I didn't wait," he says. "I started yellin' Polices! Polices! and then I began flyin' around the infield with the fans flyin' behind. They caught up with me at second base but the polices was a couple of jumps in the lead and we stood 'em off, knockin' some heads here and there.

"They wrote me up in the paper the next day," Paige said sourly. "Said I throwed the game."

II

An air of uneasiness hung over the home stadium of the last-place St. Louis Browns one day last August. Local fans, accustomed to great suffering, had the feeling that their team was about to throw away another ball game. Over six innings, the Browns had compiled a 2-0 edge over the league-leading Yankees. But now, with two out in the last of the seventh, pitcher Gene Bearden was beginning to wobble. One Yankee run scored. Then, while St. Louis supporters cringed, Bearden loaded the bases.

Among those shrinking into themselves at this critical moment was the Browns' shortstop-manager, Marty Marion. He glanced guiltily at his relief pitchers warming up in the bull pen. Then, stifling an impulse to call for volunteers, he made what seemed to be the only possible decision. He nominated Leroy (Satchel) Paige to douse the fire.

Languorous and serene, Mr. Paige, the eminent traveler, linguist, sage and relief-pitching mainstay of the Browns, rose and began his usual interminable stroll toward the mound.

In his thirty-or-so years in professional baseball, he had been in worse spots. If he failed here, at least he would not have to spring from the field before enraged masses of machete-wielding fans, as he had so often had to do in the twenty years he played winter ball in Latin America. Nor would his outfielders stroll off the diamond without his knowing it, as had happened in North Dakota in 1934. There was positively no danger of politicos threatening him with the firing squad, as they had done in the Dominican Republic in 1936.

Humming a little tune, Paige took his regular half-dozen warmup pitches on the mound, sighted on pinch hitter Irv Noren and fed him a fast curve. He smiled pleasantly as Marion gathered in a short pop-up, retiring the side.

Later, still humming contentedly, Mr. Paige did away with Phil Rizzuto, Joe Collins and Hank Bauer in the eighth, and Yogi Berra, Gil McDougald and Gene Woodling in the ninth, to save the game.

Afterward, despite the satisfactory outcome, there was some discussion among local fans over the soundness of manager Marion's strategy in selecting the aging Paige at a time of such crisis.

When these comments reached the sensitive ears of Browns owner Bill Veeck, he seemed astonished. "Well, what else was there to do?" he inquired of one doubter. "Marion needed the greatest baseball brains, experience, speed, control and coolness he could find in one man. So he put in the world's greatest relief pitcher. No particular strategy about that!"

Veeck's was a generous, but not a wildly extravagant, statement. By any yardstick, the venerable Paige, whose age is thought to lie somewhere between forty-five and fifty-three, is one of the two or three best relief men in baseball. In the first eleven games the Browns played this season, he was called upon four times. He helped save three of the games, and was compelled to retire from the fourth when a line drive struck his foot. In 1952, he pitched in almost one third of the St. Louis Browns' contests, struck out 91 batters, won twelve games, lost ten, saved ten, and ended up by making the American League All-Star team and becoming —in the opinion of most experts—the most valuable relief hurler in that circuit.

In his approximately thirty years of baseball, two lifetimes for the average pitcher, Paige has broken all records for number of games pitched and won (some 2,000 out of 2,500). Working winter and summer in many lands, often as an itinerant solo star, for some 250 different sand-lot, semipro and Negro-league teams—not to mention the Cleveland Indians and St. Louis Browns—he has also very probably broken all records for travel and number of customers drawn by any individual ballplayer.

Barred by the color line from rewriting big baseball's record book in his prime, Paige contented himself with striking out most of the traveling major-league all-stars who came his way over the years in exhibition games. Those feats not only caused Paige to be called the greatest pitcher who ever lived by such recognized authorities as Dizzy Dean and Charley Gehringer, among many others, but they did a great deal to lay the groundwork for the entry of Negro players into the major leagues in 1947.

"They was tall times, tall times," Paige says of those years. "But let whosomever wishes sit around recollecting. I'm looking up the line."

Up the line looms a busy season. Last year, Paige worked in a staggering 46 games; this year he may wind up working even more often. "If we don't have to use him in relief every other game," said Marion early in the season, "he'll get plenty of starting assignments."

That prospect does not dampen Paige's celebrated self-confidence. Now, as always, Satchel is so certain of his powers, both physical and mental, that sometimes he makes himself uneasy.

In the Browns' shower room after a recent game, for example, several players were tossing a slippery cake of soap at a wall dish, trying without success to make it stick there. Paige entered, picked up the soap casually, and tossed it. It stuck. There was a general raising of eyebrows, none higher than Satchel's. He tossed another bar, even more slippery. It stuck, too. Paige looked thoughtfully at the sober faces around him.

"Boys," he said, "there is apparently things that even I don't know I can do."

Paige's powers have raised him to a patriarchal position among the Browns. Such recognition is not easily won, but when a man can explain to a club car full of ballplayers not only what the hull and superstructure of Noah's ark were made of, but the composition of its doors and hinges as well, respect must be paid where it is due.

The elderly pitcher's abilities as a graduate student of the human race also have had frequent workouts. During spring training this year, it was noticed that one of the Browns' promising rookies was mooning around the ball field instead of trying to make the team. When management failed to diagnose the trouble, Paige cast an eye on the spaniel droop of the young man's features.

"The child is down with love," he announced flatly.

After Paige's analysis proved correct, his observations on love were naturally sought by other Browns players. For a man who has made lifelong researches into the subject, it turned out that he had a rather low opinion of it.

"Love," said Paige, "is a proposition I wouldn't advise you to mess with, as regards the general run of women. You restrict yourself to one or two lady friends and you're gonna be all right. But you expand to include the field and you're bound to get cut up. Myself," he added dismally, "I'm a passel of scars. Oh, I seen some terrible times, terrible times. . . ."

One such time overtook Paige when he was approximately twenty-three and playing for the town of Santa Clara, Cuba in his first winter season in the banana leagues. When love came, Paige was sitting in a Santa Clara park on a hot evening, eating peanuts and listening to the palms clacking. Then a lovely, huge-eyed creature, who spoke a little English, walked by.

"She dropped some Sen-Sen in my hand," he recalls sadly. "That was the signal."

Eventually, Paige called at the girl's mud-walled home and found he had to stand out in the street among snoring pigs, talking to her through a barred window because he had not known her long enough to enter. Some weeks later, when her family let him in, he was dismayed to learn that his admission was a sign he and the girl were officially engaged, and that the authorities would be so informed.

"I quit callin' immediately," Paige says, "but pretty soon the owner of the ball club comes to my hotel and says the polices is lookin' for me. So I started goin' back to her house."

Ultimately, says Paige, the strain told and he began to lose ball games. The club owner bowed to the inevitable.

"One night he phones my hotel and says it's all fixed," Paige recalls. "He's gonna get me out in a car to the mountains. Then I'll get on a horse and go on over the top and get another car. This car will take me to a place where I can catch a motorboat and go on out to a ship to take me back to the U.S.A. That's how it was gonna be."

Paige, who suffers from a nervous stomach, winced as memories of that night came back to plague him.

"The hotel telephone operator was the girl's cousin," he said miserably. "Them polices was after me when I was in the car, and on a jackass runnin' up the mountain, and on foot runnin' down the mountain, and right on out to the motorboat.

"Man," he concluded, his voice heavy with strain, "when I finally come flyin' up that gangplank, I was through with love."

When Paige made this retreat across the wilds of Cuba, he was the summer property of one of the most formidable teams then in existence, the all-Negro Pittsburgh Crawfords. The late Gus Greenlee, owner of the Crawfords, had been vaguely aware of Paige from the year 1923, when Paige's two pitches, hard and harder, had begun to terrorize semipro teams in his home town of Mobile. Greenlee had followed Paige's career from the time he joined the Chattanooga Black Lookouts in 1926 through various subsequent jumps to other teams in the Negro Southern Association. By 1930, when Greenlee offered Paige $200 a month to join the Crawfords, Satchel was winning up to 60 games a year, striking out from 10 to 18 men in every game.

In three years at Pittsburgh, he won an estimated 105 games while losing 37.

Paige's battery mate on the Crawfords was the late Josh Gibson, the *aficionado's* choice for the long-ball hitter of all time. Paige has the greatest reverence for Gibson, and it shocks him to run into people who have not heard of the great man.

Not long ago, a sassy young reporter, fuddled with the doings of the Musials, the Mantles and so on, tried Paige severely by yawning while he was recounting some of Gibson's prodigies. To fix him, Paige recalled one game.

"We was playin' the Homestead Grays in the city of Pitchburgh," he said quietly. "Josh comes up in the last of the ninth with a man on and us a run behind. Well, he hit one. The Grays waited around and waited around, but finally the empire rules it ain't comin' down. So we win.

"The next day," Paige went on, eying the youth coldly, "we was disputin' the Grays in Philadelphia when here come a ball outta the sky right in the glove of the Grays' center fielder. The empire made the only possible call.

" 'You're out, boy!' he says to Josh. 'Yesterday, in Pitchburgh.' "

Paige was quite a sight around Pittsburgh at this time—six foot three and a quarter inches tall, slow-moving, meatless and loose-limbed, with a wide-roving eye. The calm, dry, sadly comic air, the sly humor and itchy foot, the unwillingness to be pinned down by statistics, appointments or contracts were all there in embryo. So was the now famous Paige self-confidence.

Satchel thought—and still thinks—of himself as a great hitter and base runner. There is some evidence that he may once have been pretty fair in those departments, and additional evidence that he could be still. Perhaps the best measurement of his current capacity at the plate, however, is his last season's batting record—five hits in thirty-nine tries. As to his speed, there is much debate among observers. Some question that he could beat Casey Stengel to first base. Others note that he moves quickly enough afield to have handled all chances in his first four years in the majors without a single error.

"In my opinion," says White Sox manager Paul Richards, a Paige fan, "he could play shortstop."

The fact is, he has, in his time, been an infielder, and a pretty good one. Catcher Roy Campanella of the Brooklyn Dodgers tells of playing against Paige in Puerto Rico during the winter of 1939–40. "In Sunday double-headers," says Campanella, "Satch would pitch the first game and strike out maybe seventeen batters, and then play first base in the second game. Did all right, too."

Although there may have been some basis for Paige's belief while at Pittsburgh that he could run and hit with the best of them, there was less justification for another view he held at the time—that he was a danger-ous man in the ring. When Gus Greenlee had Paige under contract he was also managing the light heavy-weight champion of the world, John Henry Lewis. Watching Lewis work out, Paige became overpowered with manly urges and challenged him.

Greenlee visited the gym one day and was horrified to see his two most expensive commodities in the ring, the one weaving and laughing, the other stilting fiercely about in many-colored shorts like an enraged flamingo. Before Greenlee could get to them, Paige managed to hit Lewis on top of the head, whereupon Lewis feinted, stood off and rapped the pitcher on the chin. Some time later, while Lewis, Greenlee and the trainers worked feverishly with ammonia and massage, Paige opened his eyes.

"I stang him," he was saying happily. "Git me a shot at Joe Louis."

As a man already on the way toward becoming a legend in fields other than boxing, Paige was generally believed in Pittsburgh to have size 15 feet and to be wealthy, a wild dresser, the owner of several fiery-red cars, and a very frying pan of romance. Actually, he walked on mere size twelves and was flat broke, modestly clad except for ties and shoes, the owner of a piece of a roadster he was buying from Gus Greenlee, and a lover too winded from constant flight to be impressive when cornered.

It was the opinion of most of the local young ladies at the time that Satchel was just too ornery to settle down. Miss Janet Howard, a bright and resourceful waitress at Gus Greenlee's Crawford Grill, thought otherwise, however.

"From the minute she first set a plate of asparagus down in front of me," Satch Paige recalls, "I began to feel paralyzed."

Marriage to Janet brought responsibilities undreamed of by Paige. He had saved no money at all. When he had to bring his salary home, only to find it wasn't enough, and when Greenlee balked at giving him a raise, he began looking around. One offer of $250 a month came in, but it made Paige uncomfortable.

"It was from a car dealer named Neil Churchill away out in a place called Bismarck, North Dakota," Paige recalls. "Churchill had a semipro team of mostly white boys, but he needed pitchin' so he calls Abe Saperstein, who owns the Harlem Globetrotters, and asks who he should get. Abe says me. Well, now," said Paige, "I wasn't exactly sure that North Dakota belonged to Sam (the U.S.A.) at the time, and I didn't want to go. But Janet says jump, so we jumped."

In Bismarck, a city that contained few Negroes, Paige and his wife looked fruitlessly for housing and finally settled in a boxcar that had housed section hands. Still broke, Satchel rustled up early meals with a shotgun in the surrounding jackrabbit country.

At the time, 1934, Paige was just rounding into his prime, which is to say that he was probably the greatest pitcher then alive. When some of the other Bismarck players seemed inclined to doubt the Paige prowess, he quickly set them right. He placed a small matchbox on an upright stick beside home plate and knocked it off with thirteen of twenty pitches from the mound. That established the control. Then he pitched a fast ball which took a nasty hop near the plate, skipping off the catcher's mitt to graze his temple. The catcher called for a chest protector and mask. He needed them, for he was unable to hold the next eight pitches out of ten. That established the speed. (Satch's present receiver, the Browns' Clint Courtney, reported nine years later that Paige's fast ball was still hard to follow. "It has a hop on the end," complained Courtney, "and it keeps ticking off the top of my mitt.")

For a couple of years, the Bismarck team had been humiliated regularly by the neighboring Jamestown Red Sox. In his first game against Jamestown, Paige allowed no runs and fanned fifteen, using only Little Tom, his medium fast ball, and leaving Long Tom, his real fast ball, for future use. Paige beat Jamestown four more times that season, in addition to winning 37 other games for Bismarck, but the season was not a success, Jamestown beat Bismarck once.

The one Jamestown victory came about in a strange way. During the season, Paige had occasionally electrified the prairie fans by signaling his outfield to walk off the field, thus leaving himself with nothing but an infield for defense. The signal was easy to see. Paige stood on the mound, wiping his brow elaborately with his pitching hand.

On the night of the final game against Jamestown, Paige was off form. The opposition batters hit everything—floaters, curves, the "two-hump blooper," the chin-grazing "barber pitch," the "hesitation pitch" and even Long Tom. Luckily, Bismarck was also hitting, so Paige was able to keep a shaky lead as the score mounted.

In the last of the ninth, with the score 15 to 14 in Bismarck's favor and Jamestown's murderers' row coming up, Paige began to perspire freely. Curves got the first man. The second man singled and Paige's blood pressure rose. Long Tom dispatched the third batter, but as the cleanup man walked to the plate, Paige was seized by a premonition of evil. He mopped his brow nervously.

Paige is still outraged by the memory of that night game.

"While my outfield was strollin' off the field behind my back," he says, "I fed the cleanup man a little outcurve which I intended him to hit on the fly to right field. He did. It was some time," says Paige grumpily, "before I again visited the city of Bismarck." (Actually, he rejoined the team the next summer.)

In the autumn of 1934, Paige and his wife headed for Denver, where he had been invited to pitch for the House of David in the *Denver Post* semipro tournament. The House had a talented organization, but what impressed Paige most was the amazing growth of whiskers on all the players. Paige had never been able to grow any whiskers himself, and he felt naked and alone. Although he won his first three tournament games for the House without facial hair, he complained bitterly. Finally, his teammates presented him with a lengthy false beard of reddish hue.

Thoroughly pleased, Paige wore the red whiskers in his final appearance. While he was winding up to deliver a hesitation pitch in the fourth inning, however, the beard became entwined with his pitching arm and was torn from his jaws with the delivery.

Finding himself denuded again, Paige became so unsettled that he very nearly lost the game. He squeaked through, however, and the House went on to win the tournament.

"It was the tamperin' with nature that rattled me," Satchel says.

In California that winter, Paige commanded the Satchel Paige All-Stars, an impressive pickup team of Negro-league players. This team included catcher Josh Gibson, third baseman Judy (Sweet Juice) Johnson, the catlike Harry Williams at second base, and Cool Papa Bell, whose speed and daring in the outfield and on the bases may have surpassed that of Willie Mays. In three previous years wintering on the West Coast, the Paige Stars, with or without the members named, had won some 128 games—at least 40 of them against teams of major-league all-stars—while losing 23.

The games against big-leaguers were of tremendous importance to Paige and the others. They knew, the sports writers knew, and many of the fans knew that many of the Negro stars were better ballplayers than some of the high-salaried, internationally famous men they faced. Yet they were denied a shot at the big fame, big money, big records and big company. Paige burned with a quiet resentment at this denial. He felt that someday the color line would be broken. But his great fear, he says, was that he would be too old, his prime wasted in cow pastures, when the great day came.

The bigger the major-league stars, the more Paige bore down. According to accounts passed down by witnesses, he struck out Rogers Hornsby five times in one game, Charley Gehringer three times in another, Jimmy Foxx three times in a third. In 1934 in Hollywood, Paige pitched what Bill Veeck says is the greatest game he ever saw. In that game, which lasted 13 innings, Paige was opposed by Dizzy Dean, a 30-game winner for the Cardinals. Dean was superlative, holding the Paige Stars to one run and fanning 15. But Paige shut out the Dean Stars and fanned 17. After the game, Dean informed the press that Paige was the best pitcher in the business.

Later that winter, Paige made his usual leisurely barnstorming trip through the tropics. After a series of games in Mexico City, he and a couple of his American All-Stars were invited to the ranch of a local ball-club owner, whose side line was raising bulls for the ring. Standing behind a stone wall in a ranch pasture one day, one of the stars saw Paige gazing over into another pasture where some local *toreros* were tempting the horns of the terrible black bulls. His natural bravery seemingly aroused by the spectacle, Paige expressed to a bullfighter who was resting nearby his burning desire to defy the bulls himself someday.

"I got a way with animals," Paige is supposed to have said fiercely.

Absorbed by the violence over the wall, Paige failed to observe some animals grazing behind him. Satchel was just repeating his defiance of the bulls, according to the story, when a shape loomed at his elbow. Annoyed, Paige turned to see what it was. It was all looming bulk, black hair and horns.

Slowly, almost wearily, says the witness, Paige turned back to the bullfighter on the wall.

"Toreador," he called in a small strained voice. "Oh, toreador."

But the bullfighter was watching his fellow *toreros* work.

"Toreador!" Paige yelled suddenly. "Polices! Polices! Help!"

While the bullfighter jerked around to see what was the matter, the visiting bull, apparently alarmed by the noises issuing from Paige, turned and trotted back to the grazing herd.

"Scared?" Paige now says, in recalling the incident. "That bull was jelly. I turned the cold eye on him. The chances are, that bull never was any good when he got to the ring in Mexico City. Fear ruins 'em."

Back from Mexico in the summer of 1935, Paige rejoined Bismarck while his wife stayed in Pittsburgh. The team's problem that year was to find competition. Of the 102 games played, it lost five. In midseason, Paige pitched 29 days in a row with one loss; his total for the summer was 43 wins and two losses. As Bismarck's renown grew, the inevitable team of major-league all-stars appeared, this one boasting Earl Averill, Heinie Manush and Jimmy Foxx, among others. Bismarck beat the big-leaguers 7–4 at Grand Forks, North Dakota, 10–0 at Valley City and 16–2 at Bismarck before they could get out of the bush country.

Among the customers who sat fascinated by the sight of Paige at his peak were many Sioux Indians from nearby reservations. They named him the Long Rifle and worked him into at least one tribal legend, in which he uses the bean ball on a cantankerous local Indian commissioner. One Sioux in particular, a Dorothy Running-Deer, as Paige recalls, often hung about the grounds after game time. Paige took little notice of her; he was a married man, and also she was short and rather plain. Nevertheless, she did him a great service.

"One day," Paige recalls, "this Dorothy Deer invited me out in the hills to meet her papa who raised rattlesnakes in a deep pit in back of his hut. I looked at the snakes and said good-by. Before leavin', however, I ask the old man if he'd ever been bit, and he said lots of times, but he had an ointment that took out the harm. When he gave me a great big jug of it, I ask him if the ointment might be good for rubbin' my arm. He said he wouldn't advise it."

After heeding the warning for a couple of days, Paige finally dabbed a finger into the snake oil and cautiously rubbed a few drops on his tired biceps. Forthwith, he declares, energies and sensations of a kind he had never known vibrated from shoulder to fingers.

"My mistake was I didn't dilute it," Paige says reflectively. "Man, it's a wonder my arm didn't fly outta the room."

For many years since then, ballplayers in hundreds of locker rooms, including those of the Cleveland Indians and the St. Louis Browns, have speculated endlessly about the ingredients of the secret preparation which the Long Rifle uses to revitalize his arm. Some say it's kerosene and olive oil and some say it's wolfbane and wild cherry stems. Paige doesn't say. He just calls it Deer oil.

As the terror of the northern Midwest, the 1935 Bismarck team was invited to play in the national semipro tournament at Wichita, Kansas. En route, in McPherson, Kansas, they encountered a problem. Local citizens, apparently rendered unsteady by a winning team of their own, openly referred to the Bismarcks as hayshakers.

A six-inning challenge game was promptly arranged and the Bismarcks took an early two-run lead. In the final inning, the disgruntled McPherson fans began to hoot at Paige.

That was a mistake. Paige fanned the first man. Then, repeating his Jamestown gesture, he called in his outfield and struck out the next man. Then, outdoing the Jamestown gesture, he called in his infield. With nobody representing Bismarck but Paige and catcher Quincy Troupe, he struck out the third man. He used nine fast balls in all.

Bismarck won the Wichita tournament in seven games, and barnstormed west for new fields to conquer. In Denver, Paige confronted the House of David, which he had pitched to victory in the *Post* tournament the year before. The beards still fascinated him. One unusually lush growth so attracted him, indeed, that he fired a pitch into it, thus raising a technical baseball point so fine that no one has yet been able to settle it.

The argument took place in the seventh inning. Paige had two strikes on the owner of the great beard when he was seized by an overpowering desire to part the man's whiskers with a Long Tom. When he did, the umpire promptly ruled that the man had been hit by a pitched ball and waved him on to first.

According to an impartial witness, Paige then raised an arm to halt the game. Striding up to the struck man, he asked permission to exhibit his beard to the umpire.

"Empire," said Paige, combing the luxuriant growth with long fingers, "if you will kindly observe here, you will see that these whiskers can't rightly be called no part of a man. They is air."

The umpire, seeing the logic, began to hem and haw. After about five minutes, however, he got mad and returned to his former ground. Paige was defeated, but the crowd was with him and the question is still considered wide open.

After his second appearance in Denver, Paige's fame as a pitching phenomenon began to spread across the nation, and beyond. One Denver wire-service story, translated into Spanish, reached the eyes of Dr. José Enrique Aybar, dean of the University of Santo Domingo, deputy of the Dominican Republic's national congress, and a man with a mission. Some days before, Dr. Aybar had been given $30,000 by President Rafael L. Trujillo, absolute dictator of the country and by all odds the fiercest strong man in Central America, and told to go out and get a ball club. An election was coming up and Trujillo's opponent was showing surprising strength— due almost entirely to the fact that he had imported ballplayers who were beating everything in sight and thus ballyhooing his name.

After reading the stuff on Paige, Dr. Aybar got in touch with him at once, asking him to round up as many American Negro players as he could find and fly to Ciudad Trujillo, the capital. Thinking he'd like to spend a restful winter in the tropics, Paige recruited Josh Gibson, Cool Papa Bell, Harry Williams and some others and took off.

At Ciudad Trujillo, Paige and his teammates were met by barefoot soldiers with ammunition belts over their chests and long, bayoneted rifles in their hands. Paige thought them very distinguished. The soldiers convoyed the players to a hotel and took up posts outside their rooms. Thereafter, every place Paige and his friends went, the soldiers went with them. When Paige met Dr. Aybar, the doctor explained that the situation was very serious and that Trujillo's team must win an upcoming series of seven games against the Estrellas de Oriente, the opponent's team, at whatever cost.

When the day of the great series arrived, the city was decorated with flags and the streets were jammed with people. Gaiety and laughter, machetes and shooting irons were everywhere. At the ball park, the heavily armed followers of Trujillo bulked threateningly along the third-base line; and the heavily armed followers of Trujillo's opponent bulked just as threateningly along the first-base line.

"I knew then that whichever way the series went, I lost," says Paige.

The series went as badly as possible. With the strain giving Paige nervous stomach, the Trujillo forces dropped two straight. The reaction from the president's office was very bad. Then they lost one more, and all Dr. Aybar could do was wring his hands when Paige asked how his chances were for getting back to the States. In desperation, Paige and his mates played as never before, taking the next three in a row while tension mounted throughout the country. On the last day, with the score in games three and three, Paige might have been excused had he been unable to walk to the mound. Instead, he strode out confidently, his stomach gas all gone.

"I had it fixed with Mr. Trujillo's polices," Paige says. "If we win, their whole army is gonna run out and escort us from the place. If we lose . . ." Paige hesitated. "If we lose, there is nothin' to do but consider myself and my boys as passed over Jordan."

Paige did not lose.

Back with the all-forgiving Crawfords the next summer, Paige found that his hectic, itinerant past was beginning to catch up with him. Word-of-mouth advertising of his exploits had made his name magical in many cities and backwoods of the Western Hemisphere.

Communities he had never heard of suddenly wanted to see him pitch. Offers ranging from $100 to $500 for three innings' work began to come in. Paige began traveling around the country as a solo star, making guest appearances with one club after another, week after week. With every appearance, the pressure mounted, his fame grew and his nervous stomach got worse. He was billed as "Satchel Paige, the World's Greatest Pitcher, Guaranteed to Strike Out the First Nine Men!" The trick word was "guaranteed." Crowds jammed ball parks to see him win —all the time. He was not supposed to lose any more than Bojangles Robinson was supposed to fall down while executing a buck-and-wing. People said that Satchel Paige was not only extra-human, but that he was just rounding into his greatest years at thirty-one, or thirty-three, or thirty-seven, or whatever.

"Everything is still in front of him," they said.

In Venezuela at the height of this clamor, Paige pitched two innings of a three-inning guest shot without incident, which is to say he struck everybody out. In the third inning, throwing a routine sidearm fast ball, however, he felt a small, sharp pain in his pitching shoulder.

That evening he caught a plane for his next guest appearance in Mexico City. With the first ball he pitched in that rarefied atmosphere, his shoulder joint snapped audibly and he sat down on the mound, in the midst of a rising storm of catcalls, bewildered by the pain.

Back in Kansas City, unable to lift his right arm, Paige thought he had better see a doctor. The examination took only a couple of minutes.

"Satchel," said the doctor, briskly, "you're through."

III

Mr. Leroy (Satchel) Paige, the tall, urbane and seemingly imperish- able relief-pitching star of the St. Louis Browns, cast a startled glance at Joe DiMaggio during an all-star charity game in Hollywood a while ago. Before his eyes, the thirty-seven-year-old Clipper, who had come out of retirement to make one last appearance at bat, took a couple of swings in an elderly fashion, then popped out feebly to short. The sight abso- lutely dismayed Mr. Paige.

Back in 1926, when Paige was pitching for the Chattanooga Black Lookouts, in the Negro Southern Association, DiMaggio was a San Fran- cisco schoolboy of eleven. In 1935, when Paige was a 10-year semipro veteran and already a legend in the land, DiMaggio was still a year away from the Yankees. Thirteen years later, when Paige was just breaking into the majors as a Cleveland rookie, sports writers were calling Di- Maggio the Yankees' grand old man. Now, when Paige was being hailed as one of the best relief prospects in baseball, DiMaggio was bowing out of the game.

With time jumping around like that, no wonder Paige was confused.

Mr. Paige, whose own age is believed to fall somewhere between forty-five and fifty-three, is unalterably opposed to time. As soon as he learns the hitting weaknesses of one generation of sluggers, for example, time does away with them. Time also makes off with pitchers—a circumstance Paige feels is not only an inexcusable affront to his profession, but harmful to society in general.

"All this comin' and goin'," he says indignantly. "Rookies flyin' up the road and old-timers flyin' down, and nobody in between but me and ol' John Mize, standin' pat, watchin' 'em go by.

"And I ain't even sure about ol' John," says Paige. "Maybe he's flyin' on, too. If he is," Paige adds, accusingly, "I can always watch 'em go by myself. Time ain't gonna mess with me!"

This last seems to be indisputable fact. Paige currently is enjoying what is probably his thirtieth year as a professional pitcher. In that span, he has not only set athletic longevity records, but has pitched and won more ball games (some 2,000 out of 2,500), traveled more miles (nearly a million), drawn more customers (an estimated 10,000,000), seen more astonishing sights and thrown a faster fast ball than any other moundsman known to man.

"I've never seen anything quite like Lee-roy," says Browns owner Bill Veeck, who also was a schoolboy of eleven when Paige was with Chattanooga. "He's been my hero since 1934 when I saw him beat a Dizzy Dean All-Star team 1-0 in thirteen innings in California. Last year, when the wise men were saying he'd come apart if he pitched more than three innings once a week, he worked in almost a third of all our games and won twelve and saved ten for us. He was easily the best relief man in the league, in my opinion, and the only Brownie to make the All-Star team."

Veeck pondered. "If this keeps up," he added reflectively, "what will he be like five years from now?"

Paige is too busy with the here and now to consider such questions. Age or no age, he is the Browns' highest-paid player, at $25,000 a year. To hold this exalted status, he is obliged to keep pace with the other Browns, some of whom were born after he started pitching for pay.

The sight of Paige keeping pace can be deceptive, of course. Before games, when other players are prancing around, swinging four bats, doing knee-bends, and so on, Paige may be seen reclining gracefully in his canopied contour chair by the Browns' bull pen, throwing gently to a catcher, counting the house or possibly playing "skidoodle."

"Skidoodle is a game I invented some years ago to exercise without doin' myself permanent harm," Paige says. "I throw the ball on one bounce to another man, he bounces it back at me. We jangle around. Nobody falls down exhausted."

Paige has conditioned himself so long and so well that on a hot day he can warm up his celebrated right arm with five or six pitches. Par for most pitchers is about fifteen minutes of steady throwing. Browns manager Marty Marion never tells the old gentleman how to live or what to throw. Even Clint Courtney, the Browns' combative catcher, has given up trying to get him to follow pitching signals, since Paige will throw what he wants to, anyhow.

Courtney's restraint is doubtless wise, for what Paige wants to throw has impressed many of the American League's most formidable hitters. Mickey Mantle, who up until recently had hit Paige one for ten, says flatly that he would "rather face any other pitcher in the league in a pinch situation." Detroit's Johnny Pesky, who at last count also had just one hit off Paige in many tries, says he hesitates to think what might have happened had Paige come to the majors while in his youth. "He used to average fifteen strike-outs a game, five days a week," Pesky says wonderingly. Outfielder Bob Nieman, also of Detroit, adds that he saw Paige load the bases with none out against Cleveland last year, and then retire the next three men on twelve pitches. "That stayed with me," Nieman says.

Paige's battery mate, Courtney, gives three reasons why the elderly pitcher is a present danger instead of a disturbing memory to hitters. "You hear about pinpoint control," Courtney says, "but Paige is the only man I've ever seen who really has it. He threw me six strikes out of ten pitches over a chewing-gum wrapper one time. Also," says Courtney, "his fast ball still burns my mitt when he lets it go, which is whenever he needs it. Finally, he just thinks faster than most hitters. Satchel is a very smart man."

What Paige thinks about various hitters can usually be heard by fans some distance from the Browns' bull pen during games. Sitting in his chair, Paige keeps a running commentary going, most of it seemingly for his own benefit.

"Don't ever feed that man low outside," he cautioned himself recently, as Mantle came to bat. "He will harm you." Ferris Fain, the 1952 American League batting champion, once caused Paige to cry a rhymed warning to the man pitching to him. "Throw it high, the skin will fly," hollered Paige. When Larry Doby of the Indians is up, Paige usually suggests using "the barber." (The barber is Paige's name for a high, inside pitch that shaves the batter's chin.)

Mickey Vernon, of the Senators, is the only man who leaves Paige speechless. For some mysterious reason, Vernon hits Paige almost at will.

Because Paige is the oldest established one-man traveling baseball spectacle now active, the Browns' management feels squeamish about cramping him with rules. He is on the honor system, which is to say that he does not have to stay in hotels with the team on road trips if he wishes to stay with friends, as he does in about half the towns the Browns play. Nobody orders him to bed by midnight. He is presumed to have outlived most of the ballplayer vices and so escapes spiritual lectures. All he is expected to do, besides win, is to appear on time for trains, practice or games.

That requirement, unhappily, is the very one Paige has to struggle hardest to meet. Punctuality undermines him, somehow. When he is late nowadays, guilt sits so heavily upon him that he usually assumes some other character, completely foreign to his normal self, to help bear it.

On such occasions, Paige often comes into the dressing room in the character of a hurt or outraged man and makes some immediate and inscrutable statement, such as, "They oughta bust the clocks down there" or "The taxi drivers is in cahoots!" or "He was bound to send me air mail!" Translated, these comments mean that Paige was late because the clocks in some hotel were wrong, or that the taxi drivers were in league with the opposing team to delay him, or that some friend kept him so long he had to take a plane to catch up with the team.

Paige's real character, as opposed to his character when tardy, is an arresting blend of warmth and reserve, humor, cunning, dignity, slap-stick and competitive drive—all governed by one of the most penetrat-ing, though unschooled, intelligences in or outside baseball. Whether he appears as the soul of assurance in a desperate situation on a ball field, or as a lean, expensively dressed, rather regal, languid and melancholy-looking man on the street, the rare but unmistakable stamp of originality is upon Paige.

"I'm Satchel," he sometimes explains simply, when people try to fit him into various molds. "I do as I do."

Doing as he does, Paige communicates his personality to whole ball parks full of fans with theatrical ease. Every time he rises from his bull-pen seat, even to get a drink, an excited murmur runs through the stands. When he starts his slow, slightly bent, sadly comic amble to the mound to save a game, fans get the impression from him that the whole situation is too simple for concern. The unconcern is the essence of Paige and always causes the crowd to explode in appreciation.

Even opposing fans are for Paige. In Boston last year, for example, he went in to put down a Red Sox uprising and was promptly shelled for an unbelievable six runs before he could get the side out. Throughout this disaster, the Red Sox stands sat in stony, embarrassed silence. When he finally wobbled off the diamond, the cheers could be heard in Cam-bridge. Paige has never been booed in the majors.

Because he has pitched so long, and has disappeared so many times into backwoods baseball in this and other countries, many fans have lost track of Paige and have come to the conclusion that he is deceased. During spring training this year, he says, he was riding in a Los Angeles cab when he noticed the driver scrutinizing him in the rear-vision mir-ror. Finally the driver shook his head and exclaimed: "No, it ain't possi-ble. He's passed."

"Who's passed?" Paige inquired guardedly.

The driver explained that for a minute he could have sworn his passenger was a famous, long-gone pitcher named Satchel Paige.

"I knew Ol' Satch well," the driver sighed. "Even though I was only a little child of eight when he was in his prime."

"When was that?" asked Ol' Satch, gloomily.

"About 1913," said the driver.

Paige's mother, Mrs. Tula Paige, who is eighty-three and has never seen Satchel play, also has certain delusions about him. She thinks of him as a child who has wandered into a shiftless, sinful life. For thirty years, she has remained inexorably opposed to his playing baseball, writing him regular instructions about attending Mass and avoiding gambling, late hours, wild women and other evils.

"I sure wish she'd change her mind about baseball," Paige complains. "It's a big strain when your mama ain't with you."

Other Browns players do not share his mother's view that Paige requires protection from the hazards of life. They have heard stories about how he once made his way on foot across tropical jungles to escape romance, and how he was later feted by Venezuelan savages. They have heard how he personally intimidated a brave bull in Mexico, and how he was canonized in 1935 by the North Dakota Sioux. These stories, among dozens of others, have given Paige an aura of wisdom, experience and mystery impressive to many veteran ballplayers and practically all rookies.

Occasionally, when reminiscent moods overpower him, Paige himself gives his clubhouse admirers, and a select few others, a glimpse or two into his adventurous past. These reviews are never complete without discussion of the fans. Fans have always fascinated Paige. In South America, where he played winter ball off and on for twenty years, they were always running him around, trying either to carry him on their shoulders or decapitate him with machetes.

The fans Paige remembers best lived in the wild country of northwestern Venezuela. These fans were short, dark, fierce fellows who ran about the forest in G strings, shooting poisoned arrows at birds and occasional oil-line workers. Every so often, some of them sneaked into the Maracaibo ball park and had to be run out to keep them from scaring the customers and stealing baseballs.

"The only time I seen these fans," Paige recently recalled for some teammates, "I was on a jackass ridin' around in the jungle sightseein'. I was wearin' some cream-colored pants, a sport shirt and two-tone shoes, as I recollect. When I come to a clearin' in the forest I thought I'd get off and rest. But the clearin' was jammed with these fans, sittin' around in front of a big grass house and eatin' pig and roots and bugs and all that mess they eat. When they seen me," Paige said, "they grabbed up their blow guns and aimed right at my new Stetson hat."

For a long time, Paige gazed silently at the fans and the fans gazed silently at Paige. Then, he said, one of them ran into a hut, returned with a baseball and stood pointing from the ball to Paige and jabbering excitedly. The blowguns came down at once, Paige said, and he was thereupon obliged to dismount and join the fans in a meal of pig, roots and bugs. They gave him a blowgun of his own, and wouldn't let him leave until the day was almost gone.

"I could of been a big man in that outfit if I'd stayed on," Paige concluded offhandedly. "But I had to get on back to the States, where I also had some fans."

Paige has grown so used to autograph hunters among his stateside fans that he often fails to observe them closely. In Phoenix last spring, a slight, partially bald, agitated-looking man came bounding into the Browns' dressing room after an exhibition game. Paige was reclining in a whirl bath at the time, but he borrowed a pen from the man and signed his program obligingly. When the man suddenly began firing ad-lib witticisms, however, twitching his eyebrows and sidling around bent-kneed, Paige, who is the official humorist on the Browns, began to regard him so coolly that he finally crept away.

"Who was that character?" Paige asked Browns trainer Bob Bauman as he emerged from the bath.

"Groucho Marx," Bauman said.

Paige, who mourns this unfortunate meeting, blames it almost entirely on the fact that Marx was not wearing his stage eyebrows at the time, not on his own failure to scrutinize Marx properly. Usually, of course, Paige does not have to peer at anyone in particular, since he deals with fans mostly in groups.

On train trips, for example, other players usually arrive at stations singly, or in pairs. Paige almost inevitably appears at the center of a large and enthusiastic delegation. Friendly and relaxed, he nevertheless maintains a certain reserve toward his admirers, as befits a man who has been one of the authentic folk heroes of America's Negroes, not to mention thousands of others, for many years.

When Paige takes to the road, he usually carries one enormous bag containing four conservative suits, several pairs of shoes, bottles of pills, ointments and philters to combat anticipated ailments, and a great miscellany of other items. One of the twenty cameras he owns inevitably dangles from a shoulder strap. Redcaps compete desperately to carry his luggage. As Paige strolls regally along the train platforms on his way to the Browns' car, all the cooks and porters hang out of car windows on both sides to salute him.

"All right, brothers," Paige exclaims, waving and grinning broadly as he passes. "Let us ramble."

In the club car, Paige is inevitably surrounded by other Browns players, who consider him a library of general information and probably the most authoritative train-window commentator in the land.

Paige thinks creatively in almost any field, which is to say that even though he may not know what he is talking about on some subject, what he says nevertheless sounds more factual than the facts. Recently, for example, Paige told one teammate how to make straw hats. This man, who had once worked in a straw-hat factory, came away convinced that he had spent years laboring in error. In a conversation on the theory of engineering stresses with ex-Brownie outfielder Frank Saucier, an honor student in engineering who is now in the Navy, Paige waxed so eloquent that Saucier had to retreat to his books to reassure himself.

One subject Paige rarely discusses is his home life. The main reason is that his pretty second wife, Lahoma, does not approve of mixing his public and private affairs.

At home in one of the two large, dark-brick houses he owns in Kansas City, Missouri, Paige usually moves with the patriarchal gravity of a settled landholder. (He lives in one house, rents the other.) A restless man, he constantly prowls about the trophy room, the Chinese antique room and the twelve other rooms, including his roost on the second floor.

Paige's home activity tends to dampen the natural ebullience of the many relatives and friends always to be found in the household, several of them on a semipermanent basis. But it has little effect on Mrs. Paige, who has a strong character, or on his four children: Pamella, five; Caroline, two and a half; Linda, one and a half; and Leroy, Jr., six months. Mrs. Paige, who first caught her husband's eye as a clerk in a Kansas City camera store when he wandered in to buy film six years ago, keeps him on rather short tether, which he seems to find agreeable, since he grumbles about it all the time. Paige's first wife, Janet, a vivacious Pittsburgh waitress whom he married in 1934 and from whom he was divorced some years ago, also kept him on short rein. Too short, he says.

Outside his home life, no field of conversational inquiry is too remote for Paige to venture into. If other players have problems with love, finances, batting averages, falling hair or whatever, Paige may be counted on for remedies. Occasionally, of course, he comes upon something that ruffles his composure.

In the club car of a Chicago-bound train this year, some players presented Paige a book called *How to Pitch*, by Cleveland's wealthy squire, Bob Feller, Paige's junior by perhaps fifteen years. Retiring to a window seat with this volume, Paige, who has beaten Feller a staggering number of times in exhibition games, at once began snorting and shifting about.

"Here, now!" he exclaimed, starting up in astonishment at one point. "Is that how you do it?"

A few pages later, he leaped up and began to execute one of the illustrated techniques. But he couldn't seem to get the hang of it.

"That's a good book," he informed one of his teammates later. "Only thing is, if I start pitchin' the correct way now, I'll probably break my arm. I just about broke it once," he said, darkly, "and I can't risk it again."

When Paige just about broke his arm, he was in Mexico City, in 1938, at the peak of his fame and pitching power. Throwing a simple sidearm curve one day, he snapped his arm so badly that he couldn't lift it. Back in Kansas City, the doctor who examined him said flatly that he was through.

No news could have been more inconceivable to Paige. His arm had lifted him from poverty and childhood delinquency in Mobile. It had survived Canadian cold, 117-degree desert heat, thousands of all-night bus rides and greasy hamburger joints and cheap boardinghouses. It had stood up to every trial to which Paige could subject it, including four Negro World Series and East-West all-star games before crowds of 50,000 and up. Had it been of a different hue, major-league club owners might have paid up to $150,000 cash for it at 1938 prices.

All this notwithstanding, Satch Paige couldn't lift it. Within a month, the only job he could get was a coach for the Kansas City Monarchs. For the next year, he traveled with the Monarchs' second team, growing more and more obscure and irascible. "Man," Paige says, "it was a long year."

It was an interminable year, hard on the young players trying to expand under the brooding shadow of the former "greatest pitcher in the world," and impossible for Paige, who seemed to grow taller, thinner and grimmer-looking every day. By 1940, when he was thirty-four, or thereabouts, and hadn't pitched for fourteen months, Paige was ready to quit.

Then, just before a Monarchs game one afternoon, a queer thing happened. Someone overthrew first in a pre-game warmup and Paige ambled over, picked up the ball and threw it back to the pitcher. It was the most unobtrusive of acts, but just about every player on the field seemed to see it and to stop stockstill.

Walking thoughtfully toward the dugout, Paige picked up a glove and called for a ball. Without a word, the Monarchs' catcher left the plate and stationed himself about pitching distance from Paige. Then Paige began to throw, easily at first, then harder and harder. Nobody moved, the stands were silent, the game waiting. The catcher called, "Easy, Satchel, easy!" But Paige leaned into his pitches until the ball seemed to diminish in space. Then, abruptly, he stopped, and gazed around at all the eyes upon him.

"Well," he said, "I'm back."

The news traveled fast. Semipro club owners flocked around with contracts as soon as they heard, and the fans began to roar. Life once again became a pleasure for Paige. He traveled far and wide, showing new generations of hitters a whole new assortment of curves, floaters and so on, to go with his fast ball, which he now used only in the pinches. His fan mail was staggering. His income as a solo performer ranged up to $35,000 a year.

"It was all so nice," Paige recalls, "that I almost forgot time was passin' and I hadn't begun to do what I'd always wanted."

What Paige had always wanted was to play for a major-league club. By 1946, when every hot stove buzzed with rumors that the big-league color line was about to be broken, Paige lived at a high pitch of excitement.

"Maybe I was too eager," Paige says. "But then I figured that with all those writin' men sayin' I'm due for the Hall of Fame and all that ruckus—well, I figured I'd be the first one under the wire."

When Jackie Robinson became the first one, Paige went on pitching for semipro teams without comment. When Larry Doby and others followed Robinson, Paige spoke less and less.

"When 1948 come around," Paige says, "and I still got my nose to the window, I realized what the club owners was thinkin'. They was thinkin' that when I was with Chattanooga, Larry Doby wasn't bawn."

However, Bill Veeck, then owner of the Cleveland Indians, was not thinking just that way.

"Abe Saperstein, who owns the Harlem Globetrotters basketball team, and who always seems to turn up when Satch needs him, had been after me for a long time to sign him up," Veeck says. "But Lou Boudreau, who was managing Cleveland, didn't think it was there any more. Still, he was desperate for relief men so he put on a catcher's mitt at the stadium one day and says to Satch: 'All right, here's the plate. See if you can get it up here.' Well," Veeck says, "Lee-roy threw fifty pitches. Forty-six of them were strikes. That was that."

If the Indians management was convinced, some sports writers were not. J. G. Taylor Spink, publisher of the influential St. Louis *Sporting News,* let go as follows:

"Many well-wishers of baseball emphatically fail to see eye to eye with the signing of Satchel Paige, superannuated Negro pitcher. . . . To bring in a pitching rookie of Paige's age . . . is to demean the standards of baseball in the big circuits."

"I demeaned the big circuits considerable that year," Paige says. "I win six an' lose one."

The night that Paige walked out of a quarter century of circus baseball into the rarefied atmosphere of the big leagues, some 20,000 fans at Cleveland Stadium rose for ten minutes of unbroken roaring. Paige obliged by blanking the Browns for two innings in relief.

By the end of the season, Paige, besides his six-and-one record, had an earned-run average of 2.47, had struck out 45, made no errors afield and got himself two hits. Sports writers were so amazed that several of them voted to name him Rookie of the Year.

"I declined the position," Paige says calmly. "I wasn't sure which year the gentlemen had in mind."

When Paige joined the Indians, the news penetrated instantly to the remotest backwoods; all over the American League, crowds poured out to watch the legend in the flesh. The climax was reached on August 20th, when Paige started against eighth-place Chicago at Cleveland, and the all-time record night crowd of 78,382 paid to see him win.

Toward the end of the 1948 season, to Paige's vast surprise, certain creaks in his physical mechanism had begun to appear. "Ol' No. 1," which is what Paige calls his back muscles and diaphragm, remained in good shape. So did "Ol' No. 2," his pitching arm. But he was having a time with his nervous stomach—the product of too many years of barnstorming as "The World's Greatest Pitcher—Guaranteed to Strike Out the First Nine Men." His flat feet hurt and the emaciated calves attached to them seemed weighted with stone. On top of all this, the dentist had a message for him.

"The dentist says to me that all my teeth will have to come out," Paige recalls, with horror. "I says, doctor, I will not abide with store teeth, and he says, then you will not abide."

If emotion was on Paige's side, fact seemed to be on the dentist's. Paige felt worse and worse as the 1948 season closed, and he was full of miseries when he reported to the Indians in Arizona for the 1949 season. However, in mid-season, when the hot weather began, he felt better and began to expand and advise the young pitchers in the devious ways of the game.

During one grindingly tight game with Boston, Paige was advising Mike Garcia, a young Cleveland pitcher of great promise. It was the last of the eighth, Cleveland led by one run, the Red Sox were up with nobody out and Garcia was squirming with nervousness in the Indian bull pen. He had just been told that he might have to go in for relief.

"Boy," said Paige, lounging back on the bull-pen bench and exuding vast confidence, "I wouldn't worry about them Red Sox. There ain't a hitter among 'em."

As Paige spoke, a pinch hitter singled sharply, and lead-off man Dom DiMaggio came to bat. "Now, this fella," Paige drawled, "there is a mess." DiMaggio singled to center and Johnny Pesky came up.

"Pesky!" Paige snorted, disdainfully. "Why they say that man can hit, I don't know. You just feed him in close on his knees . . ."

Pesky hit the first pitch for a single, loading the bases. While the dreaded Ted Williams strode to the plate, Paige clapped the quaking Garcia on the shoulder and declared jovially: "Now we're gonna be all right."

As Satchel made this announcement, manager Lou Boudreau beckoned to the bull pen—not for Garcia, but for Paige. There was a moment of deep silence in the dugout. Then, as though in a trance, Paige rose from the bench.

"Son," he said, huskily, concluding his message to Garcia, "just remember, when you're disputin' the Red Sox, put your trust in the power of prayer."

Prayer got Paige out of the hole with the loss of but one run.

During the long August pull in 1949, all of Paige's miseries came back and the batters started injuring him repeatedly. Of the thirty-one games he appeared in that year, he won four and lost seven. The next winter, when Bill Veeck sold out as principal owner of the Indians, Satchel Paige's contract went up for sale. There were no takers.

"That winter, I went back to that dentist," Paige recalled with annoyance, a while ago. "Well, he come at me with them pliers, and I reared back, and then we got to rasslin' and I give him a few knocks in the excitement. But he win," said Paige, taking out his uppers and gazing at them with grudging admiration. "Couple days and the misery was gone."

The end of Paige's miseries seemed to interest nobody in the majors in 1950, however, so he started back over the old itinerant trail, pitching any- and everywhere, and nearly doubling the $20,000 a year he had made in the majors. When the Giants and Braves offered him contracts in the pennant drive, Paige had to turn them down. "I couldn't afford to lose money pitchin' for nobody but Bill Veeck," he says. "With Burr-head, I didn't feel it so much."

When Veeck bought control of the St. Louis Browns in mid-1951, one of his first acts was to sign Paige.

"Lee-roy was a must," says Veeck. "Everybody kept telling me he was through, but that was understandable. They thought he was only human.

"Later on in the season," Veeck added reflectively, "I began to think so myself. Satch won three and lost four for us. When he announced at the end of the season that it might be his last year, the wire services carried the story mostly for sentimental reasons."

When the juices of spring began to rise in Mr. Paige in early 1952, however, he set out for the Browns' training camp at Burbank, California, with no thought for last year's statements to the press. The California weather filled him with such energies that he could hardly wait for the season to begin.

When it did begin, however, the other Browns were also so steamed up that they were astonished to find themselves in first place.

"I was just a bull-pen pitcher," Paige recalls, with dismay. "Every man we put in the first four games went the route. The buck fever was among us. But I says to myself, look here, Satchel, them old-time ballplayers on them other clubs ain't loosened up yet. Wait 'til the hot weather hits them and they'll all be stompin' around up there on top, fightin' each other for that third of a game, that little piece of a game to put them in the lead. Then you'll be pitchin', I says to myself. Oh, my, yes."

By June, it seemed to Paige that he was pitching every other day.

The fast-slipping Browns would get a slim lead, watch it begin to vanish and call loudly for Paige. If the opposition had managed to tie the score before Paige went in, games would go on endlessly, because Paige would yield no runs and his teammates could never get any when they were most needed.

By July 4th, Paige had appeared in 25 games. He had pitched 10 innings of an 18-inning game at Washington, holding the Senators to a 5-5 tie until the game was called at 1:00 A.M. Against the Indians, he had gone 11 innings of an incredible 19-inning game, finally losing it when he and the fans could hardly keep their eyes open. Time and again, he had gone in to protect one-run leads for the Browns and retired the best hitters of the American League, one, two, three. Watching him do just that to the Yankees one night, Casey Stengel, manager of both the Bombers and the 1952 American League All-Star team, picked Paige as one of his pitchers for the July dream game.

"That took care of the third one of my big ambitions," Paige says. "Before I'd hardly got started in my career, I'd played for a big-league club, pitched in a World Series" (two thirds of an inning with Cleveland in 1948) "and made the All-Star team. That did my stomach gas a lot of good."

The rest of the season did his digestion little good, however. As the Browns went down and down to seventh place, Paige rose more and more often to pitch. By season's end, he had worked a staggering total of 46 games, struck out 91, and won 12 games, lost 10 and saved 10.

In the long grind, he had even worked against railroad timetables. At 9:30 one evening, with the Browns leading Washington by one run and due to catch a 10:30 train, Paige had come ambling in to stem a ninth-inning Washington rally. He retired three Senator hitters on nine called strikes and one ball. On the train later on, he had apologized for the ball.

"When the shootin' finally stopped," says Paige, "I found out I was tired. I figured a few hot baths and a few days layin' around the house would take care of that, and it did, as far as my frame was concerned. But I had another kind of tired. I was kinda tired of baseball."

This new fatigue took a long time to show up. Most of the winter, Paige took it easy around his house, doing a little carpentry and plumbing here and there, thinking he ought to fix up the back yard, and worrying about his 35 per cent income tax. Time and inaction were great problems. Winter, itself, was a problem. Satchel hated the cold—it had always driven him to the tropics in other years. In winter, time seemed to drag, leaving nothing to do but shoot some pool, or do a little after-dinner speaking around Kansas City, or answer his fan mail, or hunt, or regard the television, which wasn't much good for his pitching eye.

By early February of this year, the new fatigue really began to work on Paige. He descended the long staircase in his house like a remote chieftain, scattering relatives and friends right and left with a cold eye.

He got out his Spanish guitar and sang gloomy tunes up in his room.

Then, one gray day, things came to a head. The first thought Paige had on awakening was of a talk he was supposed to give at a luncheon in his honor that noon. The thought wearied and depressed him. He put it out of his mind until midday, when some civic leaders called for him in a limousine. On the way downtown, he sat silent and somber. At a loss to explain Paige's mood, the leaders talked around it, finally inquiring, heartily, what he intended to say at the banquet.

Paige took his time answering. He roused himself slowly from a slouched position. He stared at the gentlemen.

"I'm gonna say that they got the wrong man for this speech," he said finally. "I'm gonna say I'm through with baseball! Worn out runnin' around! Sick and tired!"

That stopped all conversation. Many blocks farther on, the limousine approached a vacant lot where some piping, stick-legged boys were rushing the season with a pickup ball game. Paige began to stir restlessly at the sight. He looked away but his eyes seemed to be drawn back. He coughed nervously. When the limousine was passing the lot, Paige suddenly sat up and ordered the driver to stop. Despite the heated protests of the civic gentlemen, he got out.

"You run on along to the lunch," he said. "I'll just set here a while."

After the lunch, says one witness, the gentlemen satisfied their curiosity by driving back past the lot. They arrived in the middle of a hot ball game. The battery was Paige, six feet three and a quarter inches tall, weight 180, age indefinite, pitching; Slattery, four feet two inches tall, weight 85, age nine, catching. The up team, the Jackson Street White Sox, was hitting Satchel Paige unmercifully. Also, the umpire, Yogi Olzewschki, wasn't giving him the corners.

After watching the game for a moment, the dignitaries looked at one another with visible dismay and told the driver to move on.

"Empire," Paige was protesting happily as they vanished down the street, "are you by any chance in need of spectacles?"

"I see fine!" Olzewschki was shouting authoritatively. "Play ball, or I'll throw you out of the game!"

HOW TO STAY YOUNG

1. Avoid fried meats which angry up the blood.
2. If your stomach disputes you, lie down and pacify it with cool thoughts.
3. Keep the juices flowing by jangling around gently as you move.
4. Go very light on the vices, such as carrying on in society. The social ramble ain't restful.
5. Avoid running at all times.
6. Don't look back. Something might be gaining on you.

(Signed) LEROY SATCHEL PAIGE

THIS STREAK of Joe D.'s was probably the greatest hitting record of major league history. This story was datelined Cleveland, July 17, 1941.

1941:
New York Yankees 4,
Cleveland Indians 3

JOHN DREBINGER

IN A BRILLIANT SETTING of lights and before 67,468 fans, the largest crowd ever to see a game of night baseball in the major leagues, the Yankees tonight vanquished the Indians, 4 to 3, but the famous hitting streak of Joe DiMaggio finally came to an end.

Officially it will go into the records as fifty-six consecutive games, the total he reached yesterday. Tonight in Cleveland's municipal stadium the great DiMag was held hitless for the first time in more than two months.

Al Smith, veteran Cleveland left-hander and a Giant castoff, and Jim Bagby, a young right-hander, collaborated in bringing the DiMaggio string to a close.

Jolting Joe faced Smith three times. Twice he smashed the ball down the third-base line, but each time Ken Keltner, Tribe third sacker, collared the ball and hurled it across the diamond for a put-out at first. In between these two tries, DiMaggio drew a pass from Smith.

Then, in the eighth, amid a deafening uproar, the streak dramatically ended, though the Yanks routed Smith with a flurry of four hits and two runs that eventually won the game.

With the bases full and only one out, Bagby faced DiMaggio and, with the count at one ball and one strike, induced the renowned slugger to crash into a double play. It was a grounder to the shortstop, and as the ball flitted from Lou Boudreau to Ray Mack to Oscar Grimes, who played first base for the Tribe, the crowd knew the streak was over.

However, there were still a few thrills to come, for in the ninth, with the Yanks leading, 4 to 1, the Indians suddenly broke loose with an attack that for a few moments threatened to send the game into extra innings and thus give DiMaggio another chance.

Gerald Walker and Grimes singled, and though Johnny Murphy here replaced Gomez, Larry Rosenthal tripled to score his two colleagues. But with the tying run on third and nobody out the Cleveland attack bogged down in a mess of bad base running and the Yanks' remaining one-run lead held.

It was on May 15 against the White Sox at the Yankee Stadium that DiMaggio began his string. As the great DiMag kept clicking in game after game, he became the central figure of the baseball world.

On June 29, in a double-header with the Senators in Washington, he tied, then surpassed the American League and modern record of forty-one games, set by George Sisler of the Browns in 1922. The target was the all-time major league high of forty-four contests set by Willie Keeler, famous Oriole star, forty-four years ago under conditions much easier for a batsman than they are today. Then there was no foul-strike rule hampering the batter.

But nothing hampered DiMaggio as he kept getting his daily hits, and on July 1 he tied the Keeler mark. The following day he soared past it for game No. 45, and he kept on soaring until tonight, in seeking his fifty-seventh game, he finally was brought to a halt.

Actually, DiMaggio hit in fifty-seven consecutive games, for on July 8 he connected safely in the All-Star game in Detroit. But that contest did not count in the official league records.

DiMaggio's mark ends five short of his own Pacific Coast League record of sixty-one consecutive games, which he set while with San Francisco in 1933. The all-time minor league high is sixty-seven, set by Joe Wilhoit of Wichita in the Western League in 1919.

GENERAL

PEOPLE have wondered whether a curve ball curves at all, and among these was the world famous aerodynamics wizard Igor Sikorsky. Mr. Sikorsky happened to have a wind tunnel, so tests were undertaken. His findings are reported in the following article.

The Sikorsky test found that a curve ball does curve, which accounts for Mr. Drury's title to his article, "The Hell It Don't Curve." The Sikorsky test also found that while a curve ball does curve in the sense that it follows a steady arc, it does not travel in a straight line and then "break." To which, I can only add, as editor of this anthology and a .240 hitter, the hell it don't.

The Hell It Don't Curve

JOSEPH F. DRURY, JR.

IN THE early 1870's, two major controversies stormed in the world of sports. One of these arguments ended in a generally accepted decision just five years later. But the other still rages spasmodically today, after more than eighty years of scientific rhubarb.

It was California's Governor Leland Stanford who, in 1878, collected a $50,000 bet by proving that all four feet of a galloping horse are off the ground at the same time. And it was Igor Sikorsky, internationally famous expert on aerodynamics, who not long ago used a wind tunnel to show that a human being *can* make a baseball curve.

Before Sikorsky approached the thesis, it had been argued and refuted, proved and exploded, sworn to and Bronx-cheered-at by scientists, photographers, and fans in general. Even the philosophers got into the act, one of them observing that "it would be at variance with every principle of philosophy" to contend that the ball does not curve.

Two of the most recent tests of the curve ball controversy were made by two national picture magazines. Each of them used an elaborate photographic technique, and the conclusions of both were regarded as more or less authoritative. But while one magazine *(Life)* claimed that its studies "raise once more the possibility that this stand-by of baseball is, after all, only an optical illusion," the other *(Look)* insisted that its own photographs proved "that a curve ball actually does curve." The high-speed cameras merely added fuel to the fires of both camps.

The pictures which purported to indicate that a baseball does *not* curve were themselves branded optical illusions by traditionalists. And when he studied pictures made to show that the ball *does* curve, Ernest Lowry, an outspoken member of the optical illusion school, called them "a most convincing demonstration of the complete *collapse* of the entire curve ball theory."

Incidentally, Mr. Lowry, who says the optical illusion is caused by "persistence of retinal impressions," also entertains some rather bitter convictions about what baseball men are doing to the country's juveniles. "The great injustice of the much publicized 'curve pitch,'" he contends, "is that of the manner in which millions of American boys have been misled on the question. They have been forced to delude themselves into thinking that their pitches do curve, or else be cruelly frustrated when they sense that their heroic efforts failed to achieve that which is now proved an impossibility."

Thus it was with righteous zeal that Sikorsky took up the scientific gauntlet. If American youth was being outrageously deceived by an unscrupulous combine of club owners and sports writers, if the curve ball religion was nothing but an opiate for the mustard-smeared masses, then he would explode the myth and rock baseballdom with his sock-dolager exposé.

At the time Sikorsky turned to the wind tunnel, major league baseball men openly propagandized the curve ball doctrine. A survey to measure their reactions to the "optical illusion" photographs brought in some interesting comments. Some were subtle. Others carried the impact of a hard-swung fungo bat.

"I am not positive whether a ball curves or not," said Eddie Sawyer, former manager of the Phillies, "but there is a pitch in baseball much different from the fast ball that 'separates the men from the boys.' If this pitch does not curve, it would be well to notify a lot of baseball players who were forced to quit the game they loved because of this certain pitch, and may be reached now at numerous gas stations, river docks, and mental institutions."

Ex-Cincinnati pilot Luke Sewell asked a very pertinent question. "Isn't it strange," he said, "that the optical illusion only happens when someone tries to throw a curve ball, and never when a fast or straight ball is attempted?" And Earl Mack, of the Athletics, followed up with this: "Is the magazine author crediting pitchers with the power of turning on optical illusions at will?"

And so the reactions went. Obviously, you would wire-tap a lot of locker rooms and subpoena many a ton of baseball records before you'd find a modern major-leaguer to support Mr. Lowry's suspicions. But he might have found a useful witness in Colonel J. B. Joyce, who, in 1877, was a ruling spirit in the old Cincinnati Red Stockings. It was to convince Joyce that the first publicized test of the curve ball issue was made. According to A. G. Spalding, who describes the test in his volume, *Baseball, America's National Game,* Colonel Joyce insisted that it was "absurd to say that any man could throw a ball other than in a straight line."

The test was made in Cincinnati in the presence of a large crowd. A surveyor set three posts in a row, twenty feet apart. Then two high fences were built, extending beyond each end post and in a direct line with all three posts. Will White, one of the league's best right-hand pitchers, stood to the left of the fence at one end of the course. When he made his throw, the fence prevented his hand from crossing the straight line between the posts.

"White pitched the ball," says Spalding, "so that it passed to the right of the middle post. This it did by three or four inches, but curved so much that it passed the third post a half foot to the left. The test was a success in everything but the conversion. Colonel Joyce would not be convinced."

Shortly after the 1877 experiment, the *Cincinnati Enquirer* printed the views of three college professors on the possibility of a pitched curve ball. Professor Stoddard, of Worcester University, wrote: "It is not only theoretically but practically impossible for any such impetus to be conveyed to a moving body as would be required . . . to control the movement of what is termed a curved ball."

But Professor Lewis Swift, of Rochester University, disagreed. "It is true that some time ago, when the subject was first broached to me," he said, "I denied that it was possible to do it. But I began to investigate the matter and soon saw that, instead of being impossible, it was in accordance with the *plainest principles of philosophy.*"

It is doubtful that principles of philosophy were in the mind of Ralph Lightfoot while he was test-flying in a helicopter over Bridgeport, Conn., some time ago. Lightfoot is chief of flight research at United Aircraft Corporation's Sikorsky plant. When he landed, he was given a message to report immediately to Mr. Sikorsky for discussion of an "important project."

Sikorsky had just received a telephone call from New York, where United Aircraft's Lauren (Deac) Lyman had been lunching with Walter H. Neff of United Air Lines. During their luncheon conversation, the topic had turned to the opening of the baseball season and the curve ball talents of leading pitchers.

"Doesn't it strike you as strange," asked Neff, "that science counts the wing-beats of insects and controls planes at supersonic speeds—but it can't seem to prove what happens when a man throws a baseball sixty feet?"

"The problem should be simple enough," said Lyman. "Just a combination of human factors and pure aerodynamics."

"Then why couldn't one of your company's engineers do it, Deac?"

Lyman smiled thoughtfully. "I wonder . . ." he said. "By gosh, why don't we phone Igor?"

When Lightfoot entered his office, Sikorsky greeted him in his soft, continental accent. "Look, Mr. Lightfoot," the helicopter genius began, gesturing with cupped hands. "Here we have a solid sphere moving rapidly in space and rotating on a vertical axis. You see?"

Lightfoot nodded. His mind raced ahead of Sikorsky's words. It sounded alarmingly like flying saucers. But as his boss continued, the engineer grinned broadly. "The object," said Sikorsky, "is to elude the man with the stick."

Whatever he lacked in baseball lingo Sikorsky made up for in scientific lore. For instance, he knew that a pitched ball, traveling in a curved path, is an example of aerodynamic action in everyday life. He realized, too, that the force which causes a ball to curve in flight is the same force known to engineers as "the Magnus effect," because it was explained by Professor G. Magnus, of Berlin, way back in 1851. Needless to say, Magnus wasn't interested in baseballs. His subject was *cannon* balls, and he was trying to find out why German artillery couldn't throw more "strikes."

But 25 years later, a British physicist named Lord John Rayleigh applied the Magnus findings to a report on the flight of a tennis ball. Briefly, what Rayleigh found was this: That when a ball is in flight but not spinning, it is exposed to a uniform air flow in one direction. So it follows a straight line. But when the ball is made to rotate sideways, friction between the ball and the air around it forms a sort of whirlpool. When this happens, the air flow is no longer in one direction. The whirlpool brings another force into play. And this double force on only one side of the ball produces a *lateral* force which drives it in the direction toward which it is spinning.

The picture magazine which favored the optical illusion explanation of the curve ball theory accepted, of course, the more obvious fact that a tennis or Ping-pong ball curves. In fact, the author wrote: "If a baseball could be spun with the same amount of power relative to its weight that a tennis ball is spun, then its path, it is agreed, would also be curved to the same extent. But," he added, "no pitcher, it seems, has a strong enough finger and wrist motion to put the necessary spin onto the ball which would materially affect its sidewise motion."

It was Sikorsky's first problem, then, to determine how much "stuff" or spin a pitcher can put on the ball in the regulation sixty-foot, six-inch distance from the mound to the plate.

To learn this, baseball fans among the plant's engineers were glad to contribute some of their off-duty time. Careful studies were made of rapid-fire flash photographs showing the progress of a single pitch. Aircraft technicians, experienced in observing the behavior of whirling propellers, examined the change in the position of the ball's stitches from picture to picture. They figured that the ball was spinning at the rate of one-third of a revolution during each one-thirtieth of a second between exposures. Since the entire pitch took less than a half second, the rate of rotation was seen to be about five revolutions for the pitch, or about 600 per minute.

So far, the engineers knew how much spin a human could put on a pitched baseball. But they still had to find out whether that was enough to make it curve. For the wind tunnel, that job was literally "a breeze."

Using official National and American League balls—identical except for their markings—Sikorsky and Lightfoot impaled them on a slender spike connected to the shaft of a small motor. During the next "stand-by time" between aircraft tests, the baseballs were inserted into the tunnel and rotated by the motor at speeds from zero to 1,200 revolutions per minute. Since official army devices had clocked Bob Feller's fast ball at 98.6 miles per hour, the forward speeds of the air moving through the tunnel were varied between 80 and 110 miles per hour. The motor was mounted on a delicately-balanced scale which measured the direction and force of all pressures brought on the balls.

To observe maximum and minimum effects, the baseballs were spiked and rotated at two different angles. In one position, four seams met the wind during each revolution. This produced the greatest amount of side force on the ball. In the other position, only two seams met the wind, producing less friction and less side force.

When the wind tunnel results were plotted on conventional engineering graph sheets, Sikorsky knew he had "something for the books." The results have so much significance that they could even cause changes in pitching and batting techniques. Here, in the order of their importance, are the findings.

1. *It can be definitely concluded that a pitched baseball does actually curve, in addition to any optical illusion which may exist.*

2. A pitched baseball travels in a *uniformly* curved path from the time it leaves the pitcher's hand until it reaches the catcher's glove. There's no such thing as a "sharp-breaking curve" in the sense that a ball can be thrown so that it flies first in a straight line and then suddenly veers off. That kind of "remote control" is strictly from *fiction*, not friction.

3. To an observer at or behind the plate, it *appears* that the ball travels fairly straight most of the way and then breaks suddenly and sharply near the plate. Actually, the curve ball *arcs* toward or away from the plate *throughout* its flight; but the batter, because he views the flight at an angle, cannot discern the gradual arc and believes the ball "breaks" at an angle.

4. Here's one for the coaches. The pitcher who learns to release the ball so that *all four* seams meet the wind each time it rotates will have the nearest thing possible to a "jug-handle" curve. If he has Feller's speed of over 80 miles per hour, and Carl Hubbell's spin of 600 revolutions per minute, his curve will "break" as much as 19 inches. With the same speed and rotation, but with only two seams meeting the wind, the amount of curve will drop to about 7½ inches.

If you're an average fan, you'll be content to measure a curve by how well it fools the batter. But for those with technical minds, here's a Sikorsky formula that will tell you how much a baseball will curve:

$$d \text{ equals } \frac{^cL \; P \; V^2 \; t^2 \; g \; C^2}{7230 \; W} \text{ feet}$$

Where: d equals displacement from a straight line; ^cL equals circulation of air generated by friction when ball is spinning; P equals the density of the air (normal at .002378); V equals the speed of the ball; t equals the time for delivery; g equals the acceleration of gravity (32.2 feet per second²); C equals the circumference of the ball (9 inches); and W equals the ball's weight (.3125 pounds); while the number 7230 relates other values of pounds, inches, feet, seconds, etc., to arrive at an answer in feet.

Sikorsky and his co-workers may well have produced the most convincing evidence yet that a pitcher can throw curves. Happily enough, their findings offer both the curve ball *and* the optical illusion squads their inning of vindication. The fact of the matter, stated simply, is that the curve ball *does* curve, but the batter—because of his angular view of the pitch—experiences the *optical illusion* that the ball curves more radically than it does.

Al Schacht, the "Clown Prince of Baseball," now runs one of the world's swankiest "cracker barrel leagues" at his New York restaurant. And to illustrate how seriously the world of baseball takes its curves, Al revives this favorite story:

A farm-belt ballplayer, locally famous for his hitting powers, won a major league tryout during spring training. Each week, as his batting average and confidence soared, he wired his mother. The first week, he said: "Dear Mom. Leading all batters. These pitchers not so tough." A week later, he boasted: "Looks like I will be regular outfielder. Now hitting .433." Early in the third week of training, the yokel's mother got a wire that led her to dismiss the new farmhand and get out her son's work clothes. "Dear Mom," it said. "They started throwing curves. Will be home Friday."

POETRY

MR. ELLARD helped organize the undefeated Cincinnati Red Stockings of 1869 as baseball's first professional club.

The Red Stockings

GEORGE ELLARD

We used no mattress on our hands,
No cage upon our face;
We stood right up and caught the ball
With courage and with grace.

From *Constitution and By-laws,* 1860

EXCELSIOR BASEBALL CLUB, BROOKLYN

9. Members, when assembled for field exercise, or for any meeting of the club, who shall use profane and improper language, shall be fined ten cents for each offense.
10. A member disputing the decisions of the umpire shall be fined twenty-five cents for each offense.
11. A member who shall audibly express his opinion on a doubtful play before the decision of the umpire (unless called upon to do so) shall be fined twenty-five cents for each offense.
13. A member wearing or using the apparel of a fellow-member, without his *written* permission, shall be fined one dollar.
14. All fines incurred for violation of Sections 9, 10, and 11 must be paid to the umpire, before leaving the field.

——————— FICTION ———————

HERE IS Danny O'Neill, in early adolescence, faced with a decision: shall he be a priest, or shall he be a ballplayer? How many boys have faced moments of similar crisis? How many have written the same letter to Mr. Connie Mack that appears in this excerpt from James T. Farrell's tetralogy on Danny O'Neill? The date in the story is 1919.

From *Father and Son*

JAMES T. FARRELL

DANNY WAS TERRIFIED. He sat alone in his bedroom, thinking about what had happened. Perhaps this man was a temptation of the Devil, and God had sent this temptation as a way of telling him that he really had the call. God had often sent the Devil to saints to tempt them. But, of course, God had given the saints the strength and grace to resist temptation. But he wasn't a saint and he had never been strong enough to resist temptation.

Could he ever be a saint?

Anybody would laugh at him if they knew he even asked himself such a question.

He couldn't be too sure that this old man had been put in his path as a way of letting him know that he was really called. He had no right to think that God was going out of His way for anybody like Danny O'Neill, did he? Of course he didn't.

Danny wandered restlessly to the parlor. He began to wonder if baseball scouts went to Washington Park. If they did, maybe one of them might see him on one of his good days. They might see how promising he was. If they did, would they get in touch with him?

But he had to give up that idea. He had to recognize that this question of the call had been on his mind for months. If it stuck in his mind so much, now mustn't it mean that it was the sign? If it kept coming back to him at so many different times, when he had so many different things in his mind or he was doing so many different things, why, didn't that mean something?

Sometimes it was like a voice inside of him talking to him, and the voice would say to him:

You know you have the call! You know you have the call! You know you got the call!

Did he? Now, there was that voice again, right now, this minute.

You know it! You know you have the call!

Suppose he did. He could first be a baseball player, and never marry, and then, when his playing days were over, he could be ordained. But if he really had the call, he wouldn't always be fighting with himself this way. If he had the call, and God had poured grace into his soul, he would want to be a priest. He wouldn't love Roslyn. He wouldn't be dreaming of being a baseball player the way he always did. Yes, he was convinced. He didn't have the call.

He jumped to his feet, happy, feeling a sudden lightness of mood.

But how could he tell Sister?

As soon as one worry left your mind, another took its place. Here was one. But then, Sister couldn't say that he had to be a priest when he didn't have the call. A person who didn't have a vocation shouldn't be a priest. That stood to reason.

Danny sat at his desk with his bedroom door closed. He was elated. Just after he had made up his mind that he didn't have the call, the idea had come to him like an inspiration. And now he had gotten the letter finished, written carefully and legibly so that it looked as if a man had written it. It ought to work, too. Connie Mack was known above all other managers as the man to pick promising players off the sand lots and develop them into stars. Well, after receiving this letter, why shouldn't Connie send a scout out to Washington Park to look him over? And maybe the scout would see him on a good day and sign him up for a tryout with the Athletics a couple of years from now when he was old enough. Players had been signed up at fifteen before. There was the case of that pitcher, Hoyt. Proud of himself, he read the letter he'd just composed.

Mr. Connie Mack
Shibe Park
The Philadelphia Athletics
Philadelphia, Pennsylvania.

DEAR MR. MACK:
I am writing you this letter to tip you off about a kid named O'Neill who is to be seen playing ball in Washington Park in Chicago all of the time. He isn't ripe just yet because he is only fifteen or sixteen

That was a smart idea, to make out that the man who was supposed to be writing this letter didn't know too much about him, so it was best not to give his exact age.

but he is coming along fast for his age, and he will be ripe soon enough and he looks like a real comer. If you look him over you can pick up a promising youngster now for nothing and he seems destined for the big show. I am a baseball fan and like to see kids get a chance, and take pride in picking them. I picked some before and was a good picker. Years ago when George Moriarity was playing on the sand lots of Chicago I picked him, and I think you must admit I picked a big leaguer then because Moriarity is a big leaguer. You can pick this kid up now for nothing and you will never regret it. He plays out in Washington Park all the time, and you can send a scout out there to look at him and easily find out who he is.
I know you will not be sorry for this tip.
                                        A baseball fan, a real one
                                        T. J. WALKER

He was pleased and satisfied with his letter. All year he'd really felt that 1919 was going to be an important year for him. Maybe this letter might begin to prove that it was. He was smart to have thought up this idea.

WHAT IS ASTOUNDING about this piece is its opening sentence. Paige, Johnson, Grove, Nolan Ryan—radar guns not available for all, but the suspicion persists that Feller threw the ball faster than any human being before or since. But here he isn't talking fast ball at all. Or is he?

How I Throw the Slider

BOB FELLER

PROBABLY THE BEST THING about the slider is that it looks like a fast ball. A good batter usually can spot a curve coming in by the early arc it describes, by its spin, or by the delivery motion of the pitcher. But he has trouble detecting a slider because it looks and spins and moves like a fast ball—except, of course, that it breaks just at the last moment. In fact, I throw my slider almost the same way as my fast ball. I grip the ball the same, except that my forefinger and index finger, instead of being placed directly over the center of the ball, are moved out a bit, just off center. I throw my slider faster and harder than I do a curve ball, and as it comes into the plate I don't think many batters can tell that it isn't going to be a fast ball. Then, as it crosses the plate, it breaks a bit and the batter doesn't meet the ball quite where he expected to. Remember that most of the time the batter swings on a slider still thinking it's a fast ball.

When I throw the slider sidearm, it hooks; when I give it the overhand delivery, it tends to break and drop. But either way you throw it, the slider is a good extra pitch, a valuable addition to your assortment of stuff. However, I don't think it is good to use as your main delivery. Personally, I don't use it too often. I have found that it tends to be hard on my arm, and it takes something off my fast ball. Your arm must be strong and finely developed in the pitching motions and strains before you can make much use of it. I do use it a lot in Boston against the Red Sox' right-hand hitters, but that's because of that short left-field fence. It is a tough pitch for the batter to pull because it breaks away from a right-hand batter (if you're a right-hand pitcher like I am). Against left-hand batters, I throw it when I want them to pull the ball foul. I let up on it and make sure it's a bad pitch. The slider then comes in a little closer than it looks, and they usually pull slightly ahead of the ball, enough to make it go foul. The reason I do this is to try to get them off balance so that when I throw my fast ball they will hold up just a bit and hit it straight away instead of pulling it.

I've noticed that most low-ball hitters are able to bang the slider pretty good for some reason, but it's the type of pitch you can throw at anyone once in a while. Of all the pitches I tried to get past Joe DiMaggio, the slider worked best. Joe had more trouble with it than with my fast ball or curve. He just couldn't hit it consistently.

A lot of people seem to think that the slider is a new pitch; others claim it's nothing more than a nickel curve with a new name. As far as I know, George Blaeholder, who pitched for the St. Louis Browns in the late twenties and early thirties, was the originator of the slider as we know it. Johnny Allen used it a lot, too. Now, of course, it appears that every pitcher has included it in his repertoire. Allie Reynolds, Early Wynn, and Bob Lemon have very good sliders. So do a lot of other pitchers. Lemon's breaks more than mine does, but I think that's because Bob has a natural break in every pitch he throws. His fast ball, for instance, is really a sinker; I think even if he tried to throw the ball straight it would sink. My slider, like my curve, doesn't have a deep break, but for the same reason, it doesn't break big, either.

I really developed my slider in the service, although I did use it as early as 1941. It takes time to learn, and it wasn't until I came back to baseball in 1945 that I had the pitch working properly. Now I almost never have a bad day with it. I don't know why this is, but on those days when my fast ball lacks zip or my curve isn't breaking, the slider still goes good. Once you've learned how to throw it properly, it seems to work all the time. That's another reason why it is a valuable asset. Quite a few times I've been able to stick in there without much of my stuff because I was able to fall back on my slider for the important pitches.

Any young fellow who wants to throw a slider should remember these points: it takes a lot of practice and training, and it's hard on your arm, so don't be in a hurry learning to throw it. I would suggest that you just get your fast ball and curve and control down pat. Then you'll find that your arm is strong enough and disciplined enough to handle the slider—and you'll have a good, dependable extra pitch to get them out with.

──────────────── FICTION ────────────────

HERE IS a classic story. Its only previous publication was in the first *Fireside Book of Baseball*. The author, a one-time Kansas City reporter who became public relations chief for United Aircraft, submitted it to a leading magazine. There was an immediate enthusiasm to publish it, but two or three changes in wording were requested. The author refused, and I don't blame him. Later a few hundred copies were printed privately for friends. Mickey Cochrane called this "the funniest and truest baseball piece" he ever read.

The Spitter

PAUL FISHER

I SAID at supper you was the first baseball writer I seen since I left the Giants. That's not strictly so. Right after the war got good and started, another baseball writer was down here to see me. I reckon I never knowed what the war was going to do to the country till then. Wimmern welders, wimmern hack drivers, wimmern rasslers, wimmern boilermakers—we was bound to have them when the young fellers marched off. But dogged if I ever expected to see a womern baseball writer.

She was on one of the St. Louie papers, and she come all the way down here to see me special. If you was out in the Pacific with the troops most of the war for your paper, then you prolly seen what she was working on. It was a book called *My Greatest Day in Baseball.* After they run it off regular style, they put it out with a paper back for the fighting boys. Real life stories. They would look up some ol' big league ballplayer like me, and he would recollect a good day he had up there, and then the writer would doll up his language and dig out the box score for that pertickler day, and that would be his greatest day in baseball.

Different writers done different players. That was because of geography. Ballplayers come from purt near every place, and they usually hit back home when they wind up, like me. This here womern baseball writer drawed me to write up, I reckon, because St. Louie is the closest big league town to the hills down here in Arkansas.

She aint a gal, but she aint a ol' womern either. I judge she was twenty-four-twenty-five, age most wimmern round here got three-four young uns. Real thin with specs. She aint going to win no prizes on her face or on her shape, but still and all I took to her right off. Intellectual grounds I reckon you'd called it. Fur four years I figger she's smartest womern I ever spent a day talking to.

She was shore well read in baseball. She knowed my record from a to izzard. She knowed what I hit all the twelve years I was up there. She knowed about the time I got three for four agin Carl Mays in the fourth series game in '21, and about the time in the '23 series I taken a three-bagger away from Bob Meusel and doubled the Babe off first from deep left center. She even knowed I murdered a titty-high pitch, except she

115

called it letter-high. That was her big difference from most of you baseball writers. She used real refined language.

She had picked out them two games to choose from as my greatest
day for this here book. She says not only was them good days for me, but
they was historic games and us Giants win 'em both.

It was a rule for this here book, she says, that the player's good days
had to be a day his club wins. She had a real nice smile and she turned
it on then. She says I could choose any of them days, of course, but like
a womern, she says, smiling, she wants to guide me and help herself a wee
bit. As my Buzzwell, she says, she perferred my day when I made the
great throw to get the Babe because that showed me, not for my great
nacheral physical gifts, but for what characterized me most—I was always out there thinking.

Up to that point we was getting along like a well-broke team. She
was setting here in the parlor, right in the rocker you're in, and she'd
fetched out a notebook and a pin and was all braced to take down my
every word. I was setting right here. I was thinking. The more I figgered,
the more I knowed in my own heart I ort not to be so muley, but I
couldn't go along with her. That day agin the Yanks wasn't my greatest
—least not in the thinking line. Finally I says so.

"Well," she says, and she aint smiling now, "certainly you have the
choice. If you perfer to select another day and another game, why, then,
most certainly that's within your perview."

"It's a game that aint never been writ up," I says. "But lots of games
down in these here hills never is. We aint like New York. Here everybody
comes to a game, so they aint no need to write 'em up."

"You mean," she says, "you are selecting a game that isn't even
recorded in organized baseball?"

"Why, yes, ma'am," I says. "In this here book you say you want my
greatest day in baseball, and you perfer me thinking. This time I'm going
to tell you about, I done some of the tallest thinking I ever done in all
my life."

"Perceed," she says, and I done so.

After I left the Giants in '24, crops down here wasn't so good, so for
a couple of summers I got together a nine called the Gray Travelers, and
we went around playing the country and town teams with us always as
the visiting club. They was good money in it—if you win. Mostly we
played winner-take-all, with a side bet I seen run as high as nine-ten
hunnert dollars. Crops was bad, but they was lots of money loose in them
days and people had real pride and dug deep for their local nines.

All through this country—not only here in Arkansas, but in Missouri,
Kansas and Oklahomy—they was sending up some great young ballplay-
ers. Fellers like Bill Dickey, Arky Vaughan, the Waner boys, Glenn
Wright, the Deans, Schoolboy Rowe. Purt near every town and pea patch

had three-four young fellers so good they made the rest of their club look real solid.

Traveling, batting agin home town empires, playing on diamonds that was mostly on the sides of mountings, we had a lot of strikes on us. The crowds was no pleasure. They wasn't above flashing mirrors in your eyes or flinging them giant firecrackers under your feet or running you lickety-split out of town if you done a little hard sliding into their favorites.

So my nine had to be a whole lot better. The first year we win about seven out of every ten games, and when I totted up the season's figgers, we done jist a little better than even. Then the second year I got ol' Heinie Aunfeldt who use to catch for the Cubs, Cornbread Jones who had been up, too, three real good young infielders, and a big farmer from Pea Ridge who was good enough finally to go up to Brooklyn. Day, this Pea Ridge feller was named. You recollect him. I heerd he always gave a hog call in Ebbets Field when he was slated to pitch and scared them Dodger fans most to death. My legs was too fur gone to play the outfield, so I took over third base.

They's things you do in the big leagues, natcher'ly, that's way past town ball, and up there they expect you to do things a certain way. That's why they's called the big leagues, I reckon. But after being up twelve years, I had to re-learn myself some ol' town ball tricks with my Travelers. I had to learn Pea Ridge to pull his cap right down over the bridge of his nose so the home-town rooters can't blind him with mirrors. I had to learn my outfielders how to run down the side of the mountings spraddle-legged to take low liners. Me and ole Heinie and the first baseman got to learn ourselves how to climb like mounting goats up on the hoods of the autos parked all along the field to catch them foul balls. In fact, by '26, I done away with spiked shoes. We played in tennis slippers. You could climb up on Fords and Dorts and Chevvies purty good in spikes, but for Marmons and Hupmobiles and Franklins in them days, tennis slippers was best.

Anyways, by the time July rolled around in my second year with the Travelers, we was going real good. We was up through Missouri and over through Kansas and we got clear down into Oklahomy before we lost a game. We was way ahead financially. We win twenty-three before we lost that game in Oklahomy. Pea Ridge Day had pitched most every other day, so we took two weeks off, and decided for me to work up a schedule in Arkansas where things was a-booming.

When I got back home here, all the people in the hills was talking about a nine over at Simmons Run, not too fur from the Oklahomy line. They was putting a railroad through there, and some oil had been sighted, so they was a kinda boom on. Folks said this Simmons Run nine was made up entirely of local fellers except for pitchers. They brung in pitchers from outside, most of the time one of the three left-handed

Indians which had made life so mizzible for us Travelers in '25. They was three Indians in three separate hearses, two black and one pearl gray. . . .

You never *heerd* of them three left-handed Indians?

No, they wasn't dead Indians. I shore wished many a time that they was. They owned them hearses personally. They was three things them three Indians liked to do that I knowed of. They liked to drive them hearses. They liked to carry their whole famblies and most of their tribe everywhere in the hearses with 'em. And they shore liked to pitch. I expect the thing they liked to do most was sit back in the hearse with a little mounting water, because when they pitched agin you, they made return trips to the closed end of the hearse. They would go back in them hearses in the third, fifth, sixth, seventh, eighth and ninth innings, and a thing I allus noticed was that all three, after the sixth inning, pitched with one eye closed, sump'n a man only does when he's shooting a fararm or drinking stimulates.

The folks said this Simmons Run nine had got both Little Rock and Fort Smith's perfessional teams to come up fur games and beat 'em both. I was told that the Indian in the gray hearse, Willie Wildflower his name was, the one who allus wore the miller's cap and the striped overhalls when he pitched, had shut both of 'em out. I knowed these Indians had oil wells over by Miami, Oklahomy, so I got in my car and went over there.

They was home all right. I seen a million Indian wimmern and young uns out in the backyards of the three big stone houses the three left-handed Indians had built, but I was real formal and went to the door of the middle house. It had a pure big silver knocker and I purt near tore that door off, knocking. Nobody answered. Finally I went around to the back, and down in a grove, maybe fifty yards away, there was the three hearses and the three Indian wrongarms. They had put up tents in the grove of trees. They wasn't living in them big stone houses at all. They had jist built them houses fur show.

They knowed me all right. We talked about how good they was the year before and they says they was even better this year. Then I done a thing that wasn't real ethical. I says I heerd the big distilleries up at Peory, Illinois, was hiring left-handed pitchers, paying regular money and a bonus of gov'ment spirits for every win. I says it was a real fast league, but having seen the three of 'em pitch, I figgered they could win. Jist by chance I had a road map and if they wanted I'd be glad to pencil out the best route. I never seen three more excited Indians. They didn't give a dang about salaries, but that bonus shore whetted 'em. Even before I walked back up to my car, they was slinging their wimmern and kids in the hearses, the hulabaloo was deaf'ning, and I knowed they was off, fur three weeks or a month, anyways.

So I clumb in my auto and drove lickety-split over to Simmons Run. The town barber was running the Simmons Run nine—funny how often in country ball you find a barber who thinks he's a Connie Mack, John McGraw, and Colonel Ruppert all rolled into one. Before we talked two minutes, I seen he thought they was going to really clean out plow. So I ast him about the very next Sunday and he says they'd have to cancel out on the Watts, Oklahomy, club, but if they did, they would have to have a tolable big side bet. I says we might scrape up five hunnert, but, no, he figgers that was purty small. Twelve hunnert dollars, he says, and winner take all the gate. He near choked on that figger, so I knowed it was the biggest bet in the history of Simmons Run.

"I reckon you'll pitch the Indians?" I says to him.

"I reckon we will," he says, real chipper. "And to win, we'll rotate 'em, three innings apiece, if we think it need be. But it won't. You fellers never beat 'em onct last year."

"They're mighty good," I says. "But it's worth a try. You figger to have much of a gate with this little notice?"

"We shore do," he says. "This is the Sunday we plan to unveil our nine in the new sateen uniforms we bought 'em fur beating Fort Smith and Little Rock. Folks have heerd so much about the nine and now about these sateen uniforms that they's coming all the way from Siloam Springs and Gravette and Fayetteville, jist to see us."

"Well," I says, "we'll be in Sunday morning, and I'll meet you here with the twelve hunnert. We know a good base empire—"

"Don't you worry about empires," he says. "Home club furnishes the empires. We allus use one on the bases, too; we wasn't born yestidday."

I lost there, but still and all, I feels purty keen. I never knowed a left-hander to leave a forrarding address, and I was purty certain left-handed Indians was no exception. But keen as I feels then, I feels keener Sunday morning as young Pea Ridge Day and me was driving toward Simmons Run. Thirty miles away, even early in the morning, the road was lined with buckboards and buggies and even ol' hayricks, with people hanging on from every which side. And I never seen so many autos out in Arkansas in my life. The traffic was all one-way to Simmons Run.

It's peculiar thing about this here hill country. You can stand up on a mounting and look fur miles and maybe you won't see more'n three-four houses. Country seems real empty. But have a fox hunt or a square dance or a fight or a ball game where the home nine is going to play some perfessionals like Cornbread and ole Heinie and I used to be, and the folks just seem to spring from the hills and the hollers. They come pouring out of every cranny, packing their young uns and their wimmern folks and follered by their hounds. Every auto and every buggy has a market basket filled plumb up with cold-fried chicken and smoked ham and 'tater salad and piccalilli, and they's stone jugs full of spring-cold buttermilk or sweet cider, and all the folks is grinning and real neighbor-like, willing to feed you till you bust. They's quick to fight, but down deep, these here folks is as good a friends as you'll find.

I drapped young Pea Ridge at the railroad commissary where our nine was dressing and picked up five hunnert dollars from both ole Heinie and Cornbread to fill out the bet. Then I went to the barber shop. Simmons Run is only two roads intersecting, you might say, but I was about tuckered out fighting my way through the crowd. They was fire-crackers going off right and left and hounds baying and dozens of young uns already lost and howling fur their folks. The barber had pervailed on Judge Damon to hold the stakes. We counted out the money and when I seen we wasn't being shortchanged none, I says to the barber.

"You starting Dryshell or Willie Wildflower?"

"Here at Simmons Run," he says, swelling up and looking real smart-alecky, "we make it a practice never to reveal our plans. Aint that right, judge?"

The judge looked sour at such high-falutin manners, but he didn't say nothing.

"Fact is," says the barber, "we may start John Bearpaw."

"Well," I says, "I didn't see their hearses. Most usually them Indians get right in the middle of all the firecracker shooting."

"Don't let it worry you none at all," this here barber says, and he winks knowing like at Judge Damon. "Whoever we pitch will purely dazzle you fellers. And we'll dazzle you some more when you see our brand new uniforms. Slickest in three states."

Going back to the commissary to get in my own monkey suit, I seen quite a few fellers I knowed personal and ast if they had seen the three Indians or even the three hearses. Nobody had. I reckon I was like every feller that's laid out a slick plan. I feared I'd missed some place. But purty soon I got to listening to our shortstop, Tommy Ringle, who says he's seen this Simmons-Run nine a couple of times and played agin' 'em onct. He was briefing Pea Ridge on how to pitch to 'em.

Tommy says they can hit but he figgers Pea Ridge is too fast for 'em —they won't get around quick enough theirselves to pull the ball fur distance. They's one exception, Tommy says—the catcher.

"He's bigger'n a horse and jist as strong," Tommy says. "His name's Ory. He's got the stutters, but it shore don't hurt his hitting none. I aint never seen a man who could hit a ball so fur. He hits 'em off his ears and off his shoe tops. You'll jist have to figger him out yourselves."

"Them kind," says ole Heinie, who's lacing up his tennis slippers, "sometimes can't hit a change-up. We'll tippy up a couple to him, Pea Ridge, and see how he likes the slow stuff."

We was the first nine on the diamond. Ball fields down here is a lot more uniform than in the big leagues, if that surprises you. They's no place with enough level ground fur a complete field, so they mostly set on the side of the mounting with home plate at the foot and the infield sloping upwards. I never seen a diamond in all these hills with home plate at the top of the mounting. Onct I figgered out why. These boys hit fur distance in these here hills, and if they was swinging down hill, it would take a mint to keep 'em in baseballs. They's another advantage. The autos and buggies and wagons can park along the foul lines, and being as one is parked a little higher than the other, right on out to the top of the mounting, it makes seeing easier fur all concerned.

I never seen a crowd in Arkansas like they had there that day at Simmons Run. The furthest auto on the left field line looked like a speck. A stand had been built back of home plate to seat eight-nine hunnert, but they musta been a full thousand packed on the seats. The Simmons Run nine was charging admission fur everything except hounds and suckling young, fifty cents each fur the grownups and a quarter fur the walking young. The gate come to eighteen hunnert and ten dollars. So I figger a good five thousand had paid to get in.

We was warming up along the third base line when I seen everybody craning their necks looking into the crowd back of first. My heart shore sunk then. Usually that's where the three left-handed Indians pulled up in their hearses and slid open the back doors fur a million Indians to fly out, most of 'em carrying greenbacks in big wads to buy sarsparilly and popcorn and hot dogs. But it turned out diff'runt. Thirty-forty Simmons Run folks was clearing a path through the crowd. Purty soon they had a big hole. A covered wagon was backed up to the hole, and all at once someone inside the wagon slung up the canvas and out jumped the Simmons Run nine, one after the other, and come running out into the middle of the field.

I never heerd sich a roar, not even at the Polo Grounds when the Babe hit one agin us in the '21 series. The noise jist growed and growed. Man, they was never a sight or sound like it in the history of baseball. They had stole a leaf from them big football colleges like Illinois U. and Michigan U. and Pennsylvania U. One by one they'd drap out of the covered wagon and run all alone over to the pitcher's mound where they squatted in a perfect line.

It was stupendjous. The folks was standing up shouting, the hounds was baying and the young uns, scared by all the hulabaloo, was screaming. Firecrackers was going off every which way, and every horn in every auto was sounding. It wasn't that they was jist the undefeated Simmons Run nine. It wasn't that they was jist local boys who wasn't afeerd to cross bats with any club, amateur or perfessional. Mostly it was them new uniforms the barber had bragged up.

They was sateen, jist as he said, and while I never seen sateen ball suits before, that didn't stun me near so much as the color. They was purely black. When the sun struck that black sateen, it purt near blinded you. I seen ball suits with lots of red and lots of green and lots of yaller, and onct when I was with Telsy on my way up to the big leagues, we had powder blue road uniforms till the fans near hooted us out of the league. But fur a real eye-catching ball suit, them black sateen outfits the Simmons Run nine had beat anything I ever hope to lay eyes on.

They was country boys so they couldn't hold on to the pose in the center of the field long. As they begun to go back to the first base line, I seen one more player crawling out of that covered wagon. He was in a gray road suit, well made, too, and when he turned around, he made two quick tugs at his cap brim and then quick wets his right finger tips with his tongue. Fur me, that was as much as if he had wrote his name. I knowed him before he follered up by tugging twice at his belt.

Yes sir, you're right, it was ol' Tug Monahan. And onct he had got onto the field, he done jist like he allus did at Forbes Field in Pittsburgh —he begin lookin all 'round, counting the house.

In country and town ball, you're expected to do a little social visiting before a game so I went right over. Ol' Tug looked at me as if it had only been yestidday since I seen him, but leastways he shook hands.

"I thought you was still with the Pirates?" I says.

"I got waived out the same year you did," he says. "And you should know it."

"Where'd these fellers find you?" I says.

"You know and they know I live in K.C.," he says, "and that's where you can always find me."

"I reckon, Tug," I says, "that it's no fun pitching without your spitter—" but I didn't get in a word more.

"They outlawed the spitter only in organized ball," he says. "This is a hell of a long ways from organized ball."

"These are jist kids, Tug," I says, "and they might walk right into that spitter."

"Some kids, Muley," Tug says. "Ole Heinie must have grandsons up there and Cornbread Jones and you both broke in before I did."

Right about then I had a feeling I was standing in the shade. I was, too. The big Simmons Run catcher, Ory he was called, has moseyed up and he was standing on the sunny side of me. He was six foot six-seven inches and built to fit. I never seen a uniform fit a man so snug. But the thing I seen about his uniform that struck me as strange was his sweat shirt. Most wrist bands on sweat shirts don't have a long bunch of ridges running from halfway up to the elbow, but his did. Then it come to me that was no sweat shirt he had on—that was the top part of long underwear sich as they was selling down in these hills fur several years. And when I looked down at his legs, I seen the legs of his long drawers had been folded under his baseball stockings. Glancing here and there, I noticed all the Simmons Run nine was wearing long underwear, and I reckoned the answer was that never having had sweat shirts, and seeing pitchers of full baseball outfits, they had reasoned that even in the big leagues, the players wore long underwear right through the heat of the summer.

I must have missed some of the talk between Ory and Tug, because when I come to, Tug was saying,

"Speak up, man, I won't bite you."

"I-I-I-I fou-fou-fou-fought we sh-sh-should t-t-talk over the s--s--s--s-
-signals," Ory says. You see, he stuttered some.

"Signals?" Tug says. "What signals?"

"He means your signs," I says. "This here is your catcher, Tug."

Ory laid a hand on my shoulder and I purt near was pushed through
the ground.

"I-I-I'll d-do my own t-t-t-talking," he says to me. "I-I-I'm b-big
enough to s--sp-speak my own m-m-mind."

"You shore are," I says and I wandered over by the water keg at the
end of the Simmons Run bench. I aint planning to listen in, but you
couldn't help yourself, what with that high squeaky voice of Ory and that
deep cellar voice of ol' Tug.

Well, it was a long conversation without much said for several minutes. I heerd Tug say he'd sign for pitchouts, and then I missed a few lines
and purty soon both their voices rose up stronger than ever.

"You mean," Tug says real loud, "that you won't catch a spitter?"

"N-n-n-no, sir-e-ee," Ory screams, and hurls his little two-bit kid's
catching glove on the ground. "A s-s-s-spitter t-t-takes off every wh-wh-
which way. A-a-and th-there's g-g-g-germs on sp-s-spit."

"What?" Tug hollers.

"G-g-g-germs," screams Ory. "S-s-s-spit is un-un-un-s-s-unsanitary."

"Gaddlemighty," Tug hollers. "You afraid of a little old germ? Don't
you know my spitter is my best pitch?"

"C-c-can't help it," Ory says. "D-d-don't th-th-th-throw that g-g-g-
gol-goldanged spitter."

"Listen, you big ape," Tug screams, "you know who's hitting agin us?
Take a look. Muley hit in the five spot for McGraw for years. Cornbread
Jones was as good a hitter as I ever hope to see in the big leagues. Ol'
Aunfeldt won more games in the clutch for the Cubs than any hitter they
had. You think I came 250 miles to have my ears pinned back?"

"I-I-I w-w-won't catch n-n-n-no sp-spitters," Ory says coldly.

Well, finally it ended up in a compromise, you might say. Tug
would throw his spitter only if he got in a bad hole and only if Ory
gave him the sign. They used the oldest set of signs in baseball, as it
worked out. One finger was for Tug's fast ball, two for his hook, the
fist for his change-up, and they decided that if Ory put down three
fingers, that was for the spitter. I slaunched off about then, and went
back to my bench.

Tug begin warming up, and he looked as loose and easy as he ever
looked up there. But he aint what took my eye. This Ory was a ballplayer
if I ever seen one. He drapped in a natural crouch on the first warmup
toss, and you could see every muscle in his body as he set there on his
toes. Fact is, so tight was his black sateen suit and his long drawers that
I could count the four buttons on the trap door of the underdrawers—
the buttons that hold up the flap. If you could forget the clo'es and the

little toy mitt he wore, you'da swore he was the purtiest catcher you ever seen in all your born days.

And one thing I knowed. Watching him, I knowed simple as their signs was, we wasn't going to steal them signs. He was one of them natcheral catchers that hide their signing hand from everyone except the pitcher and even the pitcher's got to look sharp to see how many fingers are down for the called pitch.

Well, in a ways it was a dull game the first seven innings. But purty. Ol' Tug Monahan was pulling the ball up to his mouth purty near every pitch, faking saliver on it, but he never throwed a spitter onct. He was pitchin me and Cornbread low, half-speed hooks, and he kept his stuff high and tight on ole Heinie, so none of us was getting any wood on the ball. His control was perfect and he was sneaky fast. Pea Ridge was slinging his high hard one till it jist whistled. Except to this big Ory. First time Ory came up Pea Ridge slang two fast balls way wide, then jist ante-ed a soft one up, and Ory like to broke his back sending a little toy fly down to me near the third sack. He did it again in the fifth and we went into the last of the eighth without either them or us getting a man as fur as second, much less scoring.

The sun was bearing down, and when Ory come up with one out and nobody on in the eighth, he was something to see. His black britches was so soaked with sweat that they seemed glued to him and every time he took a practice swipe with his war club, the sweat jist flew all round him. Pea Ridge throwed him a couple way wide, and then, like young pitchers jist natcherally seem to do, he let one go right down the alley but Ory jist stood there and watched her sail by for a strike.

Heinie came out from behind the plate and he was sore.

"You young fool," he shouts to Pea Ridge, "pitch like I tell you to. No more of that."

So Pea Ridge wastes another, and I reckon he was smarter'n ol' Heinie. He ra'red back and slang another right in the gut.

Ory swang and before I could even duck, the ball shot past my ear, climbing fast. I turned and seen Cornbread beginning to spin to go back on his ol' legs, but it was no use. That ball was still lifting when it went over the mounting top. In all my born days, I never seen a ball hit so fast or so fur. And as I turned back, I knowed without a piece of stupendjous luck we're gone gooses.

Ory was halfway between first and second when the real roar went up from all that mob of hill folks. He was one of them big fellers that run with all their arms and legs spraddled and their head down. All he knowed was that he had hit one on the nose, the crowd was yelling their lungs loose, and so he was putting on all his horses to run till someone tole him to stop.

Right then I figgered out two of the things in a thinking way that won that ball game.

I knowed if we could get Ory out of there, Simmons Run prolly didn't have no one to hold Tug Monahan and maybe we could push a run or two across. I knowed, too, that outside Ory, none of them is going to hit Pea Ridge, if we play a week of Sundays. Sitting here now—jist as I did seven-eight years ago when that womern baseball writer came to write up my greatest day in baseball—I can recollect jist as clear how my mind was churning and I was reaching for a solution to win by.

One thing I gave up immejiately as Ory rounded second. I knowed I couldn't give him the hip as he swang around third. He'da knocked me stem-winding, and all of us woulda got rid out of Simmons Run on a rail to boot. So to keep away from that devil idey, I begun backing toward home plate, acting as if I was going to take a relay throw and whip it home.

Ory swang round third and he was still going hell-bent with his head down. So I eased over toward the line and when he was about twenty-five feet from the plate and the panjemonium was so stupendjous I couldn't hardly think, I drawed in all the air I could and hollered as I never hollered before,

"SLIDE, ORY, SLIDE!"

He heerd me. He slud. He musta weighed 270–280 pounds and he was no Ty Cobb or Max Carey fur sliding grace. He flang hisse'f up in the air and came down square on his hine-end, with his feet up off the ground. A reg'lar explosion of dust blew in the air. He slud fifteen-twenty feet before he hit the plate and he slud right on for another ten feet. Before I got choked up on the dust, I smelled the burnt sateen he had skidded off from the friction, you might say, of all that meat hitting on that sun-baked ground.

I never expect to hear a crowd like that agin. They purely blowed that huge cloud of dust away they made so much racket. You couldn't have made a body hear you if you'da clumb right in their ear. It was that deaf'ning. And Ory was up to the occasion. He clumb to his feet after sitting there about two minutes. First he bowed to the thousand folks crammed into the stands back of home. Then he decided to dust hisse'f off with his cap and that took a couple of minutes. Presently he marched over to home plate and bows to all the folks stretched out along third base to the mounting top. After he figgered they should be satisfied, he executes a right-about-face, and makes a big long bow to the folks stretched out along the right field line.

When he made the turn-about, I seen his backside fur the first time. I knowed then why people not only was cheering but was laughing fit to kill and nudging at each others ribs and p'inting. Ory's whole hine-end was out. When he slud, he not only burned up the seat of them black sateen britches, but he created so much heat he burned the flap off his long drawers. One of the buttons was hanging by a thread, and the light brown piece of cloth—a kinda reinforcement they had on them models of underdrawers—was all that was left of the whole flap. An it was ready to break loose and fall down between his legs like a ribbon with the first strain he put on it.

You ever notice what happens when a man gits in a fix like Ory was in? Not only down here in this country—everywhere. Like the saying—not even their best friends will tell him. Ory figgered, I reckon, that the p'inting and the mixed laughing and cheering was for his homer. They was no breeze stirring to give him a idey of his raw state, and before he was done bowing, one of their men had made the last out and his own nine, pleased to be winning and maybe jist a little bit willing for Ory to look as much fool as hero, had tooken to the field.

Ory quit bowing long enough to put on his two-bit mask and his two-bit glove and get behind the plate. They was still so much noise you couldn't hear nothing. I was trying to far up our nine on the bench, but they couldn't hear me and most of 'em, anyways, was craning around, trying to get a glance at Ory's backside to see if the button still held up that brown ribbon.

With two out, Ringle worked Tug fur a free pass—the only one he given us that day. Ol' Cornbread laid into the first pitched and lined a hard single into left field. He hit a hook, I seen, which hung and I knowed Tug was tiring. Ol' Heinie come up and he didn't waste a second. He cracked one a mile a minute down the third base line. Their third-sacker knocked it down deep behind third, but it was a hit and the bases was full and I was up.

I allus had a superstition about crossing to the plate in front of the catcher, specially with men on. I wasn't thinking about Ory's bare hiney but when I went around him, I seen that there last button had bit the dust and the brown reinforcement ribbon was flapping around between his legs with his action. Om'nous as things was for Simmons Run and noisy as the crowd was, people was making half the noise, jist enjoying Ory's delicate condition. Only he never knowed it.

The first pitch Tug throwed me was around my ankles and the Simmons Run empire called it a strike. Tug faked a spitter and come in with a curve ball that was way wide. He faked twice more and they was too wide even for the Simmons Run empire to call anything but balls. Then Tug put one in there, and run the count to three and two.

You recollect how Tug allus rested his left hand on his left knee and leaned way forrard to get his signs? Well, I was watching him like a hawk and I seen his whole face light up sudden-like. He scrooched forrard to take still another look and a kinda grin comes over his face and then he r'ars back in his holding stance and puts the ball up to his mouth. He done this maybe twenty-five–thirty times through the game, faking his spitter. But this time I suspicioned from his grin and his action that it was the real spitter coming, a pitch that allus troubled me up there and I knowed would trouble me here.

I got cocked, and the second he came around, I knowed it was a spitter. All told I got maybe a fifth of a second to figger what to do. This pitch is coming right down the middle fast as a bullet, titty-high, right where I like 'em. But when it was no more than twenty feet out of Tug's hand, you could feel it getting ready to sail. I knowed when the saliver on it took a real hold, it would jump at least two feet and would be so fur outside that I'd draw me a free pass and force in the tying run.

Same time, churning through my head, was the fact Ory didn't like them there spitters. If I swang wild and lit fur first, chances was Ory would miss the ball complete, and we'd be free to take all the bases we could on a passed third strike. Maybe we'd score two-three runs and win.

All this passed through my brain in the blink of the eye. I made the most desperate swing a man ever made and knowed the minute the ball jumped by me I done the right thing. Ory was still squatting. He jist let that spitter sail by.

Everybody, natcherally, was running with the count full and two out. As I rounded first I seen Ringle and Cornbread high-tailing it in, and right behind 'em ole Heinie was chuffing. My legs was killing me time I got to second, so I slowed up to look. Ory was standing straight up, his face purple behind the little toy mask an his Adam's apple jumping up and down. The whole Simmons Run nine was standing jist friz in their tracks. The ball was way back by the backstop, so I lit out for third, and it wasn't till I was heading into home that their first-sacker woken up and started for the ball. So I scored and that made four runs for us on my strikeout.

Ory was standing about three feet in front of home plate when I crossed. Sudden-like he took off his toy mask and slang it on the ground and then he slang his toy mitt on the ground and jumped up and down on it. Then real puppusful he started marching out toward ol' Tug. Tug kin take care of hisse'f agin most people, but with this big baboon Ory I figgered I better go out to give him a hand.

When Ory gets about ten feet from Tug, he stops and screams,

"I-I-I-I f-f-f-f-f-fought I t-t-t-tole you to n-n-never to th-th-throw that sp-sp-spitter!"

"Gaddlemighty, boy!" Tug says. "You give me the spitter sign, didn't you? You showed me three fingers, didn't you?"

"S-s-s-sign?" Ory shouts. "Three f-f-f-fingers? I-I-I-I-I g-g-give you the s-s-s-sign for a curve b-b-ball. Two f-f-f-f-fingers. L-l-l-like this."

He scrooched down and wagged two fingers. But hanging right down beside his middle finger so it looked like a third finger was the brown reinforcement piece of his long drawers. Tug and me studied it for maybe a minute before the whole thing lighted up for us and then we fell down right there on the pitcher's mound and laughed till we near died.

I tole the story of that game to this here womern baseball writer, jist about word for word as I tole you. I tole her how it all ended up regulation. They had their last bats and Pea Ridge fanned the side and it ended 4–1, our favor. Shore, I got no hits and didn't do nothing mechanical to rave about. But fur pure puppusful thinking, that was my greatest day in baseball.

When she left here that afternoon, that womern baseball writer said she'd write it all up, jist as I given the facts. That was in '42. As I said, fur four years I figgered she was the smartest womern I ever talked to. Then, in '46, Hod Eaton's boy who lives down the road a piece come home from fighting all over Europe, and he brang back a paper back copy of that there book, *My Greatest Day in Baseball.* He give me the loan of it and I spent one whole winter reading it forrards and backwards.

I aint in it, so they's no use for you to put out good money for a copy. Oh, they's a couple of times I show up in box scores—Waite Hoyt's greatest day, when he beat us Giants in '21 and I went nothing fur four agin him, and Muddy Ruel's greatest day when ol' Walt Johnson comes in to stop us Giants cold in the '24 series and I only git one scratch hit that don't mean nothing in the final result. But there aint a line about me out there allus thinking.

I brooded on it some and now I figgered it out. Wimmern aint got the background fur baseball writing. This womern, I'd say, had learned herse'f the game outta books or from watching a college nine play. It was past her to see that maybe they's ten thousand games played every year in town ball and country ball that's jist as bristling with real playing and real thinking as anything you'll see up there.

So when we et, maybe it was my unconscious mind, you might say, that made me declare you was the first baseball writer I seen since I left the Giants. Come to think of it, all I had was her word for it that she was a baseball writer and wimmern aint above claiming something they really aint. Leastways, some wimmern.

Well, after us talking so long as this, how 'bout wetting your whistle with a drap of cider?

THE ARTICLE "How to Pitch" appeared in a booklet called *History of Colored Baseball*, printed in Philadelphia in 1907.

From "How to Pitch"

ANDREW FOSTER

THE REAL TEST comes when you are pitching with men on bases. Do not worry. Try to appear jolly and unconcerned. I have smiled often with the bases full with two strikes and three balls on the batter. This seems to unnerve. In other instances, where the batter appears anxious to hit, waste a little time on him and when you think he realizes his position and everybody yelling at him to hit it out, waste a few balls and try his nerve; the majority of times you will win out by drawing him into hitting at a wide one.

———— AUTOBIOGRAPHY ————

NOBODY EVER CLINCHED a World Series by a final-game score like this one. But, as ol' Diz was wont to observe, if you can do it, it ain't braggin'.

1934:
St. Louis Cardinals 11,
Detroit Tigers 0

FRANKIE F. FRISCH *as told to* KEN SMITH

I FINALLY got to sleep on the night of October 8, 1934, in my hotel in Detroit. The next day was the most important day of my whole baseball career so far, and I knew it.

When I had been a fresh kid, with John J. McGraw's Giants in the 1921, '22, '23 and '24 World Series, I never fretted about anything. Slept like a baby and played with an abandon I wish I had had in the three

Series during the '30s. McGraw and the older men like Dave Bancroft, Heinie Groh and Casey Stengel did the worrying in the old days. A young squirt isn't afraid of anything. Life's a breeze and every day is a lark.

But in the 1930, '31 and '34 Series, the responsibility was terrific. This stuff you hear about old codgers mellowing and losing the competitive urge is the bunk. It grows stronger with age, especially when you are playing second base and managing the Gashouse Gang.

Well, we were even-Stephen at three games apiece, in the 1934 Series—the Cardinals against the Tigers. You can imagine how I would feel if we blew this, of all Series, after such a donnybrook as we had been through in the first six games. I lay there in the sheets, figuring pitches for Mickey Cochrane, Charley Gehringer, Goose Goslin and Hank Greenberg, knowing that here was the one big game of my life whether I played a personal part in the playing end, or not. I don't have to thumb back and say, "Let's see, now, which *was* my biggest day?"

You can imagine what was on my mind lying there before the seventh and deciding game. Dizzy Dean had won the first for us in Detroit, 8–3. Schoolboy Rowe, who had a tremendous year with the Tigers, had beaten us the second game, 3–2, the Schoolboy retiring 22 batters in a row starting with the fourth inning. Paul Dean had won the third battle, but the Tigers had taken the fourth and fifth, and the city of Detroit was beginning to lay the red carpet for a championship celebration.

Then Paul came back and won the sixth game with a single, 4–3. I'll never forget old Dizzy hugging Paul in the dressing room after the game, wrestling him and yelping, "You're the greatest pitcher the Dean family ever had," and then Diz would pound everybody else on the back and brag about his kid brother. Diz had announced at the start of the year "me and Paul will win 50 games," and they'd darn near done it, Diz winning 30 and Paul 19. Diz had said they'd murder the Tigers in the Series, too, and now they had between them won three games—the only ones we had taken.

I remember John Carmichael coming up to me in the confusion of that dressing room after the sixth game and asking, "Dean tomorrow— the other Dean?" and me sitting there, all in from the strain, and answering, "If I last till tomorrow, maybe. It'll be Dean or Wild Bill Hallahan."

Carmichael took one look at Diz charging around the room with a white pith helmet—the kind Englishmen wear on tiger hunts—and hollering how he'd take the seventh game tomorrow. Carmichael said, "Wild horses can't keep Dean off that mound tomorrow, Frank."

I looked. Dizzy had a rubber tiger, a Detroit souvenir, by the tail and was whacking Bill DeLancey over the head with it and then throwing it into the showers at Pepper Martin. I knew inside me Diz would pitch it. He had a terrible head cold and only two days before had been knocked out running the bases, but there'd be no use fighting against it —he was the boy and the chips were sure down.

Incidentally the wolves had been on me for putting in Dizzy to run for big, slow Virgil Davis in that fourth game—the time Diz went into second so high and hard that Charley Gehringer, trying for a force-out, hit Diz in the head. But I didn't mind the criticism. We were out to win. We were the Gashouse Gang and I knew Diz would give 'em something to worry about running bases as well as pitching.

Well, morning came for the big game and then at the park Diz took the ball and warmed up with what looked like 50,000 Tiger fans hooting at him, and him grinning and yelling at each of us Cards who passed, "I'll shut 'em out. Get me a couple of runs: that's all. I'll blank the blank-blank blankety-blanks."

Dizzy said he'd shut 'em out and he did. And with the score 0–0 to start the third he singled and stretched it to get to second.

Pepper Martin, the Wild Horse, was up next and he hit a slow hopper to Greenberg and went down so fast he beat the throw. Three years before, Pepper had driven Mickey Cochrane crazy running bases in the Series between the Athletics and the Cards and now he did it again.

Then Auker walked Rothrock and the bases were full. And I was up. I couldn't let the rest of them make an old man out of the playing-manager, so I doubled and all three of 'em came in.

That was all for Auker and in came Schoolboy Rowe. Our bench stood up and gave him the "How'm-I-doin'-Edna?" chant. He had asked that during a radio interview, throwing in a little message to his girl, and the papers had been riding him about it. Rip Collins welcomed Rowe with a double and I scored. Then DeLancey doubled and Rip scored—and away went Schoolboy with a lot of others besides us asking Edna how he was doin'.

We kept on hitting, and Cochrane, who was fit to be asylumed by this time, kept bringing in more pitchers. Dizzy got his second hit of the inning by racing like Pepper to first on a slow grounder, bringing DeLancey in. By the time the inning was over we had seven runs and I figured maybe Dizzy would be winded by all that hitting and base running he'd done in the inning, but, heck, no. He beat the rest of the team out to position and could hardly take time to make his warm-up throws.

The Tigers were sore with that score standing against them and Dizzy holding them helpless. They called us plenty of names, but we had the fanciest name-callers in the game and poured it right back and, I suppose, more so.

It was like playing ball at the foot of Vesuvius. And in the sixth came the eruption. Pepper started by singling and, seeing Goslin in left juggle the throw momentarily, he went on to second. Rothrock and I went out, but Medwick lammed the ball against the screen for a double and kept on to third, sliding in hard. Marv Owen on third got the ball and stepped on Medwick's leg. Joe kicked up from his position on his back and hit Owen in the chest. They started to fight, and both teams boiled out. The panic was on, but nothing to what happened after the umpires had quieted everybody down and got the inning played out.

As Medwick went out to left field, the Tiger fans met him with cushions, bottles, lemons, and some of them took off their shoes and tried to bean him. They tried to climb the 18-foot wire fence to murder him. For 15 minutes the game was stopped and finally Commissioner Landis told Cochrane and me to bring Owen and Medwick up to his box. He asked Medwick, "Did you kick him?" and Joe said, "You're darn right, I did!" They wouldn't shake hands and the noise got worse. Cochrane would run out and beg the bleachers to be good, but they would have none of his advice. So Landis put both Medwick and Owen out of the game and we went on to finish it.

So it ended 11–0. Dizzy had done what he said he'd do and we'd done more than he asked us.

GENERAL

From *For 2¢ Plain*

HARRY GOLDEN

THE BASIC SUPERSTITION of the East Side centered around the fear that something would break the spell when everything was going all right. Too much praise was the greatest danger, because it would call attention to the evil spirits, who, out of jealousy, would harm a handsome child, a prosperous business, or a happy home. No one really knows the origin of this. We do know that the superstition is universal, including, of course, the habit of knocking on wood when you hear good news. Take an example in America where the same superstition exists. It is almost a crime to call attention to the baseball game while a pitcher is heading toward a no-hit performance. No member of the team will utter a word, or even look at the pitcher. They must talk of other matters. This is all to distract the attention of the evil spirits. Inning after inning the pitcher will go back to the players' dugout and no one will say a word. So here we have Anglo-Saxon ballplayers from Texas, Georgia, and the Carolinas steeped in the folklore which we thought was singularly an Eastern European tradition. It is interesting to note that the fear of the evil eye is automatically transferred to the spectators in the stands. No one yells while a man is pitching a no-hit game. Instinctively they try not to look at the pitcher. They talk nervously about things completely unrelated to the ball game.

Ty Cobb, the Georgia Peach, was the greatest ballplayer who ever lived. He began where all other ballplayers left off. He had a special place in my heart, along with Enrico Caruso, Franklin D. Roosevelt, Winston Churchill, Irving Berlin, Al Jolson, and John Barrymore.

I once heard a Columbia University professor deliver a lecture on Ty Cobb. He said that if Cobb had entered banking, he would have been the leading banker in America; if he had gone into politics, he would have become President; he was a born leader, a man who would always win; he would have been in the number-one spot of whatever field of endeavor he chose.

As far as teams were concerned, of course, I was always a New York Giants' man.

On warm spring days we walked from the East Side to the New York World Building on Park Row to watch the baseball game on the electrically operated board. I also saw many a game during the summer vacations. I found that I could see the game at the Polo Grounds and get back in time to sell newspapers to the home-going factory workers. On the Bowery at Houston Street was a large bakery which sold pretzels to the Polo Grounds concessionaire, Mr. Harry Stevens. We kids in the neighborhood alternated in delivering those pretzels, and I got the job as often as any of them. The pay was twenty-five cents for the errand and ten cents carfare, plus the privilege of seeing the game. The pretzels had to be delivered by twelve o'clock, with the game not scheduled to start until around three P.M.; but the only chance you had of seeing the game, without paying, was to stay inside the park. However, I did not sit in the stands for three hours just twiddling my thumbs like a dope. I moseyed around, got to know the players, ran their errands and made myself useful in many other ways around the clubhouse, and once I even helped the groundkeepers put the tarpaulin down over the infield during a sudden shower before game time. I became friends with the Giants' Captain, Larry Doyle, and players George Wiltse, Al Demaree, Leon Ames, Otis Crandall, George Burns, Buck Herzog, and Jeff Tesreau, and received many a smile from the aloof but kindly Christy Mathewson himself.

There was a billboard behind the centerfield bleachers advertising flypaper: "Last year George Burns caught 198 flys, but Ajax Flypaper caught 19 billion, 865 million, etc., flies." A good advertisement. I also recall a lady with a very large black picture hat sitting in the front row of the center-field bleachers, and often on weekdays she was all alone out yonder, and just as the Giants took the field, you could hear her battle cry in every corner of the Polo Grounds—"Come on, Artie"—and the shortstop Arthur Fletcher would wave his glove at her, everybody would applaud, and then the first visiting batter stepped up to the plate. Probably Mr. Fletcher's wife or sister. There was a big player by the name of Heinie Zimmerman playing third base and the fans behind him rode him unmercifully. Once Zimmerman ran up to the stands in New York and socked a guy for calling him names. That personal touch in baseball is gone. It is more of a business today.

The Giants represented the New York of the brass cuspidor—that old New York which was still a man's world before the advent of the League of Women Voters; the days of swinging doors, of sawdust on the barroom floor, and of rushing the growler.

The Yanks also played in the Polo Grounds in those days and the star attraction was the famous Hal Chase, who played first base for a while. Later he got into trouble with gamblers, but that was in the National League. Among the Yankee players I knew in those days was a pitcher by the name of Ray Caldwell, who was nuts about Jewish food, and I took him down to the East Side several times so he could eat knishes.

But when the Detroit Tigers came to New York, I did not go near the clubhouse if I could help it. I didn't want to speak to or meet Ty Cobb.

I wanted it left as it was—just sitting in the grandstand, watching every move of that great and wonderful man.

———————————— SPOT REPORTING ————————————

Spot reporting? General? Autobiography? Even History? Arnold Hano's rich book, *A Day in the Bleachers,* defies easy classification. Mr. Hano's day in the bleachers was the day of the first game of the 1954 World Series between the Giants and the favored Cleveland Indians at the Polo Grounds. Arnold saw one of baseball's most memorable plays—it is already known, simply and universally, as The Catch—better than anyone in the press box. This is *real* spot reporting—direct from center field. It is the top of the eighth, score 2-2, none out, Indians on first and second.

From *A Day in the Bleachers*

ARNOLD HANO

AND LIKE WOLVES drawn to our fresh play, we had already forgotten him (Maglie), eyes riveted on Liddle, while off to the side of the plate Vic Wertz studied the new Giant pitcher and made whatever estimations he had to make.

Wertz had hit three times already; nobody expected more of him. He had hit one of Maglie's fast balls in the first inning, a pitch that was headed for the outside corner but Wertz's bat was too swift and he had pulled the ball for a triple. Then he hit a little curve, a dinky affair that was either Maglie's slider or a curve that didn't break too well, and drove it into left field for a single. Finally, he had pulled another outside pitch that—by all rights—he shouldn't have been able to pull, so far from the right-field side of the plate was it. But he had pulled it, as great sluggers will pull any ball because that is how home runs are made. Wertz hadn't hit a home run on that waist-high pitch on the outside; he had rifled it to right field for another single.

But that was all off Maglie, forgotten behind a door over five hundred feet from the plate. Now it was Liddle, jerking into motion as Wertz poised at the plate, and then the motion smoothed out and the ball came sweeping in to Wertz, a shoulder-high pitch, a fast ball that probably would have been a fast curve, except that Wertz was coming around and hitting it, hitting it about as hard as I have ever seen a ball hit, on a high line to dead center field.

For whatever it is worth, I have seen such hitters as Babe Ruth, Lou Gehrig, Ted Williams, Jimmy Foxx, Ralph Kiner, Hack Wilson, Johnny Mize, and lesser-known but equally long hitters as Wally Berger and Bob Seeds send the batted ball tremendous distances. None, that I recall, ever hit a ball any harder than this one by Wertz in my presence.

And yet I was not immediately perturbed. I have been a Giant fan for years, twenty-eight years to be exact, and I have seen balls hit with violence to extreme center field which were caught easily by Mays, or Thomson before him, or Lockman or Ripple or Hank Leiber or George Kiddo Davis, that most marvelous fly catcher.

I did not—then—feel alarm, though the crack was loud and clear, and the crowd's roar rumbled behind it like growing thunder. It may be that I did not believe the ball would carry as far as it did, hard hit as it was. I have seen hard-hit balls go a hundred feet into an infielder's waiting glove, and all that one remembers is crack, blur, spank. This ball did not alarm me because it was hit to dead center field—Mays' territory—and not between the fielders, into those dread alleys in left-center and right-center which lead to the bull pens.

And this was not a terribly high drive. It was a long low fly or a high liner, whichever you wish. This ball was hit not nearly so high as the triple Wertz struck earlier in the day, so I may have assumed that it would soon start to break and dip and come down to Mays, not too far from his normal position.

Then I looked at Willie, and alarm raced through me, peril flaring against my heart. To my utter astonishment, the young Giant center fielder—the inimitable Mays, most skilled of outfielders, unique for his ability to scent the length and direction of any drive and then turn and move to the final destination of the ball—Mays was turned full around, head down, running as hard as he could, straight toward the runway between the two bleacher sections.

I knew then that I had underestimated—badly underestimated—the length of Wertz's blow.

I wrenched my eyes from Mays and took another look at the ball, winging its way along, undipping, unbreaking, forty feet higher than Mays' head, rushing along like a locomotive, nearing Mays, and I thought then: it will beat him to the wall.

Through the years I have tried to do what Red Barber has cautioned me and millions of admiring fans to do: take your eye from the ball after it's been hit and look at the outfielder and the runners. This is a terribly difficult thing to learn; for twenty-five years I was unable to do it. Then I started to take stabs at the fielder and the ball, alternately. Now I do it pretty well. Barber's advice pays off a thousand times in appreciation of what is unfolding, of what takes some six or seven seconds—that's all, six or seven seconds—and of what I can see in several takes, like a jerking motion picture, until I have enough pieces to make nearly a whole.

There is no perfect whole, of course, to a play in baseball. If there was, it would require a God to take it all in. For instance, on such a play, I would like to know what Manager Durocher is doing—leaping to the outer lip of the sunken dugout, bent forward, frozen in anxious fear? And Lopez—is he also frozen, hope high but too anxious to let it swarm through him? The coaches—have they started to wave their arms in joy, getting the runners moving, or are they half-waiting, in fear of the impossible catch and the mad scramble that might ensue on the base paths?

The players—what have they done? The fans—are they standing, or half-crouched, yelling (I hear them, but since I do not see them, I do not know who makes that noise, which of them yells and which is silent)? Has activity stopped in the Giant bull pen where Grissom still had been toiling? Was he now turned to watch the flight of the ball, the churning dash of Mays?

No man can get the entire picture; I did what I could, and it was painful to rip my sight from one scene frozen forever on my mind, to the next, and then to the next.

I had seen the ball hit; its rise; I had seen Mays' first backward sprint; I had again seen the ball and Mays at the same time, Mays still leading. Now I turned to the diamond—how long does it take the eyes to sweep and focus and telegraph to the brain?—and there was the vacant spot on the hill (how often we see what is not there before we see what is there) where Liddle had been and I saw him at the third base line, between home and third (the wrong place for a pitcher on such a play; he should be behind third to cover a play there, or behind home to back up a play there, but not in between).

I saw Doby, too, hesitating, the only man, I think, on the diamond who now conceded that Mays might catch the ball. Doby is a center fielder and a fine one and very fast himself, so he knows what a center fielder can do. He must have gone nearly halfway to third, now he was coming back to second base a bit. Of course, he may have known that he could jog home if the ball landed over Mays' head, so there was no need to get too far down the line.

Rosen was as near to second as Doby, it seemed. He had come down from first, and for a second—no, not that long, nowhere near that long, for a hundred-thousandth of a second, more likely—I thought Doby and Rosen were Dark and Williams hovering around second, making some foolish double play on this ball that had been hit three hundred and thirty feet past them. Then my mind cleared; they were in Cleveland uniforms, not Giant, they were Doby and Rosen.

And that is all I allowed my eyes on the inner diamond. Back now to Mays—had three seconds elapsed from the first ominous connection of bat and ball?—and I saw Mays do something that he seldom does and that is so often fatal to outfielders. For the briefest piece of time—I cannot shatter and compute fractions of seconds like some atom gun— Mays started to raise his head and turn it to his left, as though he were about to look behind him.

Then he thought better of it, and continued the swift race with the ball that hovered quite close to him now, thirty feet high and coming down (yes, finally coming down) and again—for the second time—I knew Mays would make the catch.

In the Polo Grounds, there are two squarish green screens, flanking the runway between the two bleacher sections, one to the left-field side of the runway, the other to the right. The screens are intended to provide a solid dark background for the pitched ball as it comes in to the batter. Otherwise he would be trying to pick out the ball from the far-off sea of shirts of many colors, jackets, balloons, and banners.

Wertz's drive, I could see now, was not going to end up in the runway on the fly; it was headed for the screen on the right-field side.

The fly, therefore, was not the longest ball ever hit in the Polo Grounds, not by a comfortable margin. Wally Berger had hit a ball over the left-field roof around the four-hundred foot marker. Joe Adcock had hit a ball into the center-field bleachers. A Giant pitcher, Hal Schumacher, had once hit a ball over the left-field roof, about as far out as Berger's. Nor—if Mays caught it—would it be the longest ball ever caught in the Polo Grounds. In either the 1936 or 1937 World Series— I do not recall which—Joe DiMaggio and Hank Leiber traded gigantic smashes to the foot of the stairs within that runway; each man had caught the other's. When DiMaggio caught Leiber's, in fact, it meant the third out of the game. DiMaggio caught the ball and barely broke step to go up the stairs and out of sight before the crowd was fully aware of what had happened.

So Mays' catch—if he made it—would not necessarily be in the realm of the improbable. Others had done feats that bore some resemblance to this.

Yet Mays' catch—if, indeed, he was to make it—would dwarf all the others for the simple reason that he, too, could have caught Leiber's or DiMaggio's fly, whereas neither could have caught Wertz's. Those balls had been towering drives, hit so high the outfielder could run forever before the ball came down. Wertz had hit his ball harder and on a lower trajectory. Leiber—not a fast man—was nearing second base when Di-Maggio caught his ball; Wertz—also not fast—was at first when . . .

When Mays simply slowed down to avoid running into the wall, put his hands up in cup-like fashion over his left shoulder, and caught the ball much like a football player catching leading passes in the end zone.

He had turned so quickly, and run so fast and truly that he made this impossible catch look—to us in the bleachers—quite ordinary. To those reporters in the press box, nearly six hundred feet from the bleacher wall, it must have appeared far more astonishing, watching Mays run and run until he had become the size of a pigmy and then he had to run some more, while the ball diminished to a mote of white dust and finally disappeared in the dark blob that was Mays' mitt.

The play was not finished, with the catch.

Now another pet theory of mine could be put to the test. For years I have criticized base runners who advance from second base while a long fly ball is in the air, then return to the base once the catch has been made and proceed to third after tagging up. I have wondered why these men have not held their base; if the ball is not caught, they can score from second. If it is, surely they will reach third. And—if they are swift—should they not be able to score from second on enormously long flies to dead center field?

Here was such a fly; here was Doby so close to second before the catch that he must have practically been touching the bag when Mays was first touching the drive, his back to the diamond. Now Doby could —if he dared—test the theory.

And immediately I saw how foolish my theory was when the thrower was Mays.

It is here that Mays outshines all others. I do not think the catch made was as sensational as some others I have seen, although no one else could have made it. I recall a catch made by Fred Lindstrom, a converted third baseman who had had legs, against Pittsburgh. Lindstrom ran to the right-center field wall beyond the Giants' bull pen and leaped high to snare the ball with his gloved hand. Then his body smashed into the wall and he fell on his back, his gloved hand held over his body, the speck of white still showing. After a few seconds, he got to his feet, quite groggy, but still holding the ball. That was the finest catch I can recall, and the account of the game in next day's New York *Herald Tribune* indicated it might have been the greatest catch ever made in the Polo Grounds.

Yet Lindstrom could not have reached the ball Mays hit and Mays would have been standing at the wall, ready to leap and catch the ball Lindstrom grabbed.

Mays never left his feet for the ball Wertz hit; all he did was outrun the ball. I do not diminish the feat; no other center fielder that I have ever seen (Joe and Dom DiMaggio, Terry Moore, Sammy West, Eddie Roush, Earle Combs, and Duke Snider are but a few that stand out) could have done it for no one else was as fast in getting to the ball. But I am of the opinion that had not Mays made that slight movement with his head as though he were going to look back in the middle of flight, he would have caught the ball standing still.

The throw to second base was something else again.

Mays caught the ball, and then whirled and threw, like some olden statue of a Greek javelin hurler, his head twisted away to the left as his right arm swept out and around. But Mays is no classic study for the simple reason that at the peak of his activity, his baseball cap flies off. And as he turned, or as he threw—I could not tell which, the two motions were welded into one—off came the cap, and then Mays himself continued to spin around after the gigantic effort of returning the ball whence it came, and he went down flat on his belly, and out of sight.

But the throw! What an astonishing throw, to make all other throws ever before it, even those four Mays himself had made during fielding practice, appear the flings of teen-age girls. This was the throw of a giant, the throw of a howitzer made human, arriving at second base—to Williams or Dark, I don't know which, but probably Williams, my memory says Dark was at the edge of the outfield grass, in deep shortstop position—just as Doby was pulling into third, and as Rosen was scampering back to first.

I wonder what will happen to Mays in the next few years. He may gain in finesse and batting wisdom, but he cannot really improve much because his finest talent lies in his reflex action. He is so swift in his reflexes, the way young Joe Louis was with his hands when, cobra-like, they would flash through the thinnest slit in a foe's defense; Louis, lashing Paulino Uzeudun with the first hard punch he threw, drilling into the tiniest opening and crushing the man who had never before been knocked out. That is Mays, too. Making a great catch and whirling and throwing, before another man would have been twenty feet from the ball.

And until those reflexes slow down, Mays must be regarded as off by himself, not merely *a* great ballplayer, but *the* great ballplayer of our time.

(I am not discussing his hitting here; for some strange reason— National League-itis, I guess—when I discuss the native ability of a ballplayer, I invariably narrow my gaze to his defensive ability. DiMaggio was a better hitter in his prime than Mays is now, maybe than Mays ever will be, although no hitter was ever as good as Mays at the same stage of their respective careers—check Ruth, Wagner, Cobb, Hornsby in their second full year of play and you will see what I mean.)

Still, Willie's 1954 season at the plate may have been some freak occurrence. It happens sometimes that a ballplayer hits all season far above his norm. I am thinking of Ferris Fain who led the league a few years ago, though he had never been an impressive hitter before. My wife inquired about this man Fain, of whom she was suddenly hearing so much. I told her that he was a pretty good ballplayer, an excellent defensive first baseman, and a fair hitter. She said, "Fair? He's leading the league, isn't he?"

I said, "Yes, but that's a fluke. He's hitting way over his head. Watch what happens next year."*

Or take Carl Furillo hitting over .340 in 1953. Furillo is a fine hitter, a solid .300 hitter who can drive in nearly a hundred runs a season, but .340 is not his normal average. Possibly .345 is nowhere near Mays' norm; nothing in the past had indicated he could hit that high.

I do not list Mays among the great hitters, though I concede that one day we all may. As a fielder, he is already supreme.

So much for Mays and the catch.

— FICTION —

HERE IS a chapter from Mark Harris' fine baseball novel, *Bang the Drum Slowly*. The narrator is Henry (Author) Wiggen, pitching hero of Harris' earlier novel, *The Southpaw*. In the sequel—specifically, in the chapter reprinted here —Wiggen has not yet come to terms with the ball club on his season's contract. It is spring-training time. Wiggen alone knows that a teammate, Bruce Pearson, is dying of an incurable disease. The doctors have made Wiggen promise to stay close to Pearson at all times. With this background material, here is the chapter. Do you agree that the third paragraph from the last is one of the truly memorable speeches of our time? And in the years since, did you see the movie version of *Bang the Drum Slowly*, starring Michael Moriarity and Robert De Niro? It may be the greatest baseball film ever made.

---

*The following year Fain led the league again. . . . (AUTHOR'S NOTE)

From *Bang the Drum Slowly*

MARK HARRIS

THE TALK of the camp last spring was a kid name of Piney Woods, a wild and crazy catcher out of a place called Good Hope, Georgia, that the writers all called "Dutch's good hope from Good Hope" until it become obvious that he could not last. Back he went to QC in April, and we went into the year with the same 3 catchers we finished 54 with, Goose and Bruce and Jonah Brooks. Jonah come up from QC when Red split his finger in St. Paul, Minnesota, that time, a fine boy, just fine, always singing. 13 runs behind and he will still be singing, calling "Wing her through, Author, wing her through," and then after a good pitch singing, "Author wung her through, he wung her through," except when now and then he thought the call was wrong, and then sung, "Oh-o-o-o Lord my big black ass," his jaw always going and his mind always working, his eye everywhere, a natural catcher if ever I seen one, except he could not hit.

For a time it looked like Piney Woods might be the answer. He can hit. But he is no natural. He is too wild and crazy. He drives in motorcycle races in the winter. Dutch was looking for a combination of a natural catcher like Jonah and a hitter like Piney, and still is. I guess there is only one Red Traphagen in a lifetime.

The first few days me and Lucky Judkins sat in the stands watching the drill and lying about money, telling each other how much we were holding out for. I don't know why you lie about money. I guess you figure people figure you are lying, so you might as well. One morning Ugly Jones clumb up from the field and said, "Author, leave me give you one piece of advice. Do not hang in the park because your eye gleams and your hand itches. You are becoming anxious to play ball, and this will cost you money," which was true. I mean it was true I was becoming gleamy, I guess. Ugly is a wild old hand, veteran of many a holdout, and I went back to the house, and we swum and laid on the beach and played badminton and waited for the telephone to ring, and every time it rung I said, "This is Old Man Moors meeting my price," but it never was, and to myself I thought, "This is Bruce. The attack come." But it never was Bruce neither. It was writers, or one of the boys, or Joe Jaros wishing to play Tegwar [a card game played by members of the team—ED.]. The boys phoned a lot, or dropped by, and I kept in touch. My weight kept going up something awful.

The real bomb-burst was Lucky getting swapped to Cincinnati for F. D. R. Caselli, a right-hand pitcher and a good boy, a cousin by marriage of Gussie Petronio, the Mammoth catcher before Red, leaving me the last and only holdout. I might of went out of my mind a little if there been any left-hand pitching in camp, but there was none, 90 boys that threw with their left hand maybe, but none that threw very hard or very smart, and I sat tight. The boys were all with me, down to the last penny.

It all dragged on so long I said to Holly ["Author's" wife—ED.], "Am I a baseball player or only a man living on the beach at Aqua Clara?" and she said, "What difference?" Everything you said to her any more she said, "What difference?" meaning lay in the sun and enjoy life. She was happy. I never seen her so still before. She is usually always running around doing 77 things at once, hanging with the wives, reading books, studying taxes, cleaning the house, gassing on the phone, but now she done nothing only laid on the beach and looked at the waves. Now and then she took a dip and flipped over and left the waves wash her in, and then she laid on the sand again and browned up, and nights she got all dressed for Bruce.

He come down every night after work. You could see him from far off, walking along and looking at the waves and whistling "Come Josephine in My Flying Machine," which the boys all sung in honor of Piney and his stupid motorcycle. Piney himself sung it every time you asked him, closing his eyes, not laughing, thinking you loved hearing it for the singing, when the reason you loved it was he took it so serious, singing—

> Come Josephine in my flying machine,
> Going up she goes, up she goes.
> Balance yourself like a bird on the beam,
> In the air she goes, there she goes.
> Up, up, a little bit higher,
> Oh my, the moon is on fire.
> Come Josephine in my flying machine,
> Going up, goodby, all on, goodby.

He always dragged a stick in the sand behind him. He parked it by the door and come in and ate, salads for me mostly, and lean meat and no bread and butter and this disgusting skim milk, my weight at 209 by now and climbing a mile a minute, and when we was done we sat out back, out of the ocean breeze, until along about 10 he went around the house for his stick, and I drove him back to the Silver Palms.

In the hotel we shoved his bed around near the phone, and I wrote my number on a piece of paper and tacked it on the wall, and he said, "I hope if it happens it will not happen at a bad hour," and I said, "It might or might not probably never happen. I have no faith in those cockeyed doctors up there. But if it happens do not stop and check the time, just call me," and he said he would.

I begin selling policies to kill the time. ["Author" has a sideline as an insurance salesman.—ED.] I drove down to St. Pete every couple days, and Tampa and Clearwater, and over to Lakeland once, never pushing, only chatting with the various boys and leaving it sell itself, which it does once you put the idea in their mind. All spring they see too many old-time ballplayers floating from camp to camp and putting the touch on old friends, maybe giving a pointer to a kid and then saying, "By the way, could you advance me 5 until the first of the month?" which kids often do, probably writing home, "Oh boy, I just had the privilege of loaning 5 to So-and-so," until after they loaned out enough 5's it did not seem so much like a privilege any more.

I drove Lucky down to Tampa the day he was traded. Lucky was the second person I ever sold an annuity to, and he said, "Well, Author, one day we will all be done working. We will just fish and look in the box once a month for the checks, me and you and Bruce and all the rest," and I almost told him, for it was getting hard to carry it around. But I smothered it back. Once you told somebody everybody would know, and once Dutch knew it would of been "Goodby, Bruce." "It is hard picturing you in a Cincinnati suit," I said. In the lobby of The Floridian I got to gassing with Brick Brickell, the manager of Cincinnati. "You are holding out serious," he said. "For what?"

"$27,500," I said.

"You will never get it," he said. Then he looked around to see if anybody was listening. "*We* would pay it," he said.

"I doubt that," I said.

"Try me," he said. "Hold out long enough and we will buy you, and I give you my verbal word we will pay you 25,000 at the least. I been trying to buy you already."

"What are they asking?" I said.

"A quarter of a million dollars and players," he said.

"What will they take?" I said.

"150,000 and players," he said.

"What will you give?" said I.

"Now, Author," he said, "I cannot reveal a thing of that sort. The trouble is that they want Sam Mott. Dutch is worried about his catching."

"Does he not worry about his left-hand pitching?" I said.

"Brooklyn will sell him Scudder," he said, "but only if you are gone, not wishing to cut their own throat."

I drove F. D. R. Caselli back with me, jabbering all the way, him I mean, and all the time he jabbered I kept making up these little conversations where Old Man Moors called me on the phone, pleading with me, "Come on and sign. I will meet your price," until I was just about ready to call him myself. But then again I told myself, "No! Do not sell yourself short!" F. D. R. had blisters on his hands, and he kept asking me what was good for them, and I told him something or other. I forget what.

All spring the wives kept pumping Holly full of miserable stories about babies born with this or that missing, and mothers suffering, which if she ever believed any of it she would of went wild. But she never believes what people say, and all that happened I kept getting as fat as a pig until what we done we bought a badminton set and played badminton all day, deductible, for my weight is a matter of business. By the middle of March I was probably the world's champion heavyweight left-hand badminton player, and still no call from the boss.

One day the club said it was definitely closing a deal with Cleveland for Rob McKenna, saying this on a Friday night for the Saturday paper and leaving no chance for anybody to deny it on Sunday, for they have no Sunday paper in Aqua Clara, and putting all the writers a little bit on the spot since they hated calling Cleveland all the way out in Arizona to check on the truth of what they already probably knew was the bunk. This scared me, though, and I went to the phone, and the instant I touched it it rung, and a voice said, "Do not touch that phone!" It was Ugly Jones. "Author," he said, "you are doing fine."

"I am fatter than a pig," I said.

"Good," he said. "That is the way to convince them, for it worries them more than it worries you. It might not even be a bad idea to show yourself around. Leave the brass see how fat you are."

What we done we went out the park the following Wednesday and sat in the stands behind first. There was about 6 left-handers warming, a few wearing QC suits that been up the spring before, the rest wearing Mammoth shirts, one kid wearing my number, 44, kids, all kids, and all full of hope.

Old Man Moors and Patricia and some automobile people up from Miami strolled in and sat down, Bradley Lord joining them soon after. Patricia said "Hello" and asked Holly how she was. Her and Holly gassed awhile, and then she went back. Old Man Moors glanced up my way, pretending he was looking over the paint job on the park, and I called for peanuts, which fat you up about about a pound for a dime, and I begun munching away.

The first left-hander set George and Perry down 1-2, and the peanuts went dry in my mouth a little. Pasquale then took 2 strikes and belted one out amongst the palms, and I give a little look down at the Moorses and scarcely had time to look back when Sid hit one that fell not 4 feet from where Pasquale's went, back-to-back homers from the power factory, always a nice sight, and Canada shot a single into left, and Piney one into right. Dutch shouted, "I seen enough of that one," waving the left-hander out of there and bringing on a new one, a tall, thin kid with a dizzy habit of wearing his glove with 3 fingers out. He walked Vincent and Ugly and hit Herb Macy on the butt until when he finally found the plate George blasted one back at him that bounced off his knee and blooped out over second base, and the poor kid was lugged off on a stretcher. Another one went out the same way the same day.

Once Dutch looked up at me, and I waved. He did not wave back. He takes it as a personal insult. Behind your back he tells you, "Sure, sock it to them for every nickel you are worth," but when you do he does not like it, though he himself was a holdout more than once in his playing days, and anyhow he was quite busy waving one left-hander out and a new one in, about 5 of them before a kid come on in the sixth and struck Sid and Canada out. The Moorses begun shaking their head "Yes" between themself, Bradley Lord shaking his, too, as soon as he seen it was safe, The World's Only Living Human Spineless Skunk. This newest kid was rather fast, but no curve whatsoever, and I said to Holly, "The boys see that he has no curve by now," which they did all right. Piney and Vincent singled. Ugly stepped in, looking up my way and giving me a kind of a wink and taking a couple and then lacing a drive down the line in right that the whole park busted out laughing over because it slammed up against the fence and stuck there, this old rat-trap fence made of boards, the drive getting jammed in between 2 boards. The right fielder went over and tried to wedge it out. But it was in tight, and Ugly trotted around the bases laughing, and even Dutch was laughing, and by then the Moorses and the people from Miami were laughing, and Bradley Lord, too, seeing all the rest, and about one minute later Lindon bounced one off the same fence that knocked the first ball through, and Mr. Left-Hander Number 6 went to the shower. You really had to laugh. I mean, when a ball slams up against a fence your eye is back out on the field, looking for the rebounce, and then when it don't you think the whole world has went flooey or something, like when you drop a shoe you hear it clunk, and if no clunk comes you quick dial the madhouse. Every so often I begun to laugh, and Holly, too, and Old Man Moors turned around and give me a look, and me and Holly got up about then and yawned and stretched and bought a couple more peanuts and went home and waited for the phone to ring.

After supper it rung, and I sat beside it and left it ring 12 or 13 times until I picked it up and said in my most boring voice, "Fishing pier. Hookworms for sale," only it wasn't Old Man Moors a-tall but Joe Jaros, and he said, "Author, how about a hand of Tegwar or 2?"

I already turned him down a number of times, not wishing to hang in the hotel and look anxious, but I was in the mood now, and I said, "We will be right down."

"Who do you mean by 'we'?" he said, and I said I meant me and Bruce. "Me and Bruce been playing quite a bit all winter," I said. "He is pretty good by now," though this was not true, for he was not.

"I will stay here," said Bruce, and that settled it, at least for now, and he stood with Holly. When I got there Joe had things set up in the lobby, a table for 3, one chair for me and one for him and one empty and waiting for the slaughter. He had a pocket full of change and little bills. Next to the empty chair he stood a lamp all lit and bright, and at the empty place a clean and shining ash tray. The empty chair stood just a little sideways so a cluck could slide in easy.

He shuffled, shuffling over and over again but never dealing, just waiting for the cluck to wander in sight. Joe knew. He can spot one a block away, or walk through a dining car and spot one, or pick one out in a crowd. He been at it 30 years, and I said, "Joe, when my wife goes home Bruce must play with us."

"Sure," he said, not thinking, but then it hit home, and he said, "Now, Author, Bruce is not the type. He is too damn dumb. Anyhow, the way Piney Woods been hitting Bruce might not last the year."

"You must promise me," I said, and he promised, for right about then he seen his party and would of promised you could hang him in the morning. He got all excited. "That looks like it," he said, and we begun to deal, and in through the lobby come a big chap wearing sun glasses, though he was indoors, and though it was night, his arms all red the way a fellow gets when he never sees the sun except a couple a weeks on vacation, a big button in his coat in the shape of a fish saying FEARED IN THE DEEP that the local people hand out by the bushel to every cluck that don't actually faint dead away at the sight of the ocean. He bought a magazine and sat down in an easy chair and begun to read, soon wondering why he could not see, and then shoving his glasses up on his head, every so often peeking at us over the top of his magazine, me and Joe dealing fast and furious now, really working, too, because I will swear if you concentrate hard enough you can bring the cluck up out of his chair and over, which we soon done, for he closed his magazine and worked up his energy and hauled himself up, his sun glasses falling back down over his eyes. Over he come, sticking his magazine in his coat and leaning his hands down on the back of the empty chair and finally saying, "Would you mind if I watch?"

We never spoke nor looked up. We played Casino, your 8 takes a 5 and a 3, your 10 takes a 6 and a 4, like that, pictures taking pictures, and when the hand was done Joe flipped his wrist around and said, "A quarter of 8."

"No," said Mr. Feared In The Deep, "I said would you mind if I watch."

"Oh," said Joe, "I thought you asked me if I had a watch," not saying another word, only dealing again, straight Casino again except with a little switch here and there, maybe a 7 taking in a 5 and a 9, or a deuce an ace and a 3, Casino, only doubled, so there was still some sort of a system to it, though not too much system to the cash sliding back and forth, the cluck watching and studying, taking off his glasses and twirling them, 2 or 3 times starting to say something but then not saying it, only saying once, "It looks like Casino," neither me nor Joe answering him nor even hearing him for all he knew until after the hand I said, "Did you speak?"

"I only said it looks like Casino," he said.

"Casino?" said Joe.

"Like the card game called Casino," said Feared In The Deep.

"You mean the game they play in boarding schools for girls?" said Joe.

"I did not know it was played there," said the cluck. "I personally played Casino myself from time to time."

"We only play men's games," said Joe.

We dealed again. "Would you mind if I sat down?" said the cluck. Nobody said "No," and he sat, and he slapped his pants where his money was and looked at his watch and sort of inched his chair around until he was finally forward over the table, his eye going from my hand to Joe's, the game becoming a little more complicated now, Joe calling once, "Goddam it, fence-board!" and slapping down his hand and showing how he fence-boarded, me laughing and gathering in the money, Joe saying, "I never fence-boarded before since one time against Babe Ruth in St. Pete," the cluck really quite confused about now and ready to go back and look at his magazine.

Right about then I was paged, and Joe went red. "Hang around," he said. "Never mind it. Hang around."

"It is the boss," I said.

"So you are Henry Wiggen," said the cluck. "I seen you was left-handed but did not know who. It is quite an honor."

"I must go, Joe," I said.

"Damn it, Author. Stick around." He was boiling inside, for Tegwar is serious business to him, the great laugh of his life. He will laugh for days after a good night of Tegwar. He will tell you Tegwar stories going back 30 years, of clucks on trains and clucks in hotels, and of great Tegwar partners he had, ballplayers now long since faded from the scene, remembering clubs not half so much by what they done but how they rode with the gag, how they gathered, like the boys even at that moment were gathering for a glimpse of the big fish on the line. It is the gathering of the boys that Joe loves, for without the watching of the crowd the laugh would be hollow. It would be like playing ball to empty stands, and the page come by, saying, "Mr. Wiggen, Mr. Wiggen," and Joe said, "Scram!" and the page scrammed.

But it was no good, and the boys knew it and Joe knew it and I knew it. It takes time. The cluck has got to lay his money on the table and leave it there awhile. He has got to think about it. It has got to be the cluck's own choice every minute of the way, and he has got to hang himself, not be hung by others. It must never be hurried. Yet with the page calling we could not play it slow, though we tried.

Then soon the boys all stepped aside, and Dutch come through and said, "I been trying for days to get some sleep and finally was just drifting off when I am told you are playing cards and too busy to talk contract. Do not push things too far, Author."

"It was my fault," said Joe. "I would not leave him go," and Dutch seen the cluck there and felt sorry for Joe, or as sorry as he can ever feel, and he said so. "What good is being sorry?" said Joe, and he slammed down the cards, and he swore, and Mr. Feared In The Deep begun back-watering as fast as he could, hearing both laughing and swearing but not understanding a word, and I went on up to the Moorses sweet, feeling sorry for Joe and yet also laughing.

Nobody else was laughing but me when I got there. I said, "Leave us not waste time talking contract unless you are willing to talk contract. I was taught in school where slavery went out when Lincoln was shot."

"I know," said Old Man Moors, "for you wrote it across the top of your contract."

"Not across *my* contract," I said. "Maybe across the contract of a turnstile turner."

"Author," said Patricia, "leave us all calm down." She was very beautiful that night, and I said so, and she thanked me. Her nose was quite sunburned. "You are looking over your weight," she said. "It will no doubt take you many weeks to get in shape."

"He looks 10 pounds over his weight at least," said Bradley Lord.

"*Mr.* Bradley Lord," said I, whipping out my loose cash. "I have $200 here which says I am no more than 2 and ⅜ pounds over my weight if you would care to go and fetch the bathroom scale."

"What do you consider your absolute minimum figure?" said Mr. Moors.

"19,000," I said.

"In that case," said he, "we can simply never do business, and I suppose I must be put to the trouble of scouring up another left-hand pitcher."

"That should not be hard," said I, "for I seen several promising boys out there this afternoon. Any one of them will win 4 or 5 games if God drops everything else."

"They are top-flight boys," said Mr. Moors. "Dutch thinks extremely high of at least 3 of them. I will tell you what I will do, Wiggen. I will jack up my absolute maximum figure to 13,500 and not a penny more, and if you have a good year we will make it back to you in 56."

"And when I have a good year in 56 you will make it back to me in 57," I said, "and I will go on being paid for the year before. This shorts me out of a year in the long run."

"We heard this one before," said Bradley Lord.

"Every time Bradley Lord opens his mouth I am raising my absolute minimum figure," I said.

"Bradley," said Patricia, "go get some drinks."

"You feel very confident about this year," said Mr. Moors, "and I will tell you what I will do." He turned my contract over and begun scratching down figures. "For the 20th victory you win this year I will pay you a bonus of 2,500, and for every game over 20 I will pay you 2,000 more, and then to show you where my heart is I will jack up my absolute maximum figure to 14,000."

"We are coming closer together," said Patricia.

"I believe we are just about there," said Old Man Moors.

Bradley come back with 3 cokes, giving one to Old Man Moors and one to Patricia and keeping one for himself.

"As a starter," said I, "I like the look of the arrangement. But instead of 20 victories you must write in 15."

"If I write in 15 I must lower the amount," he said. "You are so damn-fire sure you are going to have such a top-flight year I would think you would jump at the arrangement."

"I am sure about the year I am going to have," said I, "but I am deep in the hole, owing money left and right and Holly pregnant and the high cost of Coca-Cola. I am tired living like a sharecropper."

"Bradley," said Patricia, "go get Author a coke."

Old Man Moors was sketching out the new bonus arrangement on the back of my contract, but he looked up now. "How much do you still owe the goddam Government?" he said.

"$421.89," I said.

He wrote this down on a separate sheet. "I will throw this in," he said, "plus pay you a bonus of $1,500 for the 15th victory you win this year, and 1,000 for every victory over 15. You are better off than you were under the first arrangement."

"Not if I win 25 games," I said.

"If you win 25 games I will round out Bonus Plan Number 2 to equal Number One," said he. "But you know you are not libel to win 25 games. I do not see why you are trying to heckle me. If you win 25 games I will be so goddam pleased I will pay you a flat 5,000 bonus if I do not drop dead from surprise."

"I won 26 in 52," said I.

"Yes," said he, "but never come near it since." He mentioned my Won-and-Lost for 53 and 54, which everybody knows, so no need to repeat. Bradley Lord come back with my coke, and Old Man Moors shoved him the separate sheet, saying, "Make out a check in this amount and send it to the United States Bureau of Internal Revenue in the name of Wiggen. Very well, Henry, your base pay will be 14,000 plus Bonus Plan Number 2. I think that is fair. I know that you are going to have a grand year," and he reached out his hand. He was calling me "Henry" now, all smiles, which he had a right to be, I guess, for I believe he was ready to go much higher on his absolute maximum. But I did not push him, for the main job was yet ahead, and I did not take his hand, saying, "Sir, there is one clause yet to go in my contract."

"Shoot," said he.

"There must be a clause," said I, "saying that me and Bruce Pearson will stay with the club together, or else go together. Whatever happens to one must happen to the other, traded or sold or whatever. We must be tied in a package on any deal under the sun."

"No deals are on the fire," said he.

"I never heard of such a thing," said Bradley Lord.

Patricia was powdering her nose out of a little compact. She snapped the lid shut, and it was the only sound, and she said, "It is not a matter of whether anybody ever heard of such a thing before or not, and it is not a matter whether any deals are on the fire or not. It is a thing we could never do for many reasons, the first reason being that Dutch would never hear of it, and all the rest of the reasons second."

"Boys and girls," said Old Man Moors, "leave us be calm. Wiggen, I will give you my verbal word instead of writing it in."

"It must be wrote in," said I.

"Bradley," said Patricia, "call Dutch."

"He is asleep," said Bradley.

"He been trying for days to get some sleep," said I.

"Call him," she said.

Bradley called him, and it rung a long time, and when you heard his voice you could hear it all over the room, like he was there, and Bradley held the phone away from his ear, and then he said, "Mr. Moors wishes to see you," and after awhile he come down in his slippers and robe, pajama pants but no top. "I been trying for days to get some sleep," he said, still not awake. "Go get me a coke."

"Tell him your clause," said Patricia.

He looked at me with his eyes shut. "So it is you with a special clause, Author? I will bet it is a dilly." His voice was low and full of sleep, and he kept scrounging in his eyes with his hands, trying to wake up. "Bradley, run get me a wet rag," he said. He took a swig of his coke. "Sterling must be shot for hay fever with a special shot. Vincent Carucci must have contact lenses. Gonzalez must have a buddy along to speak Spanish with, and Goldman must go home on Passover. What do you wish, Author, the Chinese New Year off or Dick Tracy's birthday?"

"I wish a clause," said I, "tying me in a package with Pearson."

"Does he owe you money?" said Old Man Moors.

Bradley brung him the rag, and Dutch squeezed it out on the floor. "Jesus, Bradley, you ain't got much strength in your hand," he said. "How do you mean tied in a package?"

"If he is sold I must be sold," I said. "Or if he is traded I must be traded the same place. Wherever he goes I must go."

His face was covered with the rag, and when he took it away the color was gone, drained away down in his chest. I will swear the hair of his chest was red, and then slowly it drained back up again, and he said, "This is telling me who I must keep and who not, which nobody ever told me before, Author, and nobody will ever tell me again as long as I am upright. If it is money talk money, and good luck. Talking money is one thing. But talking business is another, and I will as soon trade the whole club for a tin of beans as leave anybody tell me who stays and who gets cut loose."

"I am sorry to hear it," said I, "because without that clause there will be no contract."

"Then there will be no contract," said Dutch, "and I must suffer along the best I can."

"Several of those left-handers looked good to me," said Old Man Moors.

"Good for what?" said Dutch.

"Will you go sell insurance?" said Bradley Lord. "You do not know a soul on earth to sell insurance to outside of ballplayers. Will you sell insurance to other insurance agents? Where will you run up against people with money with the language you speak? I never seen you wear a necktie."

"Shut up," said Dutch.

"I am ignoring him," said I. "I am only laying it out straight, all my cards up. I do not wish to sell insurance. Insurance is for later. I rather play baseball than anything else. I do it best. I like the trains. I like the hotels. I like the boys. I like the hours and the money. I like the fame and the glory. I like to think of 50,000 people getting up in the morning and squashing themself to death in the subway to come and see me play ball."

"That is how I feel," said Dutch.

"I am dead serious," said I.

"What is up between you 2? A roomie is a roomie, Author, not a Siamese twin brother fastened at the hip. I do not understand this a-tall, and I will investigate it. I will run it down to the end of the earth. Are you a couple fairies, Author? That can not be. It been a long time since I run across fairies in baseball, not since Will Miller and another lad that I forget his name, a shortstop, that for Christ sake when they split they went and found another friend. This is all too much for me."

"You will understand it sometime," I said.

"When?"

"No telling," I said. "Maybe soon, maybe not for 15 years."

"I am 62," said Dutch. "I will certainly be hanging by my thumb until I hear. Christ Almighty, I seen you on days when you hated Pearson, when you ate him out as bad as I myself ever ate him out. I seen you about to kill him for his stupidity. I seen you once get up from the table and walk away."

"Because he laughed without knowing why," I said.

"Such a thing can be not only hate but also love," said Patricia.

"It is not love," said I.

"I do not mean fairy love," she said.

"He laughs because he wishes to be one of the boys all the time," said Dutch. "Must this clause go on forever?" He closed his eyes again, not sleeping but thinking. "I have 4 catchers," he said. "I have a catcher that is old and another that can not hit and another that is wild and crazy and another that is just plum dumb." He opened his eyes and begun checking them off on his fingers. "I would give both my eyes for Sam Mott of Cincinnati, but they want Author, and I cannot give Author, or if I give you I must have Scudder off Brooklyn which the son of a bitches will not give me except for all my right-hand power. I could spare my right-hand power if I could swing a deal with Pittsburgh, but Pittsburgh wants Author and I have already give you to Cincinnati on paper for Sam Mott. So I must play my old catcher on days when he feels young, and my catcher that can not hit on days the power is on, and my wild and crazy catcher on days he ever comes to his senses, which so far he has give me no sign of really having any. I will ship him back to QC and see if Mike can talk him off his motorcycle. We must never have another motorcycle in camp. I been trying for days to get some sleep. When you really stop and think about it I am libel to wind up using my catcher that is just plum dumb more and more." He finished off his coke and belched a loud belch and scratched the hair on his chest.

"Some day you will understand," I said.

"No," said he. "That is too much to ask. Forget it. I will agree to this clause. I never done such a thing before and would not do it now except there is a look in your eye that tells me that I must." He looked in my eye a long time. "Yes," he said, "there is a look which tells me that I must," and that was all he said but went back out and up to bed, and Bradley Lord drew up the contract and we all signed.

FOR sheer dramatics, it's hard to beat this one in all baseball annals. Old Pete Alexander coming in to pitch to Lazzeri . . . bases loaded . . . two out . . . Remember?

1926:
St. Louis Cardinals 3,
New York Yankees 2

JAMES R. HARRISON

THE CARDINALS WON. The baseball drama had a happy ending after all, for as the last reel faded out the sentimental favorites were holding the championship. They beat the Yankees and the Yankees beat themselves, and between the two the greatest game of the series went to St. Louis, 3 to 2.

The old story can be written again. The breaks of the game decided it. To baseball history can be added one more chapter where the seventh game of the big series was decided, not by skill or courage, but by fate.

After millions of words had been scribbled and tons of white paper covered with expert calculations, the World Series worked itself down to four short words: Koenig's fumble, Meusel's muff.

If Mark Koenig, the Yankee shortstop, had gripped his fingers around the grounder in the fourth inning; if the veteran Bob Meusel had caught an easy fly that bobbed out of his hands in the same round, the Yanks would have won and would be world champions this morning.

If the Cardinals had not scored three unearned runs on those two devastating errors, Waite Hoyt would not have been robbed for the second time in his career of the glory of a shutout in the final game of the World Series. Babe Ruth would not today be mourning the fact that his home run in the third did not bring the championship to New York singlehandedly and unaided.

And St. Louis last night and through the early hours of the morning would not have been celebrating the happy ending to its wait of thirty-eight years.

Everything was incidental to those two errors. It was incidental that Herb Pennock came back to pitch in a hopeless cause. It was incidental, even though highly dramatic, that in the seventh inning, with the bases full and two out, Alexander the Great came out of the shadows of the bull pen to strike out Tony Lazzeri and throttle the Yankees' last great rally.

It was incidental, too, that Tommy Thevenow, Cardinal shortstop, drove in the winning runs with a single in the fourth.

Alexander wrote finis to the hopes of the surging Yanks with an old hand but a steady one. To his already superb work in the series he added this one climax. His pitching in the series was probably the greatest since the days of Matty and Babe Adams, but if Meusel and Koenig had held on to the ball, Alex would have been merely a gallant old pitcher on a losing ball team.

Fate made a hero of Alexander and a victim of Hoyt. Fate was the scene shifter who set the stage in the seventh, out upon which Alexander shuffled. His cap was perched on one side of his head and he was slowly chewing a quid of tobacco. He was a quaint, almost humorous, figure with his jaunty cap, his old man's gait and his quizzical face, but when he wound up his arm and threw, the Yanks had reached the end of the trail.

There was nothing more left for them. They had battled through six games and now had the championship at the ends of their fingers when suddenly they came face to face with Alex. While 40,000 went wild with delight at Yankee Stadium, he stood across the path and the Yanks took a detour to second-place money in the greatest money series of all time.

In the third, Babe Ruth hit his fourth homer, setting a new record for a single series. With Hoyt pitching the game of a lifetime, this run looked enough to win. But in the fourth Koenig fumbled and Meusel muffed, and the Yanks found themselves two runs behind.

Miller Huggins reorganized his scattered battalion and the Yanks charged on. They swirled at Jesse Haines in the sixth and luck was with them this time, for Chick Hafey played a line drive rashly and Dugan scored with the second run.

Only one to go now, and Haines, his pitching hand bruised, was weakening. In the seventh, Combs opened with a single. The Yanks were coming again. Koenig sacrificed Combs to second and Ruth was walked intentionally.

Meusel, the unfortunate lad with the feeble fingers of an earlier inning, had his chance to wipe the slate clean, but his grounder to Bell was turned into a force-out of Ruth at second while Combs dashed on to third.

Gehrig was now at bat. His single had won one game and his double helped to win another. Haines faltered after he had thrown two strikes on the native-born New Yorker. Something suddenly went wrong with the Haines right arm. He floated three bad balls up to the plate, and another high one sent Gehrig to first and filled the bases.

Rogers Hornsby called his men into a huddle. Hornsby, O'Farrell, Haines, Bottomley, Bell, Thevenow—they were all there. When the conference broke up, Haines took off his glove and walked to the bench.

The Cardinals were going to try a new pitcher. Forty thousand pairs of eyes peered anxiously through the gray mist toward the bull pen out in deep left. There was a breathless pause, and then around the corner of the stand came a tall figure in a Cardinal sweater. His cap rode rakishly on the corner of his head. He walked like a man who was going nowhere in particular and was in no hurry to get there. He was a trifle knock-kneed and his gait was not a model of grace and rhythm.

Any baseball fan would have known him a mile away. It was Grover Cleveland Alexander. Alexander the Great was coming in to pull the Cardinal machine out of the mudhole. The ancient twirler, who had gone nine full innings the day before, was shuffling in where younger men feared to tread.

On any other day he would have been sitting contentedly on the bench, chewing his quid and ruminating on life. This time he was plucked out from the bull pen and thrust into the limelight as the last hope of the Cardinals.

He warmed up in that leisurely, methodical way of his, and as he faced Tony Lazzeri, fresh young slugger from the Coast, he was outwardly as unconcerned as if it were a spring exhibition game. Throughout the park there came a silence. The fans slid forward to the edge of their seats. Hardly a mother's son of them seemed to be moving a muscle, but, although the crowd was rigid with the thrill of the moment, old Alex was undisturbed.

He had been through all that before. Apparently there wasn't a nerve in his body. Ball one to Lazzeri was low and the crowd stirred, but Alex calmly carved the outside corner with a strike, like a butcher slicing ham.

Another one outside and Lazzeri fouled it into the stand. The Yankee was now in the hole. "This lad is in a tighter fix than I am," thought Alex, and so he essayed a low curve that one of the Singer midgets couldn't have hit. Lazzeri swung and missed. The deed was done. Alex took off his glove and shuffled again to the bench. The Cardinals, young and impetuous, pounded his back and hugged him madly, but old Alex took it with placid good humor—not the shadow of a smile on his face.

Only once did he turn his head and send a half-smile toward the stand and we suspect that that was his only gesture of triumph.

In the eighth the Yanks went out one, two, three. The old arm of Alexander was now rising and falling with a steady beat, tolling off the last minutes of the World Series. Against him was Pennock, but Alex had a one-run lead and there was nothing in his mellow past which made anyone believe that Alexander would lose a one-run lead in the ninth inning of the last World Series game.

Combs and Koenig were child's play for him, as the Yankees' final turn began. Combs grounded to Bell and was out. Koenig gave the same fielder an easy roller.

And now the drama was almost done. There was only one more scene. Ruth was at bat—the Yankees' last hope. Would Alexander pitch to him as he had to lesser men?

It would have been the last great story of the series if Alex had fanned him. But Alex was not concerned with great stories, drama, climaxes, headlines or anything else of the sort. He pitched carefully and deliberately to Ruth. He brought the count to three and two, but Alex just missed the corner of the plate on the next one and the Babe walked.

Meusel rather than Ruth was on the program, but before Meusel could settle the issue Ruth did it for him by breaking for second base. O'Farrell whipped a fast throw to Hornsby and the series was over.

Now Rogers Hornsby can go back to Texas, where his mother lies dead, and Alexander the Great can go back to his easy chair, his slippers and a winter fireplace and dwell pleasantly on the October afternoon when Tony Lazzeri swung at a low ball which a Singer midget could not have hit. If Alex wants to chuckle, he is clearly entitled to it.

He can look back to the series which saw him winning two masterful victories and helping to win a third. The man who was fired by Joe McCarthy, manager of the Cubs, in midsummer, came back in October to fashion one of the greatest World Series pitching achievements.

Matty, Babe Adams, Combs and Coveleskie twirled three victories in other baseball classics, but they were all young men and full of strength. Alex was not only old but he was a baseball discard, tossed onto the scrap heap as an antique without worth.

Rogers Hornsby can go back to Texas with the comforting thought that he "stayed with the team" and won. The young man who caught the imagination and sympathy of the country as only Walter Johnson before him had done is undoubtedly glad the series is over. Not for him any triumphant celebrations; he has discharged one duty only to take on another.

The series set nineteen playing records and was the greatest ever in total receipts and attendance. Although yesterday's crowd was a miserable disappointment, with only 38,093 paid, it was enough to send the attendance up to 328,051, and the receipts to $1,207,864. When 63,600 paid to see the second game in the stadium, all marks for a single day's attendance were also passed. The total of winning and losing players' share was bigger than anything before.

The weather man is being blamed for yesterday's financial slump. Showers and an overcast sky in the morning made it certain that the crowd would be small.

Hoyt pitched fine ball all the way through. For a short spell he was again the Hoyt of 1921, when his work against the Giants earned him the brief sobriquet, a "second Matty." His fast ball was a work of art and his curve the best he has shown in five years—both wonderfully controlled and hopping through like the wind.

Hoyt came through in magnificent style, but it was again his misfortune to be beaten by the breaks of the game. His mind must have wandered back to 1921. In the last ill-fated game of that series Roger Peckinpaugh booted a ball away and Hoyt lost, 1 to 0. Once again fate came along to kick him on the shins.

Ruth had hit his homer, and when the fourth opened Hoyt was in front of Hornsby's easy grounder. Bottomley singled to left. Hoyt forced Bell to ground to Koenig, who had an easy double play in sight.

But the kid shortstop played the ball to one side, and in his eagerness to kill two birds with one stone fumbled the roller. One bad break for Hoyt followed another. With two strikes and no balls against Hafey, the left fielder lifted a weak fly which fell in left between the scurrying figures of Koenig and Meusel.

The bases were full and only one out, and fate was saving its best prank for the last. O'Farrell raised a fly to left center. Meusel, having a stronger arm than Combs, waved the Kentuckian away so that he could make the throw to the plate. There was only an outside chance of keeping Bottomley from scoring, but Meusel did not even catch the ball.

The white pill hit his outstretched hands and popped out again, like a rabbit from the magician's hat. For a minute there was a stunned silence. Even the Cardinals were so taken aback that they hardly knew what to do. Bottomley, of course, was lighting out for the plate, and the others finally got into action and ran for the next base.

There is only one explanation for the Meusel muff. He tried to throw the ball before he got it, and thereby made himself the greatest World Series goat since Fred Snodgrass of Giant fame.

With the score tied and bases still full, Hoyt settled gamely down, but the "breaks" had beaten him. He laid two strikes over on Thevenow and was pitching stanchly when the boy shortstop happened to tap the ball with the end of his bat and loop a safe hit to right center, which scored two more runs.

Hoyt, pitching like Matty of old, was beaten nevertheless. He was beaten like Matty of 1912, when Snodgrass muffed an easy fly. You have heard of the famous "$100,000 muff." You know about the time Hank Gowdy tripped over his mask and lost the deciding game of the 1924 series. You know about Peckinpaugh of last October, but they were as nothing compared to the fumble of Koenig and the muff of Meusel.

For this was the biggest money series of all, with the spoils bigger and the stake greater. There has never been a 7-game World Series without the seventh game producing its Meusels and Snodgrasses and Gowdys. Hoyt now joins the unhappy ranks with Mathewson, Virgil Barnes and Walter Johnson.

John McGraw can sympathize with Miller Huggins, for it happened to him twice.

There has also never been a full-limit series which ended satisfactorily—never a seventh game decided strictly on its merits. Invariably the breaks have decided it. For three straight years this has happened, and in each case the winner was the winner because on that afternoon the run of the cards was with him.

To Ruth as well as to Hoyt should go the heartfelt condolences of Yankee rooters. The playboy of baseball might have heard his name go ringing down the corridors of baseball as a man who won a series game with a home run.

It was the only earned run of the game. In the third Haines was going along nicely until he met Ruth. Jess fell back to his slow ball. Ruth fouled the first one into the stand, but the next one was too low and was a ball. The third was slow and inside.

The Babe's timing was perfect and the swish of his bat terrific. Remember that it was a slow ball and hard to knock for any distance. Ruth had to supply the momentum himself, yet he whaled that ball clear over the outfielders' heads and into the bleachers off right center.

Barely hurdling the fence, the ball passed directly over the words "World's Champions" in the razor ad. "A happy omen," yelled the Yankee rooters. It was a good omen until Koenig and Meusel ruined it, for with that blow Ruth would have made world champions of the Yankees.

A crowd lukewarm toward the Yanks rose to its feet and acclaimed the king as he has not been acclaimed in years. The furor and the din were earsplitting.

It was Ruth's second great moment in the series, the first being when he hit three homers in the fourth game at St. Louis. His total for the series was four, setting a record, and his total for all series is eight, two above the previous high-water mark.

George Herman started the winning rally in one game with a single, carried the flag in another with three homers, and would have won the last but for the mistakes of his teammates. In this series Ruth and Pennock were nine-tenths of the Yanks.

It was Ruth who also made the most sensational play of the closing game when he sprinted at top speed back almost to the running track and enfolded O'Farrell's terrific line drive in his glove. For this he got another tornado of cheers from the multitude. Ruth was carrying the crowd by storm. In another inning his apathetic subjects were actually rooting for the Yankees—the greatest tribute possible to the colorful personality of King George.

The series is over. The Yanks were outbatted and outfielded, but their superior experience and balance carried them along. Even those assets were failing them until Ruth completely turned the tide with his St. Louis homers. Those three pitched balls almost cost the Cardinals the title.

Ruth is still the Yankee team. The Cards made great talk about pitching to him, but in the deciding game they walked him four out of five times.

It was a series of great crowds and busy turnstiles, but not much action compared to many another series. Not a well-played series and not a thrilling one, except in spots. The breaks were evenly divided. The new champions earned what they got and old Alex earned a quiet winter in his rocking chair.

HERE IS Gabby Hartnett's own story of one of baseball's truly great moments —his "home run in the gloaming" in 1938.

1938:
Chicago Cubs 6,
Pittsburgh Pirates 5

GABBY HARTNETT *as told to* HAL TOTTEN

DO YOU know how you feel when you're real scared, or something BIG is going to happen? Well, that's the way I felt for one terrific minute of my biggest day in baseball—and I don't believe you'll have to guess very much as to just which day that was.

It was in 1938, Sept. 28, the day of "the home run in the dark." But as a matter of fact, that day—that one big moment—was the climax of a series of things that had gone on for a week or more. And every one of those incidents helped to make it the biggest day in all my years in the major leagues.

The week before—on Sunday—you'll remember we had played a double-header in Brooklyn. We lost the first game 4 to 3, and we were leading the second game by two runs along about the fifth inning. It was muddy and raining and was getting dark fast. Then big Fred Sington came up with a man on base and hit a home run to tie the score.

It was too dark to play any more, so they called the game and it ended in a tie. Now—every game meant a lot to us just then. We were three and a half games behind. Winning was the only way we could hope to catch the Pirates. And we were scheduled in Philadelphia the next day. So we couldn't play the game off then.

But MacPhail wanted to play it. We had an open date for travel at the end of the series in Philly, and he wanted us to go back to Brooklyn and play off the tie. The boys wanted to play it, too. They figured we could win it and gain on the Pirates.

Well, I couldn't make up my mind right away, so I asked MacPhail to give me 24 hours to decide. He said he would. But I'd been figuring —you see, we had to win all three games in the series with Pittsburgh if we were to win the pennant. And I had to think of my pitchers. I had to argue with the whole ball club—they wanted to play.

But I stuck my neck out and turned it down. I'll admit that I didn't feel any too easy about it. But I had to make the decision. And I felt that we might lose that game just as easy as we could win it. So I took that chance.

Well, we sat for three days in Philly and watched it rain. Of course, Pittsburgh wasn't able to play in Brooklyn, either. And they were three and a half games in front of us. On Thursday we played the Phils twice and beat 'em both times, 4 to 0 and 2 to 1. Lee won his 20th game of the season in that first one—and his fourth straight shutout. Clay Bryant was the pitcher in the second. But Pittsburgh beat Brooklyn twice, so we were still three and a half back.

The next day we won two again—and we had to come from behind to do it. Rip Collins put the second one on ice by doubling in the ninth with the bases full to drive in three runs just as they posted the score showing that Cincinnati had beaten the Pirates. That put us within two games of the leaders. We were really rollin'.

Then we came home and on Saturday we played the Cardinals—and beat 'em 9 to 3. But the Pirates won, too. On Sunday it was the same thing —we both won. Monday Pittsburgh wasn't scheduled, so the Pirates were in the stands at Wrigley Field as we played the final of the series with St. Louis. Bill Lee was scored on for the first time in five games, but we won 6 to 3. And then came the big series—with the lead cut to a game and a half.

I stuck my neck out in the very first game of the series. Several times, in fact. I started Dizzy Dean on the mound. He hadn't pitched since Sept. 13 and hadn't started a game since Aug. 13. But how he pitched! Just a slow ball, control, and a world of heart.

We got him out in front in the third when Collins tripled and Jurges drove him in with a single. For five innings Dean was superb. Then he seemed to tire. Not due to anything that happened on the field.

Lloyd Waner grounded out in that inning, and Paul Waner fouled out. Rizzo singled, but Vaughan popped to Herman. Still, I noticed that he didn't have as much on the ball.

Probably I was the only one to notice it—except maybe Diz himself. I began to worry a bit. And I made up my mind right then and there that no matter how anything else was going, the minute Dean got in trouble, I was going to get him out of there. We got another run the last half of that inning. And Diz got through the seventh and eighth, although it took a great play by Dean himself to cut down a run at the plate in the eighth.

When the ninth came around I decided to play safe and started Lee warming up in the bull pen. Bill wasn't usually a good relief pitcher, but he was the best pitcher in the league, and that was a spot for the best we had.

Dean hit Vaughan to start the ninth and I was plenty uneasy. But Suhr popped out, and Jensen batted for Young and forced Arky at second. Then came little "Jeep" Handley and he hit one clear to the wall in left center for a double. That put the tying runs on second and third, and that was my cue.

Todd was up. He always hit Dean pretty good, even when Diz had his stuff—and Diz didn't have a thing then. Not only that, but Todd never hit Lee very well. So even though Lee hadn't been a steady relief pitcher, I called him in. My neck was out again. What if Todd hit one? What if Lee had trouble getting started—after all, he'd been working day after day. But—well, when it gets to the place where it means a ball game, you've got to make a change, even if the hitter socks one into the bleachers.

I'll say this for Dean—he never complained about that. He walked right in and said I'd done the right thing—that he'd lost his stuff and his arm didn't feel so good. So Lee came in. The first pitch was a strike. Todd fouled the next one off. Then Lee cut loose with as wild a pitch as I ever saw and Jensen scored. Handley went to third with the tying run. My hunch didn't look so good. But Lee wound up again; he pitched; and Todd swung and struck out. We'd won the game and were only a half game out of first place.

That brings us up to the big day. We scored in the second inning on a couple of errors. But Pittsburgh went ahead with three in the sixth. We tied it up in our half. But the Pirates got two in the eighth and led, 5 to 3. In our half Collins opened with a single and Jurges walked.

Lazzeri batted for Lee, who had gone in again that day, and doubled, scoring Rip. They walked Hack. Then Herman drove in Jurges to tie it up again, but Joe Marty—who had run for Tony—was thrown out at the plate by Paul Waner. A double play ended that round.

It was very dark by then. But the umpires decided to let us go one more. Charlie Root got through the first half of the ninth all right. In our half Cavarretta hit one a country mile to center, but Lloyd Waner pulled it down. Reynolds grounded out. And it was my turn.

Well—I swung once—and missed; I swung again, and got a piece of it, but that was all. A foul and strike two. I had one more chance. Mace Brown wound up and let fly; I swung with everything I had and then I got that feeling I was talking about—the kind of feeling you get when the blood rushes out of your head and you get dizzy.

A lot of people have told me they didn't know the ball was in the bleachers. Well, I did—maybe I was the only one in the park who did. I knew it the minute I hit it. When I got to second base I couldn't see third for the players and fans there. I don't think I walked a step to the plate—I was carried in. But when I got there I saw George Barr taking a good look—he was going to make sure I touched that platter.

That was the shot that did it. We went into first place. And while we still had the pennant to win, we couldn't be headed. We won again the next day for Bill Lee, easy—10 to 1. The heart was gone out of Pittsburgh. And we clinched the pennant down in St. Louis the next Saturday when we won and Pittsburgh lost to Cincinnati.

FOR combination of story, subject, and writer, you would look far to beat this
one. Mr. Reiser was—I say "was"; I was almost tempted to classify this piece
under "history"—a great ballplayer. He busted more fences than busted him
—though the margin wasn't very big.

The Rocky Road of Pistol Pete

W. C. HEINZ

OUT IN Los Angeles," says Garry Schumacher, who was a New York
baseball writer for 30 years and is now assistant to Horace Stoneham,
president of the San Francisco Giants, "they think Duke Snider is the
best center fielder they ever had. They forget Pete Reiser. The Yankees
think Mickey Mantle is something new. They forget Reiser, too."

Maybe Pete Reiser was the purest ballplayer of all time. I don't
know. There is no exact way of measuring such a thing, but when a
man of incomparable skills, with full knowledge of what he is doing,
destroys those skills and puts his life on the line in the pursuit of his
endeavor as no other man in his game ever has, perhaps he is the truest
of them all.

"Is Pete Reiser there?" I said on the phone.

This was last season, in Kokomo. Kokomo has a population of about
50,000 and a ball club, now affiliated with Los Angeles and called the
Dodgers, in the Class D Midwest League. Class D is the bottom of the
barrel of organized baseball, and this was the second season that Pete
Reiser had managed Kokomo.

"He's not here right now," the woman's voice on the phone said.
"The team played a double-header yesterday in Dubuque, and they
didn't get in on the bus until 4:30 this morning. Pete just got up a few
minutes ago and he had to go to the doctor's."

"Oh?" I said. "What has he done now?"

In two and a half years in the minors, three seasons of Army ball and
ten years in the majors, Pete Reiser was carried off the field 11 times.
Nine times he regained consciousness either in the clubhouse or in hospitals. He broke a bone in his right elbow, throwing. He broke both ankles,
tore a cartilage in his left knee, ripped the muscles in his left leg, sliding.
Seven times he crashed into outfield walls, dislocating his left shoulder,
breaking his right collarbone and, five times, ending up in an unconscious
heap on the ground. Twice he was beaned, and the few who remember
still wonder today how great he might have been.

"I didn't see the old-timers," Bob Cooke, who is sports editor of the

New York *Herald Tribune,* was saying recently, "but Pete Reiser was the best ballplayer I ever saw."

"We don't know what's wrong with him," the woman's voice on the phone said now. "He has a pain in his chest and he feels tired all the time, so we sent him to the doctor. There's a game tonight, so he'll be at the ball park about 5 o'clock."

Pete Reiser is 39 years old now. The Cardinals signed him out of the St. Louis Municipal League when he was 15. For two years, because he was so young, he chauffeured for Charley Barrett, who was scouting the Midwest. They had a Cardinal uniform in the car for Pete, and he used to work out with the Class C and D clubs, and one day Branch Rickey, who was general manager of the Cardinals then, called Pete into his office in Sportsman's Park.

"Young man," he said, "you're the greatest young ballplayer I've ever seen, but there is one thing you must remember. Now that you're a professional ballplayer you're in show business. You will perform on the biggest stage in the world, the baseball diamond. Like the actors on Broadway, you'll be expected to put on a great performance every day, no matter how you feel, no matter whether it's too hot or too cold. Never forget that."

Rickey didn't know it at the time, but this was like telling Horatius that, as a professional soldier, he'd be expected someday to stand his ground. Three times Pete sneaked out of hospitals to play. Once he went back into the lineup after doctors warned him that any blow on the head would kill him. For four years he swung the bat and made the throws when it was painful for him just to shave and to comb his hair. In the 1947 World Series he stood on a broken ankle to pinch hit, and it ended with Rickey, then president of the Dodgers, begging him not to play and guaranteeing Pete his 1948 salary if he would just sit that season out.

"That might be the one mistake I made," Pete says now. "Maybe I should have rested that year."

"Pete Reiser?" Leo Durocher, who managed Pete at Brooklyn, was saying recently. "What's he doing now?"

"He's managing Kokomo," Lindsey Nelson, the TV sportcaster, said.

"Kokomo?" Leo said.

"That's right," Lindsey said. "He's riding the buses to places like Lafayette and Michigan City and Mattoon."

"On the buses," Leo said, shaking his head and then smiling at the thought of Pete.

"And some people say," Lindsey said, "that he was the greatest young ballplayer they ever saw."

"No doubt about it," Leo said. "He was the best I ever had, with the possible exception of Mays. At that, he was even faster than Willie." He paused. "So now he's on the buses."

The first time that Leo ever saw Pete on a ball field was in Clearwater that spring of '39. Pete had played one year of Class D in the Cardinal chain and one season of Class D for Brooklyn. Judge Kenesaw Mountain Landis, who was then Baseball Commissioner, had sprung Pete and 72 others from what they called the "Cardinal Chain Gang," and Pete had signed with Brooklyn for $100.

"I didn't care about money then," Pete says. "I just wanted to play."

Pete had never been in a major-league camp before, and he didn't know that at batting practice you hit in rotation. At Clearwater he was grabbing any bat that was handy and cutting in ahead of Ernie Koy or Dolph Camilli or one of the others, and Leo liked that.

One day Leo had a chest cold, so he told Pete to start at shortstop. His first time up he hit a homer off the Cards' Ken Raffensberger, and that was the beginning. He was on base his first 12 times at bat that spring, with three homers, five singles and four walks. His first time against Detroit he homered off Tommy Bridges. His first time against the Yankees he put one over the fence off Lefty Gomez.

Durocher played Pete at shortstop in 33 games that spring. The Dodgers barnstormed North with the Yankees, and one night Joe McCarthy, who was managing the Yankees, sat down next to Pete on the train.

"Reiser," he said, "you're going to play for me."

"How can I play for you?" Pete said. "I'm with the Dodgers."

"We'll get you," McCarthy said. "I'll tell Ed Barrow, and you'll be a Yankee."

The Yankees offered $100,000 and five ballplayers for Pete. The Dodgers turned it down, and the day the season opened at Ebbets Field, Larry MacPhail, who was running things in Brooklyn, called Pete on the clubhouse phone and told him to report to Elmira.

"It was an hour before game time," Pete says, "and I started to take off my uniform and I was shaking all over. Leo came in and said: 'What's the matter? You scared?' I said: 'No. MacPhail is sending me to Elmira.' Leo got on the phone and they had a hell of a fight. Leo said he'd quit, and MacPhail said he'd fire him—and I went to Elmira.

"One day I'm making a throw and I heard something pop. Every day my arm got weaker and they sent me to Johns Hopkins and took X rays. Dr. George Bennett told me: 'Your arm's broken.' When I came to after the operation, my throat was sore and there was an ice pack on it. I said: 'What happened? Your knife slip?' They said: 'We took your tonsils out while we were operating on your arm.' "

Pete's arm was in a cast from the first of May until the end of July. His first two weeks out of the cast he still couldn't straighten the arm, but a month later he played ten games as a left-handed outfielder until Dr. Bennett stopped him.

"But I can't straighten my right arm," Pete said.

"Take up bowling," the doctor said.

When he bowled, though, Pete used first one arm and then the other. Every day that the weather allowed he went out into the back yard and practiced throwing a rubber ball left-handed against a wall. Then he went to Fairgrounds Park and worked on the long throw, left-handed, with a baseball.

"At Clearwater that next spring," he says, "Leo saw me in the outfield throwing left-handed, and he said: 'What do you think you're doin'?' I said: 'Hell, I had to be ready. Now I can throw as good with my left arm as I could with my right.' He said: 'You can do more things as a right-handed ballplayer. I can bring you into the infield. Go out there and cut loose with that right arm.' I did and it was okay, but I had that insurance."

So at 5 o'clock I took a cab from the hotel in Kokomo to the ball park on the edge of town. It seats about 2,200, 1,500 of them in the white-painted fairgrounds grandstand along the first base line, and the rest in chairs behind the screen and in bleachers along the other line.

I watched them take batting practice; trim, strong young kids with their dreams, I knew, of someday getting up there where Pete once was, and I listened to their kidding. I watched the groundskeeper open the concession booth and clean out the electric popcorn machine. I read the signs on the outfield walls, advertising the Mid-West Towel and Linen Service, Basil's Nite Club, The Hoosier Iron Works, UAW Local 292 and the Around the Clock Pizza Café. I watched the Dubuque kids climbing out of their bus, carrying their uniforms on wire coat hangers.

"Here comes Pete now," I heard the old guy setting up the ticket box at the gate say.

When Pete came through the gate he was walking like an old man. In 1941 the Dodgers trained in Havana, and one day they clocked him, in his baseball uniform and regular spikes, at 9.8 for 100 yards. Five years later the Cleveland Indians were bragging about George Case and the Washington Senators had Gil Coan. The Dodgers offered to bet $1,000 that Reiser was the fastest man in baseball, and now it was taking him forever to walk to me, his shoulders stooped, his whole body heavier now, and Pete just slowly moving one foot ahead of the other.

"Hello," he said, shaking hands but his face solemn. "How are you?"

"Fine," I said, "but what's the matter with you?"

"I guess it's my heart," he said.

"When did you first notice this?"

"About eleven days ago. I guess I was working out too hard. All of a sudden I felt this pain in my chest and I got weak. I went into the clubhouse and lay down on the bench, but I've had the same pain and I'm weak ever since."

"What did the doctor say?"

"He says it's lucky I stopped that day when I did. He says I should be in a hospital right now, because if I exert myself or even make a quick motion I might go—just like that."

He snapped his fingers. "He scared me," he said. "I'll admit it. I'm scared."

"What are you planning to do?"

"I'm going home to St. Louis. My wife works for a doctor there, and he'll know a good heart specialist."

"When will you leave?"

"Well, I can't just leave the ball club. I called Brooklyn, and they're sending a replacement for me, but he won't be here until tomorrow."

"How will you get to St. Louis?"

"It's about 300 miles," Pete says. "The doctor says I shouldn't fly or go by train, because if anything happens to me they can't stop and help me. I guess I'll have to drive."

"I'll drive you," I said.

Trying to get to sleep in the hotel that night I was thinking that maybe, standing there in that little ball park, Pete Reiser had admitted out loud for the first time in his life that he was scared. I was thinking of 1941, his first full year with the Dodgers. He was beaned twice and crashed his first wall and still hit .343 to be the first rookie and the youngest ballplayer to win the National League batting title. He tied Johnny Mize with 39 doubles, led in triples, runs scored, total bases and slugging average, and they were writing on the sports pages that he might be the new Ty Cobb.

"Dodgers Win On Reiser HR," the headlines used to say. "Reiser Stars As Brooklyn Lengthens Lead."

"Any manager in the National League," Arthur Patterson wrote one day in the New York *Herald Tribune*, "would give up his best man to obtain Pete Reiser. On every bench they're talking about him. Rival players watch him take his cuts during batting practice, announce when he's going to make a throw to the plate or third base during outfield drill. They just whistle their amazement when he scoots down the first base line on an infield dribbler or a well-placed bunt."

He was beaned the first time at Ebbets Field five days after the season started. A sidearm fast ball got away from Ike Pearson of the Phillies, and Pete came to at 11:30 that night in Peck Memorial Hospital.

"I was lying in bed with my uniform on," he told me once, "and I couldn't figure it out. The room was dark, with just a little night light, and then I saw a mirror and I walked over to it and lit the light and I had a black eye and a black streak down the side of my nose. I said to myself: 'What happened to me?' Then I remembered.

"I took a shower and walked around the room, and the next morning the doctor came in. He looked me over, and he said: 'We'll keep you here for five or six more days under observation.' I said: 'Why?' He said: 'You've had a serious head injury. If you tried to get out of bed right now, you'd fall down.' I said: 'If I can get up and walk around this room, can I get out?' The doc said: 'All right, but you won't be able to do it.' "

Pete got out of bed, the doctor standing ready to catch him. He walked around the room. "I've been walkin' the floor all night," Pete said.

The doctor made Pete promise that he wouldn't play ball for a week, but Pete went right to the ball park. He got a seat behind the Brooklyn dugout, and Durocher spotted him.

"How do you feel?" Leo said.

"Not bad," Pete said.

"Get your uniform on," Leo said.

"I'm not supposed to play," Pete said.

"I'm not gonna play you," Leo said. "Just sit on the bench. It'll make our guys feel better to see that you're not hurt."

Pete suited up and went out and sat on the bench. In the eighth inning it was tied, 7–7. The Dodgers had the bases loaded, and there was Ike Pearson again, coming in to relieve.

"Pistol," Leo said to Pete, "get the bat."

In the press box the baseball writers watched Pete. They wanted to see if he'd stand right in there. After a beaning they are all entitled to shy, and many of them do. Pete hit the first pitch into the center-field stands, and Brooklyn won, 11 to 7.

"I could just barely trot around the bases," Pete said when I asked him about it. "I was sure dizzy."

Two weeks later they were playing the Cardinals, and Enos Slaughter hit one and Pete turned in center field and started to run. He made the catch, but he hit his head and his tail bone on that corner near the exit gate.

His head was cut, and when he came back to the bench they also saw blood coming through the seat of his pants. They took him into the clubhouse and pulled his pants down and the doctor put a metal clamp on the cut.

"Just don't slide," he told Pete. "You can get it sewed up after the game."

In August of that year big Paul Erickson was pitching for the Cubs and Pete took another one. Again he woke up in a hospital. The Dodgers were having some pretty good beanball contests with the Cubs that season, and Judge Landis came to see Pete the next day.

"Do you think that man tried to bean you?" he asked Pete.

"No sir," Pete said. "I lost the pitch."

"I was there," Landis said, "and I heard them holler: 'Stick it in his ear.' "

"That was just bench talk," Pete said. "I lost the pitch."

He left the hospital the next morning. The Dodgers were going to St. Louis after the game, and Pete didn't want to be left in Chicago.

Pete always says that the next year, 1942, was the year of his downfall, and the worst of it happened on one play. It was early July and Pete and the Dodgers were tearing the league apart. In a four-game series in Cincinnati he got 19 for 21. In a Sunday double-header in Chicago he went 5 for 5 in the first game, walked three times in the second game and got a hit the one time they pitched to him. He was hitting .381, and they were writing in the papers that he might end up hitting .400.

When they came into St. Louis the Dodgers were leading by ten and a half games. When they took off for Pittsburgh they left three games of that lead and Pete Reiser behind them.

"We were in the twelfth inning, no score, two outs and Slaughter hit it off Whit Wyatt," Pete says. "It was over my head and I took off. I caught it and missed that flagpole by two inches and hit the wall and dropped the ball. I had the instinct to throw it to Peewee Reese, and we just missed gettin' Slaughter at the plate, and they won, 1-0.

"I made one step to start off the field and I woke up the next morning in St. John's Hospital. My head was bandaged, and I had an awful headache."

Dr. Robert Hyland, who was Pete's personal physician, announced to the newspapers that Pete would be out for the rest of the season. "Look, Pete," Hyland told him. "I'm your personal friend. I'm advising you not to play any more baseball this year."

"I don't like hospitals, though," Pete was telling me once, "so after two days I took the bandage off and got up. The room started to spin, but I got dressed and I took off. I snuck out, and I took a train to Pittsburgh and I went to the park.

"Leo saw me and he said: 'Go get your uniform on, Pistol.' I said: 'Not tonight, Skipper.' Leo said: 'Aw, I'm not gonna let you hit. I want these guys to see you. It'll give 'em that little spark they need. Besides, it'll change the pitching plans on that other bench when they see you sittin' here in uniform.' "

In the fourteenth inning the Dodgers had a runner on second and Ken Heintzelman, the left-hander, came in for the Pirates. He walked Johnny Rizzo, and Durocher had run out of pinch hitters.

"Damn," Leo was saying, walking up and down. "I want to win this one. Who can I use? Anybody here who can hit?"

Pete walked up to the bat rack. He pulled out his stick. "You got yourself a hitter," he said to Leo.

He walked up there and hit a line drive over the second baseman's head that was good for three bases. The two runs scored, and Pete rounded first base and collapsed.

"When I woke up I was in a hospital again," he says. "I could just make out that somebody was standin' there and then I saw it was Leo. He said: 'You awake?' I said: 'Yep.' He said: 'By God, we beat 'em! How do you feel?' I said: 'How do you think I feel?' He said: 'Aw, you're better with one leg, and one eye than anybody else I've got.' I said: 'Yeah, and that's the way I'll end up—on one leg and with one eye.'

"I'd say I lost the pennant for us that year," Pete says now, although he still hit .310 for the season. "I was dizzy most of the time and I couldn't see fly balls. I mean balls I could have put in my pocket, I couldn't get near. Once in Brooklyn when Mort Cooper was pitching for the Cards I was seeing two baseballs coming up there. Babe Pinelli was umpiring behind the plate, and a couple of times he stopped the game and asked me if I was all right. So the Cards beat us out the last two days of the season."

The business office of the Kokomo ball club is the dining room of a man named Jim Deets, who sells insurance and is also the business manager of the club. His wife, in addition to keeping house, mothering six small kids, boarding Pete, an outfielder from Venezuela and a shortstop from the Dominican Republic, is also the club secretary.

"How do you feel this morning?" I asked Pete. He was sitting at the dining-room table, in a sweat shirt and a pair of light-brown slacks, typing the game report of the night before to send it to Brooklyn.

"A little better," he said.

Pete has a worn, green 1950 Chevy, and it took us eight and a half hours to get to St. Louis. I'd ask him how the pain in his chest was and he'd say that it wasn't bad or it wasn't so good, and I'd get him to talking again about Durocher or about his time in the Army. Pete played under five managers at Brooklyn, Boston, Pittsburgh and Cleveland, and Durocher is his favorite.

"He has a great mind, and not just for baseball," Pete said. "Once he sat down to play gin with Jack Benny, and after they'd played four cards Leo read Benny's whole hand to him. Benny said: 'How can you do that?' Leo said: 'If you're playin' your cards right, and I give you credit for that, you have to be holding those others.' Benny said: 'I don't want to play with this guy.'

"One spring at Clearwater there was a pool table in a room off the lobby. One night Hugh Casey and a couple of other guys and I were talking with Leo. We said: 'Gee, there's a guy in there and we've been playin' pool with him for a couple of nights, but last night he had a real hot streak.' Leo said: 'How much he take you for?' We figured it out and it was $2,000. Leo said: 'Point him out to me.'

"We went in and pointed the guy out and Leo walked up to him and said: 'Put all your money on the table. We're gonna shoot for it.' The guy said: 'I never play like that.' Leo said: 'You will tonight. Pick your own game.' Leo took him for $4,000, and then he threw him out. Then he paid us back what we'd gone for, and he said: 'Now, let that be a lesson. That guy is a hustler from New York. The next time it happens I won't bail you out.' Leo hadn't had a cue in his hands for years."

It was amazing that they took Pete into the Army. He had wanted to enlist in the Navy, but the doctors looked him over and told him none of the services could accept him. Then his draft board sent him to Jefferson Barracks in the winter of 1943, and the doctors there turned him down.

"I'm sittin' on a bench with the other guys who've been rejected," he was telling me, "and a captain comes in and says: 'Which one of you is Reiser?' I stood up and I said: 'I am.' In front of everybody he said: 'So you're trying to pull a fast one, are you? At a time like this, with a war going on, you came in here under a false name. What do you mean, giving your name as Harold Patrick Reiser? Your name's Pete Reiser, and you're the ballplayer, aren't you?' I said: 'I'm the ballplayer and they call me Pete, but my right name is Harold Patrick Reiser.' The captain says: 'I apologize. Sergeant, fingerprint him. This man is in.'"

They sent him to Fort Riley, Kansas. It was early April and raining and they were on bivouac, and Pete woke up in a hospital. "What happened?" he said.

"You've got pneumonia," the doctor said. "You've been a pretty sick boy for six days. You'll be all right, but we've been looking you over. How did you ever get into this Army?"

"When I get out of the hospital," Pete was telling me, "I'm on the board for a discharge and I'm waitin' around for about a week, and still nobody there knows who I am. All of a sudden one morning a voice comes over the bitch box in the barracks. It says: 'Private Reiser, report to headquarters immediately.' I think: 'Well, I'm out now.'

"I got over there and the colonel wants to see me. I walk in and give my good salute and he says: 'Sit down, Harold.' I sit down and he says: 'Your name really isn't Harold, is it?' I say: 'Yes, it is, sir.' He says: 'But that isn't what they call you where you're well known, is it? You're Pete Reiser the ballplayer, aren't you?' I say: 'Yes, sir.' He says: 'I thought so. Now, I've got your discharge papers right there, but we've got a pretty good ball club and we'd like you on it. We'll make a deal. You say nothing, and you won't have to do anything but play ball. How about it?' I said: 'Suppose I don't want to stay in?'

"He picked my papers up off his desk," Pete was saying, "and he tore 'em right up in my face. I can still hear that 'zip' when he tore 'em. He said: 'You see, you have no choice.'

"Then he picked up the phone and said something and in a minute a general came in. I jumped up and the colonel said: 'Don't bother to salute, Pete.' Then he said to the general: 'Major, this is Pete Reiser, the great Dodger ballplayer. He was up for a medical discharge, but he's decided to stay here and play ball for us.'

"So, the general says: 'My, what a patriotic thing for you to do, young man. That's wonderful. Wonderful.' I'm sittin' there, and when the general goes out the colonel says: 'That major, he's all right.' I said: 'But he's a general. How come you call him a major?' The colonel says: 'Well, in the regular Army he's a major and I'm a full colonel. The only reason I don't outrank him now is that I've got heart trouble. He knows it, but I never let him forget it. I always call him major.' I thought: 'What kind of an Army am I in?' "

Joe Gantenbein, the Athletics' outfielder, and George Scharein, the Phillies' infielder, were on that team with Pete, and they won the state and national semipro titles. By the time the season was over, however, the order came down to hold up all discharges.

The next season there were 17 major-league ballplayers on the Fort Riley club, and they played four nights a week for the war workers in Wichita. Pete hit a couple of walls, and the team made such a joke of the national semipro tournament that an order came down from Washington to break up the club.

"Considering what a lot of guys did in the war," Pete says, "I had no complaints, but five times I was up for discharge, and each time something happened. From Riley they sent me to Camp Livingston. From there they sent me to New York Special Services for twelve hours and I end up in Camp Lee, Virginia, in May of 1945.

"The first one I meet there is the general. He says: 'Reiser, I saw you on the list and I just couldn't pass you up.' I said: 'What about my discharge?' He says: 'That will have to wait. I have a lot of celebrities down here, but I want a good baseball team.' "

Johnny Lindell, of the Yankees, and Dave Philley, of the White Sox, were on the club and Pete played left field. Near the end of the season he went after a foul fly for the third out of the last inning, and he went right through a temporary wooden fence and rolled down a 25-foot embankment.

"I came to in the hospital, with a dislocated right shoulder," he says, "and the general came over to see me and he said: 'That was one of the greatest displays of courage I've ever seen, to ignore your future in baseball just to win a ball game for Camp Lee.' I said: 'Thanks.'

"Now it's November and the war is over, but they're still shippin' guys out, and I'm on the list to go. I report to the overseas major, and he looks at my papers and says: 'I can't send you overseas. With everything that's wrong with you, you shouldn't even be in this Army. I'll have you out in three hours.' In three hours, sure enough, I've got those papers in my hand, stamped, and I'm startin' out the door. Runnin' up to me comes a Red Cross guy. He says: 'I can get you some pretty good pension benefits for the physical and mental injuries you've sustained.' I said: 'You can?' He said: 'Yes, you're entitled to them.' I said: 'Good. You get 'em. You keep 'em. I'm goin' home.' "

When we got to St. Louis that night I drove Pete to his house and the next morning I picked him up and drove him to see the heart specialist. He was in there for two hours, and when he came out he was walking slower than ever.

"No good," he said. "I have to go to the hospital for five days for observation."

"What does he think?"

"He says I'm done puttin' on that uniform. I'll have to get a desk job."

Riding to the hospital I wondered if that heart specialist knew who he was tying to that desk job. In 1946, the year he came out of the Army, Pete led the league when he stole 34 bases, 13 more than the runner-up Johnny Hopp of the Braves. He also set a major-league record that still stands, when he stole home eight times.

"Nine times," he said once. "In Chicago I stole home and Magerkurth hollered: 'You're out!' Then he dropped his voice and he said: '_____, I missed it.' He'd already had his thumb in the air. I had nine out of nine."

I suppose somebody will beat that some day, but he'll never top the way Pete did it. That was the year he knocked himself out again trying for a diving catch, dislocated his left shoulder, ripped the muscles in his left leg and broke his left ankle.

"Whitey Kurowski hit one in the seventh inning at Ebbets Field," he was telling me. "I dove for it and woke up in the clubhouse. I was in Peck Memorial for four days. It really didn't take much to knock me out in those days. I was comin' apart all over. When I dislocated my shoulder they popped it back in, and Leo said: 'Hell, you'll be all right. You don't throw with it anyway.' "

That was the year the Dodgers tied with the Cardinals for the pennant and dropped the play-off. Pete wasn't there for those two games. He was in Peck Memorial again.

"I'd pulled a Charley horse in my left leg," Pete was saying. "It's the last two weeks of the season, and I'm out for four days. We've got the winning run on third, two outs in the ninth and Leo sends me up. He says: 'If you don't hit it good, don't run and hurt your leg.'

"The first pitch was a knockdown and, when I ducked, the ball hit the bat and went down the third base line, as beautiful a bunt as you've ever seen. Well, Ebbets Field is jammed. Leo has said: 'Don't run.' But this is a big game. I take off for first, and we win and I've ripped the muscles from my ankle to my hip. Leo says: 'You shouldn't have done it.'

"Now it's the last three days of the season and we're a game ahead of the Cards and we're playin' the Phillies in Brooklyn. Leo says to me: 'It's now or never. I don't think we can win it without you.' The first two up are outs and I single to right. There's Charley Dressen, coachin' on third, with the steal sign. I start to get my lead, and a pitcher named Charley Schanz is workin' and he throws an ordinary lob over to first. My leg is stiff and I slide and my heel spike catches the bag and I hear it snap.

"Leo comes runnin' out. He says: 'Come on. You're all right.' I said: 'I think it's broken.' He says: 'It ain't stickin' out.' They took me to Peck Memorial, and it was broken."

We went to St. Luke's Hospital in St. Louis. In the main office they told Pete to go over to a desk where a gray-haired, semistout woman was sitting at a typewriter. She started to book Pete in, typing his answer on the form. "What is your occupation, Mr. Reiser?" she said.

"Baseball," Pete said.

"Have you ever been hospitalized before?"

"Yes," Pete said.

In 1946 the Dodgers played an exhibition game in Springfield, Missouri. When the players got off the train there was a young radio announcer there, and he was grabbing them one at a time and asking them where they thought they'd finish that year.

"In first place," Reese and Casey and Dixie Walker and the rest were saying. "On top" . . . "We'll win it."

"And here comes Pistol Pete Reiser!" the announcer said. "Where do you think you'll finish this season, Pete?"

"In Peck Memorial Hospital," Pete said.

After the 1946 season Brooklyn changed the walls at Ebbets Field. They added boxes, cutting 40 feet off left field and dropping center field from 420 to 390 feet. Pete had made a real good start that season in center, and on June 5 the Dodgers were leading the Pirates by three runs in the sixth inning when Culley Rikard hit one.

"I made my turn and ran," Pete says, "and, where I thought I still had that thirty feet, I didn't."

"The crowd," Al Laney wrote the next day in the New York *Herald Tribune,* "which watched silently while Reiser was being carried away, did not know that he had held onto the ball . . . Rikard circled the bases, but Butch Henline, the umpire, who ran to Reiser, found the ball still in Reiser's glove. . . . Two outs were posted on the scoreboard after play was resumed. Then the crowd let out a tremendous roar."

In the Brooklyn clubhouse the doctor called for a priest, and the Last Rites of the Church were administered to Pete. He came to, but lapsed into unconsciousness again and woke up at 3 A.M. in Peck Memorial.

For eight days he couldn't move. After three weeks they let him out, and he made that next western trip with the Dodgers. In Pittsburgh he was working out in the outfield before the game when Clyde King, chasing a fungo, ran into him and Pete woke up in the clubhouse.

"I went back to the Hotel Schenley and lay down," he says. "After the game I got up and had dinner with Peewee. We were sittin' on the porch, and I scratched my head and I felt a lump there about as big as half a golf ball. I told Peewee to feel it and he said: 'Gosh!' I said: 'I don't think that's supposed to be like that.' He said: 'Hell, no.'"

Pete went up to Rickey's room and Rickey called his pilot and had Pete flown to Johns Hopkins in Baltimore. They operated on him for a blood clot.

"You're lucky," the doctor told him. "If it had moved just a little more you'd have been gone."

Pete was unable to hold even a pencil. He had double vision and, when he tried to take a single step, he became dizzy. He stayed for three weeks and then went home for almost a month.

"It was August," he says, "and Brooklyn was fightin' for another pennant. I thought if I could play the last two months it might make the difference, so I went back to Johns Hopkins. The doctor said: 'You've made a remarkable recovery.' I said: 'I want to play.' He said: 'I can't okay that. The slightest blow on the head can kill you.' "

Pete played. He worked out for four days, pinch hit a couple of times and then, in the Polo Grounds, made a diving catch in left field. They carried him off, and in the clubhouse he was unable to recognize anyone.

Pete was still having dizzy spells when the Dodgers went into the 1947 Series against the Yankees. In the third game he walked in the first inning, got the steal sign and, when he went into second, felt his right ankle snap. At the hospital they found it was broken.

"Just tape it, will you?" Pete said.

"I want to put a cast on it," the doctor said.

"If you do," Pete said, "they'll give me a dollar-a-year contract next season."

The next day he was back on the bench. Bill Bevens was pitching for the Yankees and, with two out in the ninth, it looked like he was going to pitch the first no-hitter in World Series history.

"Aren't you going to volunteer to hit?" Burt Shotton, who was managing Brooklyn, said to Pete.

Al Gionfriddo was on first and Bucky Harris, who was managing the Yankees, ordered Pete walked. Eddie Miksis ran for him, and when Cookie Lavagetto hit that double, the two runs scored and Brooklyn won, 3–2.

"The next day," Pete says, "the sports writers were second-guessing Harris for putting me on when I represented the winning run. Can you imagine what they'd have said if they knew I had a broken ankle?"

At the end of that season Rickey had the outfield walls at Ebbets Field padded with one-inch foam rubber for Pete, but he never hit them again. He had headaches most of the time and played little. Then he was traded to Boston, and in two seasons there he hit the wall a couple of times. Twice his left shoulder came out while he was making diving catches. Pittsburgh picked Pete up in 1951, and the next year he played into July with Cleveland and that was the end of it.

Between January and September of 1953, Pete dropped $40,000 in the used-car business in St. Louis, and then he got a job in a lumber mill for $100 a week. In the winter of 1955 he wrote Brooklyn asking for a part-time job as a scout, and on March 1, Buzzy Bavasi, the Dodger vice-president, called him on the phone.

"How would you like a manager's job?" Buzzy said.

"I'll take it," Pete said.

"I haven't even told you where it is. It's Thomasville, Georgia, in Class D."

"I don't care," Pete said. "I'll take it."

At Vero Beach that spring, Mike Gaven wrote a piece about Pete in the New York *Journal American.*

"Even in the worn gray uniform of the Class D Thomasville, Georgia, club," Mike wrote, "Pete Reiser looks, acts and talks like a big leaguer. The Dodgers pitied Pete when they saw him starting his come-back effort after not having handled a ball for two and a half years. They lowered their heads when they saw him in a chow line with a lot of other bushers, but the old Pistol held his head high. . . ."

The next spring, Sid Friedlander, of the New York *Post,* saw Pete at Vero and wrote a column about him managing Kokomo. The last thing I saw about him in the New York papers was a small item out of Tipton, Indiana, saying that the bus carrying the Kokomo team had collided with a car and Pete was in a hospital in Kokomo with a back injury.

"Managing," Pete was saying in that St. Louis hospital, "you try to find out how your players are thinking. At Thomasville one night one of my kids made a bad throw. After the game I said to him: 'What were you thinking while that ball was coming to you?' He said: 'I was saying to myself that I hoped I could make a good throw.' I said: 'Sit down.' I tried to explain to him the way you have to think. You know how I used to think?"

"Yes," I said, "but you tell me."

"I was always sayin': 'Hit it to me. Just hit it to me. I'll make the catch. I'll make the throw.' When I was on base I was always lookin' over and sayin': 'Give me the steal sign. Give me the sign. Let me go.' That's the way you have to think."

"Pete," I said, "now that it's all over, do you ever think that if you hadn't played it as hard as you did, there's no telling how great you might have been or how much money you might have made?"

"Never," Pete said. "It was my way of playin'. If I hadn't played that way I wouldn't even have been whatever I was. God gave me those legs and the speed, and when they took me into the walls that's the way it had to be. I couldn't play any other way."

A technician came in with an electrocardiograph. She was a thin, dark-haired woman and she set it up by the bed and attached one of the round metal disks to Pete's left wrist and started to attach another to his left ankle.

"Aren't you kind of young to be having pains in your chest?" she said.

"I've led a fast life," Pete said.

On the way back to New York I kept thinking how right Pete was. To tell a man who is this true that there is another way for him to do it is to speak a lie. You cannot ask him to change his way of going, because it makes him what he is.

Three days after I got home I had a message to call St. Louis. I heard the phone ring at the other end and Pete answered. "I'm out!" he said.

"Did they let you out, or did you sneak out again?" I said.

"They let me out," he said. "It's just a strained heart muscle, I guess. My heart itself is all right."

"That's wonderful."

"I can manage again. In a couple of days I can go back to Kokomo."

If his voice had been higher he would have sounded like a kid at Christmas.

"What else did they say?" I said.

"Well, they say I have to take it easy."

"Do me a favor," I said.

"What?"

"Take their advice. This time, please take it easy."

"I will," he said. "I'll take it easy."

If he does it will be the first time.

AUTOBIOGRAPHY

The Day I Batted Against Castro

DON HOAK *with* MYRON COPE

CUBA WAS an American baseball player's paradise when I played there in the winter of 1950–51. Later, as a major-league third baseman, I became one of the better-paid ballplayers, but I was just an $800-a-month minor leaguer when I went to Cuba.

There the Cienfuegos club paid me $1,000 a month plus $350 a month for expenses. I had a cottage apartment at the elegant Club Nautico on the beach near Havana. The rent, thanks to a reduced rate obtained by the owner of our team, was $150. The $150 included:

(a) A spacious living room with floor-to-ceiling windows; two bed-rooms; two baths; a screened patio in the rear; a dazzling flower garden out front.

(b) A fine old Cuban lady named Eeta, who did my housekeeping and cooking. (I had to pay her bus fare.)

(c) A guard to watch over my apartment.

Late at night, after the baseball games were over, I fished off the coral reefs for yellowtails and eels. By day, I went scuba-diving for lobster or napped on the beach or walked across the road to the golf course to shoot a round. Cuba was the best place in the world to play baseball.

But even in those days, the students at the University of Havana were politically restless. At the Havana ball park they'd frequently inter-rupt our games by staging demonstrations on the field.

They would pour down from the stands and parade across the field carrying banners. They would set off firecrackers and blow horns and shout slogans for ten or fifteen minutes and then go back to their seats. The dictator, Fulgencio Batista, tolerated them, perhaps because he did not consider them a serious threat to his power. His police allowed them to spend their energies. As a matter of fact, Batista himself sometimes witnessed the demonstrations, for he attended many games. Surrounded by bodyguards, he would sit through the commotion with arms folded across his chest and just a trace of a smile at the corner of his lips.

Another regular customer at the park was Fidel Castro. He had just received his law degree from the university, but he remained a well-known and flamboyant leader of the students. As a baseball fan, he belonged in the nut category.

I knew Castro's face well and I suspected he was something of a wild man because of the company he kept. He often came to the park with a man named Pedro Formanthael, who played right field for the Maria-nao club. Pedro was about forty but an excellent ballplayer. He stood no more than five feet ten but was built very solidly and could hit with power. He wore a great mustache and had a temper that was just as black. He always carried a pistol a foot long, and I wondered how he fit it into his jacket. Anyhow, he and Castro were great pals.

Our Cienfuegos club was playing Pedro Formanthael's team in the Havana park the night I came face to face with Castro.

It was approximately the fifth inning, as I recall, when the firecrack-ers went off. Up went the banners. The horns blared, and down from the stands came the students—perhaps 300 of them. As fate would have it, I had just stepped into the batter's box when all hell broke loose. "Here we go again," I thought as I stepped out of the box to await order.

But on this night the demonstration took an unexpected turn.

Castro marched straight out to the mound and seized a glove and ball from the Marianao pitcher, a tall Cuban whose name I can't recall. The pitcher shrugged and walked off the field.

Castro then toed the rubber, and as he did so his appearance on the mound was so ridiculous that I cannot forget a single detail of it. He wore no glasses then, but he did have a beard—a funny little beard at the point of his chin that he obviously had taken great care to groom. He was tall and rather skinny.

He wore a long-sleeved white shirt—a type of shirt many Cubans favored. It had pleats like a formal dress shirt and a square bottom which was worn outside the trousers. Castro also wore tight black slacks and black suede shoes with pointed toes. His footwear was almost dandy, and as I see pictures of today's Castro in army fatigues and combat boots I am amused by the contrast. However, I don't suppose a guy in black suede shoes would stand very well at the head of a people's revolution.

Anyhow, Castro put on the glove and ordered the Marianao catcher —a Cuban veteran named Mike Guerra, who had played for the Washington Senators and Philadelphia Athletics—to catch his repertoire. Castro wound up with a great windmill flourish, whirling his pitching arm overhead about six times. Obviously he considered himself an ace hurler, as the sportswriters say. Left-handers as a breed are eccentric, but Castro, a right-hander, looked kookier than any southpaw I have known.

I figured, "Let him have his fun," and watched him throw half a dozen pitches. The crowd was in an uproar. The students, ranged along the foul lines, were dancing with glee.

Suddenly Castro stopped throwing, glared at me, and barked the Spanish equivalent of "Batter up!"

I looked at the umpire but he only shrugged. "What the hell," I said, and stepped into the batter's box. I was not particularly anxious to defy Castro and his mob, because I knew the Latin temper to be an explosive force. Also, Castro's gunslinging buddy, Pedro Formanthael, was throwing me dirty looks from right field.

Castro gave me the hipper-dipper windup and cut loose with a curve. Actually, it was a pretty fair curve. It had a sharp inside break to it—and it came within an inch of breaking my head.

"Ball one!" said the umpire. Castro marched forward a few paces from the mound and stared daggers at him. The students expressed considerable displeasure. The umpire suggested to me that I had better start swinging or he would be compelled to call me out on strikes.

But I glanced at those students on the foul line and thought, "If I swing hard I'm liable to line a foul down there and kill somebody." I had to think fast because Castro, his floppy shirt billowing in the evening breeze, was already into his windup—a *super* hipper-dipper windup this time. I thought he would take off for the moon.

Finally he cut loose with a fast ball—a good fast ball, a regular bullet.

It came at me in the vicinity of the shins. Fortunately, I was a pretty fair bat handler, so I came around on the pitch with a short golf stroke and lofted a pop-foul over the heads of the students on the third-base line. I figured the best thing to do was to tap soft fouls into the stands.

Castro's third pitch was another fast ball. He really zinged it. It scorched its way straight for my eyeballs. I leaned away, gave my bat a quick lurch, and managed another pop-foul into the stands.

Castro had two strikes on me and he was stomping pompously around the mound as though he had just conquered Washington, D.C.

At that point, however, a new factor entered the picture. The Hoak temper.

I've got a wee trace of Comanche blood, you see, and I imagine I have a temper that can match any Latin's from Havana to Lima. To me, baseball is war. In 1956 I played winter ball in the Dominican Republic where I pleased the fans by hitting .394 and sliding into bases like a maniac. I am known there, even to this day, as Crazy Horse. When I played for Pittsburgh a broadcaster there named me The Tiger. Mind you, I don't care to fight Castro and 300 Cubans under any circumstances, but if I have a bat in my hands I know I won't be the only guy to get hurt.

So I turned to the umpire and announced, "I've got a major-league career and big money and good times ahead of me, and I am not going to stand here and let some silly punk in a pleated shirt throw at my skull. Now just get that idiot out of the game."

Here, still another factor entered the picture. The *umpire's* temper.

His name was Miastri and he was a fine umpire. He was such a firebrand that when he threw a player out of a game he often fined him on the spot, and when he fined a guy he would turn around and look up to the press box and announced the amount of the fine with vigorous hand signals. And now he had decided he, too, had had a bellyful of Castro.

He marched over to the *policía,* who were lazily enjoying the fun from the grandstands, and ordered them in no uncertain terms to clear the field. Down they came from the stands, riot clubs brandished at shoulder level.

A knot of cops moved briskly on pitcher Castro. Briefly, he made a show of standing his ground, but the cops shoved him off the mound. He shuffled meekly toward the third-base grandstands, like an impudent boy who has been cuffed by the teacher and sent to stand in the corner.

My final memory of him is one that somehow strikes me funny to this day. As he crossed the third-base line I happened to look at his shoes. He had dust on his black suede shoes.

Looking back, I think that with a little work on his control, Fidel Castro would have made a better pitcher than a prime minister.

THE TITLE to the ensuing article, which appeared in *Sports Illustrated* magazine, is most apt. Mr. Rickey and The Game go together.

Mr. Rickey and The Game

GERALD HOLLAND

"I AM ASKED to speak of the game," said Branch Rickey, restating a question that had been put to him, "I am asked to reflect upon my own part in it. At the age of 73, on the eve of a new baseball season, I am importuned to muse aloud, to touch upon those things that come first to mind."

Seated in his office at Forbes Field, the home of the Pittsburgh Pirates, Branch Rickey nibbled at an unlighted cigarette and sniffed the proposition like a man suddenly come upon a beef stew simmering on a kitchen stove.

Abruptly he threw himself back in his chair and clasped his hands over his head and stared up at the ceiling. He looked ten years younger than his actual age. Thanks to a high-protein, hamburger-for-breakfast diet, he was thirty pounds lighter than he had been three months before. His complexion was ruddy and his thick brown hair showed only a little gray at the temples. Now his great bushy eyebrows shot up and he prayed aloud:

"Lord make me humble, make me grateful . . . make me *tolerant!*"

Slowly he came down from the ceiling and put his elbows on the desk. Unconsciously, perhaps, a hand strayed across the desk to a copy of *Bartlett's Familiar Quotations*. The hand was that of an old-time catcher, big, strong and gnarled. He turned slowly in his chair and swept his eyes over the little gallery of framed photographs on the wall. Among them were George Sisler, Rickey's first great discovery, one of the greatest of the left-handed hitters, now at work down the hall as chief of Pittsburgh scouts; Rogers Hornsby, the game's greatest right-handed hitter, a betting man for whom Rickey once dared the wrath of baseball's high commissioner, Kenesaw Mountain Landis; Jackie Robinson, chosen by Rickey as the man to break down baseball's color line; Honus Wagner, the immortal Pittsburgh shortstop, now past eighty, at this moment growing weaker by the day at his sister's house across town; Charley Barrett, the old Cardinal scout, Rickey's right arm in the days when St. Louis was too poor to make a Southern training trip.

Turning back to his desk, Rickey grimaced and then spoke rapidly, almost harshly:

"Of my career in baseball, let us say first of all that there have been the appearances of hypocrisy. Here we have the Sunday school mollycoddle, apparently professing a sort of public virtue in refraining from playing or watching a game of baseball on Sunday. And yet at the same time he is not above accepting money from a till replenished by Sunday baseball."

He paused and bit the unlighted cigarette in two. He dropped his voice:

"A deeply personal thing. Something not to be exploited, not to be put forward protestingly at every whisper of criticism. No, a deeply personal thing. A man's promise, a promise to his mother. Not involving a condemnation of baseball on Sunday, nor of others who might desire to play it or watch it on Sunday. Simply one man's promise—and it might as well have been a promise not to attend the theater or band concerts in the park."

His eyes went around the room and were held for a moment by the blackboard that lists the players on the fifteen ball clubs in the Pittsburgh farm system. His lips moved and the words sounded like, "But is the boy *ready* for New Orleans?" Then, with a quick movement, he leaned across the desk and waggled an accusing finger.

"Hell's fire!" he exploded. "The Sunday school mollycoddle, the bluenose, the prohibitionist has been a *liberal!* No, no, no—this has nothing to do with Jackie Robinson, I contend that there was no element of liberalism there. I will say something about that perhaps, but now the plain everyday things—the gambling, the drinking, the . . . other things. I submit that I have been a liberal about *them!*"

He was silent. He did not mention or even hint at the names of managers who won major league pennants after everyone but Branch Rickey had quit on them; nor the men who gladly acknowledge that they are still in baseball because of the confidence Rickey placed in them.

The telephone with the private number rang. Branch Rickey picked it up and traded southpaw Paul La Palme to the St. Louis Cardinals for Ben Wade, a relief pitcher. "You announce it," he said into the phone, "and just say La Palme for Wade and an unannounced amount of cash. We'll talk about a Class A ballplayer later. Anybody but a catcher. I don't need a catcher at that level." He put down the phone and his eyes twinkled. "Later in the day I may make a deal with Brooklyn," he said, "if I can get up the nerve." As things turned out, either he did not get up the nerve or he was unable to interest the Flatbush authorities.

He whirled around in his chair and stared out the window. He could see, if he was noticing, the end of a little street that runs down from Hotel Schenley to the ball park. It is called Pennant Place, a reminder of happier days for the Pittsburgh fans, now so ashamed of their eighth-place Pirates that only a few of them show up at the ball park—even for double-headers.

Rickey ran both hands furiously through his thick hair.

"A man trained for the law," he said, "devotes his entire life and all his energies to something so cosmically unimportant as a game."

He examined minutely what was left of his cigarette. Carefully, he extracted a single strand of tobacco and looked at it closely before letting it fall to the floor. Usually he chews unlighted cigars, but this day it was a cigarette.

He began to laugh.

"The law," he chuckled, "I might have stayed in the law. I do not laugh at the great profession itself. I am laughing at a case I had one time —the only case I ever had as a full-time practicing attorney. I had gone to Boise, Idaho from Saranac to try to gain back my strength after recovering from tuberculosis. I got an office and hung out a shingle and waited for the clients. None came. Finally, I was in court one day and the judge appointed me attorney for a man who was being held on a charge the newspapers used to describe as white slavery.

"I was apprehensive, but at last I summoned enough courage to go over to the jail and see my client. Oh, he was a horrible creature. I can see him now, walking slowly up to the bars and looking me up and down with contempt. He terrified me. I began to shake like a leaf. After a minute he said, 'Who the hell are you?'

"I tried to draw myself up a little and then I said, 'Sir, my name is Branch Rickey. The court has appointed me your attorney and I would like to talk to you.' He looked me up and down again and then spat at my feet. Then he delivered what turned out to be the final words of our association. He said, 'Get the hell out of here!' "

Rickey threw back his head.

"I not only got out of there," he said, "I got out of the state of Idaho and went to St. Louis and took a job with the St. Louis Browns. I intended to stay in baseball for just one year. But when the year was up, Mr. Robert Lee Hedges, the owner, offered me a raise. There was a new baby at our house. And not much money, new or old. So I was a moral coward. I chose to stay with the game."

Rickey thought a moment.

"I might have gone into politics," he said. "As recently as fourteen years ago, there was the offer of a nomination for a political office. A governorship. The governorship, in fact, of Missouri. I was tempted, flattered. But then, as I ventured a little into the political arena, I was appalled by my own ignorance of politics. But the party leaders were persuasive. They pledged me the full support of the regular party organization. They said they could not prevent any Billy Jumpup from filing, but no Billy Jumpup would have the organization's backing. It is an overwhelming thing to be offered such prospects of reaching high office. I thought it over carefully and then tentatively agreed to run, on condition that another man—a seasoned campaigner—run on the ticket with me. He said that was utterly impossible. He invited me to go with him to New York and talk to Mr. Herbert Hoover about the situation in Missouri. But afterward I still was unable to persuade my friend to run. He was Arthur Hyde, Secretary of Agriculture under Mr. Hoover. Later I learned to my sorrow the reason for Mr. Hyde's decision. He was even then mortally ill. So, regretfully, I asked that my name be withdrawn. The man who ran in my place was elected and then went on to the United States Senate.

"So, conceivably, I might have been a governor. Instead, I chose to stay with the game."

Rickey made elaborate gestures of straightening the papers on his desk.

"A life of public service," he said, peering over his glasses, "versus a life devoted to a game that boys play with a ball and bat."

He turned and picked up a baseball from a bookcase shelf.

"This ball," he said, holding it up.

"This symbol. Is it worth a man's whole life?"

There was just time for another mussing of the hair before the phone rang again.

"Pooh," said Rickey into the phone after a moment. "Three poohs. Poohbah." He hung up.

"I was listening last night to one of the television interview programs," he said. "Senator Knowland was being interrogated. It was a discussion on a high level and the questions involved matters affecting all of us and all the world. I was listening intently and then I heard the senator say, 'Well, I think the Administration has a pretty good batting average.'"

Rickey blew out his cheeks and plucked a shred of tobacco from his lips.

"It must have been a full minute later," he went on, "and the questions had gone on to other things when I sat straight up. Suddenly I realized that to answer a somewhat difficult question this United States senator had turned naturally to the language of the game. And this language, this phrase 'a pretty good batting average,' had said exactly what he wanted to say. He had not intended to be frivolous. The reporters did not smile as though he had made a joke. They accepted the answer in the language of the game as perfectly proper. It was instantly recognizable to them. I dare say it was recognizable even in London."

He frowned, thinking hard. Then his face lit up again.

"The game invades our language!" he exclaimed. "Now, the editorial page of *The New York Times* is a serious forum, not ordinarily given to levity. Yet at the height of the controversy between the Army and Senator McCarthy, there was the line on this dignified editorial page, 'Senator McCarthy—a good fast ball, but no control.'"

Rickey slapped his thigh and leaned over the desk.

"Now, didn't that tell the whole story in a sentence?"

He waved an arm, granting himself the point.

He cherished his remnant of a cigarette.

"A man was telling me the other day," he went on, "he said he was walking through Times Square in New York one blistering day last summer. The temperature stood at 100° and the humidity made it almost unbearable. This man happened to fall in behind three postmen walking together. Their shirts were wringing wet and their mailbags were heavily laden. It struck this man that these postmen might well be irritable on such a day and, since he saw that they were talking animatedly, he drew closer so that he might hear what they were saying. He expected, of course, that they would be complaining bitterly of their dull drab jobs on this abominable day. But when he had come close enough to hear them, what were they talking about with such spirit and relish?"

He paused for effect, then with a toss of his head, he exploded:

"Leo Durocher and the New York Giants!"

Carefully, he put down his cigarette butt. Then he leaned back and rubbed his eyes with the back of his fists. He tore furiously at his hair and half swallowed a yawn.

"Mrs. Rickey and I," he said, "sat up until two o'clock this morning playing hearts."

He straightened the papers on his desk and said as an aside: "I contend it is the most scientific card game in the world."

He searched the ceiling for the point he was developing, found it and came down again.

"The three postmen, heavily laden on a hot, miserable day, yet able to find a happy, common ground in their discussion of this game of baseball. And in their free time, in their hours of leisure, if they had no other interest to turn to, still there was the game to bring color and excitement and good wholesome interest into their lives."

He took up the fragment of paper and tobacco that was left of the cigarette as though it were a precious jewel.

"Leisure," he said, sending his eyebrows aloft, "is a hazardous thing. Here in America we do not yet have a leisure class that knows what to do with it. Leisure can produce something fine. It may also produce something evil. Hell's fire! Leisure can produce a great symphony, a great painting, a great book."

He whirled around to the window and peered out at Pennant Place. Then, turning back like a pitcher who has just cased the situation at second base, he let go hard.

"Gee!" he cried. "Leisure can also produce a great dissipation! Leisure can be idleness and idleness can drive a man to his lowest!"

He recoiled, as from a low man standing at the side of his desk.

"Idleness is the worst thing in this world. Idleness is doing nothing and thinking of wrong things to do. Idleness is the evil that lies behind the juvenile delinquency that alarms us all. It's the most damnable thing that can happen to a kid—to have nothing to do."

He put the tattered cigarette butt in his mouth and spoke around it.

"The game that gives challenge to our youth points the way to our salvation. The competitive spirit, that's the all-important thing. The stultifying thing in this country is the down-pressure on competition, the something-for-nothing philosophy, the do-as-little-as-you-can creed— these are the most devastating influences today. This thinking is the kind that undermines a man's character and can undermine the national character as well."

He studied his shreds of cigarette with the deliberation of a diamond cutter.

"Labor and toil," he intoned, "by the sweat of thy brow shalt thou earn thy bread. Labor and toil—and something else. A joy in work, a zest. Zest, that is the word. Who are the great ballplayers of all time? The ones with zest. Ty Cobb. Willie Mays. The man down the hall, one of the very greatest, George Sisler. Dizzy Dean. Pepper Martin. We have one coming back to us this year here at Pittsburgh. Dick Groat. He has it. Highly intelligent, another Lou Boudreau, the same kind of hitter. He has it. Zest."

Rickey smiled. "Dick Groat will be one of the great ones. There will be others this year. We have 110 boys coming out of service, 475 players under contract on all our clubs. A total of $496,000 invested in player bonuses. There will be other good prospects for the Pirates among these boys. This ball club of ours will come in time. No promises for this year, but in '56, I think, yes."

He turned to look down the street to Pennant Place, then added: "A *contending* team in '56—at least that."

(At the barbershop in Hotel Schenley it is related that Rickey's defense of his eighth-place ball club is considerably less detailed. "Patience!" he cries, anticipating the hecklers as he enters the shop.)

The door opened and Harold Roettger, Rickey's assistant, entered the room. A round-faced, studious-looking man, Roettger has been with Rickey since the old St. Louis Cardinal days. He was in the grip of a heavy cold.

"Do you remember a boy named Febbraro?" he asked, sniffling, "in the Provincial League?"

"Febbraro, Febbraro," said Rickey, frowning. "A pitcher. I saw him work in a night game."

"That's the boy," said Roettger, wiping his eyes. "He's been released."

"Aha," said Rickey, "yes, I remember the boy well. Shall we sign him?"

"We ought to talk about it," said Roettger, fighting a sneeze.

"Harold," said Rickey, "Richardson [Tommy Richardson, president of the Eastern League] is coming down for a meeting tomorrow. I wish you could be there. I devoutly wish you were not ill."

"I, too, devoutly wish I were not ill," said Roettger. "I'll go home now and maybe I'll be ready for the meeting."

"Please try not to be ill tomorrow," said Rickey. "I desperately need you at the meeting."

"I will try very hard," said Roettger, "and will you think about Febbraro?"

"I will," said Rickey. "Go home now, Harold, and take care of yourself."

(Later, Roettger recovered from his cold and signed Febbraro for Williamsport in the Eastern League.)

As Roettger left, Rickey searched for the thread of his soliloquy.

"Hornsby," he said suddenly, "Rogers Hornsby, a man with zest for the game. And Leo, of course.

"Leo Durocher has come a long way, off the field as well as on. A quick mind, a brilliant mind, an indomitable spirit. A rugged ballplayer —and I like rugged ballplayers. But when he came to St. Louis, Leo was in trouble. No fewer than 32 creditors were breathing down his neck, suing or threatening to sue. An impossible situation. I proposed that I go to his creditors and arrange for weekly payments on his debts. This meant a modest allowance of spending money for Leo himself. But he agreed.

"There were other matters to be straightened out. Leo's associates at the time were hardly desirable ones. But he was not the kind of man to take kindly to any criticism of his friends. I thought a lot about Leo's associations, but I didn't see what I could do about them.

"Then one day during the winter I received a call from the United States Naval Academy at Annapolis. The Academy needed a baseball coach and they asked if I could recommend a man. I said I thought I could and would let them know.

"I knew my man. But I didn't dare tell him right away. Instead, I called his wife [Durocher was then married to Grace Dozier, a St. Louis fashion designer] and asked her to drop in at the office. When she arrived, I told her that I intended to recommend Leo as baseball coach at the Naval Academy.

"She looked at me a moment. Then she said, 'Would they take Leo?' I said they would if I recommended him. Then I told her I proposed to get a copy of the Naval Academy manual. I said I knew that if I handed it to Leo myself, he was quite likely to throw it back in my face. But if she were to put it in his hands, he might agree to look it over. Mrs. Durocher thought again. Then she said, 'Get the manual.' "

(Rickey has a habit of presenting ballplayers with what he considers to be worth-while reading. When Pee Wee Reese was made captain of the Dodgers, Rickey sent him Eisenhower's *Crusade in Europe*.)

"When I told Leo," Rickey continued, "he was stunned and un-believing, then enormously but quietly pleased. I told him that I would arrange for him to report late for spring training. I made it clear that he was to decline any payment for his services. Treading softly, I mentioned that the boys he would be coaching were the finest our country had to offer. I suggested gently that any leader of such boys would, of course, have to be letter perfect in his conduct. Leo didn't blow up. He just nodded his head.

"When he reported to spring training camp, he was bursting with pride. He showed me a wrist watch the midshipmen had given him. He said, 'Mr. Rickey, I did it, I did it!'

"I said, 'You did half of it, Leo.'

" 'What do you mean, half!' he demanded.

" 'To be a complete success in this undertaking, Leo, you must be invited back. If they ask you back for next season, then you may be sure you have done the job well.' "

Rickey smiled.

"They did invite him back," he said. "And this time the midshipmen gave him a silver service. He had done the job—the whole job—and I rather think that this experience was a big turning point for Leo. It lifted him into associations he had never known before and he came away with increased confidence and self-assurance and, I am quite sure, a greater measure of self-respect."

(Years later, just before Leo Durocher was suspended from baseball for a year by Commissioner A. B. Chandler, Rickey called his staff to-gether in the Brooklyn Dodgers' offices to say of his manager: "Leo is down. But we are going to stick by Leo. We are going to stick by Leo until hell freezes over!" Today, in a manner of speaking, it is Rickey who is down—in eighth place—and Leo who is up, riding high as manager of the world champions.)

Rickey straightened his tie. He was wearing a four-in-hand. Ordinar-ily, he wears a bow tie, but once a month he puts on a four-in-hand as a gesture of neckwear independence.

"More than a half-century spent in the game," Rickey mused, "and now it is suggested that I give thought to some of the ideas and innova-tions with which I have been associated. The question arises, 'Which of these can be said to have contributed most to making baseball truly our national game?'

"First, I should say, there was the mass production of ballplayers. The Cardinals were three years ahead of all the other clubs in establish-ing tryout camps. We looked at 4,000 boys a year. Then, of course, we had to have teams on which to place boys with varying degrees of ability and experience. That brought into being the farm system.

"There were other ideas not ordinarily remembered. With the St. Louis Browns, under Mr. Hedges, we originated the idea of Ladies'

Day, a very important step forward. Probably no other innovation did so much to give baseball respectability, as well as thousands of new fans.

"With the Cardinals, we developed the idea of the Knot Hole Gang. We were the first major league team to admit boys free to the ball park and again the idea was soon copied."

(In the beginning, boys joining the Cardinal Knot Hole Gang were required to sign a pledge to refrain from smoking and profanity—clearly the hand of Rickey.)

"These were ideas," Rickey went on, "and baseball was a vehicle in which such ideas might comfortably ride."

Rickey's eyes strayed to a framed motto hanging on the wall. It read: "He that will not reason is a bigot; he that cannot reason is a fool and he that dares not reason is a slave."

Rickey bent down and went rummaging through the lower drawers of his desk. In a moment he came up holding a slender book. The jacket read: *Slave and Citizen: the Negro in the Americas.* By Frank Tannenbaum."

"This book," said Rickey, "is by a Columbia University professor. Let me read now just the concluding paragraph. It says, 'Physical proximity, slow cultural intertwining, the growth of a middle group that stands in experience and equipment between the lower and upper class; and the slow process of moral identification work their way against all seemingly absolute systems of values and prejudices. Society is essentially dynamic, and while the mills of God grind slow, they grind exceeding sure. Time will draw a veil over the white and black in this hemisphere, and future generations will look back upon the record of strife as it stands revealed in the history of the people of this New World of ours with wonder and incredulity. For they will not understand the issues that the quarrel was about.' "

Rickey reached for a pencil, wrote on the flyleaf of the book and pushed it across the desk. He leaned back in his chair and thought a moment. Then he sat straight up.

"Some honors have been tendered," he said, "some honorary degrees offered because of my part in bringing Jackie Robinson into the major leagues."

He frowned and shook his head vigorously.

"No, no, no. I have declined them all. To accept honors, public applause for signing a superlative ballplayer to a contract? I would be *ashamed!*"

He turned to look out the window and turned back.

"Suppose," he demanded, "I hear that Billy Jones down the street has attained the age of 21. Suppose I go to Billy and say, 'You come with me to the polling place.' And then at the polling place I take Billy by the arm and march up to the clerks and say, 'This is Billy Jones, native American, 21 years of age,' and I demand that he be given the right to cast a ballot!"

Rickey leaned over the desk, his eyes flashing.

"Would anyone but a lunatic expect to be applauded for that?"

It immediately became clear that although Rickey deprecated his right to applause, he had never minimized the difficulties of bringing the first Negro into organized baseball.

"I talked to sociologists," he said, "and to Negro leaders. With their counsel, I worked out what I considered to be the six essential points to be considered."

He started to count on his fingers.

"Number one," he said, "the man we finally chose had to be right off the field. *Off* the field.

"Number two, he had to be right *on* the field. If he turned out to be a lemon, our efforts would fail for that reason alone.

"Number three, the reaction of his own race had to be right.

"Number four, the reaction of press and public had to be right.

"Number five, we had to have a place to put him.

"Number six, the reaction of his fellow players had to be right.

"In Jackie Robinson, we found the man to take care of points one and two. He was eminently right off and on the field. We did not settle on Robinson until after we had invested $25,000 in scouting for a man whose name we did not then know.

"Having found Robinson, we proceeded to point five. We had to have a place to put him. Luckily, in the Brooklyn organization, we had exactly the spot at Montreal where the racial issue would not be given undue emphasis.

"To take care of point three, the reaction of Robinson's own race, I went again to the Negro leaders. I explained that in order to give this boy his chance, there must be no demonstrations in his behalf, no excursions from one city to another, no presentations or testimonials. He was to be left alone to do this thing without any more hazards than were already present. For two years the men I talked to respected the reasoning behind my requests. My admiration for these men is limitless. In the best possible way, they saw to it that Jackie Robinson had his chance to make it on his own.

"Point four, the reaction of press and public, resolved itself in the course of things, and point six, the reaction of his fellow players, finally —if painfully—worked itself out."

Rickey reached across the desk and tapped the Tannenbaum book. "Time," he said, "time."

He despaired of his cigarette now and tossed it into the wastebasket. His eyes moved around the room and he murmured half to himself: "We are not going to let anything spoil sports in this country. Some of the things I read about boxing worry me, but things that are wrong will be made right . . . in time."

He laughed.

"I don't think anyone is worried about wrestling. Isn't it a rather good-natured sort of entertainment?"

He chuckled a little more, then frowned again.

"I am asked about the minor leagues. The cry is heard, 'The minors are dying!' I don't think so. The minors are in trouble but new ways will be found to meet new situations and new problems. Up to now, I confess, the major leagues have been unable to implement any effort to protect the minor leagues from the encroachment of major league broadcasts."

(A baseball man once said that Branch Rickey is constitutionally unable to tell a falsehood. "However," this man said, "sometimes he pours over the facts of a given case such a torrent of eloquence that the truth is all but drowned.")

The door opened and Rickey jumped to his feet. His eyes lit up as he cried: "Mother!"

In the doorway stood Mrs. Rickey, carrying a box of paints the size of a brief case.

"Well, Mother!" cried Rickey, coming around from behind the desk. "How did it go? Did you get good marks?"

Mrs. Rickey, a small, smiling woman, stood looking at her husband. Childhood sweethearts in Ohio, they have been married for 49 years.

Rickey pointed dramatically to the paintbox.

"Mother has joined a painting class!" he exclaimed. "At 73 years of age, Mother has gone back to school! Well, Mother? Did you recite or what? Do they give marks? What is the teacher like?"

Mrs. Rickey walked to a chair and sat down. It was plain that she was accustomed to pursuing a policy of containment toward her husband.

"They don't give marks," she said quietly. "The teacher is very nice. He was telling us that painting opens up a whole new world. You see things and colors you never saw before."

Rickey was aghast.

"Wonderful!" he cried. "Isn't that just wonderful! Mother, we must celebrate. I'll take you to lunch!"

"All right," said Mrs. Rickey. "Where will we go?"

"The Duquesne Club," said Rickey.

"That'll be fine," said Mrs. Rickey.

(In sharply stratified Pittsburgh society, there are two standards by which to measure a man who stands at the very top: one is membership in the Duquesne Club, the other is a residence at Fox Chapel, the ultra-exclusive Pittsburgh suburb. Rickey has both; the residence is an 18-room house set down on 100 acres.)

Rickey was the first to reach the sidewalk. He paced up and down waiting for Mrs. Rickey, flapping his arms against the cold, for he had forgotten to wear an overcoat that morning. Guido Roman, a tall, handsome Cuban who is Rickey's chauffeur, opened the car door.

"You want to get inside, Mr. Rickey?" he asked.

"No, Guido," said Rickey, blowing on his fingers, "I'm not cold."

A car drew up and stopped across the street. A tall, muscular young man got out.

Rickey peered sharply and ducked his head. "A thousand dollars this lad is a ballplayer," he muttered out of the side of his mouth. "But who is he, who is he?"

The young man came directly to Rickey.

"Mr. Rickey, you don't remember me," he said. "My name is George—!"

"Sure, I remember you, George!" Rickey exploded, thrusting out his hand. "You're a first baseman, right?"

"Yes, sir," said George, blushing with pleasure.

"Go right in the office and make yourself at home, George," Rickey said, beaming. "There's another first baseman in there named George—George Sisler. Say hello to him!"

"Say, thanks, Mr. Rickey," George said, hurrying to the office door.

In a moment Mrs. Rickey came out and the ride downtown in Rickey's Lincoln began. As the car pulled away from the curb, Rickey, a notorious back-seat driver, began a series of barked directions: "Right here, Guido! Left at the next corner, Guido! Red light, Guido!"

Guido, smiling and unperturbed, drove smoothly along. As the car reached the downtown business district, Rickey peering this way and that, shouted, "Slow down, Guido!"

Guido slowed down and then Rickey whispered hoarsely: "There it is, Mother! Look!"

"What?" smiled Mrs. Rickey.

"The largest lamp store in the world! Right there! I inquired about the best place to buy a lamp and I was told that this place is the largest in the whole wide world! Right there!"

"We only want a two-way bed lamp," said Mrs. Rickey.

"I know," said Rickey. "But there's the place to get it. You could go all over the world and not find a bigger lamp store. Right turn here, Guido!"

"One way, Mr. Rickey," said Guido, cheerfully.

That was the signal for a whole comedy of errors, with Rickey directing and traffic cops vetoing a series of attempts to penetrate one-way streets and to execute left turns. Rickey grew more excited, Mrs. Rickey more calm, Guido more desperate as the Duquesne Club loomed and faded as a seemingly unattainable goal.

"Judas Priest!" Rickey finally exclaimed. "It's a perfectly simple problem! We want to go to the Duquesne Club!"

"I know how!" Guido protested, "I know the way!"

"Then turn, man, turn!"

"Get out of here!" yelled a traffic cop.

"For crying out loud!" roared Rickey. "Let's get out and walk."

"I'm not going to walk," said Mrs. Rickey, mildly. "We have a car. Let Guido go his way."

"Oh, all right," Rickey pouted. "But you'd think I'd never been downtown before!"

In a moment the car pulled up at the Duquesne Club and Rickey, serene again, jumped out and helped Mrs. Rickey from the car.

"Take the car home, Guido," he said pleasantly. "We'll call you later."

"Yes, Mr. Rickey," said Guido, mopping his brow.

A group of women came out of the Duquesne Club as the Rickeys entered. The women nodded and smiled at Mrs. Rickey. Raising his hat, Rickey bowed low, then crouched to whisper hoarsely behind his hand:

"Classmates of yours, Mother?"

He stamped his foot and slapped his thigh, choking with laughter.

"One of them is in the painting class," said Mrs. Rickey placidly. "The others are in the garden club."

At the luncheon table on the second floor, Rickey ordered whitefish for Mrs. Rickey and roast beef for himself. There were no cocktails, of course; Rickey is a teetotaler.

("I shudder to think what might have happened if Branch had taken up drinking," a former associate has said. "He does nothing in moderation and I can see him facing a bottle of whiskey and shouting: 'Men, we're going to hit that bottle and hit it *hard!*'")

The luncheon order given, Rickey excused himself and made a brief telephone call at the headwaiter's desk. Returning to the table, he sat down and began to speak of pitchers.

"The greatest pitchers I have ever seen," he said, "were Christy Mathewson and Jerome Dean."

(Rickey likes to address a man by his proper given name. He is especially fond of referring to Dizzy Dean as "Jerome.")

"Mathewson," Rickey continued, "could throw every pitch in the book. But he was economical. If he saw that he could win a game with three kinds of pitches, he would use only three. Jerome, on the other hand, had a tendency to run in the direction of experimentation. Murry Dickson (formerly of the Pirates, now of the Phillies) has a fine assortment of pitches, but he feels an obligation to run through his entire repertory in every game."

The food had arrived and Rickey picked up knife and fork and, eying Mrs. Rickey closely, began to speak more rapidly.

"Yes," he said loudly, "Murry is the sort of pitcher who will go along splendidly until the eighth inning and then apparently say to himself:

'Oh, dear me, I have forgotten to throw my half-speed ball!' And then and there he will throw it."

Abruptly, Rickey made a lightning thrust with his fork in the direction of a pan-browned potato on the platter. Mrs. Rickey, alert for just such a stratagem, met the thrust with her own fork and they fenced for a few seconds in mid-air.

"Jane!" pleaded Rickey, abandoning the duel.

Mrs. Rickey deposited the potato on her own plate and passed over a small dish of broccoli.

"This will be better for you," she said quietly. "You know you're not to have potatoes."

Rickey grumbled: "I am weary of this diet. It is a cruel and inhuman thing."

"Eat the broccoli," Mrs. Rickey said.

"Jane," said Rickey, "there are times in a man's life when he wants above everything else in the world to have a potato."

"You get plenty to eat," said Mrs. Rickey. "Didn't you enjoy the meat patty at breakfast?"

Rickey shrugged his shoulders, conceding the point, and attacked his roast beef and broccoli with gusto.

"That subject of my retirement comes up from time to time," he said. "And to the direct question, 'When will you retire from baseball?' my answer is, 'Never!' But I qualify that. Now. I do foresee the day, likely next year, when I shall spend less time at my desk, at my office. I shall spend more time in the field, scouting, looking at prospects, and leave the arduous responsibilities of the general manager's position to other hands."

He looked admiringly at the baked apple before him. He put his hand on the pitcher of rich cream beside it and glanced inquiringly across the table. This time the veto was not invoked and, happily, Rickey drained the pitcher over his dessert.

After he had dropped a saccharin tablet in his coffee, he leaned back and smiled at Mrs. Rickey. Then he leaned forward again and rubbed his chin, seeming to debate something with himself. He grasped the sides of the table and spoke with the air of a conspirator.

"Here is something I intend to do," he said. "My *next* thing. A completely new idea in spring training."

He arranged the silverware to illustrate the story.

"A permanent training camp, designed and built for that purpose. Twin motels—not hotels, *motels*—with four playing fields in between as a sort of quadrangle. A public address system. Especially designed press accommodations. *Now.* One motel would be occupied by the Pittsburgh club, the other by an *American League* club. They would play a series of exhibition games and would draw better than two teams from the same league. Everything that went into the camp would be the result of our experience with training camps all through the years. It would be foolproof. And it would pay for itself because it would be operated for tourists after spring training. I *have* the land. At Fort Myers, Florida, the finest training site in the country for my money. I *have* an American League Club ready to go along with me. I *have* two thirds of the financial backing necessary."

Rickey leaned back in triumph, then came forward quickly again.

"Everybody concerned is ready to put up the cash now," he whispered, *"except me!"*

He paused for effect, then suddenly realized he had not said exactly what he intended. He burst into laughter.

"Sh-h-h," said Mrs. Rickey.

"What I mean," he said, sobering, "is that I can't go along with the plan until we have a contending ball club. But we'll get there. We'll put over this thing. It will revolutionize spring training."

It was time to get back to the office. Rickey was for sprinting down the stairs to the first floor, but Mrs. Rickey reminded him of his trick knee.

"Ah, yes, Mother," he said. "We will take the elevator."

On the street outside, Rickey remembered he had sent his car home.

"We'll get a cab down at the corner," he said. "I've got a meeting at the office. Where can I drop you, Mother?"

"Well," said Mrs. Rickey, "I thought I'd go look at some lamps."

"Oh, yes," Rickey exclaimed. "Go to that store I showed you. Mother, I understand they have the largest selection of lamps in town."

Mrs. Rickey looked at him and shook her head and smiled.

Rickey, already thinking of something else, studied the sidewalk. He raised his head and spoke firmly over the traffic.

"The game of baseball," he said, "has given me a life of joy. I would not have exchanged it for any other."

He took Mrs. Rickey by the arm. They turned and walked down the street together and vanished into the crowd.

From *Papa Hemingway*

A. E. HOTCHNER

AFTER THE HAMBURGER DINNER, Adriana returned to the Gritti with us for the get-away party; Federico and a group of well-wishers were already waiting. Although I could tell he was occasionally in pain, Ernest stretched out on the couch and managed to enjoy himself. There was plenty to drink and someone had thoughtfully brought a portable phonograph. Along about midnight, for what reason I cannot now remember, I was called upon to demonstrate American baseball. It had something to do with a discussion Ernest was having with a British friend who was a cricket nut. Ernest suggested that a pair of his wool socks be rolled up and used as the baseball, and it was my bright idea to use the ornamental doorstop as a bat. The doorstops at the Gritti, like everything else there, are very elaborate. They are hand-carved mahogany with a heavy leaded base and a thin upright shaft that resembles a table leg. This shaft, when grasped at the end, with the round base at the top, made an excellent bat. Federico, who had seen baseball played, undertook the pitching assignment and I stationed myself at an improvised home plate.

I smacked the first pitch on a dead line to center field, and to my shocked surprise the baseball socks went sailing through the highly arched glass window and out into the Venetian night. The glass broke with a terrible clatter, and from the sidewalk below we heard angry voices. For a few minutes I basked in the glory of having belted a pair of wool socks so hard that they had shattered a glass window, but then we discovered that what had really happened was that the leaded base of the doorstop had come loose and gone flying out of the window along with the socks. I still have a piece of that glass, autographed by everyone who was there.

That was the end of the party; the next day when we checked out Ernest offered to pay for the broken glass.

"Ah, yes, the window," the manager said. "The flying saucer barely missed the nose of a gentleman who unfortunately is a member of the City Council. This gentleman, trembling with rage, came in with the disk, but we calmed him successfully. As for paying for the window, in the three-hundred-year history of the Gritti, no one, to our knowledge, has ever played baseball in any of its rooms, and in commemoration of the event, Signor Hemingway, we are reducing your bill ten percent."

The 1934 All-Star Game

CARL HUBBELL *as told to* JOHN P. CARMICHAEL

I CAN REMEMBER Frankie Frisch coming off the field behind me at the end of the third inning, grunting to Bill Terry: "I could play second base fifteen more years behind that guy. He doesn't need any help. He does it all by himself." Then we hit the bench, and Terry slapped me on the arm and said: "That's pitching, boy!" and Gabby Hartnett let his mask fall down and yelled at the American League dugout: "We gotta look at that all season," and I was pretty happy.

As far as control and "stuff" is concerned, I never had any more in my life than for that All-Star game in 1934. But I never was a strikeout pitcher like Bob Feller or "Dizzy" Dean or "Dazzy" Vance. My style of pitching was to make the other team hit the ball, but on the ground. It was as big a surprise to me to strike out all those fellows as it probably was to them. Before the game, Hartnett and I went down the lineup— Gehringer, Manush, Ruth, Gehrig, Foxx, Simmons, Cronin, Dickey and Gomez. There wasn't a pitcher they'd ever faced that they hadn't belted one off him somewhere, sometime.

We couldn't discuss weaknesses . . . they didn't have any, except Gomez. Finally Gabby said: "We'll waste everything except the screwball. Get that over, but keep your fast ball and hook outside. We can't let 'em hit in the air." So that's the way we started. I knew I had only three innings to work and could bear down on every pitch.

They talk about those All-Star games being exhibition affairs and maybe they are, but I've seen very few players in my life who didn't want to win, no matter whom they were playing or what for. If I'm playing cards for pennies, I want to win. How can you feel any other way? Besides, there were 50,000 fans or more there, and they wanted to see the best you've got. There was an obligation to the people, as well as to ourselves, to go all out. I can recall walking out to the hill in the Polo Grounds that day and looking around the stands and thinking to myself: "Hub, they want to see what you've got."

Gehringer was first up and Hartnett called for a waste ball just so I'd get the feel of the first pitch. It was a little too close, and Charley singled. Down from one of the stands came a yell: "Take him out!"

I had to laugh.

Terry took a couple of steps off first and hollered: "That's all right," and there was Manush at the plate. If I recollect rightly, I got two strikes on him, but then he refused to swing any more, and I lost him. He walked. This time Terry and Frisch and Pie Traynor and Travis Jackson all came over to the mound and began worrying. "Are you all right?" Bill asked me. I assured him I was. I could hear more than one voice now from the stands: "Take him out before it's too late."

Well, I could imagine how they felt with two on, nobody out and Ruth at bat. To strike him out was the last thought in my mind. The thing was to make him hit on the ground. He wasn't too fast, as you know, and he'd be a cinch to double. He never took the bat off his shoulder. You could have pushed me over with your little finger. I fed him three straight screwballs, all over the plate, after wasting a fast ball, and he stood there. I can see him looking at the umpire on "You're out," and he wasn't mad. He just didn't believe it, and Hartnett was laughing when he threw the ball back.

So up came Gehrig. He was a sharp hitter. You could double him, too, now and then, if the ball was hit hard and straight at an in-fielder. That's what we hoped he'd do, at best. Striking out Ruth and Gehrig in succession was too big an order. By golly, he fanned . . . and on four pitches. He swung at the last screwball, and you should have heard that crowd. I felt a lot easier then, and even when Gehringer and Manush pulled a double steal and got to third and second, with Foxx up, I looked down at Hartnett and caught the screwball sign, and Jimmy missed. We were really trying to strike Foxx out, with two already gone, and Gabby didn't bother to waste any pitches. I threw three more screwballs, and he went down swinging. We had set down the side on twelve pitches, and then Frisch hit a homer in our half of the first, and we were ahead.

It was funny, when I thought of it afterwards, how Ruth and Gehrig looked as they stood there. The Babe must have been waiting for me to get the ball up a little so he could get his bat under it. He always was trying for that one big shot at the stands, and anything around his knees, especially a twisting ball, didn't let him get any leverage. Gehrig apparently decided to take one swing at least and he beat down at the pitch, figuring to take a chance on being doubled if he could get a piece of the ball. He whispered something to Foxx as Jim got up from the batter's circle and while I didn't hear it, I found out later he said: "You might as well cut . . . it won't get any higher." At least Foxx wasted no time.

Of course the second inning was easier because Simmons and Cronin both struck out with nobody on base and then I got too close to Dickey and he singled. Simmons and Foxx, incidentally, both went down swinging and I know every pitch to them was good enough to hit at and those they missed had a big hunk of the plate. Once Hartnett kinda shook his head at me as if to say I was getting too good. After Dickey came Gomez and as he walked into the box he looked down at Gabby and said: "You are now looking at a man whose batting average is .104. What the hell am I doing up here?" He was easy after all those other guys and we were back on the bench again.

We were all feeling pretty good by this time and Traynor began counting on his fingers: "Ruth, Gehrig, Foxx, Simmons, Cronin! Hey, Hub, do you put anything on the ball?" Terry came over to see how my arm was, but it never was stronger. I walked one man in the third . . . don't remember who it was . . . but this time Ruth hit one on the ground and we were still all right. You could hear him puff when he swung. That was all for me. Afterward, they got six runs in the fifth and licked us, but for three innings I had the greatest day in my life. One of the writers who kept track told me that I'd pitched 27 strikes and 21 balls to 13 men and only 5 pitches were hit in fair territory.

POETRY

ONE OF America's foremost poets, Rolfe Humphries, was awarded the 1956 Fellowship of the Academy of American Poets, largest award of its kind, for outstanding achievement.

Polo Grounds

ROLFE HUMPHRIES

Time is of the essence. This is a highly skilled
And beautiful mystery. Three or four seconds only
From the time that Riggs connects till he reaches first,
And in those seconds Jurges goes to his right,
Comes up with the ball, tosses to Witek at second
For the force on Reese, Witek to Mize at first,
In time for the out—a double play.

(Red Barber crescendo. Crowd noises, obbligato;
Scattered staccatos from the peanut boys,
Loud in the lull, as the teams are changing sides . . .)

Hubbell takes the sign, nods, pumps, delivers—
A foul into the stands. Dunn takes a new ball out,
Hands it to Danning, who throws it down to Werber;
Werber takes off his glove, rubs the ball briefly,
Tosses it over to Hub, who goes to the rosin bag,
Takes the sign from Danning, pumps, delivers—

Low, outside, ball three. Danning goes to the mound,
Says something to Hub, Dunn brushes off the plate,
Adams starts throwing in the Giant bull pen,
Hub takes the sign from Danning, pumps, delivers,
Camilli gets ahold of it, a *long* fly to the outfield,
Ott goes back, back, back, against the wall, gets under it,
Pounds his glove, and takes it for the out.
That's all for the Dodgers. . . .

Time is of the essence. The rhythms break,
More varied and subtle than any kind of dance;
Movement speeds up or lags. The ball goes out
In sharp and angular drives, or long, slow arcs,
Comes in again controlled and under aim;
The players wheel or spurt, race, stoop, slide, halt,
Shift imperceptibly to new positions,
Watching the signs, according to the batter,
The score, the inning. Time is of the essence.

Time is of the essence. Remember Terry?
Remember Stonewall Jackson, Lindstrom, Frisch,
When they were good? Remember Long George Kelly?
Remember John McGraw and Benny Kauff?
Remember Bridwell, Tenney, Merkle, Youngs,
Chief Meyers, Big Jeff Tesreau, Shufflin' Phil?
Remember Mathewson, and Ames, and Donlin,
Buck Ewing, Rusie, Smiling Mickey Welch?
Remember a left-handed catcher named Jack Humphries,
Who sometimes played the outfield, in '83?

Time is of the essence. The shadow moves
From the plate to the box, from the box to second base,
From second to the outfield, to the bleachers.

Time is of the essence. The crowd and players
Are the same age always, but the man in the crowd
Is older every season. Come on, play ball!

OF COURSE, the small type in the title here is on purpose. This is from Miss Jackson's marvelous book *Raising Demons*.

braves 10, giants 9

SHIRLEY JACKSON

BEFORE THE CHILDREN were able to start counting days till school was out, and before Laurie had learned to play more than a simple scale on the trumpet, and even before my husband's portable radio had gone in for its annual checkup so it could broadcast the Brooklyn games all summer, we found ourselves deeply involved in the Little League. The Little League was new in our town that year. One day all the kids were playing baseball in vacant lots and without any noticeable good sportsmanship, and the next day, almost, we were standing around the grocery and the post office wondering what kind of a manager young Johnny Cole was going to make, and whether the Weaver boy—the one with the strong arm—was going to be twelve this August, or only eleven as his mother said, and Bill Cummings had donated his bulldozer to level off the top of Sugar Hill, where the kids used to go sledding, and we were all sporting stickers on our cars reading "We have contributed" and the fund-raising campaign was over the top in forty-eight hours. There are a thousand people in our town, and it turned out, astonishingly, that about sixty of them were boys of Little League age. Laurie thought he'd try out for pitcher and his friend Billy went out for catcher. Dinnertime all over town got shifted to eight-thirty in the evening, when nightly baseball practice was over. By the time our family had become accustomed to the fact that no single problem in our house could be allowed to interfere in any way with the tempering of Laurie's right arm, the uniforms had been ordered, and four teams had been chosen and named, and Laurie and Billy were together on the Little League Braves. My friend Dot, Billy's mother, was learning to keep a box score. I announced in family assembly that there would be no more oiling of baseball gloves in the kitchen sink.

We lived only a block or so from the baseball field, and it became the amiable custom of the ballplayers to drop in for a snack on their way to the practice sessions. There was to be a double-header on Memorial Day, to open the season. The Braves would play the Giants; the Red Sox would play the Dodgers. After one silent, apoplectic moment my husband agreed, gasping, to come to the ball games and root against the Dodgers. A rumor got around town that the Red Sox were the team to watch, with Butch Weaver's strong arm, and several mothers believed absolutely that the various managers were putting their own sons into all the best positions, although everyone told everyone else that it didn't matter, really, *what* position the boys held so long as they got a chance to play ball, and show they were good sports about it. As a matter of fact, the night before the double-header which was to open the Little League, I distinctly recall that I told Laurie it was only a game. "It's only a game, fella," I said. "Don't *try* to go to sleep; read or something if you're nervous. Would you like an aspirin?"

"I forgot to tell you," Laurie said, yawning. "He's pitching Georgie tomorrow. Not me."

"What?" I thought, and then said heartily, "I mean, he's the manager, after all. I know you'll play your best in *any* position."

"I could go to sleep now if you'd just turn out the light," Laurie said patiently. "I'm really quite tired."

I called Dot later, about twelve o'clock, because I was pretty sure she'd still be awake, and of course she was, although Billy had gone right off about nine o'clock. She said she wasn't the least bit nervous, because of course it didn't really matter except for the kids' sake, and she hoped the best team would win. I said that that was just what I had been telling my husband, and she said *her* husband had suggested that perhaps she had better not go to the game at all because if the Braves lost she ought to be home with a hot bath ready for Billy and perhaps a steak dinner or something. I said that even if Laurie wasn't pitching I was sure the Braves would win, and of course I wasn't one of those people who always wanted their own children right out in the center of things all the time but if the Braves lost it would be my opinion that their lineup ought to be revised and Georgie put back into right field where he belonged. She said *she* thought Laurie was a better pitcher, and I suggested that she and her husband and Billy come over for lunch and we could all go to the game together.

I spent all morning taking movies of the Memorial Day parade, particularly the Starlight 4-H Club, because Jannie was marching with them, and I used up almost a whole film magazine on Sally and Barry, standing at the curb, wide-eyed and rapt, waving flags. Laurie missed the parade because he slept until nearly twelve, and then came downstairs and made himself an enormous platter of bacon and eggs and toast, which he took out to the hammock and ate lying down.

"How do you feel?" I asked him, coming out to feel his forehead. "Did you sleep all right? How's your arm?"

"Sure," he said.

We cooked lunch outdoors, and Laurie finished his breakfast in time to eat three hamburgers. Dot had only a cup of coffee, and I took a little salad. Every now and then she would ask Billy if he wanted to lie down for a little while before the game, and I would ask Laurie how he felt. The game was not until two o'clock, so there was time for Jannie and Sally and Barry to roast marshmallows. Laurie and Billy went into the barn to warm up with a game of ping-pong, and Billy's father remarked that the boys certainly took this Little League setup seriously, and my husband said that it was the best thing in the world for the kids. When the boys came out of the barn after playing three games of ping-pong I asked Billy if he was feeling all right and Dot said she thought Laurie ought to lie down for a while before the game. The boys said no, they had to meet the other guys at the school at one-thirty and they were going to get into their uniforms now. I said please to be careful, and Dot said if they needed any help dressing just call down and we would come up, and both boys turned and looked at us curiously for a minute before they went indoors.

"My goodness," I said to Dot, "I hope they're not nervous."

"Well, they take it so seriously," she said.

I sent the younger children in to wash the marshmallow off their faces, and while our husbands settled down to read over the Little League rule book, Dot and I cleared away the paper plates and gave the leftover hamburgers to the dog. Suddenly Dot said, "Oh," in a weak voice and I turned around and Laurie and Billy were coming through the door in their uniforms. "They look so—so—*tall*," Dot said, and I said, "Laurie?" uncertainly. The boys laughed, and looked at each other.

"Pretty neat," Laurie said, looking at Billy.

"Some get-up," Billy said, regarding Laurie.

Both fathers came over and began turning the boys around and around, and Jannie and Sally came out onto the porch and stared worshipfully. Barry, to whom Laurie and his friends have always seemed incredibly tall and efficient, gave them a critical glance and observed that this was truly a baseball.

It turned out that there was a good deal of advice the fathers still needed to give the ballplayers, so they elected to walk over to the school with Billy and Laurie and then on to the ball park, where they would find Dot and me later. We watched them walk down the street; not far away they were joined by another boy in uniform and then a couple more. After that, for about half an hour, there were boys in uniform wandering by twos and threes toward the baseball field and the school, all alike in a kind of unexpected dignity and new tallness, all walking with self-conscious pride. Jannie and Sally stood on the front porch watching, careful to greet by name all the ballplayers going by.

A few minutes before two, Dot and I put the younger children in her car and drove over to the field. Assuming that perhaps seventy-five of the people in our town were actively engaged in the baseball game, there should have been about nine hundred and twenty-five people in the audience, but there seemed to be more than that already; Dot and I both remarked that it was the first town affair we had ever attended where there were more strange faces than familiar ones.

Although the field itself was completely finished, there was only one set of bleachers up, and that was filled, so Dot and I took the car robe and settled ourselves on top of the little hill over the third-base line, where we had a splendid view of the whole field. We talked about how it was at the top of this hill the kids used to start their sleds, coasting right down past third base and on into center field, where the ground flattened out and the sleds would stop. From the little hill we could see the roofs of the houses in the town below half hidden in the trees, and far on to the hills in the distance. We both remarked that there was still snow on the high mountain.

Barry stayed near us, deeply engaged with a little dump truck. Jannie and Sally accepted twenty-five cents each, and melted into the crowd in the general direction of the refreshment stand. Dot got out her pencil and box score, and I put a new magazine of film in the movie camera. We could see our husbands standing around in back of the Braves' dugout, along with the fathers of all the other Braves players. They were all in a group, chatting with great humorous informality with the manager and the two coaches of the Braves. The fathers of the boys on the Giant team were down by the Giant dugout, standing around the manager and the coaches of the Giants.

Marian, a friend of Dot's and mine whose boy Artie was first baseman for the Giants, came hurrying past looking for a seat, and we offered her part of our car robe. She sat down, breathless, and said she had mislaid her husband and her younger son, so we showed her where her husband was down by the Giant dugout with the other fathers, and her younger son turned up almost at once to say that Sally had a popsicle and so could he have one, too, and a hot dog and maybe some popcorn?

Suddenly, from far down the block, we could hear the high-school band playing "The Stars and Stripes Forever," and coming closer. Everyone stood up to watch and then the band turned the corner and came through the archway with the official Little League insignia and up to the entrance of the field. All the ballplayers were marching behind the band. I thought foolishly of Laurie when he was Barry's age, and something of the sort must have crossed Dot's mind, because she reached out and put her hand on Barry's head. "There's Laurie and Billy," Barry said softly. The boys ran out onto the field and lined up along the base lines, and then I discovered that we were all cheering, with Barry jumping up and down and shouting, "Baseball! Baseball!"

"If you cry I'll tell Laurie," Dot said to me out of the corner of her mouth.

"Same to you," I said, blinking.

The sky was blue and the sun was bright and the boys stood lined up soberly in their clean new uniforms holding their caps while the band played "The Star-Spangled Banner" and the flag was raised. From Laurie and Billy, who were among the tallest, down to the littlest boys in uniform, there was a straight row of still, expectant faces.

I said, inadequately, "It must be hot out there."

"They're all chewing gum," Dot said.

Then the straight lines broke and the Red Sox, who had red caps, and the Dodgers, who had blue caps, went off into the bleachers and the Giants, who had green caps, went into their dugout, and at last the Braves, who had black caps, trotted out onto the field. It was announced over the public-address system that the Braves were the home team, and when it was announced that Georgie was going to pitch for the Braves I told Marian that I was positively relieved, since Laurie had been so nervous anyway over the game that I was sure pitching would have been a harrowing experience for him, and she said that Artie had been perfectly willing to sit out the game as a substitute, or a pinch hitter, or something, but that his manager had insisted upon putting him at first base because he was so reliable.

"You know," she added with a little laugh, "*I* don't know one position from another, but of course Artie is glad to play anywhere."

"I'm sure he'll do very nicely," I said, trying to put some enthusiasm into my voice.

Laurie was on second base for the Braves, and Billy at first. Marian leaned past me to tell Dot that first base was a *very* responsible position, and Dot said oh, was it? Because of course Billy just wanted to do the best he could for the team, and on the *Braves* it was the *manager* who assigned the positions. Marian smiled in what I thought was a nasty kind of way and said she hoped the best team would win. Dot and I both smiled back and said we hoped so, too.

When the umpire shouted, "Play Ball!" people all over the park began to call out to the players, and I raised my voice slightly and said, "Hurray for the Braves." That encouraged Dot and *she* called out, "Hurray for the Braves," but Marian, of course, had to say, "Hurray for the Giants."

The first Giant batter hit a triple, although, as my husband explained later, it would actually have been an infield fly if the shortstop had been looking and an easy out if he had thrown it anywhere near Billy at first. By the time Billy got the ball back into the infield the batter—Jimmie Hill, who had once borrowed Laurie's bike and brought it back with a flat tire—was on third. I could see Laurie out on second base banging his hands together and he looked so pale I was worried. Marian leaned around me and said to Dot, "That was a nice try Billy made. I don't think even *Artie* could have caught that ball."

"He looks *furious,*" Dot said to me. "He just *hates* doing things wrong."

"They're all terribly nervous," I assured her. "They'll settle down as soon as they really get playing." I raised my voice a little. "Hurray for the Braves," I said.

The Giants made six runs in the first inning, and each time a run came in Marian looked sympathetic and told us that really, the boys were being quite good sports about it, weren't they? When Laurie bobbled an easy fly right at second and missed the out, she said to me that Artie had told her that Laurie was really quite a good little ballplayer and I mustn't blame him for an occasional error.

By the time little Jerry Hart finally struck out to retire the Giants, Dot and I were sitting listening with polite smiles. I had stopped saying "Hurray for the Braves." Marian had told everyone sitting near us that it was her boy who had slid home for the sixth run, and she had explained with great kindness that Dot and I had sons on the other team, one of them the first baseman who missed that long throw and the other one the second baseman who dropped the fly ball. The Giants took the field and Marian pointed out Artie standing on first base slapping his glove and showing off.

Then little Ernie Harrow, who was the Braves' right fielder and lunched frequently at our house, hit the first pitched ball for a fast grounder which went right through the legs of the Giant center fielder, and when Ernie came dancing onto second Dot leaned around to remark to Marian that if Artie had been playing closer to first the way Billy did he might have been ready for the throw if the Giant center fielder had managed to stop the ball. Billy came up and smashed a long fly over the left fielder's head and I put a hand on Marian's shoulder to hoist myself up. Dot and I stood there howling, "Run run run," Billy came home, and two runs were in. Little Andy placed a surprise bunt down the first-base line, Artie never even saw it, and I leaned over to tell Marian that clearly Artie did not understand all the refinements of playing first base. Then Laurie got a nice hit and slid into second. The Giants took out their pitcher and put in Buddy Williams, whom Laurie once beat up on the way to school. The score was tied with two out and Dot and I were both yelling. Then little Ernie Harrow came up for the second time and hit a home run, right over the fence where they put the sign advertising his father's sand and gravel. We were leading eight to six when the inning ended.

Little League games are six innings, so we had five more innings to go. Dot went down to the refreshment stand to get some hot dogs and soda; she offered very politely to bring something for Marian, but Marian said thank you, no; she would get her own. The second inning tightened up considerably as the boys began to get over their stage fright and play baseball the way they did in the vacant lots. By the middle of the fifth inning the Braves were leading nine to eight, and then in the bottom of the fifth Artie missed a throw at first base and the Braves scored another run. Neither Dot nor I said a single word, but Marian got up in a disagreeable manner, excused herself, and went to sit on the other side of the field.

"Marian looks very poorly these days," I remarked to Dot as we watched her go.

"She's at *least* five years older than *I* am," Dot said.

"More than that," I said. "She's gotten very touchy, don't you think?"

"Poor little Artie," Dot said. "You remember when he used to have temper tantrums in nursery school?"

In the top of the sixth the Braves were winning ten to eight, but then Georgie, who had been pitching accurately and well, began to tire, and he walked the first two batters. The third boy hit a little fly which fell in short center field, and one run came in to make it ten to nine. Then Georgie, who was by now visibly rattled, walked the next batter and filled the bases.

"Three more outs and the Braves can win it," some man in the crowd behind us said. "I don't *think*," and he laughed.

"Oh, *lord*," Dot said, and I stood up and began to wail, "No, no." The manager was gesturing at Laurie and Billy. "No, no," I said to Dot, and Dot said, "He can't do it, don't let him." "It's too much to ask of the children," I said. "What a terrible thing to do to such little kids," Dot said.

"New pitcher," the man in the crowd said. "He better be good," and he laughed.

While Laurie was warming up and Billy was getting into his catcher's equipment, I suddenly heard my husband's voice for the first time. This was the only baseball game my husband had ever attended outside of Ebbets Field. "Put it in his ear, Laurie," my husband was yelling, "put it in his ear."

Laurie was chewing gum and throwing slowly and carefully. Barry took a minute off from the little truck he was placidly filling with sand and emptying again to ask me if the big boys were still playing baseball. I stood there, feeling Dot's shoulder shaking against mine, and I tried to get my camera open to check the magazine of film but my finger kept slipping and jumping against the little knob. I said to Dot that I guessed I would just enjoy the game for a while and not take pictures, and she said earnestly that Billy had had a little touch of fever that morning and the manager was taking his life in his hands putting Billy up there in all that catcher's equipment in that hot shade. I wondered if Laurie could see that I was nervous.

"*He* doesn't look very nervous," I said to Dot, but then my voice failed, and I finished, "does he?" in a sort of gasp.

The batter was Jimmie Hill, who had already had three hits that afternoon. Laurie's first pitch hit the dust at Billy's feet and Billy sprawled full length to stop it. The man in the crowd behind us laughed. The boy on third hesitated, unsure whether Billy had the ball; he started for home and then, with his mother just outside the third-base line yelling, "Go back, go back," he retreated to third again.

Laurie's second pitch sent Billy rocking backward and he fell; "Only way he can stop it is fall on it," the man in the crowd said, and laughed.

Dot stiffened, and then she turned around slowly. For a minute she stared and then she said, in the evilest voice I have ever heard her use, "Sir, that catcher is my son."

"I beg your pardon, ma'am, I'm sure," the man said.

"Picking on little boys," Dot said.

The umpire called Laurie's next pitch ball three, although it was clearly a strike, and I was yelling, "You're blind, you're blind." I could hear my husband shouting to throw the bum out.

"Going to see a new pitcher pretty soon," said the man in the crowd, and I clenched my fist, and turned around and said in a voice that made Dot's sound cordial, "Sir, that pitcher is *my* son. If you have any more personal remarks to make about any member of my family—"

"Or mine," Dot added.

"I will immediately call Mr. Tillotson, our local constable, and see personally that you are put out of this ball park. People who go around attacking ladies and innocent children—"

"Strike," the umpire said.

I turned around once more and shook my fist at the man in the crowd, and he announced quietly and with some humility that he hoped both teams would win, and subsided into absolute silence.

Laurie then pitched two more strikes, his nice fast ball, and I thought suddenly of how at lunch he and Billy had been tossing hamburger rolls and Dot and I had made them stop. At about this point, Dot and I abandoned our spot up on the hill and got down against the fence with our faces pressed against the wire. "Come on, Billy boy," Dot was saying over and over, "come on, Billy boy," and I found that I was telling Laurie, "Come on now, only two more outs to go, only two more, come on, Laurie, come on. . ." I could see my husband now but there was too much noise to hear him; he was pounding his hands against the fence. Dot's husband had *his* hands over his face and his back turned to the ball field. "He can't hit it, Laurie," Dot yelled, "this guy can't hit," which I thought with dismay was not true; the batter was Butch Weaver and he was standing there swinging his bat and sneering. "Laurie, Laurie, Laurie," screeched a small voice; I looked down and it was Sally, bouncing happily beside me. "Can I have another nickel?" she asked. "Laurie, Laurie."

"Strike," the umpire said and I leaned my forehead against the cool wire and said in a voice that suddenly had no power at all, "Just two strikes, Laurie, just two more strikes."

Laurie looked at Billy, shook his head, and looked again. He grinned and when I glanced down at Billy I could see that behind the mask he was grinning too. Laurie pitched, and the batter swung wildly. "Laurie, Laurie," Sally shrieked. "Strike two," the umpire said. Dot and I grabbed at each other's hands and Laurie threw the good fast ball for strike three.

One out to go, and Laurie, Billy, and the shortstop stood together on the mound for a minute. They talked very soberly, but Billy was grinning again as he came back to the plate. Since I was incapable of making any sound, I hung onto the wire and promised myself that if Laurie struck out this last batter I would never never say another word to him about the mess in his room, I would not make him paint the lawn chairs, I would not even mention clipping the hedge. . . . "Ball one," the umpire said, and I found that I had my voice back. "Crook," I yelled, "blind crook."

Laurie pitched, the batter swung, and hit a high foul ball back of the plate; Billy threw off his mask and tottered, staring up. The batter, the boys on the field, and the umpire, waited, and Dot suddenly spoke.

"William," she said imperatively, *"you catch that ball."*

Then everyone was shouting wildly; I looked at Dot and said, "Golly." Laurie and Billy were slapping and hugging each other, and then the rest of the team came around them and the manager was there. I distinctly saw my husband, who is not a lively man, vault the fence to run into the wild group and slap Laurie on the shoulder with one hand and Billy with the other. The Giants gathered around their manager and gave a cheer for the Braves, and the Braves gathered around *their* manager and gave a cheer for the Giants, and Laurie and Billy came pacing together toward the dugout, past Dot and me. I said, "Laurie?" and Dot said, "Billy?" They stared at us, without recognition for a minute, both of them lost in another world, and then they smiled and Billy said, "Hi, Ma," and Laurie said, "You see the game?"

I realized that my hair was over my eyes and I had broken two fingernails. Dot had a smudge on her nose and had torn a button off her sweater. We helped each other up the hill again and found that Barry was asleep on the car robe. Without speaking any more than was absolutely necessary, Dot and I decided that we could not stay for the second game of the double-header. I carried Barry asleep and Dot brought his dump truck and the car robe and my camera and the box score which she had not kept past the first Giant run, and we headed wearily for the car.

We passed Artie in his green Giant cap and we said it had been a fine game, he had played wonderfully well, and he laughed and said tolerantly, "Can't win 'em all, you know." When we got back to our house I put Barry into his bed while Dot put on the kettle for a nice cup of tea. We washed our faces and took off our shoes, and finally Dot said hesitantly that she certainly hoped that Marian wasn't really offended with us.

"Well, of course she takes this kind of thing terribly hard," I said.

"I was just thinking," Dot said after a minute, "we ought to plan a kind of victory party for the Braves at the end of the season."

"A hot-dog roast, maybe?" I suggested.

"Well," Dot said, "I *did* hear the boys talking one day. They said they were going to take some time this summer and clean out your barn, and set up a record player in there and put in a stock of records and have some dances."

"You mean . . ." I faltered. "With *girls?*"

Dot nodded.

"Oh," I said.

When our husbands came home two hours later we were talking about old high-school dances and the time we went out with those boys from Princeton. Our husbands reported that the Red Sox had beaten the Dodgers in the second game and were tied for first place with the Braves. Jannie and Sally came idling home, and finally Laurie and Billy stopped in, briefly, to change their clothes. There was a pickup game down in Murphy's lot, they explained, and they were going to play some baseball.

--- GENERAL ---

IF YOU THINK Ann Landers has advice only for the lovelorn, kindly think again.

"We Can't Afford a Lawyer"

ANN LANDERS

DEAR ANN: This letter is being written by seven baseball players, 11 and 12 years old. We can't afford a lawyer.

This afternoon we were playing ball in a lot behind this big house. I was at bat. The next thing I knew the ball sailed right through a great big plate glass window.

The owner of the house came running out like the place was on fire. We tried to explain it was an accident but the man said we had no business playing there in the first place. Then he took down all our names on a piece of paper.

Nothing has happened so far but we are going to have a meeting about it tomorrow. Do you think I should pay for the window because I was at bat? Is the pitcher partly to blame? Should the whole team pitch in? Or should the man be a real good sport and say, "Forget it, kids, I was young once myself?"—JR. CARDINALS.

DEAR JR. CARDS: I believe it would be very brotherly if the whole team pitched in and bought a new window.

It would be downright bright if you all went to the man and asked if you could earn some money by working on his lawn this summer—in shifts, say two or three at a time. Such a suggestion might jog his memory a little that he was young once himself.

SELECTING one article by John Lardner for inclusion in a collection such as this is like deciding, as Lefty Gomez once had to, what kind of pitch to throw Jimmy Foxx. Lardner, like Foxx, is good for extra bases any time, but my choice was considerably more pleasant and less hazardous than the one confronting Gomez, who finally told catcher Bill Dickey he preferred not to throw the ball at all. The following Lardner, which appeared in *Sport*, is a personal favorite of mine.

The Unbelievable Babe Herman

JOHN LARDNER

FLOYD CAVES HERMAN, known as Babe, did not always catch fly balls on the top of his head, but he could do it in a pinch. He never tripled into a triple play, but he once doubled into a double play, which is the next best thing. For seven long years, from 1926 through 1932, he was the spirit of Brooklyn baseball. He spent the best part of his life upholding the mighty tradition that anything can happen at Ebbets Field, the mother temple of daffiness in the national game.

Then he went away from there. He rolled and bounced from town to town and ball club to ball club. Thirteen years went by before he appeared in a Brooklyn uniform again. That was in the wartime summer of 1945, when manpower was so sparse that the desperate Dodger scouts were snatching beardless shortstops from the cradle and dropping their butterfly nets over Spanish War veterans who had played the outfield alongside Willie Keeler. In the course of the great famine, Branch Rickey and Leo Durocher lured Babe Herman, then 42, from his turkey farm in Glendale, California, to hit a few more for the honor of Flatbush. A fine crowd turned out to watch the ancient hero on the first day of his reincarnation.

"It looks like they haven't forgotten you here, Babe," said one of the players, glancing around the grandstand.

Mr. Herman shook his head. "How could they?" he said with simple dignity.

And he went on to show what he meant. In his first time at bat he was almost thrown out at first base on a single to right field. The Babe rounded the bag at a high, senile prance, fell flat on his face on the baseline, and barely scrambled back to safety ahead of the throw from the outfield. The crowd roared with approval. Fifteen years earlier they would have booed themselves into a state of apoplexy, for that was a civic ritual at Ebbets Field—booing Herman. But this was 1945. You don't boo a legend from out of the past, a man who made history.

Before he went home to California to stay, a few weeks later, the Babe gathered the younger players around his knee and filled them with blood-curdling stories about his terrible past.

"You know that screen on top of the right-field fence," he said. "They put that there on account of me. I was breaking all the windows on the other side of Bedford Avenue."

Looking around to see if this had sunk in, he added: "There used to be a traffic tower on Bedford Avenue there. Once I hit one over the wall that broke a window in the tower and cut a cop's hand all to pieces. Wasn't my fault," said the Babe philosophically. "When I busted 'em, there was no telling where they'd go."

It's beyond question that Mr. Herman could bust them. He always admitted it. He used to be irritated, though, by the rumor that he was the world's worst outfielder, and a constant danger to his own life. He was also sensitive about his base-running.

"Don't write fresh cracks about my running," he once told an interviewer, "or I won't give you no story. I'm a great runner."

He proceeded to tell why he stole no bases in 1926, his first year with Brooklyn, until the very end of the season. It seems that the late Uncle Wilbert Robinson, then managing the Dodgers, came up to Mr. Herman one day and said, sourly: "What's the matter, can't you steal?"

"Steal?" said the Babe. "Why, hell, you never asked me to."

So then he stole a couple of bases, to prove he could do everything.

One talent for which Babe never gave himself enough public credit was making money. He was one of the highest-salaried players of his time, year after year. He got these salaries by holding out all through the training season. Other players, starving slowly on the ball club's regular bill of fare in Southern hotels, used to go down the street to the restaurants where Herman, the holdout, ate, and press their noses against the window like small boys, watching the Babe cut huge sirloin steaks to ribbons. It wasn't just the food that kept Babe from signing early. Holding out is a common practice with good-hit-no-field men, like Herman, Zeke Bonura, and Rudy York, in his outfielding days. The reason is obvious. The longer they postpone playing ball in the spring (for nothing), the less chance there is of getting killed by a fly ball.

Mr. Herman had such ambitious ideas about money that one year, returning his first contract to the Brooklyn office unsigned, he enclosed an unpaid bill from his dentist for treatment during the winter. The ball club ignored the bill. After all, Herman didn't hit with his teeth.

The Babe, as a player, was a gangling fellow with spacious ears who walked with a slouch that made him look less than his true height, six feet, four inches. He was born in Buffalo in 1903. Leaving there for the professional baseball wars in 1921, Mr. Herman worked for eighteen different managers before he met up with Uncle Robbie, and for nine more after that. It is said that he broke the hearts of 45 percent of these gentlemen. The rest avoided cardiac trouble by getting rid of the Babe as fast as they could.

He came up from Edmonton, in the Western Canada League, to Detroit, in the year 1922, and was promptly fired by Ty Cobb, the Tigers' idealistic manager.

"The Detroit club," said the Babe, his feelings wounded, "has undoubtedly made some bad mistakes in its time, but this is the worst they ever made."

He was fired from the Omaha club later in the same year while batting .416. A pop fly hit him on the head one day, and the Omaha owner lost his temper. The owner and the manager began to argue.

"Much as I would like to," said the manager, "I can't send away a man who is hitting .416."

"I don't care if he's hitting 4,000!" yelled the owner. "I am not going to have players who field the ball with their skulls. Fire him!"

The Babe explained later that the incident was greatly exaggerated.

"It was a foul ball," he said, "that started to go into the stands. The minute I turned my back, though, the wind caught the ball and blew it out again, and it conked me. It could happen to anybody."

Just the same, Mr. Herman was fired.

The Babe tried baseball in Boston briefly, when Lee Fohl managed the Red Sox. He never played an inning there. Studying his form on the bench, Mr. Fohl fired him. The Babe was just as well pleased. He said the Boston climate did not suit him. He went to Atlanta, where Otto Miller, later a Brooklyn coach, managed the team. Every morning for five days in a row, Mr. Miller resolved to fire Mr. Herman. Every afternoon of those five days, Mr. Herman got a hit that drove in runs and changed Mr. Miller's mind for the night. On the fifth day, playing against Nashville, he had four hits in his first four times at bat. He was robbed of a fifth hit by a sensational catch by Kiki Cuyler. After the game, Mr. Miller told the Babe that they might have won the game but for Cuyler's catch. He meant it kindly, but Mr. Herman took it as a personal criticism of himself. He was hurt. He began a loud quarrel with Otto, and was traded to Memphis on one bounce.

The Brooklyn club bought the Babe for $15,000 a couple of years later, while he was causing nervous breakdowns and busting up ball games in Seattle. Then Brooklyn tried to get rid of him for nothing, and failed. This gross insult to the name of Herman occurred as follows: The Dodgers wanted a Minneapolis player of no subsequent consequence, named Johnny Butler. They traded Herman and eight other men to Minneapolis for Butler. Minneapolis took the eight other men, but refused to take Herman. Brooklyn was stuck with the Babe, and history began to be made.

Jacques Fournier, the Dodger first baseman, hurt his leg one day in the summer of 1926. Herman replaced him. He had a good season at bat that year and the Brooklyn fans began to take to the Babe, wide ears, chewing tobacco, and all. Uncle Robbie took to him some days. Other days gave him pause—like the day famous in ballad and prose when Mr. Herman smote a two-base hit that ended in a double play.

The bases were full of Brooklyns, with one out, when the Babe strode to the plate on that occasion, swinging his bat like a cane in his right hand. He was a phenomenon physically, a left-handed hitter with most of his power in his right arm. Scattered around the landscape before him were Hank DeBerry, the Brooklyn catcher, on third base; Dazzy Vance, the immortal Dodger fireball pitcher, on second; and Chick Fewster, an outfielder, on first. Mr. Herman swung ferociously and the ball hit the right-field wall on a line. DeBerry scored. Vance, however, being a man who did not care to use his large dogs unnecessarily, hovered between second and third for a moment on the theory that the ball might be caught. When it rebounded off the wall, he set sail again, lumbered to third base, and made a tentative turn toward home. Then, deciding he couldn't score, he stepped back to third. This move confounded Fewster, who was hard on Vance's heels. Fewster started back toward second base. At that moment, a new character, with blond hair and flapping ears, came into their lives.

Mr. Herman has described himself as a great runner. What he meant was, he was a hard runner. He forgot to mention that he ran with blinkers on, as they say at the race track. He concentrated on running and ignored the human and animal life around and ahead of him. Passing Fewster like the Limited passing a whistle stop, the Babe slid into third just as Vance returned there from the opposite direction. Herman was automatically out for passing Fewster on the baseline, though nobody realized it at once but the umpire, who made an "out" sign. The third baseman, not knowing who was out, began frantically to tag Herman, who was already dead, and Vance, who stood perfectly safe on third base.

"What a spectacle!" observed Vance nonchalantly to Herman, as the third baseman looked in vain to the umpire for the sign of another out. Fewster, confused, stood a little distance away. His proper move was to go back to second and stay there, but Herman's slide had destroyed his powers of thought. Finally, the third baseman caught on. He began to chase Fewster, who ran in a panic and did not even stop at second, where he would have been safe. He was tagged in the outfield for the third out of the inning.

Cheap detractors may say what they like about Herman merely doubling into a double play. It's obvious that what he really did—the rule-book to the contrary—was triple into a double play.

It's also obvious that Vance and Fewster were as much at fault as Herman. That is the old, true spirit of Brooklyn co-operation. But Vance regarded Herman as the star of the act. A few years afterward, when

Chicago officials announced that they expected a Chicago pennant in 1933 to make things complete for the Century of Progress exposition, Vance announced his counter-plan for that year in Brooklyn. Instead of a Century of Progress, said Dazzy, they would feature "A Cavalcade of Chaos; or, the Headless Horsemen of Ebbets Field." Herman was to be the star. Unfortunately, by the time the year 1933 rolled into Brooklyn, Herman had rolled out of there, to quieter pastures.

Uncle Robbie's comment on the celebrated double play of 1926 was "#$&%$%!!" However, that was Robbie's comment on practically everything, and he meant it in a friendly way. He was tolerant of Herman, for he understood that criticism or scolding drove the Babe crazy. When 30,000 people booed him in unison—and that happened often enough in 1927, when his batting average slipped to .272, and 1929, when he led the league's outfielders in errors—the Babe would sulk for days. It took Robbie a little while, at that, to learn patience with Herman. He asked waivers on him in 1927, but changed his mind and kept the Babe when John McGraw, of the New York Giants, refused to waive.

"If that crafty blank-blank McGraw wants him," reasoned Mr. Robinson, "there must be something in him."

As time went on, the Brooklyn crowds became more sympathetic, too. That's understandable. After 1927, Herman hit for averages of .340, .381, .393, .313, and .326. In 1930, he had 241 hits for a total of 426 bases, including 35 home runs. He scored 143 runs and batted in 130. The fans barbecued him one moment and cheered him the next.

"Not only is that fellow a funny-looking blank-blank-blank," said the manager, "but he is blankety-blank unlucky. Other men, when they're on third base, can sometimes beat the outfielder's catch when they start home on a fly ball. But not this blankety-blank Herman. He always gets called for it."

The wailing and the keening were great in Brooklyn when the Babe, called by Rogers Hornsby, "the perfect free swinger," was traded to Cincinnati in December 1932, in a six-player deal. It was not a bad deal for Brooklyn, in a strictly practical way. Herman never hit in high figures again after that year, while some of the players from Cincinnati helped the Dodgers into the first division. But the fans, in the main, never forgave Max Carey, who had replaced Uncle Robbie as manager, for sending Herman away. They didn't care about being practical. They wanted salt in their stew.

Removed from the choice Brooklyn atmosphere, where he flourished, the Babe began to bounce from place to place again as he had in the days of his youth. Managers resumed the practice of firing him to save their health. He went from Cincinnati to Chicago to Pittsburgh to Cincinnati to Detroit to Toledo to Syracuse to Jersey City, and finally, with a strong tail wind, clear out to the Pacific Coast. The slower he got as a player, the more money he asked, and the more loudly he asked for it.

However, the Babe did not like the word "holdout." Once, in the early spring of 1934, he denounced the press of Los Angeles, near his home, for using that term to describe him.

"You got the wrong idea entirely," he told the reporters sternly. "I am not holding out. I just don't want to sign this _____ contract the Cubs have sent me, because the dough ain't big enough."

On his second time around in Cincinnati, in 1936, Mr. Herman came into contract with baseball's leading genius, Leland Stanford MacPhail, who was the Reds' general manager. They were bound to get together sometime, even though the Babe left Brooklyn before MacPhail was ripe for that city. It was also inevitable that MacPhail should some day fine Herman, and some day fire him. They were not made to be soulmates. MacPhail fined him, and Paul Derringer, the pitcher, $200 each, one day in July. It was a true Herman episode. With hostile runners on first and third, Derringer made a balk. The runner on third went home, and the runner on first went to second. Herman, communing with nature in the outfield, missed the play completely. He thought there were still men on first and third. When the next hitter singled to the Babe on one bounce, he studied the stitches on the ball and lobbed it back to the infield. The runner on second scored standing up. MacPhail turned purple, and levied his fines on both the pitcher and the Babe.

It's a matter of record that Derringer got his fine canceled, by throwing an inkwell at MacPhail, which impressed the great man. Mr. Herman was less direct, and therefore less successful. He waited a few weeks after being fined. Then he demanded from MacPhail a cash bonus over and above his salary. It was an ill-timed request.

"A bonus!" yelled the genius. "Why, you're not even good enough to play on the team!" He added that Herman was fired. And he was.

Right to the end of his playing days, the Babe retained his fresh young affection for cash money. He was farming turkeys at his home in Glendale by the time he landed with the Hollywood club of the Pacific Coast League in the twilight of his career. One day in 1942— just a short while before that final, nostalgic, wartime bow in Brooklyn—he arranged to have his turkeys advertised on the scorecards in the Hollywood ball park. He then announced that he was holding out. The holdout kept him home in comfort among the turkeys, but not so far away from Hollywood that he couldn't drive over from time to time to negotiate. When he finally got his price and signed up to play ball, the Babe was fat and his reflexes were slow. So he made his season's debut at a disadvantage.

Hollywood was playing a game with Seattle. The score was tied going into the tenth inning. Seattle's young pitcher, a kid named Soriano, had already struck out ten men. Hollywood filled the bases on him, with two out, in the last of the 10th, but the boy was still strong and fast. The manager asked Mr. Herman if he was in shape to go in and pinch-hit.

"I may not be sharp," said the Babe, reaching for a bat, "and maybe I can't hit him. But I won't have to. I'll paralyze him."

He walked to the plate. He glowered at the pitcher, and held his bat at a menacing angle. He never swung it. Five pitches went by—three of them balls, two of them strikes. Then Mr. Herman pounded the plate, assumed a fearful scowl, and made as though his next move would tear a hole in the outfield wall. The last pitch from the nervous Soriano hit the ground in front of the Babe's feet for ball four. A run was forced in, and the ball game was over.

"That's a boy with an education," said the Babe, as he threw away his bat. "I see he's heard of Herman."

— FICTION —

HERE's the big baby right here.

Alibi Ike

RING W. LARDNER

HIS RIGHT NAME was Frank X. Farrell, and I guess the X stood for "Excuse me." Because he never pulled a play, good or bad, on or off the field, without apologizin' for it.

"Alibi Ike" was the name Carey wished on him the first day he reported down South. O' course we all cut out the "Alibi" part of it right away for the fear he would overhear it and bust somebody. But we called him "Ike" right to his face and the rest of it was understood by everybody on the club except Ike himself.

He ast me one time, he says:

"What do you all call me Ike for? I ain't no Yid."

"Carey give you the name," I says. "It's his nickname for everybody he takes a likin' to."

"He mustn't have only a few friends then," says Ike. "I never heard him say 'Ike' to nobody else."

But I was goin' to tell you about Carey namin' him. We'd been workin' out two weeks and the pitchers was showin' somethin' when this bird joined us. His first day out he stood up there so good and took such

a reef at the old pill that he had everyone lookin'. Then him and Carey
was together in left field, catchin' fungoes, and it was after we was
through for the day that Carey told me about him.

"What do you think of Alibi Ike?" ast Carey.

"Who's that?" I says.

"This here Farrell in the outfield," says Carey.

"He looks like he could hit," I says.

"Yes," says Carey, "but he can't hit near as good as he can apologize."

Then Carey went on to tell me what Ike had been pullin' out there.
He'd dropped the first fly ball that was hit to him and told Carey his glove
wasn't broke in good yet, and Carey says the glove could easy of been
Kid Gleason's gran'father. He made a whale of a catch out o' the next one
and Carey says "Nice work!" or somethin' like that, but Ike says he could
of caught the ball with his back turned only he slipped when he started
after it and, besides that, the air currents fooled him.

"I thought you done well to get to the ball," says Carey.

"I ought to been settin' under it," says Ike.

"What did you hit last year?" Carey ast him.

"I had malaria most o' the season," says Ike. "I wound up with .356."

"Where would I have to go to get malaria?" says Carey, but Ike
didn't wise up.

I and Carey and him set at the same table together for supper. It took
him half an hour longer'n us to eat because he had to excuse himself
every time he lifted his fork.

"Doctor told me I needed starch," he'd say, and then toss a shovelful
o' potatoes into him. Or, "They ain't much meat on one o' these chops,"
he'd tell us, and grab another one. Or he'd say: "Nothin' like onions for
a cold," and then he'd dip into the perfumery.

"Better try that apple sauce," says Carey. "It'll help your malaria."

"Whose malaria?" says Ike. He'd forgot already why he didn't only
hit .356 last year.

I and Carey begin to lead him on.

"Whereabouts did you say your home was?" I ast him.

"I live with my folks," he says. "We live in Kansas City—not right
down in the business part—outside a ways."

"How's that come?" says Carey. "I should think you'd get rooms in
the post office."

But Ike was too busy curin' his cold to get that one.

"Are you married?" I ast him.

"No," he says. "I never run round much with girls, except to shows
onet in a wile and parties and dances and roller skatin'."

"Never take 'em to the prize fights, eh?" says Carey.

"We don't have no real good bouts," says Ike. "Just bush stuff. And
I never figured a boxin' match was a place for the ladies."

Well, after supper he pulled a cigar out and lit it. I was just goin' to ask him what he done it for, but he beat me to it.

"Kind o' rests a man to smoke after a good workout," he says. "Kind o' settles a man's supper, too."

"Looks like a pretty good cigar," says Carey.

"Yes," says Ike. "A friend o' mine give it to me—a fella in Kansas City that runs a billiard room."

"Do you play billiards?" I ast him.

"I used to play a fair game," he says. "I'm all out o' practice now— can't hardly make a shot."

We coaxed him into a four-handed battle, him and Carey against Jack Mack and I. Say, he couldn't play billiards as good as Willie Hoppe; not quite. But to hear him tell it, he didn't make a good shot all evenin'. I'd leave him an awful-lookin' layout and he'd gather 'em up in one try and then run a couple o' hundred, and between every carom he'd say he put too much stuff on the ball, or the English didn't take, or the table wasn't true, or his stick was crooked, or somethin'. And all the time he had the balls actin' like they was Dutch soldiers and him Kaiser William. We started out to play fifty points, but we had to make it a thousand so as I and Jack and Carey could try the table.

The four of us set round the lobby a wile after we was through playin', and when it got along toward bedtime Carey whispered to me and says:

"Ike'd like to go to bed, but he can't think up no excuse."

Carey hadn't hardly finished whisperin' when Ike got up and pulled it.

"Well, good night, boys," he says. "I ain't sleepy, but I got some gravel in my shoes and it's killin' my feet."

We knowed he hadn't never left the hotel since we'd came in from the grounds and changed our clo'es. So Carey says:

"I should think they'd take them gravel pits out o' the billiard room."

But Ike was already on his way to the elevator, limpin'.

"He's got the world beat," says Carey to Jack and I. "I've knew lots o' guys that had an alibi for every mistake they made; I've heard pitchers say that the ball slipped when somebody cracked one off'n 'em; I've heard infielders complain of a sore arm after heavin' one into the stand, and I've saw outfielders tooken sick with a dizzy spell when they've misjudged a fly ball. But this baby can't even go to bed without apologizin', and I bet he excuses himself to the razor when he gets ready to shave."

"And at that," says Jack, "he's goin' to make us a good man."

"Yes," says Carey, "unless rheumatism keeps his battin' average down to .400."

Well, sir, Ike kept whalin' away at the ball all through the trip till everybody knowed he'd won a job. Cap had him in there regular the last

few exhibition games and told the newspaper boys a week before the
season opened that he was goin' to start him in Kane's place.

"You're there, kid," says Carey to Ike, the night Cap made the
'nnouncement. "They ain't many boys that wins a big league berth their
third year out."

"I'd of been up here a year ago," says Ike, "only I was bent over all
season with lumbago."

II

It rained down in Cincinnati one day and somebody organized a
little game o' cards. They was shy two men to make six and ast I and
Carey to play.

"I'm with you if you get Ike and make it seven-handed," says Carey.

So they got a hold of Ike and we went up to Smitty's room.

"I pretty near forgot how many you deal," says Ike. "It's been a long
wile since I played."

I and Carey give each other the wink, and sure enough, he was just
as ig'orant about poker as billiards. About the second hand, the pot was
opened two or three ahead of him, and they was three in when it come
his turn. It cost a buck, and he throwed in two.

"It's raised, boys," somebody says.

"Gosh, that's right, I did raise it," says Ike.

"Take out a buck if you didn't mean to tilt her," says Carey.

"No," says Ike, "I'll leave it go."

Well, it was raised back at him, and then he made another mistake
and raised again. They was only three left in when the draw come.
Smitty'd opened with a pair o' kings and he didn't help 'em. Ike stood
pat. The guy that'd raised him back was flushin' and he didn't fill. So
Smitty checked and Ike bet and didn't get no call. He tossed his hand
away, but I grabbed it and give it a look. He had king, queen, jack and
two tens. Alibi Ike he must have seen me peekin', for he leaned over and
whispered to me.

"I overlooked my hand," he says. "I thought all the wile it was a
straight."

"Yes," I says, "that's why you raised twice by mistake."

They was another pot that he come into with tens and fours. It was
tilted a couple o' times and two o' the strong fellas drawed ahead of Ike.
They each drawed one. So Ike throwed away his little pair and come out
with four tens. And they was four treys against him. Carey'd looked at
Ike's discards and then he says:

"This lucky bum busted two pair."

"No, no, I didn't," says Ike.

"Yes, yes, you did," says Carey, and showed us the two fours.

"What do you know about that?" says Ike. "I'd of swore one was a
five spot."

Well, we hadn't had no pay day yet, and after a wile everybody except Ike was goin' shy. I could see him gettin' restless and I was wonderin' how he'd make the get-away. He tried two or three times. "I got to buy some collars before supper," he says.

"No hurry," says Smitty. "The stores here keeps open all night in April."

After a minute he opened up again.

"My uncle out in Nebraska ain't expected to live," he says. "I ought to send a telegram."

"Would that save him?" says Carey.

"No, it sure wouldn't," says Ike, "but I ought to leave my old man know where I'm at."

"When did you hear about your uncle?" says Carey.

"Just this mornin'," says Ike.

"Who told you?" ast Carey.

"I got a wire from my old man," says Ike.

"Well," says Carey, "your old man knows you're still here yet this afternoon if you was here this mornin'. Trains leavin' Cincinnati in the middle o' the day don't carry no ball clubs."

"Yes," says Ike, "that's true. But he don't know where I'm goin' to be next week."

"Ain't he got no schedule?" ast Carey.

"I sent him one openin' day," says Ike, "but it takes mail a long time to get to Idaho."

"I thought your old man lived in Kansas City," says Carey.

"He does when he's home," says Ike.

"But now," says Carey, "I s'pose he's went to Idaho so as he can be near your sick uncle in Nebraska."

"He's visitin' my other uncle in Idaho."

"Then how does he keep posted about your sick uncle?" ast Carey.

"He don't," says Ike. "He don't even know my other uncle's sick. That's why I ought to wire and tell him."

"Good night!" says Carey.

"What town in Idaho is your old man at?" I says.

Ike thought it over.

"No town at all," he says. "But he's near a town."

"Near what town?" I says.

"Yuma," says Ike.

Well, by this time he'd lost two or three pots and he was desperate. We was playin' just as fast as we could, because we seen we couldn't hold him much longer. But he was tryin' so hard to frame an escape that he couldn't pay no attention to the cards, and it looked like we'd get his whole pile away from him if we could make him stick.

The telephone saved him. The minute it begun to ring, five of us jumped for it. But Ike was there first.

"Yes," he says, answerin' it. "This is him. I'll come right down."

And he slammed up the receiver and beat it out o' the door without even sayin' good-by.

"Smitty'd ought to locked the door," says Carey.

"What did he win?" ast Carey.

We figured it up—sixty-odd bucks.

"And the next time we ask him to play," says Carey, "his fingers will be so stiff he can't hold the cards."

Well, we set round a wile talkin' it over, and pretty soon the telephone rung again. Smitty answered it. It was a friend of his'n from Hamilton and he wanted to know why Smitty didn't hurry down. He was the one that had called before and Ike had told him he was Smitty.

"Ike'd ought to split with Smitty's friend," says Carey.

"No," I says, "he'll need all he won. It costs money to buy collars and to send telegrams from Cincinnati to your old man in Texas and keep him posted on the health o' your uncle in Cedar Rapids, D.C."

III

And you ought to heard him out there on that field! They wasn't a day when he didn't pull six or seven, and it didn't make no difference whether he was goin' good or bad. If he popped up in the pinch he should of made a base hit and the reason he didn't was so-and-so. And if he cracked one for three bases he ought to had a home run, only the ball wasn't lively, or the wind brought it back, or he tripped on a lump o' dirt, roundin' first base.

They was one afternoon in New York when he beat all records. Big Marquard was workin' against us and he was good.

In the first innin' Ike hit one clear over that right field stand, but it was a few feet foul. Then he got another foul and then the count come to two and two. Then Rube slipped one acrost on him and he was called out.

"What do you know about that!" he says afterward on the bench. "I lost count. I thought it was three and one, and I took a strike."

"You took a strike all right," says Carey. "Even the umps knowed it was a strike."

"Yes," says Ike, "but you can bet I wouldn't of took it if I'd knew it was the third one. The scoreboard had it wrong."

"That scoreboard ain't for you to look at," says Cap. "It's for you to hit that old pill against."

"Well," says Ike, "I could of hit that one over the scoreboard if I'd knew it was the third."

"Was it a good ball?" I says.

"Well, no, it wasn't," says Ike. "It was inside."

"How far inside?" says Carey.

"Oh, two or three inches or half a foot," says Ike.

"I guess you wouldn't of threatened the scoreboard with it then," says Cap.

"I'd of pulled it down the right foul line if I hadn't thought he'd call it a ball," says Ike.

Well, in New York's part o' the innin' Doyle cracked one and Ike run back a mile and a half and caught it with one hand. We was all sayin' what a whale of a play it was, but he had to apologize just the same as for gettin' struck out.

"That stand's so high," he says, "that a man don't never see a ball till it's right on top o' you."

"Didn't you see that one?" ast Cap.

"Not at first," says Ike; "not till it raised up above the roof o' the stand."

"Then why did you start back as soon as the ball was hit?" says Cap.

"I knowed by the sound that he'd got a good hold of it," says Ike.

"Yes," says Cap, "but how'd you know what direction to run in?"

"Doyle usually hits 'em that way, the way I run," says Ike.

"Why don't you play blindfolded?" says Carey.

"Might as well, with that big high stand to bother a man," says Ike. "If I could of saw the ball all the time I'd of got it in my hip pocket."

Along in the fifth we was one run to the bad and Ike got on with one out. On the first ball throwed to Smitty, Ike went down. The ball was outside and Meyers throwed Ike out by ten feet.

You could see Ike's lips movin' all the way to the bench and when he got there he had his piece learned.

"Why didn't he swing?" he says.

"Why didn't you wait for his sign?" says Cap.

"He give me his sign," says Ike.

"What's his sign with you?" says Cap.

"Pickin' up some dirt with his right hand," says Ike.

"Well, I didn't see him do it," Cap says.

"He done it all right," says Ike.

Well, Smitty went out and they wasn't no more argument till they come in for the next innin'. Then Cap opened it up.

"You fellas better get your signs straight," he says.

"Do you mean me?" says Smitty.

"Yes," Cap says. "What's your sign with Ike?"

"Slidin' my left hand up to the end o' the bat and back," says Smitty.

"Do you hear that, Ike?" ast Cap.

"What of it?" says Ike.

"You says his sign was pickin' up dirt and he says it's slidin' his hand. Which is right?"

"I'm right," says Smitty. "But if you're arguin' about him goin' last innin', I didn't give him no sign."

"You pulled your cap down with your right hand, didn't you?" ast Ike.

"Well, s'pose I did," says Smitty. "That don't mean nothin'. I never told you to take that for a sign, did I?"

"I thought maybe you meant to tell me and forgot," says Ike.

They couldn't none of us answer that and they wouldn't of been no more said if Ike had of shut up. But wile we was settin' there Carey got on with two out and stole second clean.

"There!" says Ike. "That's what I was tryin' to do and I'd of got away with it if Smitty'd swang and bothered the Indian."

"Oh!" says Smitty. "You was tryin' to steal then, was you? I thought you claimed I give you the hit and run."

"I didn't claim no such a thing," says Ike. "I thought maybe you might of gave me a sign, but I was goin' anyway because I thought I had a good start."

Cap prob'ly would of hit him with a bat, only just about that time Doyle booted one on Hayes and Carey come acrost with the run that tied.

Well, we go into the ninth finally, one and one, and Marquard walks McDonald with nobody out.

"Lay it down," says Cap to Ike.

And Ike goes up there with orders to bunt and cracks the first ball into that right-field stand! It was fair this time, and we're two ahead, but I didn't think about that at the time. I was too busy watchin' Cap's face. First he turned pale and then he got red as fire and then he got blue and purple, and finally he just laid back and busted out laughin'. So we wasn't afraid to laugh ourselfs when we seen him doin' it, and when Ike come in everybody on the bench was in hysterics.

But instead o' takin' advantage, Ike had to try and excuse himself. His play was to shut up and he didn't know how to make it.

"Well," he says, "if I hadn't hit quite so quick at that one I bet it'd of cleared the center-field fence."

Cap stopped laughin'.

"It'll cost you plain fifty," he says.

"What for?" says Ike.

"When I say 'bunt' I mean 'bunt,'" says Cap.

"You didn't say 'bunt,'" says Ike.

"I says 'Lay it down,'" says Cap. "If that don't mean 'bunt,' what does it mean?"

"'Lay it down' means 'bunt' all right," says Ike, "but I understood you to say 'Lay on it.'"

"All right," says Cap, "and the little misunderstandin' will cost you fifty."

Ike didn't say nothin' for a few minutes. Then he had another bright idear.

"I was just kiddin' about misunderstandin' you," he says. "I knowed you wanted me to bunt."

"Well, then, why didn't you bunt?" ast Cap.

"I was goin' to on the next ball," says Ike. "But I thought if I took a good wallop I'd have 'em all fooled. So I walloped at the first one to fool 'em, and I didn't have no intention o' hittin' it."

"You tried to miss it, did you?" says Cap.

"Yes," says Ike.

"How'd you happen to hit it?" ast Cap.

"Well," Ike says, "I was lookin' for him to throw me a fast one and I was goin' to swing under it. But he come with a hook and I met it right square where I was swingin' to go under the fast one."

"Great!" says Cap. "Boys," he says, "Ike's learned how to hit Marquard's curve. Pretend a fast one's comin' and then try to miss it. It's a good thing to know and Ike'd ought to be willin' to pay for the lesson. So I'm goin' to make it a hundred instead o' fifty."

The game wound up 3 to 1. The fine didn't go, because Ike hit like a wild man all through that trip and we made pretty near a clean-up. The night we went to Philly I got him cornered in the car and I says to him:

"Forget them alibis for a wile and tell me somethin'. What'd you do that for, swing that time against Marquard when you was told to bunt?"

"I'll tell you," he says. "That ball he throwed me looked just like the one I struck out on in the first innin' and I wanted to show Cap what I could of done to that other one if I'd knew it was the third strike."

"But," I says, "the one you struck out on in the first innin' was a fast ball."

"So was the one I cracked in the ninth," says Ike.

IV

You've saw Cap's wife, o' course. Well, her sister's about twict as good-lookin' as her, and that's goin' some.

Cap took his missus down to St. Louis the second trip and the other one come down from St. Joe to visit her. Her name is Dolly, and some doll is right.

Well, Cap was goin' to take the two sisters to a show and he wanted a beau for Dolly. He left it to her and she picked Ike. He'd hit three on the nose that afternoon—of'n Sallee, too.

They fell for each other that first evenin'. Cap told us how it come off. She begin flatterin' Ike for the star game he'd played and o' course he begin excusin' himself for not doin' better. So she thought he was modest and it went strong with her. And she believed everything he said and that made her solid with him—that and her make-up. They was together every mornin' and evenin' for the five days we was there. In the afternoons Ike played the grandest ball you ever see, hittin' and runnin' the bases like a fool and catchin' everything that stayed in the park.

I told Cap, I says: "You'd ought to keep the doll with us and he'd make Cobb's figures look sick."

But Dolly had to go back to St. Joe and we come home for a long serious.

Well, for the next three weeks Ike had a letter to read every day and he'd set in the clubhouse readin' it till mornin' practice was half over. Gap didn't say nothin' to him, because he was goin' so good. But I and Carey wasted a lot of our time tryin' to get him to own up who the letters was from. Fine chanct!

"What are you readin'?" Carey'd say. "A bill?"

"No," Ike'd say, "not exactly a bill. It's a letter from a fella I used to go to school with."

"High school or college?" I'd ask him.

"College," he'd say.

"What college?" I'd say.

Then he'd stall a wile and then he'd say:

"I didn't go to the college myself, but my friend went there."

"How did it happen you didn't go?" Carey'd ask him.

"Well," he'd say, "they wasn't no colleges near where I lived."

"Didn't you live in Kansas City?" I'd say to him.

One time he'd say he did and another time he didn't. One time he says he lived in Michigan.

"Where at?" says Carey.

"Near Detroit," he says.

"Well," I says, "Detroit's near Ann Arbor and that's where they got the university."

"Yes," says Ike, "they got it there now, but they didn't have it there then."

"I come pretty near goin' to Syracuse," I says, "only they wasn't no railroads runnin' through there in them days."

"Where'd this friend o' yours go to college?" says Carey.

"I forget now," says Ike.

"Was it Carlisle?" ast Carey.

"No," says Ike, "his folks wasn't very well off."

"That's what barred me from Smith," I says.

"I was goin' to tackle Cornell's," says Carey, "but the doctor told me I'd have hay fever if I didn't stay up North."

"Your friend writes long letters," I says.

"Yes," says Ike; "he's tellin' me about a ballplayer."

"Where does he play?" ast Carey.

"Down in the Texas League—Fort Wayne," says Ike.

"It looks like a girl's writin'," Carey says.

"A girl wrote it," says Ike. "That's my friend's sister, writin' for him."

"Didn't they teach writin' at this here college where he went?" says Carey.

"Sure," Ike says, "they taught writin', but he got his hand cut off in a railroad wreck."

"How long ago?" I says.

"Right after he got out o' college," says Ike.

"Well," I says, "I should think he'd of learned to write with his left hand by this time."

"It's his left hand that was cut off," says Ike; "and he was left-handed."

"You get a letter every day," says Carey. "They're all the same writin'. Is he tellin' you about a different ballplayer every time he writes?"

"No," Ike says. "It's the same ballplayer. He just tells me what he does every day."

"From the size o' the letters, they don't play nothin' but double-headers down there," says Carey.

We figured that Ike spent most of his evenins answerin' the letters from his "friend's sister," so we kept tryin' to date him up for shows and parties to see how he'd duck out of 'em. He was bugs over spaghetti, so we told him one day that they was goin' to be a big feed of it over to Joe's that night and he was invited.

"How long'll it last?" he says.

"Well," we says, "we're goin' right over there after the game and stay till they close up."

"I can't go," he says, "unless they leave me come home at eight bells."

"Nothin' doin'," says Carey. "Joe'd get sore."

"I can't go then," says Ike.

"Why not?" I ast him.

"Well," he says, "my landlady locks up the house at eight and I left my key home."

"You can come and stay with me," says Carey.

"No," he says, "I can't sleep in a strange bed."

"How do you get along when we're on the road?" says I.

"I don't never sleep the first night anywheres," he says. "After that I'm all right."

"You'll have time to chase home and get your key right after the game," I told him.

"The key ain't home," says Ike. "I lent it to one o' the other fellas and he's went out o' town and took it with him."

"Couldn't you borry another key off'n the landlady?" Carey ast him.

"No," he says, "that's the only one they is."

Well, the day before we started East again, Ike come into the club-house all smiles.

"Your birthday?" I ast him.

"No," he says.

"What do you feel so good about?" I says.

"Got a letter from my old man," he says. "My uncle's goin' to get well."

"Is that the one in Nebraska?" says I.

"Not right in Nebraska," says Ike. "Near there."

But afterwards we got the right dope from Cap. Dolly'd blew in from Missouri and was going to make the trip with her sister.

V

Well, I want to alibi Carey and I for what come off in Boston. If we'd of had any idear what we was doin', we'd never did it. They wasn't nobody outside o' maybe Ike and the dame that felt worse over it than I and Carey.

The first two days we didn't see nothin' of Ike and her except out to the park. The rest o' the time they was sight-seein' over to Cambridge and down to Revere and out to Brook-a-line and all the other places where the rubes go.

But when we come into the beanery after the third game Cap's wife called us over.

"If you want to see somethin' pretty," she says, "look at the third finger on Sis's left hand."

Well, o' course we knowed before we looked that it wasn't goin' to be no hangnail. Nobody was su'prised when Dolly blew into the dinin' room with it—a rock that Ike'd bought off'n Diamond Joe the first trip to New York. Only o' course it'd been set into a lady's-size ring instead o' the automobile tire he'd been wearin'.

Cap and his missus and Ike and Dolly ett supper together, only Ike didn't eat nothin', but just set there blushin' and spillin' things on the tablecloth. I heard him excusin' himself for not havin' no appetite. He says he couldn't never eat when he was clost to the ocean. He'd forgot about them sixty-five oysters he destroyed the first night o' the trip before.

He was goin' to take her to a show, so after supper he went upstairs to change his collar. She had to doll up, too, and o' course Ike was through long before her.

If you remember the hotel in Boston, they's a little parlor where the piano's at and then they's another little parlor openin' off o' that. Well, when Ike come down Smitty was playin' a few chords and I and Carey was harmonizin'. We seen Ike go up to the desk to leave his key and we called him in. He tried to duck away, but we wouldn't stand for it.

We ast him what he was all duded up for and he says he was goin' to the theayter.

"Goin' alone?" says Carey.

"No," he says, "a friend o' mine's goin' with me."

"What do you say if we go along?" says Carey.

"I ain't only got two tickets," he says.

"Well," says Carey, "we can go down there with you and buy our own seats; maybe we can all get together."

"No," says Ike. "They ain't no more seats. They're all sold out."

"We can buy some off'n the scalpers," says Carey.

"I wouldn't if I was you," says Ike. "They say the show's rotten."

"What are you goin' for, then?" I ast.

"I didn't hear about it bein' rotten till I got the tickets," he says.

"Well," I says, "if you don't want to go I'll buy the tickets from you."

"No," says Ike, "I wouldn't want to cheat you. I'm stung and I'll just have to stand for it."

"What are you goin' to do with the girl, leave her here at the hotel?" I says.

"What girl?" says Ike.

"The girl you ett supper with," I says.

"Oh," he says, "we just happened to go into the dinin' room together, that's all. Cap wanted I should set down with 'em."

"I noticed," says Carey, "that she happened to be wearin' that rock you bought off'n Diamond Joe."

"Yes," says Ike. "I lent it to her for a wile."

"Did you lend her the new ring that goes with it?" I says.

"She had that already," says Ike. "She lost the set out of it."

"I wouldn't trust no strange girl with a rock o' mine," says Carey.

"Oh, I guess she's all right," Ike says. "Besides, I was tired o' the stone. When a girl asks you for somethin', what are you goin' to do?"

He started out toward the desk, but we flagged him.

"Wait a minute!" Carey says. "I got a bet with Sam here and it's up to you to settle it."

"Well," says Ike, "make it snappy. My friend'll be here any minute."

"I bet," says Carey, "that you and that girl was engaged to be married."

"Nothin' to it," says Ike.

"Now look here," says Carey, "this is goin' to cost me real money if I lose. Cut out the alibi stuff and give it to us straight. Cap's wife just as good as told us you was roped."

Ike blushed like a kid.

"Well, boys," he says, "I may as well own up. You win, Carey."

"Yatta boy!" says Carey. "Congratulations!"

"You got a swell girl, Ike," I says.

"She's a peach," says Smitty.

"Well, I guess she's O.K.," says Ike. "I don't know much about girls."

"Didn't you never run round with 'em?" I says.

"Oh, yes, plenty of 'em," says Ike. "But I never seen none I'd fall for."

"That is, till you seen this one," says Carey.

"Well," says Ike, "this one's O.K., but I wasn't thinkin' about gettin' married yet a wile."

"Who done the askin', her?" says Carey.

"Oh, no," says Ike, "but sometimes a man don't know what he's gettin' into. Take a good-lookin' girl, and a man gen'ally almost always does about what she wants him to."

"They couldn't no girl lasso me unless I wanted to be lassoed," says Smitty.

"Oh, I don't know," says Ike. "When a fella gets to feelin' sorry for one of 'em it's all off."

Well, we left him go after shakin' hands all round. But he didn't take Dolly to no show that night. Some time wile we was talkin' she'd came into that other parlor and she'd stood there and heard us. I don't know how much she heard. But it was enough. Dolly and Cap's missus took the midnight train for New York. And from there Cap's wife sent her on her way back to Missouri.

She'd left the ring and note for Ike with the clerk. But we didn't ask Ike if the note was from his friend in Fort Wayne, Texas.

VI

When we'd came to Boston Ike was hittin' plain .397. When we got back home he'd fell off to pretty near nothin'. He hadn't drove one out o' the infield in any o' them other Eastern parks, and he didn't even give no excuse for it.

To show you how bad he was, he struck out three times in Brooklyn one day and never opened his trap when Cap ast him what was the matter. Before, if he'd whiffed oncet in a game he'd of wrote a book tellin' why.

Well, we dropped from first place to fifth in four weeks and we was still goin' down. I and Carey was about the only ones in the club that spoke to each other, and all as we did was to remind ourself o' what a boner we'd pulled.

"It's goin' to beat us out o' the big money," says Carey.

"Yes," I says. "I don't want to knock my own ball club, but it looks like a one-man team, and when that one man's dauber's down we couldn't trim our whiskers."

"We ought to knew better," says Carey.

"Yes," I says, "but why should a man pull an alibi for bein' engaged to such a bearcat as she was?"

"He shouldn't," says Carey. "But I and you knowed he would or we'd never started talkin' to him about it. He wasn't no more ashamed o' the girl than I am of a regular base hit. But he just can't come clean on no subjec'."

Cap had the whole story, and I and Carey was as pop'lar with him as an umpire.

"What do you want me to do, Cap?" Carey'd say to him before goin' up to hit.

"Use your own judgment," Cap'd tell him. "We want to lose another game."

But finally, one night in Pittsburgh, Cap had a letter from his missus and he come to us with it.

"You fellas," he says, "is the ones that put us on the bum, and if you're sorry I think they's a chancet for you to make good. The old lady's out to St. Joe and she's been tryin' her hardest to fix things up. She's explained that Ike don't mean nothin' with his talk; I've wrote and explained that to Dolly, too. But the old lady says that Dolly says that she can't believe it. But Dolly's still stuck on this baby, and she's pinin' away just the same as Ike. And the old lady says she thinks if you two fellas would write to the girl and explain how you was always kiddin' with Ike and leadin' him on, and how the ball club was all shot to pieces since Ike quit hittin', and how he acted like he was goin' to kill himself, and this and that, she'd fall for it and maybe soften down. Dolly, the old lady says, would believe you before she'd believe I and the old lady, because she thinks it's her we're sorry for, and not him."

Well, I and Carey was only too glad to try and see what we could do. But it wasn't no snap. We wrote about eight letters before we got one that looked good. Then we give it to the stenographer and had it wrote out on a typewriter and both of us signed it.

It was Carey's idear that made the letter good. He stuck in somethin' about the world's serious money that our wives wasn't goin' to spend unless she took pity on a "boy who was so shy and modest that he was afraid to come right out and say that he had asked such a beautiful and handsome girl to become his bride."

That's prob'ly what got her, or maybe she couldn't of held out much longer anyway. It was four days after we sent the letter that Cap heard from his missus again. We was in Cincinnati.

"We've won," he says to us. "The old lady says that Dolly says she'll give him another chance. But the old lady says it won't do no good for Ike to write a letter. He'll have to go out there."

"Send him tonight," says Carey.

"I'll pay half his fare," I says.

"I'll pay the other half," says Carey.

"No," says Cap, "the club'll pay his expenses. I'll send him scoutin'."

"Are you goin' to send him tonight?"

"Sure," says Cap. "But I'm goin' to break the news to him right now. It's time we win a ball game."

So in the clubhouse, just before the game, Cap told him. And I certainly felt sorry for Rube Benton and Red Ames that afternoon! I and Carey was standin' in front o' the hotel that night when Ike come out with his suitcase.

"Sent home?" I says to him.

"No," he says, "I'm goin' scoutin'."

"Where to?" I says. "Fort Wayne?"

"No, not exactly," he says.

"Well," says Carey, "have a good time."

"I ain't lookin' for no good time," says Ike. "I says I was goin' scoutin'."

"Well, then," says Carey, "I hope you see somebody you like."

"And you better have a drink before you go," I says.

"Well," says Ike, "they claim it helps a cold."

SPOT REPORTING

MANY WILL consider this a shocking piece. Many others will, after reading it together with John Updike's coverage of the same event later in this book, be even more shocked—and regret, perhaps, that they did not read the Updike first. Perhaps that is not a bad idea. Why not turn to the Updike now, then return to this one, written by a master at the baseball-writing craft, who was assigned, by the editors of *Sport* magazine, "to deliver benediction on Ted Williams."

1960: The Kid's Last Game

ED LINN

WEDNESDAY, SEPTEMBER 26, was a cold and dreary day in Boston, a curious bit of staging on the part of those gods who always set the scene most carefully for Ted Williams. It was to be the last game Ted would ever play in Boston. Not until the game was over would Williams let it be known that it was the last game he would play anywhere.

Ted came into the locker room at 10:50, very early for him. He was dressed in dark brown slacks, a yellow sport shirt and a light tan pullover sweater, tastily brocaded in the same color. Ted went immediately to his locker, pulled off the sweater, then strolled into the trainer's room.

Despite all the triumphs and the honors, it had been a difficult year for him. As trainer Jack Fadden put it, "It hasn't been a labor of love for Ted this year; it's just been labor." On two separate occasions, he had come very close to giving it all up.

The spring-training torture had been made no easier for Ted by manager Billy Jurges. Jurges believed that the only way for a man Ted's age to stay in condition was to reach a peak at the beginning of the season and hold it by playing just as often as possible. "The most we can expect from Williams," Jurges had said, at the time of Ted's signing, "is 100 games. The least is pinch-hitting." Ted played in 113 games.

Throughout the training season, however, Ted seemed to be having trouble with his timing. Recalling his .254 average of the previous season, the experts wrote him off for perhaps the 15th time in his career. But on his first time at bat in the opening game, Ted hit a 500-foot home run, possibly the longest of his career, off Camilo Pascual, probably the best pitcher in the league. The next day, in the Fenway Park opener, he hit a second homer, this one off Jim Coates. Ted pulled a leg muscle running out that homer, though, and when a man's muscles go while he is doing nothing more than jogging around the bases, the end is clearly in sight.

It took him almost a month to get back in condition, but the mysterious virus infection that hits him annually, a holdover from his service in Korea, laid him low again almost immediately. Since the doctors have never been able to diagnose this chronic illness, the only way they can treat him is to shoot a variety of drugs and antibiotics into him, in the hope that one of them takes hold. Ted, miserable and drugged when he finally got back in uniform, failed in a couple of pinch-hitting attempts and was just about ready to quit. Against the Yankees, Ralph Terry struck him out two straight times. The third time up, the count went to 3-2 when Williams unloaded on a waist-high fast ball and sent it into the bullpen in right-center, 400 feet away.

The blast triggered the greatest home-run spurt of Ted's career. Seven days later, he hit his 500th home run. He had started only 15 1960 games and he had hit eight 1960 homers. When he hit his 506th (and 11th of the year), he had homered once in every 6.67 times at bat.

Cold weather always bothered Ted, even in his early years, and so when he strained his shoulder late in August, he was just about ready to announce his retirement again. He had found it difficult to loosen up even in fairly warm weather, and to complicate matters he had found it necessary—back in the middle of 1959—to cut out the calisthenics routine he had always gone through in the clubhouse. The exercising had left him almost too weary to play ball.

Ted started every game so stiff that he was forced to exaggerate an old passion for swinging at balls only in the strike zone. In his first time at bat, he would look for an inside pitch between the waist and knees, the only pitch he could swing at naturally. In the main, however, Ted was more than willing to take the base on balls his first time up.

He stayed on for two reasons. Mike Higgins, who had replaced Jurges as Sox manager, told him bluntly, "You're paid to play ball, so go out and play." The strength behind those words rested in the fact that both Williams and Higgins knew very well that owner Tom Yawkey would continue to pay Ted whether he played or not.

In addition, the Red Sox had two series remaining with the Yankees and Orioles, who were still locked together in the pennant race. Ted did not think it fair to eliminate himself as a factor in the two-team battle. He announced his retirement just after the Yankees clinched the pennant.

Four days earlier, Ted had been called to a special meeting with Yawkey, Higgins, Dick O'Connell (who was soon to be named business manager) and publicity director Jack Malaney. This was to offer Ted the job of general manager, a position that had been discussed occasionally in the past.

Ted refused to accept the title until he proved he could do the job. He agreed, however, to work in the front office in 1961, assisting Higgins with player personnel, and O'Connell with business matters.

The coverage of Ted's last game was at a minimum. It was thought for a while that *Life* magazine wanted to send a crew down to cover the game, but it developed that they only wanted to arrange for Ted to represent them at the World Series. Dave Garroway's *Today* program tried to set up a telephone interview the morning of the game, but they couldn't get in touch with Ted. The Red Sox, alone among big-league clubs, have offered little help to anyone on the public relations front— and never any help at all where Ted Williams was concerned. Ted didn't live at the Kenmore Hotel with the rest of the unattached players. He lived about 100 yards down Commonwealth Avenue, at the Somerset. All calls and messages for him were diverted to the manager's office.

The ceremonies that were to mark his departure were rather limited, too. The Boston Chamber of Commerce had arranged to present him with a silver bowl, and the mayor's office and governor's office had quickly muscled into the picture. By Wednesday morning, however, the governor's office—which had apparently anticipated something more spectacular—begged off. The governor's spokesman suggested the presentation of a scroll at Ted's hotel, a suggestion which Ted simply ignored.

The only civilian in the clubhouse when Ted entered was the man from *Sport,* and he was talking to Del Baker, who was about to retire, too, after 50 years in the game. Ted looked over, scowled, seemed about to say something but changed his mind.

Our man was well aware what Ted was about to say. The Red Sox have a long-standing rule—also unique in baseball—that no reporter may enter the dressing room before the game, or for the first 15 minutes after the game. It was a point of honor with Ted to pick out any civilian who wasn't specifically with a ballplayer and to tell him, as loudly as possible, "You're not supposed to be in here, you know."

Sure enough, when our man started toward Ted's locker in the far corner of the room, Ted pointed a finger at him and shouted, "You're not supposed to be in here, you know."

"The same warm, glad cry of greeting I always get from you," our man said. "It's your last day. Why don't you live a little?"

Ted started toward the trainer's room again, but wheeled around and came back. "You've got a nerve coming here to interview me after the last one you wrote about me!"

Our man wanted to know what was the matter with the last one.

"You called me 'unbearable,' that's what's the matter."

The full quote, it was pointed out, was that he "was sometimes unbearable but never dull," which holds a different connotation entirely.

"You've been after me for twelve years, that flogging magazine," he said, in his typically well-modulated shout. "Twelve years. I missed an appointment for some kind of luncheon. I forgot what happened . . . it doesn't matter anyway . . . but I forgot some appointment twelve years ago and *Sport* magazine hasn't let up on me since."

Our man, lamentably eager to disassociate himself from this little magazine, made it clear that while he had done most of *Sport's* Williams articles in the past few years he was not a member of the staff. "And," our man pointed out, "I have been accused of turning you into a combination of Paul Bunyan and Santa Claus."

"Well, when you get back there tell them what . . . (he searched for the appropriate word, the *mot juste* as they say in the dugouts) . . . what *flog-heads* they are. Tell them that for me."

Our man sought to check the correct spelling of the adjectives with him but got back only a scowl. Ted turned around to fish something out of a cloth bag at the side of his locker. "Why don't you just write your story without me?" he said. "What do you have to talk to me for?" And then, in a suddenly weary voice: "What can I tell you now that I haven't told you before?"

"Why don't you let me tell you what the story is supposed to be?" our man said. "Then you can say yes or no." It was an unfortunate way to put the question since it invited the answer it brought.

"I can tell you before you tell me," Ted shouted. "No! No, no, no."

Our man had the impression Williams was trying to tell him something. He was right. "Look," Williams said. "If I tell you I don't want to talk to you, why don't you just take my word for it?"

The clubhouse boy had come over with a glossy photo to be signed, and Ted sat down on his stool, turned his back and signed it.

Although we are reluctant to bring *Sport* into the context of the story itself, Ted's abiding hatred toward us tells much about him and his even longer feud with Boston sportswriters. Twelve years ago, just as Ted said, an article appeared on these pages to which he took violent exception. (The fact that he is so well aware that it *was* twelve years ago suggests that he still has the magazine around somewhere, so that he can fan the flames whenever he feels them dying.) What Ted objected to in that article was an interview with his mother in San Diego. Ted objects to any peering into his private life. When he holes himself up in his hotel, when he sets a barrier around the clubhouse, when he disappears into the Florida Keys at the end of the season, he is deliberately removing himself from a world which he takes to be dangerous and hostile. His constant fighting with the newspapermen who cover him most closely is a part of the same pattern. What do newspapermen represent except the people who are supposed to pierce personal barriers? Who investigate, who pry, *who find out?*

Ted's mother has been a Salvation Army worker in San Diego all her life. She is a local character, known—not without affection—as "Salvation May." Ted himself was dedicated to the Salvation Army when he was a baby. His generosity, his unfailing instinct to come to the aid of any underdog, is in direct line with the teachings of the Army, which is quite probably the purest charitable organization in the world. Even as a boy, Ted regularly gave his 30-cent luncheon allowance to classmates he considered more needy than himself, a considerable sacrifice since the Williams family had to struggle to make ends meet.

When Ted signed with San Diego at the age of seventeen, he was a tall, skinny kid (six-three, 146 pounds). He gave most of his $150-a-month salary toward keeping up the family house and he tried to build up his weight by gorging himself on the road where the club picked up the check. One day Ted was coming into the clubhouse when Bill Lane, the owner of the Padres, motioned him over. In his deep, foghorn voice, Lane said, "Well, kid, you're leading the list. You've got the others beat."

Ted, pleased that his ability was being noted so promptly, smiled and asked, "Yeah, what list?"

"The dining room list," Lane said. "Hasn't anyone told you that your meal allowance is supposed to be five dollars a day?"

Nobody had. "Okay, Bill," Ted said, finally. "Take anything over five dollars off my salary."

Bill did, too.

Even before *Sport* went into details about his background, the Boston press had discovered his weak point and hit him hard and—it must be added—most unfairly. During Ted's second season with the Sox, one reporter had the ill grace to comment, in regard to a purely personal dispute, "But what can you expect of a youth so abnormal that he didn't go home in the off season to see his own mother?"

When Williams' World War II draft status was changed from 1A to 3A after he claimed his mother as a dependent, one Boston paper sent a private investigator to San Diego to check on her standard of living; another paper sent reporters out onto the street to ask casual passersby to pass judgment on Ted's patriotism.

Reporters were sent galloping out into the street to conduct a public-opinion poll once again when Williams was caught fishing in the Everglades while his wife was giving birth to a premature baby.

A press association later sent a story out of San Diego that Ted had sold the furniture out from under his mother—although a simple phone call could have established that it wasn't true. Ted had bought the house and the furniture for his mother. His brother—who had been in frequent trouble with the law—had sold it. The Boston papers picked up that story and gave it a big play, despite the fact that every sports editor in the city had enough background material on Ted's family to know—even without checking—that it couldn't possibly be true. It was, Ted's friends believed, their way of punishing him for not being "cooperative."

Ted had become so accustomed to looking upon any reference to his family as an unfriendly act that when *Sport* wrote about his mother, he bristled—even though her final quote was "Don't say anything about Teddy except the highest and the best. He's a wonderful son." And when he searched for some reason why the magazine would do such a thing to him, he pounced upon that broken appointment, which everybody except himself had long forgotten.

After Ted had signed the photograph the day of his last game, he sat on his stool, his right knee jumping nervously, his right hand alternately buttoning and unbuttoning the top button of his sport shirt.

When he stripped down to his shorts, there was no doubt he was forty-two. The man once called the Splendid Splinter—certainly one of the most atrocious nicknames ever committed upon an immortal—was thick around the middle. A soft roll of loose fat, drooping around the waist, brought on a vivid picture of Archie Moore.

Williams is a tall, handsome man. If they ever make that movie of his life that keeps being rumored around, the guy who plays Bret Maverick would be perfect for the part. But ballplayers age quickly. Twenty years under the sun had baked Ted's face and left it lined and leathery. Sitting there, Ted Williams had the appearance of an old Marine sergeant who had been to the battles and back.

Sal Maglie, who had the end locker on the other side of the shower-room door, suddenly caught Ted's attention. "You're a National Leaguer, Sal," Ted said, projecting his voice to the room at large. "I got a hundred dollars that the Yankees win the World Series. The Yankees will win it in four or five games."

"I'm an American Leaguer now," Sal said, quietly.

"A hundred dollars," Ted said. "A friendly bet."

"You want a friendly bet? I'll bet you a friendly dollar."

"Fifty dollars," Ted said.

"All right," Sal said. "Fifty dollars." And then, projecting his own voice, he said, "I like the Pirates, anyway."

Williams went back to his mail, as the others dressed and went out onto the field.

At length, Ted picked up his spikes, wandered into the trainer's room again, and lifting himself onto the table, carefully began to put a shine on them. A photographer gave him a ball to sign.

Ted gazed at it with distaste, then looked up at the photographer with loathing. "Are you crazy?" he snapped.

The photographer backed away, pocketed the ball and began to adjust his camera sights on Ted. "You don't belong in here," Ted shouted. And turning to the clubhouse boy, he barked, "Get him out of here."

The locker room had emptied before Ted began to dress. For Ted did not go out to take batting practice or fielding practice. He made every entrance onto the field a dramatic event. He did not leave the locker room for the dugout until 12:55, only 35 minutes before the game was scheduled to start. By then, most of the writers had already gone up to Tom Yawkey's office to hear Jackie Jensen announce that he was returning to baseball.

As Ted came quickly up the stairs and into the dugout, he almost bumped into his close friend and fishing companion, Bud Leavitt, sports editor of the Bangor *Daily News*. "Hi, Bud," Ted said, as if he were surprised Leavitt was there. "You drive up?"

A semicircle of cameramen closed in on Williams, like a bear trap, on the playing field just up above. Ted hurled a few choice oaths at them, and as an oath-hurler Ted never bats below .400. He guided Leavitt against the side of the dugout, just above the steps, so that he could continue the conversation without providing a shooting angle for the photographers. The photographers continued to shoot him in profile, though, until Ted took Leavitt by the elbow and walked him the length of the dugout. "Let's sit down," he said, as he left, "so we won't be bothered by all these blasted cameramen."

If there had been any doubt back in the locker room that Ted had decided to bow out with typical hardness, it had been completely dispelled by those first few minutes in the dugout. On his last day in Fenway Park, Ted Williams seemed resolved to remain true to his own image of himself, to permit no sentimentality or hint of sentimentality to crack that mirror through which he looks at the world and allows the world to look upon him.

And yet, in watching this strange and troubled man—the most remarkable and colorful and full-blooded human being to come upon the athletic scene since Babe Ruth—you had the feeling that he was overplaying his role, that he had struggled through the night against the impulse to make his peace, to express his gratitude, to accept the great affection that the city had been showering upon him for years. In watching him, you had the clear impression that in resisting this desire he was overreacting and becoming more profane, more impossible and—yes— more unbearable than ever.

Inside Ted Williams there has always been a struggle of two opposing forces, almost two different persons. (We are fighting the use of the word schizophrenia.) The point we are making is best illustrated through Williams' long refusal to tip his hat in acknowledgment of the cheering crowds. It has always been his contention that the people who cheered him when he hit a home run were the same people who booed him when he struck out—which, incidentally, is probably not true at all. More to our point, Ted has always insisted that although he would rather be cheered than booed, he really didn't care what the fans thought of him, one way or the other.

Obviously, though, if he really didn't care he wouldn't have bothered to make such a show of not caring. He simply would have touched his finger to his cap in that automatic, thoughtless gesture of most players and forgotten about it. Ted, in short, has always had it both ways. He gets the cheers and he pretends they mean nothing to him. He is like a rich man's nephew who treats his uncle with disrespect to prove he is not interested in his money, while all the time he is secretly dreaming that the uncle will reward such independence by leaving him most of the fortune.

Ted has it even better than that. The fans of Boston have always wooed him ardently. They always cheered him all the louder in the hope that he would reward them, at last, with that essentially meaningless tip of the hat.

This clash within Williams came to the surface as he sat and talked with Leavitt, alone and undisturbed. For, within a matter of minutes, the lack of attention began to oppress him; his voice began to rise, to pull everybody's attention back to him. The cameramen, getting the message, drifted toward him again, not in a tight pack this time but in a loose and straggling line.

With Ted talking so loudly, it was apparent that he and Leavitt were discussing how to get together, after the World Series, for their annual post-season fishing expedition. The assignment to cover the Series for *Life* had apparently upset their schedule.

"After New York," Ted said, "I'll be going right to Pittsburgh." He expressed his hope that the Yankees would wrap it all up in Yankee Stadium, so that he could join Leavitt in Bangor at the beginning of the following week. "But, dammit," he said, "if the Series goes more than five games, I'll have to go back to Pittsburgh again."

Leavitt reminded Ted of an appearance he had apparently agreed to make in Bangor. "All right," Ted said. "But no speeches or anything."

A young, redheaded woman, in her late twenties, leaned over from her box seat alongside the dugout and asked Ted if he would autograph her scorecard.

"I can't sign it, dear," Ted said. "League rules. Where are you going to be after the game?"

"You told me that once before," she said, unhappily.

"Well, where are you going to be?" Ted shouted, in the impatient way one would shout at an irritating child.

"Right here," she said.

"All right."

"But I waited before and you never came."

He ignored her.

Joe Cronin, president of the American League, came down the dugout aisle, followed by his assistant, Joe McKenney. Through Cronin's office, the local nine-o'clock news-feature program which follows the *Today* program in Boston had scheduled a filmed interview with Ted. The camera had already been set up on the home-plate side of the dugout, just in front of the box seats. Cronin talked to Ted briefly and went back to reassure the announcer that Ted would be right there. McKenney remained behind to make sure Ted didn't forget. At last Ted jumped up and shouted, "Where is it, Joe, dammit?"

When Ted followed McKenney out, it was the first time he had stuck his head onto the field all day. There were still not too many fans in the stands, although far more than would have been there on any other day to watch a seventh-place team on a cold and threatening Wednesday afternoon. At this first sight of Ted Williams, they let out a mighty roar.

As he waited alongside interviewer Jack Chase, Ted bit his lower lip, and looked blankly into space, both characteristic mannerisms. At a signal from the cameraman, Chase asked Ted how he felt about entering "the last lap."

All at once Ted was smiling. "I want to tell you, Jack, I honestly feel good about it," he said, speaking in that quick charming way of his. "You can't get blood out of a turnip, you know. I've gone as far as I can and I'm sure I wouldn't want to try it any more."

"Have we gone as far as we can with the Jimmy Fund?" he was asked.

Ted was smiling more broadly. "Oh, no. We could never go far enough with the Jimmy Fund."

Chase reminded Ted that he was scheduled to become a batting coach.

"Can you take a .250 hitter and make a .300 hitter out of him?"

"There has always been a saying in baseball that you can't make a hitter," Ted answered. "But I think you can *improve* a hitter. More than you can improve a fielder. More mistakes are made in hitting than in any other part of the game."

At this point Williams was literally encircled by photographers, amateur and pro. The pros were taking pictures from the front and from the sides. Behind them, in the stands, dozens of fans had their cameras trained on Ted, too, although they could hardly have been getting anything except the number 9 on his back.

Ted was asked if he were going to travel around the Red Sox farm system in 1961 to instruct the young hitters.

"All I know is that I'm going to spring training," he said. "Other than that, I don't know anything."

The interview closed with the usual fulsome praise of Williams, the inevitable apotheosis that leaves him with a hangdog, embarrassed look upon his features. "I appreciate the kind words," he said. "It's all been fun. Everything I've done in New England from playing left field and getting booed, to the Jimmy Fund."

The Jimmy Fund is the money-raising arm of the Children's Cancer Hospital in Boston, which has become the world center for research into cancer and for the treatment of its young victims. Ted has been deeply involved with the hospital since its inception in 1947, serving the last four years as general chairman of the fund committee. He is an active chairman, not an honorary one. Scarcely a day goes by, when Ted is in Boston, that he doesn't make one or two stops for the Jimmy Fund somewhere in New England. He went out on the missions even on days when he was too sick to play ball. (This is the same man, let us emphasize, who refuses to attend functions at which he himself is to be honored.) He has personally raised something close to $4,000,000 and has helped to build a modern, model hospital not far from Fenway Park.

But he has done far more than that. From the first, Williams took upon himself the agonizing task of trying to bring some cheer into the lives of these dying children and, perhaps even more difficult, of comforting their parents. He has, in those years, permitted himself to become attached to thousands of these children, knowing full well that they were going to die, one by one. He has become so attached to some of them that he has chartered special planes to bring him to their deathbeds.

Whenever one of these children asks to see him, whatever the time, he comes. His only stipulation is that there must be no publicity, no reporters, no cameramen.

We once suggested to Ted that he must get some basic return from all this work he puts into the Jimmy Fund. Ted considered the matter very carefully before he answered: "Look," he said finally, "it embarrasses me to be praised for anything like this. The embarrassing thing is that I don't feel I've done anything compared to the people at the hospital who are doing the important work. It makes me happy to think I've done a little good; I suppose that's what I get out of it.

"Anyway," he added thoughtfully, "it's only a freak of fate, isn't it, that one of those kids isn't going to grow up to be an athlete and I wasn't the one who had the cancer."

At the finish of the filmed interview he had to push his way through the cameramen between him and the dugout. "Oh _____," he said.

But when one of them asked him to pose with Cronin, Ted switched personalities again and asked, with complete amiability, "Where is he?"

Cronin was in the dugout. Ted met Joe at the bottom of the steps and threw an arm around him. They grinned at each other while the pictures were being taken, talking softly and unintelligibly. After a minute, Ted reached over to the hook just behind him and grabbed his glove. The cameramen were still yelling for another shot as he started up the dugout steps. Joe, grinning broadly, grabbed him by the shoulder and yanked him back down. While Cronin was wrestling Ted around and whacking him on the back, the cameras clicked. "I got to warm up, dammit," Ted was saying. He made a pawing gesture at the cameramen, as if to say, "I'd like to belt you buzzards." This, from all evidence, was the picture that went around the country that night, because strangely enough, it looked as if he were waving a kind of sad goodbye.

When he finally broke away and raced up to the field, he called back over his shoulder, "See you later, Joe." The cheers arose from the stands once again.

The Orioles were taking infield practice by then, and the Red Sox were warming up along the sideline. Ted began to play catch with Pumpsie Green. As he did—sure enough—the cameramen lined up just inside the foul line for some more shots, none of which will ever be used. "Why don't you cockroaches get off my back?" Ted said, giving them his No. 1 sneer. "Let me breathe, will you?"

The bell rang before he had a chance to throw two dozen balls. Almost all the players went back to the locker room. Remaining on the bench were only Ted Williams, buttoned up in his jacket, and Vic Wertz. One of the members of the ground crew came over with a picture of Williams. He asked Ted if he would autograph it. "Sure," Ted said. "For you guys, anything."

Vic Wertz was having his picture taken with another crew member. Wertz had his arm around the guy and both of them were laughing. "How about you, Ted?" the cameraman asked. "One with the crewmen?"

Ted posed willingly with the man he had just signed for, with the result that the whole herd of cameramen came charging over again. Ted leaped to his feet. "Twenty-two years of this bull_____," he cried.

The redhead was leaning over the low barrier again, but now three other young women were alongside her. One of them seemed to be crying, apparently at the prospect of Ted's retirement. An old photographer, in a long, weatherbeaten coat, asked Ted for a special pose. "Get lost," Ted said. "I've seen enough of you, you old goat."

Curt Gowdy, the Red Sox broadcaster, had come into the dugout to pass on some information about the pregame ceremonies. Ted shouted, "The devil with all you miserable cameramen." The women continued to stare, in fascination, held either by the thrill of having this last long look at Ted Williams or by the opportunity to learn a few new words.

A Baltimore writer came into the dugout, and Ted settled down beside him. He wanted to know whether the writer could check on the "King of Swat" crown that had been presented to him in his last visit to Baltimore. Ted wasn't sure whether he had taken it back to Boston with him or whether the organization still had it.

"You know," he told the writer, "Brown's a better pitcher now than he's ever been. Oh, he's a great pitcher. Never get a fat pitch from him. When he does, it comes in with something extra on it. Every time a little different. He knows what he's doing."

Ted is a student of such things. He is supposed to be a natural hitter, blessed with a superhuman pair of eyes. We are not about to dispute this. What we want to say is that when Ted first came to the majors, the book on him was that he would chase bad balls. "All young sluggers do," according to Del Baker, who was managing Detroit when Ted came up. "Ted developed a strike zone of his own, though, by the second year."

When Ted took his physical for the Naval reserve in World War II, his eyes tested at 20/10 and were so exceptional in every regard that while he was attending air gunnery school he broke all previous Marine records for hitting the target sleeve. But Ted has a point of his own here: "My eyesight," he says, "is now 20/15. Half the major-leaguers have eyes as good as that. It isn't eyesight that makes a hitter; it's practice. *Con-sci-en-tious* practice. I say that Williams has hit more balls than any guy living, except maybe Ty Cobb. I don't say it to brag; I just state it as a fact. From the time I was 11 years old, I've taken every possible opportunity to swing at a ball. I've swung and I've swung and I've swung."

Ted always studied every little movement a pitcher made. He always remained on the bench before the game to watch them warming up. From his first day to his last, he hustled around to get all possible information on a new pitcher.

It has always been his theory that we are all creatures of habit, himself included. Pitchers, he believes, fall into observable patterns. A certain set of movements foretells a certain pitch. In a particular situation, or on a particular count, they go to a particular pitch. There were certain pitchers, Ted discovered, who would inevitably go to their big pitch, the pitch they wanted him to swing at, on the 2-2 count.

And so Ted would frequently ask a teammate, "What was the pitch he struck you out on?" or "What did he throw you on the 2-2 pitch?"

When a young player confessed he didn't know what the pitch had been, Ted would grow incredulous. "You don't know the pitch he struck you out on? I'm not talking about last week or last month. I'm not even talking about yesterday. Today! Just now! I'm talking about the pitch he struck you out on just now!"

Returning to his seat on the bench, he'd slump back in disgust and mutter, "What a rockhead. The guy's taking the bread and butter out of his mouth and he don't even care how."

In a very short time, the player would have an answer ready for

Williams. Ted always got the young hitters thinking about their craft. He always tried to instruct them, to build up their confidence. "When you want to know who the best hitter in the league is," he'd tell the rookies, "just look into the mirror."

Among opposing players, Williams was always immensely popular. Yes, even among opposing pitchers. All pitchers love to say, "Nobody digs in against *me.*" Only Ted Williams was given the right to dig in without getting flipped. Around the American League, there seemed to be a general understanding that Williams had too much class to be knocked down.

Waiting in the dugout for the ceremonies to get under way, Ted picked up a bat and wandered up and down the aisle taking vicious practice swings.

The photographers immediately swooped in on him. One nice guy was taking cameras from the people in the stands and getting shots of Ted for them.

As Ted put the bat down, one of them said, "One more shot. Teddy, as a favor."

"I'm all done doing any favors for you guys," Williams said. "I don't have to put up with you any more, and you don't have to put up with me."

An old woman, leaning over the box seats, was wailing, "Don't leave us, Ted. Don't leave us."

"Oh hell," Ted said, turning away in disgust.

The redhead asked him plaintively, "Why don't you act nice?"

Ted strolled slowly toward her, grinning broadly. "Come on, dear," he drawled, "with that High Street accent you got there."

Turning back, he stopped in front of the man from *Sport,* pointed over his shoulder at the cameramen and asked, "You getting it all? You getting what you came for?"

"If you can't make it as a batting coach," our man said, "I understand you're going to try it as a cameraman."

"What does *Sport* magazine think I'm going to do?" Ted asked. "That's what I want to know. What does *Sport* magazine think I'm going to be?"

Speaking for himself, our man told him, he had not the slightest doubt that Ted was going to be the new general manager.

"*Sport* magazine," Ted said, making the name sound like an oath. "Always honest. Never prejudiced."

At this point he was called onto the field. Taking off his jacket, he strode out of the dugout. The cheers that greeted him came from 10,454 throats.

Curt Gowdy, handling the introductions, began: "As we all know, this is the final home game for—in my opinion and most of yours—the greatest hitter who ever lived. Ted Williams."

There was tremendous applause.

"Twenty years ago," Gowdy continued, "a skinny kid from San Diego came to the Red Sox camp . . ."

Ted first came to the Red Sox training camp at Sarasota in the spring of 1938. General manager Eddie Collins, having heard that Ted was a creature of wild and wayward impulse, had instructed second baseman Bobby Doerr to pick him up and deliver him, shining and undamaged.

It was unthinkable, of course, that Ted Williams would make a routine entrance. Just before Doerr was set to leave home, the worst flood of the decade hit California and washed out all the roads and telephone lines. When Williams and Doerr finally arrived in Sarasota, ten days late, there was a fine, almost imperceptible drizzle. Williams, still practically waterlogged from the California floods, held out a palm, looked skyward, shivered and said in a voice that flushed the flamingos from their nests, "So this is Florida, is it? Do they always keep this state under a foot of water?"

Williams suited up for a morning workout out in the field, jawed good-naturedly with the fans and got an unexpected chance to hit when a newsreel company moved in to take some batting-cage shots.

The magic of Ted Williams in a batter's box manifested itself that first day in camp. The tall, thin rookie stepped into the box, set himself in his wide stance, let his bat drop across the far corner of the plate, wiggled his hips and shoulders and jiggled up and down as if he were trying to tamp himself into the box. He moved his bat back and forth a few times, then brought it back into position and twisted his hands in opposite directions as if he were wringing the neck of the bat. He was set for the pitch.

And somehow, as if by some common impulse, all sideline activity stopped that day in 1938. Everybody was watching Ted Williams.

"Controversial, sure," Gowdy said, in bringing his remarks about Ted to a close, "but colorful."

The chairman of the Boston Chamber of Commerce presented Ted a shining, silver Paul Revere bowl "on behalf of the business community of Boston." Ted seemed to force his smile as he accepted it.

A representative of the sports committee of the Chamber of Commerce then presented him with a plaque "on behalf of visits to kids' and veterans' hospitals."

Mayor John Collins, from his wheelchair, announced that "on behalf of all citizens" he was proclaiming this day "Ted Williams Day." The mayor didn't know how right he was.

As Mayor Collins spoke of Ted's virtues ("nature's best, nature's nobleman"), the muscle of Ted's upper left jaw was jumping, constantly and rhythmically. The mayor's contribution to Ted Williams Day was a $1,000 donation to the Jimmy Fund from some special city fund.

Gowdy brought the proceedings to a close by proclaiming, "Pride is what made him great. He's a champion, a thoroughbred, a champion of sports." Curt then asked for "a round of applause, an ovation for No. 9 on his last game in his Boston." Needless to say, he got it.

Ted waited, pawed at the ground with one foot. Smilingly, he thanked the mayor for the money. "Despite the fact of the disagreeable things that have been said of me—and I can't help thinking about it— by the Knights of the Keyboard out there (he jerked his head toward the press box), baseball has been the most wonderful thing in my life. If I were starting over again and someone asked me where is the one place I would like to play, I would want it to be in Boston, with the greatest owner in baseball and the greatest fans in America. Thank you."

He walked across the infield to the dugout, where the players were standing, applauding along with the fans. Ted winked and went on in.

In the press box, some of the writers were upset by his gratuitous rap at them. "I think it was bush," one of them said. "Whatever he thinks, this wasn't the time to say it."

Others made a joke of it. "Now that he's knighted me," one of them was saying, "I wonder if he's going to address me as Sir."

In the last half of the first inning, Williams stepped in against Steve Barber with Tasby on first and one out. When Barber was born—February 22, 1939—Ted had already taken the American Association apart, as it has never been taken apart since, by batting .366, hitting 43 home runs and knocking in 142 runs.

Against a left-hander, Williams was standing almost flush along the inside line of the batter's box, his feet wide, his stance slightly closed. He took a curve inside, then a fast ball low. The fans began to boo. The third pitch was also low. With a 3-0 count, Ted jumped in front of the plate with the pitch, like a high-school kid looking for a walk. It was ball four, high.

He got to third the easy way. Jim Pagliaroni was hit by a pitch, and everybody moved up on a wild pitch. When Frank Malzone walked, Jack Fisher came in to replace Barber. Lou Clinton greeted Jack with a rising liner to dead center. Jackie Brandt started in, slipped as he tried to reverse himself, but recovered in time to scramble back and make the catch. His throw to the plate was beautiful to behold, a low one-bouncer that came to Gus Triandos chest high. But Ted, sliding hard, was in under the ball easily.

Leading off the third inning against the right-handed Fisher, Ted moved back just a little in the box. Fisher is even younger than Barber, a week younger. When Fisher was being born—March 4, 1939—Ted was reporting to Sarasota again, widely proclaimed as the super-player of the future, the Red Sox' answer to Joe DiMaggio.

Ted hit Fisher's 1-1 pitch straightaway, high and deep. Brandt had plenty of room to go back and make the catch, but still, as Williams returned to the bench, he got another tremendous hand.

Up in the press box, publicity man Jack Malaney was announcing that uniform No. 9 was being retired "after today's game." This brought on some snide remarks about Ted wearing his undershirt at Yankee Stadium for the final three games of the season. Like Mayor Collins, Malaney was righter than he knew. The uniform was indeed going to be retired after the game.

Williams came to bat again in the fifth inning, with two out and the Sox trailing, 3–2. And this time he unloaded a tremendous drive to right center. As the ball jumped off the bat, the cry "He did it!" arose from the stands. Right fielder Al Pilarcik ran back as far as he could, pressed his back against the bullpen fence, well out from the 380-foot sign, and stood there, motionless, his hands at his sides.

Although it was a heavy day, there was absolutely no wind. The flag hung limply from the pole, stirring very occasionally and very faintly.

At the last minute, Pilarcik brought up his hands and caught the ball chest high, close to 400 feet from the plate. A moan of disappointment settled over the field, followed by a rising hum of excited conversation and then, as Ted came back toward the first-base line to get his glove from Pumpsie Green, a standing ovation.

"Damn," Ted said, when he returned to the bench at the end of the inning. "I hit the living hell out of that one. I really stung it. If that one didn't go out, nothing is going out today!"

In the top of the eighth, with the Sox behind 4–2, Mike Fornieles came to the mound for the 70th time of the season, breaking the league record set by another Red Sox relief star, Ellis Kinder. Kinder set this mark in 1953, the year Williams returned from Korea.

As Fornieles was warming up, three teenagers jumped out of the grandstand and ran toward Ted. They paused only briefly, however, and continued across the field to the waiting arms of the park police.

Ted was scheduled to bat second in the last of the eighth, undoubtedly his last time at bat. The cheering began as soon as Willie Tasby came out of the dugout and strode to the plate, as if he was anxious to get out of there and make way for the main event. Ted, coming out almost directly behind Tasby, went to the on-deck circle. He was down on one knee and just beginning to swing the heavy, lead-filled practice bat as Tasby hit the first pitch to short for an easy out.

The cheering seemed to come to its peak as Ted stepped into the box and took his stance. Everybody in the park had come to his feet to give Ted a standing ovation.

Umpire Eddie Hurley called time. Fisher stepped off the rubber and Triandos stood erect. Ted remained in the box, waiting, as if he were oblivious to it all. The standing ovation lasted at least two minutes, and even then Fisher threw into the continuing applause. Only as the ball approached the plate did the cheering stop. It came in low, ball one. The spectators remained on their feet, but very suddenly the park had gone very quiet.

If there was pressure on Ted, there was pressure on Fisher, too. The Orioles were practically tied for second place, so he couldn't afford to be charitable. He might have been able to get Ted to go after a bad pitch, and yet he hardly wanted to go down in history as the fresh kid who had walked Ted Williams on his last time at bat in Boston.

The second pitch was neck high, a slider with, it seemed, just a little off it. Ted gave it a tremendous swing, but he was just a little out in front of the ball. The swing itself brought a roar from the fans, though, since it was such a clear announcement that Ted was going for the home run or nothing.

With a 1-1 count, Fisher wanted to throw a fast ball, low and away. He got it up too much and in too much, a fast ball waist high on the outside corner. From the moment Ted swung, there was not the slightest doubt about it. The ball cut through the heavy air, a high line drive heading straightaway to center field toward the corner of the special bullpen the Red Sox built for Williams back in 1941.

Jackie Brandt went back almost to the barrier, then turned and watched the ball bounce off the canopy above the bullpen bench, skip up against the wire fence which rises in front of the bleachers and bounce back into the bullpen.

It did not seem possible that 10,000 people could make that much noise.

Ted raced around the bases at a pretty good clip. Triandos had started toward the mound with the new ball, and Fisher had come down to meet him. As Ted neared home plate, Triandos turned to face him, a big smile on his face. Ted grinned back.

Ted didn't exactly offer his hand to Pagliaroni after he crossed the plate, but the young catcher reached out anyway and made a grab for it. He seemed to catch Ted around the wrist. Williams ran back into the dugout and ducked through the runway door to get himself a drink of water.

The fans were on their feet again, deafening the air with their cheers. A good four or five minutes passed before anybody worried about getting the game under way again.

When Ted ducked back into the dugout, he put on his jacket and sat down at the very edge of the bench alongside Mike Higgins and Del Baker. The players, still on their feet anyway, crowded around him, urging him to go out and acknowledge the cheers.

The fans were now chanting. "We want Ted . . . we want Ted . . . we want Ted." Umpire Johnny Rice, at first base, motioned for Ted to come out. Manager Mike Higgins urged him to go on out. Ted just sat there, his head down, a smile of happiness on his face.

"We wanted him to go out," Vic Wertz said later, "because we felt so good for him. And we could see he was thrilled, too. For me, I have to say it's my top thrill in baseball."

But another player said, "I had the impression—maybe I shouldn't say this because it's just an impression—that he got just as much a kick out of refusing to go out and tip his hat to the crowd as he did out of the homer. What I mean is he wanted to go out with the home run, all right, but he also wanted the home run so he could sit there while they yelled for him and tell them all where to go."

Mike Higgins had already told Carroll Hardy to replace Ted in left field. As Clinton came to bat, with two men out, Higgins said, "Williams, left field." Ted grabbed his glove angrily and went to the top step. When Clinton struck out, Ted was the first man out of the dugout. He sprinted out to left field, ignoring the cheers of the fans, who had not expected to see him again. But Higgins had sent Hardy right out behind him. Ted saw Carroll, and ran back in, one final time. The entire audience was on its feet once again, in wild applause.

Since it is doubtful that Higgins felt Williams was in any great need of more applause that day, it is perfectly obvious that he was giving Ted one last chance to think about the tip of the hat or the wave of the hand as he covered the distance between left field and the dugout.

Ted made the trip as always, his head down, his stride unbroken. He stepped on first base as he crossed the line, ducked down into the dugout, growled once at Higgins and headed through the alleyway and into the locker room.

He stopped only to tell an usher standing just inside the dugout, "I guess I forgot to tip my hat."

To the end, the mirror remained intact.

After the game, photographers were permitted to go right into the clubhouse, but writers were held to the 15-minute rule. One writer tried to ride in with the photographers, but Williams leveled that finger at him and said, "You're not supposed to be here."

Somehow or other, the news was let out that Ted would not be going to New York, although there seems to be some doubt as to whether it was Williams or Higgins who made the announcement. The official Boston line is that it had been understood all along that Ted would not be going to New York unless the pennant race was still on. The fact of the matter is that Williams made the decision himself, and he did not make it until after he hit the home run. It would have been foolish to have gone to New York or anywhere else, of course. Anything he did after the Boston finale would have been an anticlimax.

One of the waiting newspapermen, a pessimist by nature, expressed the fear that by the time they were let in, Ted would be dressed and gone.

"Are you kidding?" a member of the anti-Williams clique said. "This is what he lives for. If the game had gone 18 innings, he'd be in there waiting for us."

He was indeed waiting at his locker, with a towel wrapped around his middle. The writers approached him, for the most part, in groups. Generally speaking, the writers who could be called friends reached him first, and to these men Ted was not only amiable but gracious and modest.

Was he going for the home run?

"I was gunning for the big one," he said with a grin. "I let everything I had go. I really wanted that one."

Did he know it was out as soon as it left his bat?

"I knew I had really given it a ride."

What were his immediate plans?

"I've got some business to clean up here," he said. "Then I'll be covering the World Series for *Life*. After that, I'm going back to Florida to see how much damage the hurricane did to my house."

The other players seemed even more affected by the drama of the farewell homer than Ted. Pete Runnels, practically dispossessed from his locker alongside Ted's by the shifts of reporters, wandered around the room shaking his head in disbelief. "How about that?" he kept repeating. "How about that? How about that?"

As for Ted, he seemed to be in something of a daze. After the first wave of writers had left, he wandered back and forth between his locker and the trainer's room. Back and forth, back and forth. Once he came back with a bottle of beer, turned it up to his lips and downed it with obvious pleasure. For Ted, this is almost unheard of. He has always been a milk and ice-cream man, and he devours them both in huge quantities. His usual order after a ball game is two quarts of milk.

Williams remained in the locker room, making himself available, until there were no more than a half-dozen other players remaining. Many of the writers did not go over to him at all. From them, there were no questions, no congratulations, no good wishes for the future. For all Ted's color, for all the drama and copy he had supplied over 22 years, they were glad to see him finally retire.

When Ted finally began to get dressed, our man went over and said, "Ted, you must have known when Higgins sent you back out that he was giving you a final chance to think about tipping the hat or making some gesture of farewell. Which meant that Higgins himself would have liked you to do it. While you were running back, didn't you have any feeling that it might be nice to go out with a show of good feeling?"

"I felt nothing," he said.

"No sentimentality? No gratitude? No sadness?"

"I said *nothing*," Ted said. "Nothing, nothing!"

As our man was toting up the nothings, Ted snarled, "And when you get back there tell them for me that they're full of . . ." There followed a burst of vituperation which we cannot even begin to approximate, and then the old, sad plaint about those twelve years of merciless persecution.

Fenway Park has an enclosed parking area so that the players can get to their cars without beating their way through the autograph hunters. When Ted was dressed, though, the clubhouse boy called to the front office in what was apparently a prearranged plan to bring Williams' car around to a bleacher exit.

At 4:40, 45 minutes after the end of the game and a good hour after Ted had left the dugout, he was ready to leave. "Fitzie," he called out, and the clubhouse boy came around to lead the way. The cameramen came around, too.

The locker-room door opens onto a long corridor, which leads to another door, which in turn opens onto the back walks and understructure of the park. It is this outer door which is always guarded.

Waiting in the alleyway, just outside the clubhouse door, however, was a redheaded, beatnik-looking man, complete with the regimental beard and the beachcomber pants. He handed Ted a ball and mentioned a name that apparently meant something to him. Ted took the ball and signed it.

"How come you're not able to get in?" he said. "If they let the damn newspapermen in, they ought to let you in." Walking away, trailed by the platoon of cameramen, he called out to the empty air, "If they let the newspapermen in, they should have let him in. If they let the newspapermen in, they should let everybody in."

He walked on through the backways of the park, past the ramps and pillars, at a brisk clip, with Fitzie bustling along quickly to stay up ahead. Alongside of Williams, the cameramen were scrambling to get their positions and snap their pictures. Williams kept his eyes straight ahead, never pausing for one moment. "Hold it for just a minute, Ted," one of them said.

"I've been here for 22 years," Ted said, walking on. "Plenty of time for you to get your shot."

"This is the last time," the cameraman said. "Cooperate just this one last time."

"I've cooperated with you," Ted said. "I've cooperated too much."

Fitzie had the bleacher entrance open, and as Ted passed quickly through, a powder-blue Cadillac pulled up to the curb. A man in shirtsleeves was behind the wheel. He looked like Dick O'Connell, whose appointment as business manager had been announced the previous night.

Fitzie ran ahead to open the far door of the car for Ted. Three young women had been approaching the exit as Ted darted through, and one of them screamed, "It's him!" One of the others just let out a scream, as if Ted had been somebody of real worth, like Elvis or Fabian. The third woman remained mute. Looking at her, you had to wonder whether she would ever speak again.

Fitzie slammed the door, and the car pulled away. "It was him," the first woman screamed. "Was it *really* him? Was it *him?*"

Her knees seemed to give away. Her girl friends had to support her. "I can't catch my breath," she said. "I can hear my heart pounding." And then, in something like terror: "I CAN'T BREATHE."

Attracted by the screams, or by some invisible, inexplicable grapevine, a horde of boys and men came racing up the street. Ted's car turned the corner just across from the bleacher exit, but it was held up momentarily by a red light and a bus. The front line of pursuers had just come abreast of the car when the driver swung around the bus and pulled away.

There are those, however, who never get the word. Down the street, still surrounding the almost empty parking area, were still perhaps 100 loyal fans waiting to say their last farewell to Ted Williams.

In Boston that night, the talk was all of Williams. Only 10,454 were at the scene, but the word all over the city was: "I knew he'd end it with a home run . . ." and "I was going to go to the game, but—"

In future years, we can be sure, the men who saw Ted hit that mighty shot will number into the hundreds of thousands. The wind will grow strong and mean, and the distance will grow longer. Many of the reports of the game, in fact, had the ball going into the centerfield bleachers.

The seeds of the legend have already been sown. George Carens, an elderly columnist who is more beloved by Ted than by his colleagues, wrote:

"Ted was calm and gracious as he praised the occupants of the Fenway press penthouse at home plate before the game began. Afterwards he greeted all writers in a comradely way, down through his most persistent critics. In a word, Ted showed he can take it, and whenever the spirit moves him he will fit beautifully into the Fenway PR setup."

Which shows that people hear what they want to hear and see what they want to see.

In New York the next day, Phil Rizzuto informed his television audience that Ted had finally relented and tipped his hat after the home run.

And the *Sporting News* headline on its Boston story was:

SPLINTER TIPS CAP
TO HUB FANS AFTER
FAREWELL HOMER

A New York Sunday paper went so far as to say that Ted had made "a tender and touching farewell speech" from home plate at the end of the game.

All the reports said that Ted had, in effect, called his shot because it was known that he was shooting for a home run. Who wants to bet that, in future years, there will not be a story or two insisting that he *did* point?

The legend will inevitably grow, and in a way it is a shame. A man should be allowed to die the way he lived. He should be allowed to depart as he came. Ted Williams chose his course early, and his course was to turn his face from the world around him. When he walked out of the park, he kept his eyes to the front and he never looked back.

The epitaph for Ted Williams remains unchanged. He was sometimes unbearable but he was never dull. Baseball will not be the same without him. Boston won't be quite the same either. Old Boston is acrawl with greening statues of old heroes and old patriots, but Ted has left a monument of his own—again on his own terms—in the Children's Cancer Hospital.

He left his own monument in the record books too. For two decades he made the Red Sox exciting in the sheer anticipation of his next time at bat.

He opened his last season with perhaps the longest home run of his career and he closed it with perhaps the most dramatic. It was typical and it was right that the Williams era in Boston should end not with a whimper. It was entirely proper that it should end with a bang.

So, the old order passeth and an era of austerity has settled upon the Red Sox franchise.

And now Boston knows how England felt when it lost India.

HISTORY

From *The American Language,* Supplement II

H. L. MENCKEN

Charley horse: Muscular soreness in a player's leg.

Traced by Nichols to 1891. Dr. H. H. Bender, chief etymologist of Webster, 1934, sent an agent to Bill Clarke, first baseman of the Baltimore Orioles, who said that it came from the name of *Charley* Esper, a left-handed pitcher, who walked like a lame horse. Lawrence C. Salter (private communication, January 14, 1944) sent another agent to Billy Earle, an old-time catcher in the Western League, who said that it was suggested by a horse worked by one *Charley,* ground-keeper at Sioux City. The late Dr. Logan Clendening wrote to me on November 20, 1943: *"Charley horse* is a ruptured muscle. It has exactly the same pathology as string-halt in a horse." In *Treatment of Charley Horse, Journal of the American Medical Association,* November 30, 1946, p. 821, it is described as "injury to a muscle, usually the *quadriceps femoris."* This injury "consists first in a contusion, which results in a *hematoma.* Later the *hematoma* may organize into a *myositis ossificans,* forming soft bone in the muscle."

HISTORY

THE CAREER of a ballplayer named Mike Kelly began in 1873 when he joined the Troy, New York, Haymakers. He was quite a fellow. So was the late Frank G. Menke, whose *Encyclopedia of Sports* is a monument.

From *Slide, Kelly, Slide*

FRANK G. MENKE

THE INSPIRATION of the immortal poem, "Slide, Kelly, Slide," was that most idolized ballplayer, Mike Kelly, one of the most fascinating figures ever to dig a cleated shoe into the diamond.

He was a slashing, dashing, devil-may-care athlete, good-natured, big-hearted, sincere. He had perhaps the keenest brain that baseball ever knew. He devised new plays in the twinkling of an eye. His strategy was superb, and wherever he went, during his baseball years, he was the beloved titan of the game. He fought for victory every inch of the way, through every game that he played, yet never had an enemy. No umpire ever found it necessary to discipline him. Millions of words were written about him in prose. The song, or poem, "Slide, Kelly, Slide," was written to honor him for his base-running skill.

Kelly was not a fast man. Hovey, Hamilton and Sunday, and the speed marvels who came in the later days, could have given him an eight-yard start and beaten him in the one hundred. Yet he was a superb base-runner because he created the "Fadeaway Slide" and timed his thefts so accurately that he was rarely caught. Before "King Kel's" day, thievery on the sacks was almost an unknown art. Kelly saw the worth of base-stealing. For many weeks, he practiced in private. Then he startled the baseball world with his wild dashes and swift slides to the next bag. He was balldom's pioneer base burglar.

When "Slide, Kelly, Slide" was written, the fans memorized it and chanted it wherever he went. When he reached first, the crowd would begin to yell "Slide, Kelly, Slide" and "King Kel" always tried to oblige. Home-town rooters and rival fans of Kelly's era went to see him and encourage him to attempt the play which, then, was a superb thriller.

Kelly originated the trick of "cutting the bases." Before then, all base-runners religiously touched each bag en route to home. Kelly decided there wasn't any use in doing it—if he could get away with it. On every occasion, when the lone umpire wasn't looking, Kelly would take advantage of the situation and would scamper across the diamond in a direct line from first to third. Once Kelly was on first and the batter hit to right. Kelly ran for second. As he reached there, he noticed that the umpire was absorbed in watching the progress of the ball. Kelly deliberately ignored the existence of third and ran from second, through the pitcher's box, to home plate.

Of course, the opposition team protested, but the game's only umpire had not seen the act. The run stood and won the game.

POETRY

LIVING in Brooklyn can affect almost anybody. So did the Dodgers affect Miss Marianne Moore, a Brooklyn resident who won the Pulitzer Prize, the Bollingen Prize, and the gold medal from the National Institute of Arts and Letters, and who was called by T. S. Eliot "the most accomplished poetess in the English-speaking world today." The following was done at World Series time, 1956.

Hometown Piece for Messrs. Alston and Reese

MARIANNE MOORE

To the tune:
Li'l baby, don't say a word: Mama goin' to buy you a mocking-bird.
Bird don't sing: Mama goin' to sell it and buy a brass ring.

"Millennium, yes; pandemonium!"
Roy Campanella leaps high. Dodgerdom

crowned, had Johnny Podres on the mound.
Buzzie Bavasi and the Press gave ground;

the team slapped, mauled, and asked the Yankees' match,
"How did you feel when Sandy Amoros made the catch?"

"I said to myself"—pitcher for all innings—
"as I walked back to the mound I said, 'everything's

getting better and better.' " (Zest, they've zest.
" 'Hope springs eternal in the Brooklyn breast.' "

And would the Dodger Band in 8, row 1, relax
if they saw the Collector of income-tax?

Ready with a tune if that should occur:
"Why not take All of Me—All of Me, Sir?")

Another series. Round-tripper Duke at bat,
"four hundred feet from home-plate"; more like that.

A neat bunt, please; a cloud-breaker, a drive
like Jim Gilliam's great big one. Hope's alive.

Homered, flied out, Fouled? Our "stylish stout"
so nimble Campanella will have him out.

A-squat in double-headers four hundred times a day,
he says that in a measure the pleasure is the pay:

catcher to pitcher, a nice easy throw
almost as if he had told it to go.

Willie Mays should be a Dodger. He should—
a lad for Roger Craig and Clem Labine to elude;

but you have an omen, pennant-winning Peewee,
on which we are looking superstitiously

Ralph Branca has Preacher Roe's number; recall?
and there's Don Bessent; he can really fire the ball.

As for Gil Hodges, in custody of first—,
"he'll do it by himself"; already versed

in the reach, he makes that great foul catch far into the box seats—
gloves the ball, straightens up, and defeats

expectation by a whisker. The modest star,
irked by one misplay, is no hero by a hair;

in a strikeout slaughter when what could matter more,
he lines a homer to the signboard and has changed the score.

Then for his nineteenth season, a home run—
with four of six runs batted in—Carl Furillo is big gun;

almost dehorned the foe—has fans dancing in delight.
Jake Pitler and his Playground "get a Night"—

Jake, that hearty man, made heartier by a harrier
who can bat as well as field—Don Demeter.

Holding them hitless for nine innings—a hitter too—
Carl Erskine leaves Cimoli nothing to do.

Take off the goat-horns, Dodgers, that egret
which two very fine base-stealers can offset.

You've got plenty: Jackie Robinson
and Campy and big Newk, and Dodgerdom again
watching everything you do. You won last year.
Come on.

POETRY

THERE was a wild rhyming to the lyrics of Cole Porter's *Kiss Me, Kate* that delighted Mr. Wolcott Gibbs, drama critic of *The New Yorker* magazine. Mr. Gibbs was particularly taken with Porter's rhyming "ambassador" with "Cressida." About the same time, however, the master himself, Ogden Nash, was not only rhyming "Memphis" with "overemphis . . ." he also was blandly asserting that U stands for Hubbell, something not even Cole Porter had previously insisted. Baseball was Mr. Nash's subject, of course.

Line-up for Yesterday
An ABC of Baseball Immortals

OGDEN NASH

A is for Alex
The great Alexander;
More goose eggs he pitched
Than a popular gander.

B is for Bresnahan
Back of the plate;
The Cubs were his love,
And McGraw was his hate.

C is for Cobb,
Who grew spikes and not corn,
And made all the basemen
Wish they weren't born.

D is for Dean.
The grammatical Diz,
When they asked, Who's the tops?
Said correctly, I is.

E is for Evers,
His jaw in advance;
Never afraid
To Tinker with Chance.

F is for Fordham
And Frankie and Frisch;
I wish he were back
With the Giants, I wish.

G is for Gehrig,
The Pride of the Stadium;
His record pure gold,
His courage, pure radium.

H is for Hornsby;
When pitching to Rog,
The pitcher would pitch,
Then the pitcher would dodge.

I is for Me,
Not a hard-sitting man,
But an outstanding all-time
Incurable fan.

J is for Johnson
The Big Train in his prime
Was so fast he could throw
Three strikes at a time.

K is for Keeler,
As fresh as green paint,
The fustest and mostest
To hit where they ain't.

L is Lajoie
Whom Clevelanders love,
Napoleon himself,
With glue in his glove.

M is for Matty,
Who carried a charm
In the form of an extra
Brain in his arm.

N is for Newsom,
Bobo's favorite kin.
If you ask how he's here,
He talked himself in.

O is for Ott
Of the restless right foot.
When he leaned on the pellet,
The pellet stayed put.

P is for Plank,
The arm of the A's;
When he tangled with Matty
Games lasted for days.

Q is Don Quixote
Cornelius Mack;
Neither Yankees nor years
Can halt his attack.

R is for Ruth.
To tell you the truth,
There's no more to be said,
Just R is for Ruth.

S is for Speaker,
Swift center-field tender;
When the ball saw him coming,
It yelled, "I surrender."

T is for Terry
The Giant from Memphis
Whose 400 average
You can't overemphis.

U would be Ubbell
If Carl were a cockney;
We say Hubbell and baseball
Like football and Rockne.

V is for Vance
The Dodgers' own Dazzy;
None of his rivals
Could throw as fast as he.

W, Wagner,
The bowlegged beauty;
Short was closed to all traffic
With Honus on duty.

X is the first
Of two x's in Foxx

Who was right behind Ruth
With his powerful soxx.

Y is for Young
The magnificent Cy;
People batted against him,
But I never knew why.

Z is for Zenith,
The summit of fame.
These men are up there,
These men are the game.

POETRY

To THE INNUMERABLE theories as to how baseball originated, it's unique to add
this one. Mr. Patchen's idea of how the game began (it appeared in his *Selected
Poems,* published by New Directions) might be, as good poetry often is, disqui-
etingly close to the truth.

The Origin of Baseball

KENNETH PATCHEN

Someone had been walking in and out
Of the world without coming
To much decision about anything.
The sun seemed too hot most of the time.
There weren't enough birds around
And the hills had a silly look
When he got on top of one.
The girls in heaven, however, thought
Nothing of asking to see his watch
Like you would want someone to tell
A joke—"Time," they'd say, "what's
That mean—time?," laughing with the edges
Of their white mouths, like a flutter of paper
In a madhouse. And he'd stumble over
General Sherman or Elizabeth B.
Browning, muttering "Can't you keep
Your big wings out of the aisle?" But down

Again, there'd be millions of people without
Enough to eat and men with guns just
Standing there shooting each other.

So he wanted to throw something—
And he picked up a baseball.

POETRY

THE ACCIDENT of alphabetical order here brings forth a fourth consecutive poem. Is this incompatible? I think not. If anything, it expresses one of the great verities of the game, as true for the Toronto Blue Jays of today as it was for the teams that underwent Phair's inspection nearly half a century ago.

The Magic Number

GEORGE E. PHAIR

If the Giants win but two of four
And the Dodgers six of ten
The Phillies, as in days of yore,
Will finish last again.

SPOT REPORTING

1956:
New York Yankees 2,
Brooklyn Dodgers 0

SHIRLEY POVICH

THE MILLION-TO-ONE shot came in. Hell froze over. A month of Sundays hit the calendar. Don Larsen today pitched a no-hit, no-run, no-man-reach-first game in a World Series.

On the mound at Yankee Stadium, the same guy who was knocked out in two innings by the Dodgers on Friday came up today with one for the record books, posting it there in solo grandeur as the only Perfect Game in World Series history.

With it, the Yankee right-hander shattered the Dodgers, 2-0, and beat Sal Maglie, while taking 64,519 suspense-limp fans into his act.

First there was mild speculation, then there was hope, then breaths were held in slackened jaws in the late innings as the big mob wondered if the big Yankee right-hander could bring off for them the most fabulous of all World Series games.

He did it, and the Yanks took the Series lead three games to two, to leave the Dodgers as thunderstruck as Larsen himself appeared to be at the finish of his feat.

Larsen whizzed a third strike past pinch hitter Dale Mitchell in the ninth. That was all. It was over. Automatically, the massive 226-pounder from San Diego started walking from the mound toward the dugout, as pitchers are supposed to do at the finish.

But this time there was a woodenness in his steps and his stride was that of a man in a daze. The spell was broken for Larsen when Yogi Berra ran onto the infield to embrace him.

It was not Larsen jumping for joy. It was the more demonstrative Berra. His battery mate leaped full tilt at the big guy. In self-defense, Larsen caught Berra in mid-air as one would catch a frolicking child, and that's how they made their way toward the Yankee bench, Larsen carrying Berra.

There wasn't a Brooklyn partisan left among the 64,519, it seemed, at the finish. Loyalties to the Dodgers evaporated in sheer enthrallment at the show big Larsen was giving them, for this was a day when the fans could boast that they were there.

So at the finish, Larsen had brought it off, and erected for himself a special throne in baseball's Hall of Fame, with the first Perfect Game pitched in major-league baseball since Charlie Robertson of the White Sox against Detroit 34 years ago.

But this was one more special. This one was in a World Series. Three times, pitchers had almost come through with no-hitters, and there were three one-hitters in the World Series books, but never a no-man-reach-base classic.

The tragic victim of it all, sitting on the Dodger bench, was sad Sal Maglie, himself a five-hit pitcher today in his bid for a second Series victory over the Yankees. He was out of the game, technically, but he was staying to see it out and it must have been in disbelief that he saw himself beaten by another guy's World Series no-hitter.

Mickey Mantle hit a home run today in the fourth inning and that was all the impetus the Yankees needed, but no game-winning home run ever wound up with such emphatic second billing as Mantle's this afternoon.

It was an exciting wallop but in the fourth inning only, because after that Larsen was the story today, and the dumbfounded Dodgers could wonder how this same guy who couldn't last out two innings in the second game could master them so thoroughly today.

He did it with a tremendous assortment of pitches that seemed to have five forward speeds, including a slow one that ought to have been equipped with back-up lights.

Larsen had them in hand all day. He used only 97 pitches, not an abnormally low number because 11 pitches an inning is about normal for a good day's work. But he was the boss from the outset. Only against Peewee Reese in the first inning did he lapse to a three-ball count, and then he struck Reese out. No other Dodger was ever favored with more than two called balls by Umpire Babe Pinelli.

Behind him, his Yankee teammates made three spectacular fielding plays to put Larsen in the Hall of Fame. There was one in the second inning that calls for special description. In the fifth, Mickey Mantle ranged far back into left center to haul in Gil Hodges' long drive with a backhand shoetop grab that was a beaut. In the eighth, the same Hodges made another bid to break it up, but Third Baseman Andy Carey speared his line drive.

Little did Larsen, the Yankees, the Dodgers or anybody among the 64,519 in the stands suspect that when Jackie Robinson was robbed of a line-drive hit in the second inning, the stage was being set for a Perfect Game.

Robinson murdered the ball so hard that Third Baseman Andy Carey barely had time to fling his glove upward in a desperate attempt to get the ball. He could only deflect it. But, luckily, Shortstop Gil McDougald was backing up, and able to grab the ball on one bounce. By a half-step, McDougald got Robinson at first base, and Larsen tonight can be grateful that it was not the younger, fleeter Robinson of a few years back but a heavy-legged, 40-year-old Jackie.

As the game wore on, Larsen lost the edge that gave him five strike-outs in the first four innings, and added only two in the last five. He had opened up by slipping called third strikes past both Gilliam and Reese in the first inning.

Came the sixth, and he got Furillo and Campanella on pops, fanned Maglie. Gilliam, Reese and Snider were easy in the seventh. Robinson tapped out, Hodges lined out and Amoros flied out in the eighth. And now it was the ninth, and the big Scandinavian-American was going for the works with a calm that was exclusive with him.

Furillo gave him a bit of a battle, fouled off four pitches, then flied mildly to Bauer. He got two quick strikes on Campanella, got him on a slow roller to Martin.

Now it was the left-handed Dale Mitchell, pinch hitting for Maglie. Ball one came in high. Larsen got a called strike.

On the next pitch, Mitchell swung for strike two.

Then the last pitch of the game. Mitchell started to swing, but didn't go through with it.

But it made no difference because Umpire Pinelli was calling it Strike Number Three, and baseball history was being made.

Maglie himself was a magnificent figure out there all day, pitching hitless ball and leaving the Yankees a perplexed gang, until suddenly with two out in the fourth, Mickey Mantle, with two called strikes against him, lashed the next pitch on a line into the right-field seats to give the Yanks a 1-0 lead.

There was doubt about that Mantle homer because the ball was curving and would it stay fair? It did. In their own half of the inning, the Dodgers had no such luck. Duke Snider's drive into the same seats had curved foul by a few feet. The disgusted Snider eventually took a third strike.

The Dodgers were a luckless gang and Larsen a fortunate fellow in the fifth. Like Mantle, Sandy Amoros lined one into the seats in right, and that one was a near thing for the Yankees. By what seemed only inches, it curved foul, the umpires ruled.

Going into the sixth, Maglie was pitching a one-hitter—Mantle's homer—and being outpitched. The old guy lost some of his stuff in the sixth, though, and the Yankees came up with their other run.

Carey led off with a single to center, and Larsen sacrificed him to second on a daring third-strike bunt. Hank Bauer got the run in with a single to left. There might have been a close play at the plate had Amoros come up with the ball cleanly, but he didn't and Carey scored unmolested.

Now there were Yanks still on first and third with only one out, but they could get no more. Hodges made a scintillating pickup of Mantle's smash, stepped on first and threw to home for a double play on Bauer, who was trying to score. Bauer was trapped in a rundown and caught despite a low throw by Campanella that caused Robinson to fall into the dirt.

But the Yankees weren't needing any more runs for Larsen today. They didn't even need their second one, because they were getting a pitching job for the books this memorable day in baseball.

THE TIME is out of joint when the late Grantland Rice should be thought to merit no more than three stanzas of verse in an anthology of this kind and size. In truth, he merits more than any book can give—even his own, called *The Tumult and the Shouting*, which every fan should read. Rice was so much more than his fecklessly assigned title, "Dean of American Sports Writers," conveyed. He was a warm and joyful person, who used to observe that he was the only man in North America who could send a poem via Western Union collect. More too, he was one hell of a writer.

It is hoped that the following piece, brief though it is, will be found as memorable as any in this collection. It is the spirit of Grantland Rice in a time of sadness. The date: August 14, 1948. Babe Ruth is dead.

Game Called

GRANTLAND RICE

Game called by darkness—let the curtain fall,
No more remembered thunder sweeps the field.
No more the ancient echoes hear the call
To one who wore so well both sword and shield.
The Big Guy's left us with the night to face,
And there is no one who can take his place.

Game called—and silence settles on the plain.
Where is the crash of ash against the sphere?
Where is the mighty music, the refrain
That once brought joy to every waiting ear?
The Big Guy's left us, lonely in the dark,
Forever waiting for the flaming spark.

Game called—what more is there for one to say?
How dull and drab the field looks to the eye.
For one who ruled it in a golden day
Has waved his cap to bid us all good-by.
The Big Guy's gone—by land or sky or foam
May the Great Umpire call him "safe at home."

JACKIE ROBINSON'S BOOK *Baseball Has Done It*, edited by Charles Dexter, is a remarkable compendium of both the history and the circumstances of the Negro in baseball. It was Robinson, of course, who broke baseball's color line in 1945, when Branch Rickey assigned him to the Montreal club of the International League as the first Negro ever to play officially in organized ball. Youngsters of today find it hard to believe there ever was a time when things were different than they are now. But it is worth remembering.

From *Baseball Has Done It*

JACKIE ROBINSON *edited by* CHARLES DEXTER

July 4, 1906
In no other profession has the color line been drawn more rigidly than in baseball. Colored players are not only barred from white clubs; at times exhibition games are canceled for no other reason than objections raised by a Southern player. These Southerners are, as a rule, fine players, and managers refuse to book colored teams rather than lose their services.

The colored player suffers great inconveniences while traveling. All hotels are generally filled from garret to cellar when they strike a town. It is a common occurrence for them to arrive in a city late at night and to walk around for several hours before finding lodging.

The situation is far different today than it was in the 1870s, when colored players were accommodated in the best hotels in the country. The cause of this change is no doubt the sad condition of things from a racial standpoint today. The color question is uppermost in the minds of Americans at the present time.

The average pay of colored players is $466 a year, compared to an average of $2,000 for white major leaguers and $571 for white minor leaguers. The disparity in salaries is enormous when it is apparent that many colored stars would be playing in the majors but for the color line.

This picture was drawn by Sol White in 1906 in his *History of Colored Baseball*. With minor modifications it was true in 1945 when I was on the Kansas City Monarchs of the Negro National League. Sol White was a hero of Negro baseball in the 1880s and 1890s, a .400 hitter on the original Cuban Giants and later manager of the invincible Philadelphia Giants. In the yellowed pages of his little book are valuable instructions in hitting and pitching, the histories of many fine teams of the times, as well as an exhortation to Negro youths to play hard, cleanly, and with respect for their opponents and the game.

According to White, baseball came late to Negroes. Bud Fowler was the first Negro to play on an otherwise white team, starring at second base for the New Castle champions of western Pennsylvania in 1872.

By 1880 twenty Negroes were on minor-league rosters. I was not the first Negro in the major leagues. In 1884 Fleetwood Walker caught 41 games for the Toledo Mudhens of the big-league American Association, while his brother Weldon played the outfield in six games.

That June the Chicago White Stockings rolled into Toledo for an exhibition game. They were champions of the rival National League, a bruising crew of sluggers, four of whom batted over .340. Their manager and first baseman was Cap Anson, who would turn handsprings in his grave if he knew that I share a niche with him in baseball's Hall of Fame.

During his 27-year big-league career Anson played all nine positions. He batted over .300 in 22 seasons; his average was .394 in 1894, when he was forty-three years old. He was a great ballplayer but a heartless man.

In 1884 the nation was still recovering from the aftermath of the Civil War. Southern senators and congressmen were whipping up a fury of bigotry against Negroes in much the same vituperative language that many Southern demagogues use today. Whether Cap Anson was poisoned by their venom I do not know, but he walked on the field in Toledo that June day, saw the Walker brothers in uniform and stalked off, taking his team with him. A large crowd was in the stands. Charlie Morton, Toledo's manager, promised to fire the Walkers the next morning. The game was played.

Thereafter Anson saw red at the mere mention of a Negro in baseball. He launched a one-man crusade to rid the game of all but whites.

The following season John Montgomery Ward of the New York Giants watched George Stovy fan fifteen batters in an Eastern League game and recommended Stovy's purchase. When Anson heard about the pending deal, his howls of rage could be heard from Chicago to New York. Negotiations were called off. Stovy spent the remainder of his career in segregated ball.

Anson's vendetta reached a climax in the winter of 1887–88. He appeared at major- and minor-league meetings, urging the adoption of a rule that would require owners to fire Negroes on their rosters and never again to contract with them. None was then in the majors; twenty-five in the minors were deprived of their jobs, among them Sol White and Weldon Walker.

Walker had played for Akron in the Tri-State League in 1887. He refused to take banishment lying down. His letter to President George McDermitt of the Tri-State League is a relic of one man's struggle for equality in that far-off day:

I have grievances, sir. I question whether my individual loss serves the public good. I write you not because I have been denied making my bread and butter, but in the hope that the league's action will be reserved. The rule that you have passed is a public disgrace! It casts derision on the laws of Ohio, the voice of the people, which says that all men are equal. There is now the same accommodation for colored and white men and women in your ball parks, and the same disposition is made of the moneys of both. I would suggest to your honorable body that if your rule is not repealed, you should make it criminal for black men and women to be admitted to your ball park.

There should be some sounder cause for dismissal, such as lack of intelligence or misbehavior. Ability, intelligence, should be recognized first, last and at all times by everyone. I ask this question—why was this rule passed?

Weldy Walker received no reply.

John J. McGraw loved victory so passionately that he would have ordered his pitchers to dust off his grandmother if she'd been a .350 hitter with a home-run bat. As the third baseman of the rough and tough Baltimore Orioles of the 1890s he had been one of an invincible crew. But as their manager in the infant American League in 1901 he was in desperate need of players. That February he went to Hot Springs, Arkansas, to drown his worries in the thermal baths.

On a diamond near McGraw's hotel two Negro teams were playing. His eye was caught by the smart hitting and slick fielding of a copper-skinned second-sacker, Charlie Grant. After the game McGraw invited Grant to his suite.

Grant was a Negro, under contract to the Chicago Columbia Giants. He emerged from McGraw's suite a full-blooded Indian chief and an Oriole.

Newspapers reported Grant's signing. On March 5 a delegation of Chicago Negroes arrived in Hot Springs. As Baltimore baseball writers watched, they presented a floral tribute to their hero.

The following day McGraw received a telegram from National League president Nick Young, reminding him of the anti-Negro rule adopted at Cap Anson's instigation in 1888.

McGraw released Grant later that day.

In the long years between the late 1880s and the mid-1940s dark-skinned Americans played ball in a world of their own. Hundreds of independent Negro teams sprang up in the 1910s, some booking as many as 200 games a year. Leagues were formed, dissolved, and re-formed. During the sports-conscious 1920s, the Negro National League and the Negro American League took firm root east and west. It was *apartheid* as in South Africa, except that occasionally a big-league team, barnstorming after the season, met a Negro team and had a heck of a time holding its own. Negro ball was almost a carbon copy of the white game, with a regular schedule, an annual All-Star game and World Series. Attendance was high, often over 20,000 at World Series contests. Among those present were many enthusiastic white fans.

Negroes regarded their stars as the equals if not the superiors of many whites whose names they read daily in the box scores. In those days we had our own press, our theaters, churches and, of course, our segregated schools. Some progress toward integration in sports was taking place in the 1930s as Jesse Owens triumphed in the 1936 Olympics and during Joe Louis' dignified reign as heavyweight king. But organized baseball was closed to us.

Few of our own diamond stars were known to white fans. Josh Gibson, the hammering home-run slugger, and Satchel Paige received occasional comment on white sports pages. Negro teams played in big- and minor-league parks, but white newspapers seldom reported their doings.

As for Negro fans—they longed to see the Homestead Grays or Kansas City Monarchs pitted against white world champions. How would Josh Gibson fare against Lefty Grove or Carl Hubbell? Could Satch stop Babe Ruth or Jimmy Foxx? No one will ever know.

Terris McDuffie was one of the many top-notch Negro hurlers of that period, a burly right-hander with a busy baseball brain. Says Terris:

I'm Alabama-born and Florida-raised. Back in '29, when I was 18, I enlisted and they put me on the ball team at Fort Benning, Georgia. I was just a beginner. I played the outfield when I wasn't pitching for the regimental club, the 24th Infantry it was. The Colonel wanted winning sports teams, so he got officers to come down from West Point to coach us in special duties like baseball, basketball and track. Well, Satchel Paige and the Birmingham Black Barons—that's the team Willie Mays was on later—come over to play us. Satch must of liked what he saw of me. He told me he was going to keep his eye on me. The day he pitched at Fort Benning he threw so hard an average hitter couldn't get his bat around for a full swing. The only way to hit Satch was to choke the bat and half swing —that's how quick he was! In all my years I never seen anyone who threw like him. Feller? No comparison! By the time Satch got on the Indians with Feller in '48 he'd lost his fast ball, but he knew so much about pitching he could still make big leaguers look silly.

When I finished my Army bit in '31 the Barons signed me. I pitched against Satch in '37 when he was with the Kansas City Monarchs and I was on the Newark Eagles. He shut me out, 6 to 0. That winter he fixed for me to go to Puerto Rico. I faced him on the Puerto Rico All-Stars . . . he was on an all-star colored team from the States. I beat 'em 4 to 0 with one hit. I lost two other games to Satch years later in Mexico. I concentrated on control. I had a sinker, a slider, a curve and different speeds and a good fast ball. My favorite pitch was my sliding sinker. I never had to use off-pitches like the knuckler or sneaky slow stuff. I started 27 games with the Eagles in '38 and finished 'em all without relief, 27 complete games in succession! I played the outfield days when I wasn't pitching. That year I was the Most Valuable Player in the Negro National League. In '41 with the Homestead Grays I won 27 games and lost 5.

After the war I was getting the highest pay in the East, though not as high as Satch in the American League out West. I had a contract for $800 a month, with a $2,000 bonus at the end of the season, about $6,000 a year. That's not *much compared to what the boys were getting in white ball, so when the Pasquel brothers offered me higher pay to jump to their Mexican League, I jumped along with Sal Maglie, Lou Klein, Max Lanier, Mickey Owen, Fred Martin and Danny Gardella. In Mexico I played on mixed teams with players of big reputations in the majors for the first time. Well, as you know, the Mexican League didn't last long, and by 1950, when it broke up, the colored leagues in the States were busting up because the majors were taking their best players. I was forty or forty-one then, but I won the Most Valuable Player award in Venezuela, pitching for Caracas in '51. The next year I went to Santo Domingo and won their MVP award, too. Just before the '54 season the big push for colored stars was on in the States. I was forty-five but my arm was still good, so the Dallas Eagles of the Texas League sent for me. That was the only time I pitched for a mixed team. My stuff was as good as ever. I worked in 14 games, won three, lost four and held my earned-run average down to 3.04. Then I badly injured my leg, could hardly walk on it for three or four years, and was finished. All told I played 24 years in professional ball.*

Our home runs were not made off the jackrabbit ball. Our hitters lambasted a ball inferior to the one used in the majors. We had no soreheads, swelled heads or braggarts. We trained in March like big leaguers, but we didn't travel like them. If they'd traveled in cars and buses like we did, lost nights on the road trying to reach the next town, riding until game time the next day, eating the wrong food, how long do you think those highly touted stars would've lasted? We stood more wear and tear and hard knocks than them.

What's happening in baseball today is very impressive. I'm glad our boys are getting a chance to prove what they can do. I think they're extraordinary. They give fans what they want, they believe in themselves; they produce.

Bill Yancey is one of the few stars of Negro ball now employed in the big leagues. In the 1930s he was the All-Star shortstop for the Philadelphia Giants, New York Lincoln Giants and the all but invincible Hilldales of Darby, Pennsylvania. Wintertimes he was the stonewall guard of the famous Renaissance Five which was recently admitted en masse to basketball's Hall of Fame. Today he is a scout for the New York Yankees, his most impressive protégé Al Downing, the strikeout prodigy.

I was born in Philadelphia and attended Central High from 1918 to 1922 but couldn't play on the basketball or baseball teams because I was a Negro. In fact, I never played on an organized team until after I was graduated.

The Philadelphia Giants tried me out in 1923, but I was too inexperienced to make the Negro big leagues then. They were owned by Bert Williams, who'd broken the Broadway color line with the Ziegfeld Follies. We had no Negro minor leagues to develop players in so I had to do my own developing where I could. I caught on with the Boston Giants as a shortstop. I didn't master that position until '28 when John Henry Lloyd, old Pop Lloyd—they've named a ball park for him in Atlantic City—taught me position play, showed me the right moves on the pivot, and how to work cutoffs and relays.

In 1929 I signed with the Lincoln Giants and was the first Negro player to put his foot on the grass at Yankee Stadium. We were scheduled to meet the Baltimore Black Sox in the first Negro game at the Stadium. I suited up early, ran out to right field and stood where the Babe stood and pretended to catch fly balls like him. Then I took a bat and went to the plate and pretended I was hitting one into the right-field seats like him. It was a bigger thrill than hitting my own first home run against the Paterson Silk Sox back in '24.

Thirty years ago Negro ball was at its peak. The Lincoln Giants often beat the Bushwicks when they were barnstorming with stars such as Lou Gehrig, Jimmy Foxx and others. White baseball writers didn't cover our league games although we often drew 10,000 to 15,000 fans and filled Comiskey Park in Chicago for our 1934 All-Star game, which was run off as smoothly and was certainly as well played as the big-league show.

No one scouted me. No one scouted Josh Gibson. I've seen 'em all since the 1920s and Josh was the greatest right-hand hitter of all time, including Jimmy Foxx and Rogers Hornsby. Take Foxx—Josh could wrap him up! They say that Jimmy's homer to the last box in the third tier in left field at Yankee Stadium was the longest blow ever made there. I was playing in the Stadium against Josh's Homestead Grays when he lifted one two stories over the bullpen and out of the ball park! The Grays used Griffith Stadium in Washington while the Senators were on the road. That old park was the toughest in the majors on home-run hitters. But Josh hit eight homers in ten games in one span, more than all the Senators hit in 77 games. Josh had great pride. Dizzy Dean often pitched post-season games against Negro teams Josh played on. One day the crowd was small and Diz was in a hurry to get away. He would never have done this in a regular game, but this was only an exhibition, so before the ninth inning he called to Josh, "Let's get the side out quick and get the heck out of here! Let three strikes go past you, will ya, Josh?" "Okay with me," grinned Josh. So Diz fogged one up to the plate. Josh swung. The ball went winging far over the fence. Josh laughed as he jogged around the bases. "That's more fun than taking three strikes!" he called to Diz.

Josh earned the top salary in the Negro leagues, $1,000 a month. He was still catching for the Homestead Grays in '47, the year Jackie Robinson became a Dodger. He was tickled to death the color line was broken, but he was a frustrated man, too old for the majors. Poor Josh let himself go. He got fat and quit in '48. Two years later he died.

--------------------------------- FICTION ---------------------------------

ALONGSIDE all the other characters, real and fancied, who populate these pages, comes now Alexander Portnoy to spin his own private fantasy.

From *Portnoy's Complaint*

PHILIP ROTH

SO I RAN all right, out of the hospital and up to the playground and right out to center field, the position I play for a softball team that wears silky blue-and-gold jackets with the name of the club scrawled in big white felt letters from one shoulder to the other: S E A B E E S, A.C. Thank God for the Seabees A.C.! Thank God for center field! Doctor, you can't imagine how truly glorious it is out there, so alone in all that space . . . Do you know baseball at all? Because center field is like some observation post, a kind of control tower, where you are able to see everything and everyone, to understand what's happening the instant it happens, not only by the sound of the struck bat, but by the spark of movement that goes through the infielders in the first second that the ball comes flying at them; and once it gets beyond them, "It's mine," you call, "it's mine," and then after it you go. For in center field, if you can get to it, it *is* yours. Oh, how unlike my home it is to be in center field, where no one will appropriate unto himself anything that I say is *mine!*

Unfortunately, I was too anxious a hitter to make the high school team—I swung and missed at bad pitches so often during the tryouts for the freshman squad that eventually the ironical coach took me aside and said, "Sonny, are you sure you don't wear glasses?" and then sent me on my way. But did I have form! did I have style! And in my playground softball league, where the ball came in just a little slower and a little bigger, I am the star I dreamed I might become for the whole school. Of course, still in my ardent desire to excel I too frequently swing and miss, but when I connect, it goes great distances, Doctor, it flies over fences and is called a home run. Oh, and there is really nothing in life, nothing at all, that quite compares with that pleasure of rounding second base at a nice slow clip, because there's just no hurry any more, because that ball you've hit has just gone sailing out of sight . . . And I could field, too, and the farther I had to run, the better. "I got it! I got it! I got it!" and tear in toward second, to trap in the webbing of my glove—and barely an inch off the ground—a ball driven hard and low and right down the middle, a base hit, someone thought . . . Or back I go, "*I* got it, *I* got it—" back easily and gracefully toward that wire fence, moving practically in slow motion, and then that delicious Di Maggio sensation of grabbing it like something heaven-sent over one shoulder . . . Or running! turning! leaping! like little Al Gionfriddo—a baseball player, Doctor, who once did a very great thing . . . Or just standing nice and calm—nothing trembling, everything serene—standing there in the sunshine (as though in the middle of an empty field, or passing the time on the street corner), standing without a care in the world in the sunshine, like my king of kings, the Lord my God, The Duke Himself (Snider, Doctor, the name may come up again), standing there as loose and as easy, as happy as I will ever be, just waiting by myself under a high fly ball *(a towering fly ball,* I hear Red Barber say, as he watches from behind his microphone —hit out toward Portnoy; *Alex under it, under it),* just waiting there for the ball to fall into the glove I raise to it, and yup, there it is, *plock,* the third out of the inning *(and Alex gathers it in for out number three, and, folks, here's old C.D. for P. Lorillard and Company),* and then in one motion, while old Connie brings us a message from Old Golds, I start in toward the bench, holding the ball now with the five fingers of my bare left hand, and when I get to the infield—having come down hard with one foot on the bag at second base—I shoot it gently, with just a flick of the wrist, at the opposing team's shortstop as he comes trotting out onto the field, and still without breaking stride, go loping in all the way, shoulders shifting, head hanging, a touch pigeon-toed, my knees coming slowly up and down in an altogether brilliant imitation of The Duke. Oh, the unruffled nonchalance of that game! There's not a movement that I don't know still down in the tissue of my muscles and the joints between my bones. How to bend over to pick up my glove and how to toss it away, how to test the weight of the bat, how to hold it and carry it and swing it around in the on-deck circle, how to raise that bat above my head and flex and loosen my shoulders and my neck before stepping in and plant-ing my two feet exactly where my two feet belong in the batter's box— and how, when I take a called strike (which I have a tendency to do, it balances off nicely swinging at bad pitches), to step out and express, if only through a slight poking with the bat at the ground, just the right amount of exasperation with the powers that be ... yes, every little detail so thoroughly studied and mastered, that it is simply beyond the realm of possibility for any situation to arise in which I do not know how to move, or where to move, or what to say or leave unsaid ... And it's true, is it not?—incredible, but apparently true—there are people who feel in life the ease, the self-assurance, the simple and essential affiliation with what is going on, that I used to feel as the center fielder for the Seabees? Because it wasn't, you see, that one was the best center fielder imagin-able, only that one knew exactly, and down to the smallest particular, how a center fielder should conduct himself. And there are people like that walking the streets of the U.S. of A.? I ask you, why can't I be one! Why can't I exist now as I existed for the Seabees out there in center field! Oh, to be a center fielder, a center fielder—and nothing more!

WITH THE COMING of the tape recorder, journalism has taken on a new look, and the spoken word has become as much a part of the archives as the written. In the case of baseball broadcasts, that means, of course, the *unrehearsed* spoken word.

Anyone who has heard Russ Hodges' description of Bobby Thomson's "homer heard' round the world" in 1951 knows how brilliant and dramatic such treatment can be, in the right hands (or mouth). And Dodger broadcaster Vin Scully gives us further proof here, in his description of the final inning of Sandy Koufax's perfect game.

Koufax's masterwork was his fourth no-hitter in four straight years (Bob Hendley, who pitched against him this night, threw a one-hitter but no cigar). And as you read Scully's spontaneous description, it will become hard to believe that this wasn't written, but is indeed the unrehearsed spoken word instead.

1965:
Los Angeles Dodgers 1, Chicago Cubs 0

VIN SCULLY

THREE TIMES in his sensational career has Sandy Koufax walked out to the mound to pitch a fateful ninth when he turned in a no-hitter. But tonight, September 9th, 1965, he made the toughest walk of his career, I'm sure, because through eight innings he has pitched a perfect game. He has struck out eleven, has retired 24 consecutive batters.

And the first man he will look at is catcher Chris Krug—big, right-handed hitter—flied to center, grounded to short.

Dick Tracewski is now at second base; and Koufax ready—and delivers: curve ball for a strike—0-and-1 the count to Chris Krug.

Out on deck to pinch-hit is one of the men we mentioned as a "possible": Joe Amalfitano. Here's the strike-one pitch: fast ball, swung on and missed, strike two.

And you can almost taste the pressure now. Koufax lifted his cap, ran his fingers through his black hair, and pulled the cap back down, fussing at the bill. Krug must feel it too, as he backs out, heaves a sigh, took off his helmet, put it back on, and steps back up to the plate.

Tracewski is over to his right to fill up the middle. Kennedy is deep to guard the line. The strike-two pitch on the way: fast ball outside, ball one. Krug started to go after it but held up, and Torborg held the ball high in the air trying to convince Vargo, but Eddy said, "No, sir."

One-and-two the count to Chris Krug. It is 9:41 P.M. on September the ninth. The 1-2 pitch on the way: curve ball tapped foul off to the left of the plate. The Dodgers defensively in this spine-tingling moment: Sandy Koufax and Jeff Torborg—the boys who will try to stop anything hit their way: Wes Parker, Dick Tracewski, Maury Wills and John Kennedy—the outfield of Lou Johnson, Willie Davis and Ron Fairly.

There are 29,000 people in the ball park and a million butterflies; 29,139 paid. Koufax into his windup and the 1-2 pitch: fast ball, fouled back out of play.

In the Dodger dugout Al Ferrara gets up and walks down near the runway and it begins to get tough to be a teammate and sit in the dugout and have to watch.

Sandy back of the rubber now, toes it. All the boys in the bullpen straining to get a better look as they look through the wire fence in left field. One-and-two the count to Chris Krug. Koufax, feet together, now to his windup, and the 1-2 pitch: ball, outside, ball two. [*The crowd boos*]

A lot of people in the ball park now are starting to see the pitches with their hearts. The pitch was outside. Torborg tried to pull it in over the plate, but Vargo, an experienced umpire, wouldn't go for it. Two-and-two the count to Chris Krug. Sandy reading signs. Into his windup, 2-2 pitch: fast ball got him swinging! Sandy Koufax has struck out twelve. He is two outs away from a perfect game.

Here is Joe Amalfitano to pinch-hit for Don Kessinger. Amalfitano is from southern California, from San Pedro. He was an original bonus boy with the Giants. Joey's been around, and as we mentioned earlier, he has helped to beat the Dodgers twice. And on deck is Harvey Kuenn.

Kennedy is tight to the bag at third. The fast ball for a strike: 0-and-1 with one out in the ninth inning, 1 to 0 Dodgers.

Sandy ready, into his windup, and the strike-one pitch: curve ball tapped foul, 0-and-2, and Amalfitano walks away and shakes himself a little bit, and swings the bat. And Koufax, with a new ball, takes a hitch at his belt and walks behind the mound. I would think that the mound at Dodger Stadium right now is the loneliest place in the world. Sandy, fussing, looks in to get his sign; 0-and-2 to Amalfitano—the strike-two pitch to Joe: fast ball, swung on and missed, strike three!

He is one out away from the promised land, and Harvey Kuenn is coming up. So Harvey Kuenn is batting for Bob Hendley. The time on the scoreboard is 9:44, the date September the ninth, 1965. And Koufax working on veteran Harvey Kuenn.

Sandy into his windup, and the pitch: fast ball for a strike. He has struck out, by the way, five consecutive batters, and this has gone unnoticed.

Sandy ready, and the strike-one pitch: very high, and he lost his hat. He really forced that one. That was only the second time tonight where I have had the feeling that Sandy threw instead of pitched, trying to get that little extra, and that time he tried so hard his hat fell off. He took an extremely long stride toward the plate, and Torborg had to go up to get it. One-and-one to Harvey Kuenn. Now he's ready: fast ball high, ball two.

You can't blame the man for pushing just a little bit now. Sandy backs off, mops his forehead, runs his left index finger along his forehead, dries it off on his left pants-leg. All the while, Kuenn just waiting.

Now Sandy looks in. Into his windup, and the 2-1 pitch to Kuenn: swung on and missed, strike two. It is 9:46 P.M. Two-and-two to Harvey Kuenn—one strike away.

Sandy into his windup. Here's the pitch: *swung on and missed, a perfect game! [Long wait as crowd noise takes over.]*

On the scoreboard in right field it is 9:46 P.M. in the city of the angels, Los Angeles, California, and a crowd of 29,139 just sitting in to see the only pitcher in baseball history to hurl four no-hit, no-run games. He has done it four straight years, and now he capped it: on his fourth no-hitter, he made it a perfect game.

And Sandy Koufax, whose name will always remind you of strikeouts, did it with a flourish. He struck out the last six consecutive batters. So, when he wrote his name in capital letters in the record book, the "K" stands out even more than the "O-U-F-A-X."

─────────── SPOT REPORTING ───────────

HERE IS a column by Red Smith, whose greatness as a sports writer may be traced in part to the fact that he does not indulge in exaggerated phraseology. He was not exaggerating when he entitled this column, "Miracle of Coogan's Bluff." We kid you not.

1951:
New York Giants 5,
Brooklyn Dodgers 4

RED SMITH

NOW IT IS DONE. Now the story ends. And there is no way to tell it. The art of fiction is dead. Reality has strangled invention. Only the utterly impossible, the inexpressibly fantastic, can ever be plausible again.

Down on the green and white and earth-brown geometry of the playing field, a drunk tries to break through the ranks of ushers marshaled along the foul lines to keep profane feet off the diamond. The ushers thrust him back and he lunges at them, struggling in the clutch of two or three men. He breaks free, and four or five tackle him. He shakes them off, bursts through the line, runs head-on into a special park cop, who brings him down with a flying tackle.

Here comes a whole platoon of ushers. They lift the man and haul him, twisting and kicking, back across the first-base line. Again he shakes loose and crashes the line. He is through. He is away, weaving out toward center field, where cheering thousands are jammed beneath the windows of the Giants' clubhouse.

At heart, our man is a Giant, too. He never gave up.

From center field comes burst upon burst of cheering. Pennants are waving, uplifted fists are brandished, hats are flying. Again and again the dark clubhouse windows blaze with the light of photographers' flash bulbs. Here comes that same drunk out of the mob, back across the green turf to the infield. Coattails flying, he runs the bases, slides into third. Nobody bothers him now.

And the story remains to be told, the story of how the Giants won the 1951 pennant in the National League. The tale of their barreling run through August and September and into October. . . . Of the final day of the season, when they won the championship and started home with it from Boston, to hear on the train how the dead, defeated Dodgers had risen from the ashes in the Philadelphia twilight. . . . Of the three-game play-off in which they won, and lost, and were losing again with one out in the ninth inning yesterday when—Oh, why bother?

Maybe this is the way to tell it: Bobby Thomson, a young Scot from Staten Island, delivered a timely hit yesterday in the ninth inning of an enjoyable game of baseball before 34,320 witnesses in the Polo Grounds. . . . Or perhaps this is better:

"Well!" said Whitey Lockman, standing on second base in the second inning of yesterday's play-off game between the Giants and Dodgers.

"Ah, there," said Bobby Thomson, pulling into the same station after hitting a ball to left field. "How've you been?"

"Fancy," Lockman said, "meeting you here!"

"Ooops!" Thomson said. "Sorry."

And the Giants' first chance for a big inning against Don Newcombe disappeared as they tagged Thomson out. Up in the press section, the voice of Willie Goodrich came over the amplifiers announcing a macabre statistic: "Thomson has now hit safely in fifteen consecutive games." Just then the floodlights were turned on, enabling the Giants to see and count their runners on each base.

It wasn't funny, though, because it seemed for so long that the Giants weren't going to get another chance like the one Thomson squandered by trying to take second base with a playmate already there. They couldn't hit Newcombe, and the Dodgers couldn't do anything wrong. Sal Maglie's most splendrous pitching would avail nothing unless New York could match the run Brooklyn had scored in the first inning.

The story was winding up, and it wasn't the happy ending that such a tale demands. Poetic justice was a phrase without meaning.

Now it was the seventh inning and Thomson was up, with runners on first and third base, none out. Pitching a shutout in Philadelphia last Saturday night, pitching again in Philadelphia on Sunday, holding the Giants scoreless this far, Newcombe had now gone twenty-one innings without allowing a run.

He threw four strikes to Thomson. Two were fouled off out of play. Then he threw a fifth. Thomson's fly scored Monte Irvin. The score was tied. It was a new ball game.

Wait a minute, though. Here's Pee Wee Reese hitting safely in the eighth. Here's Duke Snider singling Reese to third. Here's Maglie wild-pitching a run home. Here's Andy Pafko slashing a hit through Thomson for another score. Here's Billy Cox batting still another home. Where does his hit go? Where else? Through Thomson at third.

So it was the Dodgers' ball game, 4 to 1, and the Dodgers' pennant. So all right. Better get started and beat the crowd home. That stuff in the ninth inning? That didn't mean anything.

A single by Al Dark. A single by Don Mueller. Irvin's pop-up, Lockman's one-run double. Now the corniest possible sort of Hollywood schmaltz—stretcher-bearers plodding away with an injured Mueller between them, symbolic of the Giants themselves.

There went Newcombe and here came Ralph Branca. Who's at bat? Thomson again? He beat Branca with a home run the other day. Would Charley Dressen order him walked, putting the winning run on base, to pitch to the dead-end kids at the bottom of the batting order? No, Branca's first pitch was a called strike.

The second pitch—well, when Thomson reached first base he turned and looked toward the left-field stands. Then he started jumping straight up in the air, again and again. Then he trotted around the bases, taking his time.

Ralph Branca turned and started for the clubhouse. The number on his uniform looked huge. Thirteen.

On July 9, 1958, hearings were held in Washington by the Subcommittee on Antitrust and Monopoly of the Committee of the Judiciary of the United States Senate. The Subcommittee was considering H.R. 10378 and S. 4070, to limit antitrust laws so as to exempt professional baseball, football, basketball, and hockey. Before them as an expert witness came Casey Stengel, whose verbal cuneiform has added the word "Stengelese" to our language. They say there was nothing like it, in all the history of Congressional hearings, since the time the midget sat in J. P. Morgan's lap.

From *The Congressional Record*

CASEY STENGEL

Senator Kefauver: Mr. Stengel, you are the manager of the New York Yankees. Will you give us very briefly your background and your views about this legislation?

Mr. Stengel: Well, I started in professional ball in 1910. I have been in professional ball, I would say, for forty-eight years. I have been employed by numerous ball clubs in the majors and in the minor leagues.

I started in the minor leagues with Kansas City. I played as low as Class D ball, which was at Shelbyville, Kentucky, and also Class C ball and Class A ball, and I have advanced in baseball as a ball-player.

I had many years that I was not so successful as a ballplayer, as it is a game of skill. And then I was no doubt discharged by baseball in which I had to go back to the minor leagues as a manager, and after being in the minor leagues as a manager, I became a major-league manager in several cities and was discharged, we call it discharged because there was no question I had to leave.

And I returned to the minor leagues at Milwaukee, Kansas City and Oakland, California, and then returned to the major leagues.

In the last ten years, naturally, in major-league baseball with the New York Yankees; the New York Yankees have had tremendous success, and while I am not a ballplayer who does the work, I have no doubt worked for a ball club that·is very capable in the office.

I have been up and down the ladder. I know there are some things in baseball thirty-five to fifty years ago that are better now than they were in those days. In those days, my goodness, you could not transfer a ball club in the minor leagues, Class D, Class C ball, Class A ball.

How could you transfer a ball club when you did not have a

highway? How could you transfer a ball club when the railroad then would take you to a town, you got off and then you had to wait and sit up five hours to go to another ball club?

How could you run baseball then without night ball?

You had to have night ball to improve the proceeds, to pay larger salaries, and I went to work, the first year I received $135 a month.

I thought that was amazing. I had to put away enough money to go to dental college. I found out it was not better in dentistry. I stayed in baseball. Any other question you would like to ask me?

SENATOR KEFAUVER: Mr. Stengel, are you prepared to answer particularly why baseball wants this bill passed?

MR. STENGEL: Well, I would have to say at the present time, I think that baseball has advanced in this respect for the player help. That is an amazing statement for me to make, because you can retire with an annuity at fifty and what organization in America allows you to retire at fifty and receive money?

I want to further state that I am not a ballplayer, that is, put into that pension fund committee. At my age, and I have been in baseball, well, I will say I am possibly the oldest man who is working in baseball. I would say that when they start an annuity for the ballplayers to better their conditions, it should have been done, and I think it has been done.

I think it should be the way they have done it, which is a very good thing.

The reason they possibly did not take the managers in at that time was because radio and television or the income to ball clubs was not large enough that you could have put in a pension plan.

Now I am not a member of the pension plan. You have young men here who are, who represent the ball clubs.

They represent the players and since I am not a member and don't receive pension from a fund which you think, my goodness, he ought to be declared in that, too, but I would say that is a great thing for the ballplayers.

That is one thing I will say for the ballplayers, they have an advanced pension fund. I should think it was gained by radio and television or you could not have enough money to pay anything of that type.

Now the second thing about baseball that I think is very interesting to the public or to all of us that it is the owner's own fault if he does not improve his club, along with the officials in the ball club and the players.

Now what causes that?

If I am going to go on the road and we are a traveling ball club and you know the cost of transportation now—we travel sometimes with three Pullman coaches, the New York Yankees and remember I am just a salaried man, and do not own stock in the New York Yankees. I found out that in traveling with the New York Yankees on the road and all, that it is the best, and we have broken records in Washington this year, we have broken them in every city but New York and we have lost two clubs that have gone out of the city of New York.

Of course, we have had some bad weather, I would say that they are mad at us in Chicago, we fill the parks.

They have come out to see good material. I will say they are mad at us in Kansas City, but we broke their attendance record.

Now on the road we only get possibly 27 cents. I am not positive of these figures, as I am not an official.

If you go back fifteen years or so if I owned stock in the club, I would give them to you.

SENATOR KEFAUVER: Mr. Stengel, I am not sure that I made my question clear.

MR. STENGEL: Yes, sir. Well, that is all right. I am not sure I am going to answer yours perfectly, either.

SENATOR O'MAHONEY: How many minor leagues were there in baseball when you began?

MR. STENGEL: Well, there were not so many at that time because of this fact: Anybody to go into baseball at that time with the educational schools that we had were small, while you were probably thoroughly educated at school, you had to be—we only had small cities that you could put a team in and they would go defunct.

Why, I remember the first year I was at Kankakee, Illinois, and a bank offered me $550 if I would let them have a little notice. I left there and took a uniform because they owed me two weeks' pay. But I either had to quit but I did not have enough money to go to dental college so I had to go with the manager down to Kentucky.

What happened there was if you got by July, that was the big date. You did not play night ball and you did not play Sundays in half of the cities on account of a Sunday observance, so in those days when things were tough, and all of it was, I mean to say, why they just closed up July 4 and there you were sitting there in the depot.

You could go to work someplace else, but that was it.

So I got out of Kankakee, Illinois, and I just go there for the visit now.

SENATOR CARROLL: The question Senator Kefauver asked you was what, in your honest opinion, with your forty-eight years of experience, is the need for this legislation in view of the fact that baseball has not been subject to antitrust laws?

MR. STENGEL: No.

SENATOR LANGER: Mr. Chairman, my final question. This is the Antimonopoly Committee that is sitting here.

MR. STENGEL: Yes, sir.

SENATOR LANGER: I want to know whether you intend to keep on monopolizing the world's championship in New York City.

MR. STENGEL: Well, I will tell you. I got a little concern yesterday in the first three innings when I saw the three players I had gotten rid of, and I said when I lost nine what am I going to do and when I had a couple of my players I thought so great of that did not do so good up to the sixth inning I was more confused but I finally had to go and call on a young man in Baltimore that we don't own and the Yankees don't own him, and he is doing pretty good, and I would actually have to tell you that I think we are more the Greta Garbo type now from success.

We are being hated, I mean, from the ownership and all, we are being hated. Every sport that gets too great or one individual—but if we made 27 cents and it pays to have a winner at home, why would not you have a good winner in your own park if you were an owner?

That is the result of baseball. An owner gets most of the money at home and it is up to him and his staff to do better or they ought to be discharged.

SENATOR KEFAUVER: Thank you very much, Mr. Stengel. We appreciate your presence here. Mr. Mickey Mantle, will you come around? . . . Mr. Mantle, do you have any observations with reference to the applicability of the antitrust laws to baseball?

MR. MANTLE: My views are just about the same as Casey's.

WE LABEL THIS a profile, for so it is—a stark characterization of an all-time baseball immortal in the last year of his life.

Ty Cobb's Wild Ten-Month Fight to Live

AL STUMP

EVER SINCE SUNDOWN the Nevada intermountain radio had been crackling warnings: "Route 50 now highly dangerous. Motorists stay off. Repeat: *Avoid Route 50.*"

By 1 in the morning the 21-mile, steep-pitched passage from Lake Tahoe's 7,000 feet into Carson City, a snaky grade most of the way, was snow-struck, ice-sheeted, thick with rock slides and declared unfit for all transport vehicles by the State Highway Patrol.

Such news was right down Ty Cobb's alley. Anything that smacked of the impossible brought an unholy gleam to his eye. The gleam had been there in 1959 when a series of lawyers advised Cobb that he stood no chance against the sovereign State of California in a dispute over income taxes, whereupon he bellowed defiance and sued the commonwealth for $60,000 and damages. It had been there more recently when doctors warned that liquor would kill him. From a pint of whiskey per day he upped his consumption to a quart and more.

Sticking out his chin, he told me, "I think we'll take a little run into town tonight."

A blizzard rattled the windows of Cobb's luxurious hunting lodge on the crest of Lake Tahoe, but to forbid him anything—even at the age of seventy-three—was to tell an ancient tiger not to snarl. Cobb was both the greatest of all ballplayers and a multimillionaire whose monthly income from stock dividends, rents and interest ran to $12,000. And he was a man contemptuous, all his life, of any law other than his own.

"We'll drive in," he announced, "and shoot some craps, see a show and say hello to Joe DiMaggio—he's in Reno at the Riverside Hotel."

I looked at him and felt a chill. Cobb, sitting there haggard and unshaven in his pajamas and a fuzzy old green bathrobe at 1 o'clock in the morning, wasn't fooling.

"Let's not," I said. "You shouldn't be anywhere tonight but in bed."

"Don't argue with me!" he barked. "There are fee-simple sonsof-

282

bitches all over the country who've tried it and wish they hadn't." He glared at me, flaring the whites of his eyes the way he'd done for twenty-four years to quaking pitchers, basemen, umpires and fans.

"If you and I are going to get along," he went on ominously, *"don't increase my tension."*

We were alone in his isolated ten-room $75,000 lodge, having arrived six days earlier, loaded with a large smoked ham, a 20-pound turkey, a case of Scotch and another of champagne, for purposes of collaborating on Ty's book-length autobiography—a book which he'd refused to write for thirty years, but then suddenly decided to place on record before he died. In almost a week's time we hadn't accomplished thirty minutes of work.

The reason: Cobb didn't need a risky auto trip into Reno, but immediate hospitalization, and by the emergency-door entrance. He was desperately ill and had been even before we'd left California.

We had traveled 250 miles to Tahoe in Cobb's black Imperial limousine, carrying with us a virtual drugstore of medicines. These included Digoxin (for his leaky heart), Darvon (for his aching back), Tace (for a recently-operated-upon malignancy of the pelvic area), Fleet's compound (for his infected bowels), Librium (for his "tension"—that is, his violent rages), codeine (for his pain) and an insulin needle-and-syringe kit (for his diabetes), among a dozen other panaceas which he'd substituted for doctors. Cobb despised the medical profession.

At the same time, his sense of balance was almost gone. He tottered about the lodge, moving from place to place by grasping the furniture. On any public street, he couldn't navigate 20 feet without clutching my shoulder, leaning most of his 208 pounds upon me and shuffling along at a spraddle-legged gait. His bowels wouldn't work: they impacted, repeatedly, an almost total stoppage which brought moans of agony from Cobb when he sought relief. He was feverish, with no one at his Tahoe hideaway but the two of us to treat this dangerous condition.

Everything that hurts had caught up with his big, gaunt body at once and he stuffed himself with pink, green, orange, yellow and purple pills —guessing at the amounts, often, since labels had peeled off many of the bottles. But he wouldn't hear of hospitalizing himself.

"The hacksaw artists have taken $50,000 from me," he said, "and they'll get no more." He spoke of "a quack" who'd treated him a few years earlier. "The joker got funny and said he found urine in my whiskey: I fired him."

His diabetes required a precise food-insulin balance. Cobb's needle wouldn't work. He'd misplaced the directions for the needed daily insulin dosage and his hands shook uncontrollably when he went to plunge the needle into a stomach vein. He spilled more of the stuff that he injected.

He'd been warned by experts from Johns Hopkins to California's

Scripps Clinic—that liquor was deadly. Tyrus snorted and began each day with several gin-and-orange-juices, then switched to Old Rarity Scotch, which held him until the night hours, when sleep was impossible, and he tossed down cognac, champagne or "Cobb Cocktails"—Southern Comfort stirred into hot water and honey.

A careful diet was essential. Cobb wouldn't eat. The lodge was without a cook or manservant—since, in the previous six months, he had fired two cooks, a male nurse and a handyman in fits of anger—and any food I prepared for him he pushed away. As of the night of the blizzard, the failing, splenetic old king of ballplayers hadn't touched food in three days, existing solely on quarts of booze and booze mixtures.

My reluctance to prepare the car for the Reno trip burned him up. He beat his fists on the arms of his easy chair. "I'll go alone!" he threatened.

It was certain he'd try it. The storm had worsened, but once Cobb set his mind on an idea, nothing could change it. Beyond that I'd already found that to oppose or annoy him was to risk a violent explosion. An event of a week earlier had proved *that* point. It was then I discovered that he carried a loaded Luger wherever he went and looked for opportunities to use it.

En route to Lake Tahoe, we'd stopped overnight at a motel near Hangtown, California. During the night a party of drunks made a loud commotion in the parking lot. In my room next to Cobb's, I heard him cursing and then his voice, booming out the window.

"Get out of here, you—heads!"

The drunks replied in kind. Then everyone in the motel had his teeth jolted.

Groping his way to the door, Tyrus the Terrible fired three shots into the dark that resounded like cannon claps. There were screams and yells. Reaching my door, I saw the drunks climbing each other's backs in their rush to flee. The frightened motel manager, and others, arrived. Before anyone could think of calling the police, the manager was cut down by the most caustic tongue ever heard in a baseball clubhouse.

"What kind of a pest house is this?" roared Cobb. "Who gave you a license, you mugwump? Get the hell out of here and see that I'm not disturbed! I'm a sick man and I want it quiet!"

"B-b-beg your pardon, Mr. Cobb," the manager said feebly. He apparently felt so honored to have baseball's greatest figure as a customer that no police were called. When we drove away the next morning, a crowd gathered and stood gawking with open mouths.

Down the highway, with me driving, Cobb checked the Luger and re-loaded its nine-shell clip. "Two of those shots were in the air," he remarked. "The *third* kicked up gravel. I've got permits for this gun from governors of three states. I'm an honorary deputy sheriff of California and a Texas Ranger. So we won't be getting any complaints."

He saw nothing strange in his behavior. Ty Cobb's rest had been disturbed—therefore he had every right to shoot up the neighborhood.

About then I began to develop a twitch of the nerves, which grew worse with time. In past years, I'd heard reports of Cobb's weird and violent ways, without giving them much credence. But until early 1960 my own experience with the legendary Georgian had been slight, amounting only to meetings in Scottsdale, Arizona, and New York to discuss book-writing arrangements and to sign the contract.

Locker-room stories of Ty's eccentricities, wild temper, ego and miserliness sounded like the usual scandalmongering you get in sports. I'd heard that Cobb had flattened a heckler in San Francisco's Domino Club with one punch; had been sued by Elbie Felts, an ex-Coast League player, after assaulting Felts; that he boobytrapped his Spanish villa at Atherton, California, with high-voltage wires; that he'd walloped one of his ex-wives; that he'd been jailed in Placerville, California, at the age of sixty-eight for speeding, abusing a traffic cop and then inviting the judge to return to law school at his, Cobb's, expense.

I passed these things off. The one and only Ty Cobb was to write his memoirs and I felt highly honored to be named his collaborator.

As the poet Cowper reflected, "The innocents are gay." I was eager to start. Then—a few weeks before book work began—I was taken aside and tipped off by an in-law of Cobb's and one of Cobb's former teammates with the Detroit Tigers that I hadn't heard the half of it. "Back out of this book deal," they urged. "You'll never finish it and you might get hurt."

They went on: "Nobody can live with Ty. Nobody ever has. That includes two wives who left him, butlers, housekeepers, chauffeurs, nurses and a few mistresses. He drove off all his friends long ago. Max Fleischmann, the yeast-cake heir, was a pal of Ty's until the night a house guest of Fleischmann's made a remark about Cobb spiking other players when he ran the bases. The man only asked if it was true. Cobb knocked the guy into a fish pond and after that Max never spoke to him again. Another time, a member of Cobb's family crossed him—a woman, mind you. He broke her nose with a ball bat.

"Do you know about the butcher? Ty didn't like some meat he bought. In the fight, he broke up the butcher shop. Had to settle $1,500 on the butcher out of court."

"But I'm dealing with him strictly on business," I said.

"So was the butcher," replied my informants. "In baseball, a few of us who really knew him well realized that he was wrong in the head— unbalanced. He played like a demon and had everybody hating him because he *was* a demon. That's how he set all those records that nobody has come close to since 1928. It's why he was always in a brawl on the field, in the clubhouse, behind the stands and in the stands. The public's never known it, but Cobb's always been off the beam where other people are concerned. Sure, he made millions in the stock market—but that's only cold business. He carried a gun in the

big league and scared hell out of us. He's mean, tricky and dangerous. Look out he doesn't blow up some night and clip you with a bottle. He specializes in throwing bottles.

"Now that he's sick he's worse than ever. And you've signed up to
stay with him for months. You poor sap."

Taken aback, but still skeptical, I launched the job—with my first
task to drive Cobb to his Lake Tahoe retreat, where, he declared, we
could work uninterrupted.

As indicated, nothing went right from the start. The Hangtown
gunplay incident was an eye-opener. Next came a series of events, such as
Cobb's determination to set forth in a blizzard to Reno, which were too
strange to explain away. Everything had to suit his pleasure or he had a tan-
trum. He prowled about the lodge at night, suspecting trespassers, with the
Luger in hand. I slept with one eye open ready to move fast if necessary.

At 1 o'clock of the morning of the storm, full of pain and 90-proof,
he took out the Luger, letting it casually rest between his knees. I had
continued to object to a Reno excursion in such weather.

He looked at me with tight fury and said, biting out the words: "In
1912—and you can write this down—I killed a man in Detroit. He and
two other hoodlums jumped me on the street early one morning with a
knife. I was carrying something that came in handy in my early days—
a Belgian-made pistol with a heavy raised sight at the barrel end.

"Well, the damned gun wouldn't fire and they cut me up the back."

Making notes as fast as he talked, I asked, "Where in the back?"

"Well, dammit all to hell, if you don't believe me, come and look!"
Cobb flared, jerking up his shirt. When I protested that I believed him
implicitly, only wanted a story detail, he picked up a half-full whiskey
glass and smashed it against the brick fireplace. So I gingerly took a look.
A faint whitish scar ran about five inches up the lower left back.

"Satisfied?" jeered Cobb.

He described how, after a battle, the men fled before his fists.

"What with you wounded and the odds three to one," I said, "that
must have been a relief."

"Relief? Do you think they could pull that on *me? I went after them!*"

Where anyone else would have felt lucky to be out of it, Cobb chased
one of the mugs into a dead-end alley. "I used that gunsight to rip and
slash and tear him for about ten minutes until he had no face left,"
related Ty, with relish. "Left him there, not breathing, in his own rotten
blood."

"What was the situation—where were you going when it happened?"

"To catch a train to a ball game."

"You saw a doctor, instead?"

*"I did nothing of the sort, dammit! I played the next day and got
two hits in three times up!"*

Records I later inspected bore out every word of it: on June 3, 1912, in a blood-soaked, makeshift bandage, Ty Cobb hit a double and triple for Detroit, and only then was treated for the knife wound. He was that kind of ballplayer through a record 3,033 games. No other player burned with Cobb's flame. Boze Bulger, a great old-time baseball critic, said, "He was possessed by the Furies."

Finishing his tale, Cobb looked me straight in the eye.

"You're driving me into Reno tonight," he said softly. The Luger was in his hand.

Even before I opened my mouth, Cobb knew he'd won. He had a sixth sense about the emotions he produced in others: in this case, fear. As far as I could see (lacking expert diagnosis and as a layman understands the symptoms), he wasn't merely erratic and trigger-tempered, but suffering from megalomania, or acute self-worship; delusions of persecution; and more than a touch of dipsomania.

Although I'm not proud of it, he scared hell out of me most of the time I was around him.

And now he gave me the first smile of our association. "As long as you don't aggravate my tension," he said, "we'll get along."

Before describing the Reno expedition, I would like to say in this frank view of a mighty man that the greatest, and strangest, of all American sport figures had his good side, which he tried to conceal. During the final ten months of his life I was his one constant companion. Eventually, I put him to bed, prepared his insulin, picked him up when he fell down, warded off irate taxi drivers, bartenders, waiters, clerks and private citizens whom Cobb was inclined to punch, cooked what food he could digest, drew his bath, got drunk with him and knelt with him in prayer on black nights when he knew death was near. I ducked a few bottles he threw, too.

I think, because he forced upon me a confession of his most private thoughts, that I knew the answer to the central, overriding secret of his life: was Ty Cobb psychotic throughout his baseball career?

Kids, dogs and sick people flocked to him and he returned their instinctive liking. Money was his idol, but from his $4-million fortune he assigned large sums to create the Cobb Educational Foundation, which financed hundreds of needy youngsters through college. He built and endowed a first-class hospital for the poor of his backwater home town, Royston, Georgia. When Ty's spinster sister, Florence, was crippled, he tenderly cared for her until her last days. The widow of a onetime American League batting champion would have lived in want but for Ty's steady money support. A Hall of Fame member, beaned by a pitched ball and enfeebled, came under Cobb's wing for years. Regularly he mailed dozens of anonymous checks to indigent old ballplayers (relayed by a third party)—a rare act among retired tycoons in other lines of business.

If you believe such acts didn't come hard for Cobb, guess again: he was the world's champion pinchpenny.

Some 150 fan letters reached him each month, requesting his autograph. Many letters enclosed return-mail stamps. Cobb used the stamps for his own outgoing mail. The fan letters he burned.

"Saves on firewood," he'd mutter.

In December of 1960, Ty hired a one-armed "gentleman's gentleman" named Brownie. Although constantly criticized, poor Brownie worked hard as cook and butler. But when he mixed up the grocery order one day, he was fired with a check for a week's pay—$45—and sent packing.

Came the middle of that night and Cobb awakened me.

"We're driving into town *right now*," he stated, "to stop payment on Brownie's check. The bastard talked back to me when I discharged him. He'll get no more of my money."

All remonstrations were futile. There was no phone, so we had to drive the 20 miles from Cobb's Tahoe lodge into Carson City, where he woke up the president of the First National Bank of Nevada and arranged for a stop-pay on the piddling check. The president tried to conceal his anger—Cobb was a big depositor in his bank.

"Yes, sir, Ty," he said, "I'll take care of it first thing in the morning."

"You goddamn well better," snorted Cobb. And then we drove through the 3 A.M. darkness back to the lake.

But this trip was a light workout compared to that Reno trip.

Two cars were available at the lodge. Cobb's 1956 Imperial had no tire chains, but the other car did.

"We'll need both for this operation," he ordered. "One car might get stuck or break down. I'll drive mine and you take the one with chains. You go first. I'll follow your chain marks."

For Cobb to tackle precipitous Route 50 was unthinkable in every way. The Tahoe road, with 200-foot drop-offs, has killed a recorded eighty motorists. Along with his illness, his drunkenness, and no chains, he had bad eyes and was without a driver's license. California had turned him down at his last test; he hadn't bothered to apply in Nevada.

Urging him to ride with me was a waste of breath.

A howling wind hit my car a solid blow as we shoved off. Sleet stuck to the windshield faster than the wipers could work. For the first three miles, snowplows had been active and at 15 mph, in second gear, I managed to hold the road. But then came Spooner's Summit, 7,000 feet high, and then a steep descent of nine miles. Behind me, headlamps blinking, Cobb honked his horn, demanding more speed. Chainless, he wasn't getting traction. *The hell with him,* I thought. Slowing to first gear, fighting to hold a roadbed I couldn't see even with my head stuck out the window, I skidded along. No other traffic moved as we did our crazy tandem around icy curves, at times brushing the guardrails. Cobb was blaring his horn steadily now.

And then here came Cobb.

Tiring of my creeping pace, he gunned the Imperial around me in one big skid. I caught a glimpse of an angry face under a big Stetson hat and a waving fist. He was doing a good 30 mph when he'd gained 25 yards on me, fishtailing right and left, but straightening as he slid out of sight in the thick sleet.

I let him go. Suicide wasn't in my contract.

The next six miles was a matter of feeling my way and praying. Near a curve, I saw taillights to the left. Pulling up, I found Ty swung sideways and buried, nose down, in a snowbank, his hind wheels two feet in the air. Twenty yards away was a sheer drop-off into a canyon.

"You hurt?" I asked.

"Bumped my —— head," he muttered. He lit a cigar and gave four-letter regards to the Highway Department for not illuminating the "danger" spot. His forehead was bruised and he'd broken his glasses.

In my car, we groped our way down-mountain, a nightmare ride, with Cobb alternately taking in Scotch from a thermos jug and telling me to step on it. At 3 A.M. in Carson City, an all-night garageman used a broom to clean the car of snow and agreed to pick up the Imperial— "when the road's passable." With dawn breaking, we reached Reno. All I wanted was a bed and all Cobb wanted was a craps table.

He was rolling now, pretending he wasn't ill, and with the Scotch bracing him, Ty was able to walk into the Riverside Hotel casino with a hand on my shoulder and without staggering so obviously as usual. Everybody present wanted to meet him. Starlets from a film unit on location in Reno flocked around and comedian Joe E. Lewis had the band play "Sweet Georgia Brown"—Ty's favorite tune.

"Hope your dice are still honest," he told Riverside co-owner Bill Miller. "Last time I was here I won $12,000 in three hours."

"How I remember, Ty," said Miller. "How I remember."

A scientific craps player who'd won and lost huge sums in Nevada in the past, Cobb bet $100 chips, his eyes alert, not missing a play around the board. He soon decided that the table was "cold" and we moved to another casino, then a third. At this last stop, Cobb's legs began to grow shaky. Holding himself up by leaning on the table edge with his forearms, he dropped $300, then had a hot streak in which he won over $800. His voice was a croak as he told the other players, "Watch 'em and weep."

But then suddenly his voice came back. When the stickman raked the dice his way, Cobb loudly said, "You touched the dice with your hand."

"No, sir," said the stickman. "I did *not.*"

"I don't lie!" snarled Cobb.

"I don't lie either," insisted the stickman.

"Nobody touches my dice!" Cobb, swaying on his feet, eyes blazing, worked his way around the table toward the croupier. It was a weird tableau. In his crumpled Stetson and expensive camel's-hair coat, stained and charred with cigarette burns, a three-day beard grizzling his face, the gaunt old giant of baseball towered over the dapper gambler.

"You fouled the dice, I saw you," growled Cobb, and then he swung.

The blow missed, as the stickman dodged, but, cursing and almost falling, Cobb seized the wooden rake and smashed it over the table. I jumped in and caught him under the arms as he sagged.

And then, as quickly as possible, we were put into the street by two large uniformed guards. "Sorry, Mr. Cobb," they said, unhappily, "but we can't have this."

A crowd had gathered and as we started down the street, Cobb swearing and stumbling and clinging to me, I couldn't have felt more conspicuous if I'd been strung naked from the neon arch across Reno's main drag, Virginia Street. At the street corner, Ty was struck by an attack of breathlessness. "Got to stop," he gasped. Feeling him going limp on me, I turned his six-foot body against a lamppost, braced my legs and with an underarm grip held him there until he caught his breath. He panted and gulped for air.

His face gray, he murmured, "Reach into my left-hand coat pocket." Thinking he wanted his bottle of heart pills, I did. But instead pulled out a six-inch-thick wad of currency, secured by a rubber band. "Couple of thousand there," he said weakly. "Don't let it out of sight."

At the nearest motel, where I hired a single, twin-bed room, he collapsed on the bed in his coat and hat and slept. After finding myself some breakfast, I turned in. Hours later I heard him stirring. "What's this place?" he muttered.

I told him the name of the motel—Travelodge.

"Where's the bankroll?"

"In your coat. You're wearing it."

Then he was quiet.

After a night's sleep, Cobb felt well enough to resume his gambling. In the next few days, he won more than $3,000 at the tables, and then we went sight-seeing in historic Virginia City. There as in all places, he stopped traffic. And had the usual altercation. This one was at the Bucket of Blood, where Cobb accused the bartender of serving watered Scotch. The bartender denied it. Crash! Another drink went flying.

Back at the lodge a week later, looking like the wrath of John Barleycorn and having refused medical aid in Reno, he began to suffer new and excruciating pains—in his hips and lower back. But between groans he forced himself to work an hour a day on his autobiography. He told inside baseball tales never published:

". . . . Frank Navin, who owned the Detroit club for years, faked his turnstile count to cheat the visiting team and Uncle Sam. So did Big Bill

Devery and Frank Farrell, who owned the New York Highlanders—later called the Yankees.

". . . . Walter Johnson, the Big Train, tried to kill himself when his wife died."

". . . . Grover Cleveland Alexander wasn't drunk out there on the mound, the way people thought—he was an epileptic. Old Pete would fall down with a seizure between innings, then go back and pitch another shutout."

". . . . John McGraw hated me because I tweaked his nose in broad daylight in the lobby of the Oriental Hotel, in Dallas, after earlier beating the hell out of his second baseman, Buck Herzog, upstairs in my room."

But before we were well started, Cobb suddenly announced we'd go riding in his 23-foot Chris-Craft speedboat, tied up in a boathouse below the lodge. When I went down to warm it up, I found the boat sunk to the bottom of Lake Tahoe in 15 feet of water.

My host broke all records for blowing his stack when he heard the news. He saw in this a sinister plot. "I told you I've got enemies all around here! It's sabotage as sure as I'm alive!"

A sheriff's investigation turned up no clues. Cobb sat up all night for three nights with his Luger. "I'll salivate the first dirty skunk who steps foot around here after dark," he swore.

Parenthetically, Cobb had a vocabulary all his own. To "salivate" something meant to destroy it. Anything easy was "soft-boiled," to outsmart someone was to "slip him the oskafagus," and all doctors were "truss-fixers." People who displeased him—and this included almost everyone he met—were "fee-simple sonsofbitches," "mugwumps" or (if female) "lousy slits."

Lake Tahoe friends of Cobb's had stopped visiting him long before, but one morning an attractive blonde of about fifty came calling. She was an old chum—in a romantic way, I was given to understand, of bygone years—but Ty greeted her coldly. "Lost my sexual powers when I was sixty-nine," he said, when she was out of the room. "What the hell use to me is a woman?"

The lady had brought along a three-section electric vibrator bed, which she claimed would relieve Ty's back pains. We helped him mount it. He took a twenty-minute treatment. Attempting to dismount, he lost balance, fell backward, the contraption jackknifed, and Cobb was pinned, yelling and swearing, under a pile of machinery.

When I freed him and helped him to a chair, he told the lady—in the choicest gutter language—where she could put her bed. She left, sobbing.

"That's no way to talk to an old friend, Ty," I said. "She was trying to do you a favor."

"And you're a hell of a poor guest around here, too!" he thundered.

"You can leave any old time!" He quickly grabbed a bottle and heaved it in my direction.

"Thought you could throw straighter than that!" I yelled back.

Fed up with him, I started to pack my bags. Before I'd finished, Cobb broke out a bottle of vintage Scotch, said I was "damned sensitive," half apologized, and the matter was forgotten.

While working one morning on an outside observation deck, I heard a thud inside. On his bedroom floor, sprawled on his back, lay Ty. He was unconscious, his eyes rolled back, breathing shallowly. I thought he was dying.

There was no telephone. "Eavesdroppers on the line," Cobb had told me. "I had it cut off." I ran down the road to a neighboring lodge and phoned a Carson City doctor, who promised to come immediately.

Back at the lodge, Ty remained stiff and stark on the floor, little bubbles escaping his lips. His face was bluish-white. With much straining, I lifted him halfway to the bed and by shifting holds finally rolled him onto it, and covered him with a blanket. Twenty minutes passed. No doctor.

Ten minutes later, I was at the front door, watching for the doctor's car, when I heard a sound. There stood Ty, swaying on his feet. "You want to do some work on the book?" he said.

His recovery didn't seem possible. "But you were out cold a minute ago," I said.

"Just a dizzy spell. Have 'em all the time. Must have hit my head on the bedpost when I fell."

The doctor, arriving, found Cobb's blood pressure standing at a grim 210 on the gauge. His temperature was 101 degrees and from gross neglect of his diabetes, he was in a state of insulin shock, often fatal if not quickly treated. "I'll have to hospitalize you, Mr. Cobb," said the doctor.

Weaving his way to a chair, Cobb angrily waved him away. "Just send me your bill," he grunted. "I'm going home."

"Home" was the multimillionaire's main residence at Atherton, California, on the San Francisco Peninsula, 250 miles away, and it was there he headed later that night. With some hot soup and insulin in him, Cobb recovered with the same unbelievable speed he'd shown in baseball. In his heyday, trainers often sewed up deep spike cuts in his knees, shins and thighs, on a clubhouse bench, without anesthetic, and he didn't lose an inning. Grantland Rice one 1920 day sat beside a bedridden, feverish Cobb, whose thighs, from sliding, were a mass of raw flesh. Sixteen hours later, he hit a triple, double, three singles and stole two bases to beat the Yankees. On the Atherton ride, he yelled insults at several motorists who moved too slowly to suit him. Reaching Atherton, Ty said he felt ready for another drink.

My latest surprise was Cobb's eighteen-room, two-story richly landscaped Spanish-California villa at 48 Spencer Lane, an exclusive neighborhood. You could have held a ball game on the grounds.

But the $90,000 mansion had no lights, no heat, no hot water.

"I'm suing the Pacific Gas & Electric Company," he explained, "for overcharging me on the service. Those rinky-dinks tacked an extra $16 on my bill. Bunch of crooks. When I wouldn't pay, they cut off my utilities. Okay—I'll see them in court."

For months previously, Ty Cobb had lived in a totally dark house. The only illumination was candlelight. The only cooking facility was a portable Coleman stove, such as campers use. Bathing was impossible, unless you could take it cold. The electric refrigerator, stove, deep-freeze, radio and television, of course, didn't work. Cobb had vowed to "hold the fort" until his trial of the P.G.&E. was settled. Simultaneously, he had filed a $60,000 suit in San Francisco Superior Court against the State of California to recover state income taxes already collected—on the argument that he wasn't a permanent resident of California, but of Nevada, Georgia, Arizona and other way-points. State's attorneys claimed he spent at least six months per year in Atherton, thus had no case.

"I'm gone so much from here," he claimed, "that I'll win hands down." All legal opinion, I later learned, held just the opposite view, but Cobb ignored their advice.

Next morning, I arranged with Ty's gardener, Hank, to turn on the lawn sprinklers. In the outdoor sunshine, a cold-water shower was easier to take. From then on, the back yard became my regular washroom.

The problem of lighting a desk so that we could work on the book was solved by stringing 200 feet of cord, plugged into an outlet of a neighboring house, through hedges and flower gardens and into the window of Cobb's study, where a single naked bulb hung over the chandelier provided illumination.

The flickering shadows cast by the single light made the vast old house seem haunted. No ghost writer ever had more ironical surroundings.

At various points around the premises, Ty showed me where he'd once installed high-voltage wires to stop trespassers. "Curiosity seekers?" I asked. "Hell, no," he said. "Detectives broke in here once looking for evidence against me in a divorce suit. After a couple of them got burned, they stopped coming."

To reach our bedrooms, Cobb and I groped our way down long, black corridors. Twice he fell in the dark. And then, collapsing completely, he became so ill that he was forced to check in at Stanford Hospital in nearby Palo Alto. Here another shock was in store.

One of the physicians treating Ty's case, a Dr. E. R. Brown, said, "Do you mean to say that this man has traveled 700 miles in the last month without medical care?"

"Doctor," I said, "I've hauled him in and out of saloons, motels, gambling joints, steam baths and snowbanks. There's no holding him."

"It's a miracle he's alive. He has almost every major ailment I know about."

Dr. Brown didn't reveal to me Ty's main ailment, which news Cobb, himself, broke late one night from his hospital bed. "It's cancer," he said, bluntly. "About a year ago I had most of my prostate gland removed when they found it was malignant. Now it's spread up into the back bones. These pill-peddlers here won't admit it, but I haven't got a chance."

Cobb made me swear I'd never divulge the fact before he died. "If it gets in the papers, the sob sisters will have a field day. I don't want sympathy from anybody."

At Stanford, where he absorbed seven massive doses of cobalt radiation, the ultimate cancer treatment, he didn't act like a man on his last legs. Even before his strength returned, he was in the usual form.

"They won't let me have a drink," he said indignantly. "I want you to get me a bottle. Smuggle it in in your tape-recorder case."

I tried, telling myself that no man with terminal cancer deserves to be dried up, but sharp-eyed nurses and orderlies were watching. They searched Ty's closet, found the bottle and over his roars of protest appropriated it.

"We'll have to slip them the oskafagus," said Ty.

Thereafter, a drink of Scotch-and-water sat in plain view in his room, on his bedside table, under the very noses of his physicians—and nobody suspected a thing. The whiskey was in an ordinary water glass, and in the liquid reposed Ty's false teeth.

There were no dull moments while Cobb was at the hospital. He was critical of everything. He told one doctor that he was not even qualified to be an intern, and told the hospital dietician—at the top of his voice —that she and the kitchen workers were in a conspiracy to poison him with their "foul" dishes. To a nurse he snapped, "If Florence Nightingale knew about you, she'd spin in her grave."

(Stanford Hospital, incidentally, is one of the largest and top-rated medical plants in the United States.)

But between blasts he did manage to buckle down to work on the book, dictating long into the night into a microphone suspended over his bed. Slowly the stormy details of his professional life came out. He spoke often of having "forgiven" his many baseball enemies, then lashed out at them with such passionate phrases that it was clear he'd done no such thing. High on his "hate" list were McGraw; New York sportswriters; Hub Leonard, a pitcher who in 1926 accused Cobb and Tris Speaker of "fixing" a Detroit-Cleveland game; American League president Ban Johnson; one-time Detroit owner Frank Navin; former Baseball Commissioner Kenesaw Mountain Landis; and all those who intimated that Cobb ever used his spikes on another player without justification.

After a night when he slipped out of the hospital, against all orders, and we drove to a San Francisco Giants-Cincinnati Reds game at Candlestick Park, 30 miles away, Stanford Hospital decided it couldn't help Tyrus R. Cobb, and he was discharged. For extensive treatment his bill ran to more than $1,200.

"That's a nice racket you boys have here," he told the discharging doctors. "You clip the customers and then every time you pass an undertaker, you wink at him."

"Good-bye, *Mr.* Cobb," snapped the medical men.

Soon after this Ty caught a plane to his native Georgia and I went along. "I want to see some of the old places again before I die," he said.

It now was Christmas Eve of 1960 and I'd been with him for three months and completed but four chapters. The project had begun to look hopeless. In Royston, a village of 1,200, Cobb headed for the town cemetery. I drove him there, we parked, and I helped him climb a windswept hill through the growing dusk. Light snow fell. Faintly, Yule chimes could be heard.

Among the many headstones, Ty looked for the plot he'd reserved for himself while in California and couldn't locate it. His temper began to boil. "Dammit, I ordered the biggest damn mausoleum in the graveyard! I know it's around here somewhere." On the next hill, we found it: a large marble, walk-in-size structure with "Cobb" engraved over the entrance.

"You want to pray with me?" he said gruffly. We knelt and tears came to his eyes.

Within the tomb, he pointed to crypts occupied by the bodies of his father, Professor William Herschel Cobb, his mother, Amanda (Chitwood) Cobb, and his sister Florence, whom he'd had disinterred and placed here. "My father," he said reverently, "was the greatest man I ever knew. He was a scholar, state senator, editor and philosopher. I worshiped him. So did all the people around here. He was the only man who ever made me do his bidding."

Arising painfully, Ty braced himself against the marble crypt that soon would hold his body. There was an eerie silence in the tomb. He said deliberately: "My father had his head blown off with a shotgun when I was eighteen years old—*by a member of my own family.* I didn't get over that. I've never gotten over it."

We went back down the hill to the car. I asked no questions that day.

Later, from family sources and old Georgia friends of the baseball idol, I learned about the killing. One night in August of 1905, they related, Professor Cobb announced that he was driving from Royston to a neighboring village and left home by buggy. But later that night, he doubled back and crept into his wife's bedroom by way of the window. "He suspected her of being unfaithful to him," said these sources. "He thought he'd catch her in the act. But Amanda Cobb was a good woman. She was all alone when she saw a menacing figure climb through her window and approach her bed. In the dark, she assumed it to be a robber. She kept a shotgun handy by her bed and she used it. Everybody around here knew the story, but it was hushed up when Ty became famous."

News of the killing reached Ty in Augusta, where he was playing minor-league ball, on August 9. A few days later he was told that he'd been purchased by the Detroit Tigers, and was to report immediately. "In my grief," Cobb says in the book, "it didn't matter much. . . ."

Came March of 1961 and I remained stuck to the Georgia Peach like court plaster. He'd decided that we were born pals, meant for each other, that we'd complete a baseball book beating anything ever published. He had astonished doctors by rallying from the spreading cancer and, between bouts of transmitting his life and times to a tape recorder, was raising more whoopee than he had at Lake Tahoe and Reno.

Spring-training time for the big leagues had arrived and we were ensconced in a $30-a-day suite at the Ramada Inn at Scottsdale, Arizona, close by the practice parks of the Red Sox, Indians, Giants and Cubs. Here, each year, Cobb held court. He didn't go to see anybody; Ford Frick, Joe Cronin, Ted Williams, and other diamond notables came to him. While explaining to sportswriters why modern stars couldn't compare to the Wagners, Lajoies, Speakers, Jacksons, Mathewsons and Planks of his day, Ty did other things.

For one, he commissioned a noted Arizona artist to paint him in oils. He was emaciated, having dropped from 208 pounds to 176. The preliminary sketches showed up his sagging cheeks and thin neck.

"I wouldn't let you calcimine my toilet," ripped out Ty, and fired the artist.

But at analyzing the Dow-Jones averages and playing the stock market, he was anything but eccentric. Twice a week he phoned experts around the country, determined good buys and bought in blocks of 500 to 1,500 shares. He made money consistently, even when bedridden, with a mind that read behind the fluctuations of a dozen different issues. "The State of Georgia," Ty remarked, "will realize about one million dollars from inheritance taxes when I'm dead. But there isn't a man alive who knows what I'm worth." According to the *Sporting News,* there was evidence upon Cobb's death that his worth approximated $12 million. Whatever the true figure, he did not confide the amount to me—or, most probably, to anyone except attorneys who drafted his last will and testament. And Cobb fought off making his will until the last moment.

His fortune began in 1908, when he bought into United (later General) Motors; as of 1961, he was "Mr. Coca-Cola," holding more than 20,000 shares of that stock, valued at $85 per share. Wherever we traveled, he carried with him, stuffed into an old brown bag, more than $1 million in stock certificates and negotiable government bonds. The bag never was locked up. Cobb assumed nobody would dare rob him. He tossed the bag into any handy corner of a room, inviting theft. And in Scottsdale it turned up missing.

Playing Sherlock, he narrowed the suspects to a room maid and a man he'd hired to cook meals. When questioned, the maid broke into tears and the cook quit (fired, said Cobb). Hours later, I discovered the bag under a pile of dirty laundry.

Major-league owners and league officials hated to see him coming, for he thought their product was putrid and said so, incessantly. "Today they hit for ridiculous averages, can't bunt, can't steal, can't hit-and-run, can't place-hit to the opposite field and you can't call them ballplayers." He told sportswriters, "I blame Frick, Cronin, Bill Harridge, Horace Stoneham, Dan Topping and others for wrecking baseball's traditional league lines. These days, any tax-dodging mugwump with a bankroll can buy a franchise, field some semipros and get away with it. Where's our integrity? Where's *baseball?*"

No one could quiet Cobb. Who else had a lifetime average of .367, made 4,191 hits, scored 2,244 runs, won 12 batting titles, stole 892 bases, repeatedly beat whole teams single-handedly? Who was first into the Hall of Fame? Not Babe Ruth—but Cobb, by a landslide vote.

By early April, he could barely make it up the ramp of the Scottsdale Stadium, even hanging onto me. He had to stop, gasping for breath, every few steps. But he kept coming to games—loving the sounds of the ball park. His courage was tremendous. "Always be ready to catch me if I start to fall," he said. "I'd hate to go down in front of the fans."

People of all ages were overcome with emotion upon meeting him; no sports figure I've known produced such an effect upon the public.

We went to buy a cane. At a surgical supply house, Cobb inspected a dozen $25 malacca sticks, bought the cheapest, $4, white-ash cane they had. "I'm a plain man," he informed the clerk, the $7,500 diamond ring on his finger glittering.

But pride kept the old tiger from ever using the cane, any more than he'd wear the $600 hearing aid built into the bow of his glasses.

One day a Mexican taxi driver aggravated Cobb with his driving. Throwing the fare on the ground, he waited until the cabby had bent to retrieve it, then tried to punt him like a football.

"What's your sideline," he inquired, "selling opium?"

It was all I could do to keep the driver from swinging on him. Later, a lawyer called on Cobb, threatening a damage suit. "Get in line, there's five hundred ahead of you," said Tyrus, waving him away.

Every day was a new adventure. He was fighting back against the pain that engulfed him again—cobalt treatments no longer helped—and

I could count on trouble anywhere we went. He threw a saltshaker at a Phoenix waiter, narrowly missing. One of his most treasured friendships —with Ted Williams—came to an end.

From the early 1940s, Williams had sat at Ty Cobb's feet. They often met, exchanged long letters on the art of batting. At Scottsdale one day, Williams dropped by Ty's rooms. He hugged Ty, fondly rumpled his hair and accepted a drink. Presently the two greatest hitters of past and present fell into an argument over what players should comprise the all-time, All-Star team. Williams declared, "I want DiMaggio and Hornsby on my team over anybody you can mention."

Cobb's face grew dark. "Don't give me that! Hornsby couldn't go back for a pop fly and he lacked smartness. DiMaggio couldn't hit with Speaker or Joe Jackson."

"The hell you say!" came back Williams jauntily. "Hornsby outhit *you* a couple of years."

Almost leaping from his chair, Cobb shook a fist. He'd been given the insult supreme—for Cobb always resented, and finally hated, Rogers Hornsby. Not until Cobb was in his sixteenth season did Hornsby top him in the batting averages. "Get . . . away from me!" choked Cobb. "Don't come back!"

Williams left with a quizzical expression, not sure how much Cobb meant it. The old man meant it all the way. He never invited Williams back, nor talked to him, nor spoke his name again. "I cross him off," he told me.

We left Arizona shortly thereafter for my home in Santa Barbara, California. Now failing fast, Tyrus had accepted my invitation to be my guest. Two doctors inspected him at my beach house by the Pacific and gave their opinions: he had a few months of life left, no more. The cancer had invaded the bones of his skull. His pain was intense, unrelenting— requiring heavy sedation—yet with teeth bared and sweat pouring down his face, he fought off medical science. "They'll never get me on their damned hypnotics," he swore. "I'll never die an addict . . . an idiot. . . ."

He shouted, "Where's anybody who cares about me? Where are they? The world's lousy . . . no good."

One night later, on May 1, Cobb sat propped up in bed, over-looking a starlit ocean. He had a habit, each night, of rolling up his trousers and placing them under his pillow—an early-century ball-player's trick, dating from the time when Ty slept in strange places and might be robbed. I knew that his ever-present Luger was tucked into that pants roll.

I'd never seen him so sunk in despair. At last the fire was going out. "Do we die a little at a time, or all at once?" he wondered aloud. "I think Max had the right idea."

The reference was to his onetime friend, multimillionaire Max Fleischmann, who'd cheated lingering death by cancer some years earlier by putting a bullet through his brain. Ty spoke of Babe Ruth, another cancer victim. "If Babe had been told what he had in time, he could've got it over with."

Had I left Ty that night, I believe he would have pulled the trigger. His three living children (two were dead) had withdrawn from him. In the wide world that had sung his fame, he had not one intimate friend remaining.

But we talked, and prayed, until dawn, and then sleep came; in the morning, aided by friends, I put him into a car and drove him home, to the big, gloomy house in Atherton. He spoke only twice during the six-hour drive.

"Have you got enough to finish the book?" he asked.

"More than enough."

"Give 'em the word then. I had to fight all my life to survive. They all were against me . . . tried every dirty trick to cut me down. But I beat the bastards and left them in the ditch. Make sure the book says that. . . ."

I was leaving him now, permanently, and I had to ask one question I'd never put to him before.

"Why did you fight so hard in baseball, Ty?"

He'd never looked fiercer than then, when he answered. "I did it for my father, who was an exalted man. They killed him when he was still young. They blew his head off the same week I became a major leaguer. He never got to see me play. But I knew he was watching me and I never let him down."

You can make what you want of that. Keep in mind what Casey Stengel said, later: "I never saw anyone like Cobb. No one even close to him. When he wiggled those wild eyes at a pitcher, you knew you were looking at the one bird nobody could beat. It was like he was superhuman."

To me it seems that the violent death of a father whom a sensitive, highly talented boy loved deeply, and feared, engendered, through some strangely supreme desire to vindicate that father, the most violent, successful, thoroughly maladjusted personality ever to pass across American sports. The shock tipped the eighteen-year-old mind, making him capable of incredible feats.

Off the field, he was still at war with the world. For the emotionally disturbed individual, in most cases, does not change his pattern. To reinforce that pattern, he was viciously hazed by Detroit Tiger veterans when he was a rookie. He was bullied, ostracized and beaten up—in one instance, a 210-pound catcher named Charlie Schmidt broke the 165-pound Ty Cobb's nose. It was persecution immediately heaped upon the deepest desolation a young man can experience.

Yes, Ty Cobb was a badly disturbed personality. It is not hard to understand why he spent his entire life in deep conflict. Nor why a member of his family, in the winter of 1960, told me, "I've spent a lot of time terrified of him . . . I think he was psychotic from the time that he left Georgia to play in the big league."

"Psychotic" is not a word I'd care to use. I believe that he was far more than the fiercest of all competitors. He was a vindicator who believed that "Father was watching" and who could not put that father's terrible fate out of his mind. The memory of it threatened his sanity.

The fact that he recognized and feared this is revealed in a tape recording he made, in which he describes his own view of himself: "I was like a steel spring with a growing and dangerous flaw in it. If it is wound too tight or has the slightest weak point, the spring will fly apart and then it is done for. . . ."

The last time I saw him, he was sitting in his armchair in the Atherton mansion. The place still was without lights or heat. I shook his hand in farewell, and he held it a moment longer.

"What about it? Do you think they'll remember me?" He tried to say it as if it didn't matter.

"They'll always remember you," I said.

On July 8, I received in the mail a photograph of Ty's mausoleum on the hillside in the Royston cemetery with the words scribbled on the back: *"Any time now."* Nine days later he died in an Atlanta hospital. Before going, he opened the brown bag, piled $1 million in negotiable securities beside his bed and placed the Luger atop them.

From all of major-league baseball, three men and three only appeared for his funeral.

POETRY

WHEN the following stanzas first appeared, in the *San Francisco Examiner* of June 3, 1888, they bore the author's own subtitle "A Ballad of the Republic." Remarkable prophecy! Remarkable ballad!

Casey at the Bat

ERNEST L. THAYER

The outlook wasn't brilliant for the Mudville nine that day;
The score stood four to two with but one inning more to play;
And then, when Cooney died at first, and Barrows did the same,
A sickly silence fell upon the patrons of the game.

A struggling few got up to go, in deep despair. The rest
Clung to that hope which "springs eternal in the human breast";
They thought, If only Casey could but get a whack at that,
We'd put up even money now, with Casey at the bat.

But Flynn preceded Casey, as did also Jimmy Blake,
And the former was a lulu and the latter was a cake;
So, upon that stricken multitude grim melancholy sat,
For there seemed but little chance of Casey's getting to the bat.

But Flynn let drive a single, to the wonderment of all,
And Blake, the much despised, tore the cover off the ball,
And when the dust had lifted and men saw what had occurred,
There was Jimmy safe at second, and Flynn a-huggin' third.

Then from five thousand throats and more there rose a lusty yell,
It rumbled through the valley; it rattled in the dell;
It knocked upon the mountain and recoiled upon the flat,
For Casey, mighty Casey, was advancing to the bat.

There was ease in Casey's manner as he stepped into his place;
There was pride in Casey's bearing and a smile on Casey's face,
And when, responding to the cheers, he lightly doffed his hat,
No stranger in the crowd could doubt 'twas Casey at the bat.

Ten thousand eyes were on him as he rubbed his hands with dirt;
Five thousand tongues applauded when he wiped them on his shirt.
Then, while the writhing pitcher ground the ball into his hip,
Defiance gleamed in Casey's eye, a sneer curled Casey's lip.

And now the leather-covered sphere came hurtling through the air,
And Casey stood a-watching it in haughty grandeur there,
Close by the sturdy batsman the ball unheeded sped—
"That ain't my style," said Casey. "Strike one," the umpire said.

From the benches, black with people, there went up a muffled roar,
Like the beating of the storm-waves on a stern and distant shore.
"Kill him; kill the umpire!" shouted someone from the stand,—
And it's likely they'd have killed him had not Casey raised his hand.

With a smile of Christian charity great Casey's visage shone;
He stilled the rising tumult; he bade the game go on;
He signaled to the pitcher, and once more the spheroid flew;
But Casey still ignored it, and the umpire said, "Strike two."

"Fraud," cried the maddened thousands, and echo answered "Fraud,"
But one scornful look from Casey, and the multitude was awed.
They saw his face grow stern and cold; they saw his muscles strain,
And they knew that Casey wouldn't let that ball go by again.

The sneer is gone from Casey's lip; his teeth are clenched in hate;
He pounds with cruel violence his bat upon the plate.
And now the pitcher holds the ball, and now he lets it go,
And now the air is shattered by the force of Casey's blow.

Oh! somewhere in this favored land the sun is shining bright;
The band is playing somewhere, and somewhere hearts are light.
And somewhere men are laughing, and somewhere children shout;
But there is no joy in Mudville—mighty Casey has Struck Out.

HISTORY

ALBERT G. SPALDING, a star pitcher of the 1860s and recognized in the Hall of Fame as "organizational genius of baseball's pioneer days," issued in 1911 a remarkably complete baseball almanac, called *America's National Game.* From that book comes this letter, which to me is absolute delight, not only for its contents but for the sheer musicality of the line "Thatcher was the catcher," and the fact that the wording bears striking resemblance to a Sherlock Holmes adventure.

A Letter to A. G. Spalding

FRED W. THAYER

116 FEDERAL STREET
BOSTON, MAY 18, 1911

MY DEAR MR. SPALDING:

I am in receipt of your favor of the 9th instant. You shall have the facts in regard to the catcher's mask, and I think you can feel assured that the data are all correct.

In order to give you the whole story I shall have to ask you to go back to the year '76 that you may know what the conditions were in Harvard Base Ball matters.

Thatcher was the catcher in the season of '76. He left college at the end of the year.

You will recall the fact that college nines especially had rarely more than one, possibly two, substitutes, and these were "general utility" men.

Tyng was the best all-around natural ballplayer of my time. He had played third base, center field, and helped out in other positions, including catcher, in the season of '76. In one or two games in which he caught behind the bat he had been hit by foul tips and had become more or less timid.

He was, by all odds, the most available man as catcher for the season of '77, and it was up to me to find some way to bring back his confidence.

The fencing mask naturally gave me the hint as to the protection for the face, and then it was up to me to devise some means of having the impact of the blow kept from driving the mask onto the face. The forehead and chin rest accomplished this and also made it possible for me to secure a patent, which I did in the winter of 1878.

Tyng practiced catching with the mask, behind the bat, in the gymnasium during the winter of '77, and became so thoroughly proficient that foul tips had no further terrors for him.

The first match game in which the mask was used was on Fast Day, in Lynn, against the Live Oaks, in April 1877. Thereafter the Harvard catcher used it in all games.

I hope this will give you the data which you wish. At all events it gives you the real facts in regard to the Base Ball mask.

Yours faithfully,
(signed) FRED W. THAYER

FICTION

DOES LIFE IMITATE ART? It sure did in this case. Ten years after the publication of this Thurber short story, Bill Veeck, then owner of the St. Louis Browns, sent a midget up to bat against the Detroit Tigers. He walked.

You Could Look It Up

JAMES THURBER

IT ALL BEGUN when we dropped down to C'lumbus, Ohio, from Pittsburgh to play a exhibition game on our way out to St. Louis. It was gettin' on into September, and though we'd been leadin' the league by six, seven games most of the season, we was now in first place by a margin you could 'a' got it into the eye of a thimble, bein' only a half a game ahead of St. Louis. Our slump had given the boys the leapin' jumps, and they was like a bunch a old ladies at a lawn fete with a thunderstorm comin' up, runnin' around snarlin' at each other, eatin' bad and sleepin' worse, and battin' for a team average of maybe .186. Half the time nobody'd speak to nobody else, without it was to bawl 'em out.

Squawks Magrew was managin' the boys at the time, and he was darn near crazy. They called him "Squawks" 'cause when things was goin' bad he lost his voice, or perty near lost it, and squealed at you like a little girl you stepped on her doll or somethin'. He yelled at everybody and wouldn't listen to nobody, without maybe it was me. I'd been trainin' the boys for ten year, and he'd take more lip from me than from anybody else. He knowed I was smarter'n him, anyways, like you're goin' to hear.

This was thirty, thirty-one year ago; you could look it up, 'cause it was the same year C'lumbus decided to call itself the Arch City, on account of a lot of iron arches with electric-light bulbs into 'em which stretched acrost High Street. Thomas Albert Edison sent 'em a telegram, and they was speeches and maybe even President Taft opened the celebration by pushin' a button. It was a great week for the Buckeye capital, which was why they got us out there for this exhibition game.

Well, we just lose a double-header to Pittsburgh, 11 to 5 and 7 to 3, so we snarled all the way to C'lumbus, where we put up at the Chittaden Hotel, still snarlin'. Everybody was tetchy, and when Billy Klinger took a sock at Whitey Cott at breakfast, Whitey threw marmalade all over his face.

"Blind each other, whatta I care?" says Magrew. "You can't see nothin' anyways."

C'lumbus win the exhibition game, 3 to 2, whilst Magrew set in the dugout, mutterin' and cursin' like a fourteen-year-old Scotty. He bad-mouthed everybody on the ball club and he bad-mouthed everybody offa the ball club, includin' the Wright brothers, who, he claimed, had yet to build a airship big enough for any of our boys to hit it with a ball bat.

"I wisht I was dead," he says to me. "I wisht I was in heaven with the angels."

I told him to pull hisself together, 'cause he was drivin' the boys crazy, the way he was goin' on, sulkin' and bad-mouthin' and whinin'. I was older'n he was and smarter'n he was, and he knowed it. I was ten times smarter'n he was about this Pearl du Monville, first time I ever laid eyes on the little guy, which was one of the saddest days of my life.

Now, most people name of Pearl is girls, but this Pearl du Monville was a man, if you could call a fella a man who was only thirty-four, thirty-five inches high. Pearl du Monville was a midget. He was part French and part Hungarian, and maybe even part Bulgarian or some-thin'. I can see him now, a sneer on his little pushed-in pan, swingin' a bamboo cane and smokin' a big cigar. He had a gray suit with a big black check into it, and he had a gray felt hat with one of them rainbow-colored hatbands onto it, like the young fellas wore in them days. He talked like he was talkin' into a tin can, but he didn't have no foreign accent. He might 'a' been fifteen or he might 'a' been a hundred, you couldn't tell. Pearl du Monville.

After the game with C'lumbus, Magrew headed straight for the Chittaden bar—the train for St. Louis wasn't goin' for three, four hours —and there he set, drinkin' rye and talkin' to this bartender.

"How I pity me, brother," Magrew was tellin' this bartender. "How I pity me." That was alwuz his favorite tune. So he was settin' there, tellin' this bartender how heartbreakin' it was to be manager of a bunch a blindfolded circus clowns, when up pops this Pearl du Monville outa nowheres.

It give Magrew the leapin' jumps. He thought at first maybe the D.T.'s had come back on him; he claimed he'd had 'em once, and little guys had popped up all around him, wearin' red, white and blue hats.

"Go on, now!" Magrew yells. "Get away from me!"

But the midget clumb up on a chair acrost the table from Magrew and says, "I seen that game today, Junior, and you ain't got no ball club. What you got there, Junior," he says, "is a side show."

"Whatta ya mean, 'Junior'?" says Magrew, touchin' the little guy to satisfy hisself he was real.

"Don't pay him no attention, mister," says the bartender. "Pearl calls everybody 'Junior,' 'cause it alwuz turns out he's a year older'n anybody else."

"Yeh?" says Magrew. "How old is he?"

"How old are you, Junior?" says the midget.

"Who, me? I'm fifty-three," says Magrew.

"Well, I'm fifty-four," says the midget.

Magrew grins and asts him what he'll have, and that was the beginnin' of their beautiful friendship, if you don't care what you say.

Pearl du Monville stood up on his chair and waved his cane around and pretended like he was ballyhooin' for a circus. "Right this way, folks!" he yells. "Come on in and see the greatest collection of freaks in the world! See the armless pitchers, see the eyeless batters, see the infielders with five thumbs!" and on and on like that, feedin' Magrew gall and handin' him a laugh at the same time, you might say.

You could hear him and Pearl du Monville hootin' and hollerin' and singin' way up to the fourth floor of the Chittaden, where the boys was packin' up. When it come time to go to the station, you can imagine how disgusted we was when we crowded into the doorway of that bar and seen them two singin' and goin' on.

"Well, well, well," says Magrew, lookin' up and spottin' us. "Look who's here. . . . Clowns, this is Pearl du Monville, a monseer of the old, old school. . . . Don't shake hands with 'em, Pearl, 'cause their fingers is made of chalk and would bust right off in your paws," he says, and he starts guffawin' and Pearl starts titterin' and we stand there givin' 'em the iron eye, it bein' the lowest ebb a ball-club manager'd got hisself down to since the national pastime was started.

Then the midget begun givin' us the ballyhoo. "Come on in!" he says, wavin' his cane. "See the legless base runners, see the outfielders with the butter fingers, see the southpaw with the arm of a little chee-ild!"

Then him and Magrew begun to hoop and holler and nudge each other till you'd of thought this little guy was the funniest guy than even Charlie Chaplin. The fellas filed outa the bar without a word and went on up to the Union Depot, leavin' me to handle Magrew and his new-found crony.

Well, I got 'em outa there finely. I had to take the little guy along, 'cause Magrew had a holt onto him like a vise and I couldn't pry him loose.

"He's comin' along as masket," says Magrew, holdin' the midget in the crouch of his arm like a football. And come along he did, hollerin' and protestin' and beatin' at Magrew with his little fists.

"Cut it out, will ya, Junior?" the little guy kept whinin'. "Come on, leave a man loose, will ya, Junior?"

But Junior kept a holt onto him and begun yellin', "See the guys with the glass arm, see the guys with the cast-iron brains, see the fielders with the feet on their wrists!"

So it goes, right through the whole Union Depot, with people starin' and catcallin', and he don't put the midget down till he gets him through the gates.

"How'm I goin' to go along without no toothbrush?" the midget asts. "What'm I goin' to do without no other suit?" he says.

"Doc here," says Magrew, meanin' me—"doc here will look after you like you was his own son, won't you, doc?"

I give him the iron eye, and he finely got on the train and prob'ly went to sleep with his clothes on.

This left me alone with the midget. "Lookit," I says to him. "Why don't you go on home now? Come mornin', Magrew'll forget all about you. He'll prob'ly think you was somethin' he seen in a nightmare maybe. And he ain't goin' to laugh so easy in the mornin', neither," I says. "So why don't you go on home?"

"Nix," he says to me. "Skiddoo," he says, "twenty-three for you," and he tosses his cane up into the vestibule of the coach and clam'ers on up after it like a cat. So that's the way Pearl du Monville come to go to St. Louis with the ball club.

I seen 'em first at breakfast the next day, settin' opposite each other; the midget playin' "Turkey in the Straw" on a harmonium and Magrew starin' at his eggs and bacon like they was a uncooked bird with its feathers still on.

"Remember where you found this?" I says, jerkin' my thumb at the

midget. "Or maybe you think they come with breakfast on these trains,"
I says, bein' a good hand at turnin' a sharp remark in them days.

The midget puts down the harmonium and turns on me. "Sneeze,"
he says; "your brains is dusty." Then he snaps a couple drops of water at
me from a tumbler. "Drown," he says, tryin' to make his voice deep.

Now, both them cracks is Civil War cracks, but you'd of thought they
was brand-new and the funniest than any crack Magrew'd ever heard in
his whole life. He started hoopin' and hollerin', and the midget started
hoopin' and hollerin', so I walked on away and set down with Bugs
Courtney and Hank Metters, payin' no attention to this weak-minded
Damon and Phidias acrost the aisle.

Well, sir, the first game with St. Louis was rained out, and there we
was facin' a double-header next day. Like maybe I told you, we lose the
last three double-headers we play, makin' maybe twenty-five errors in
the six games, which is all right for the intimates of a school for the blind,
but is disgraceful for the world's champions. It was too wet to go to the
zoo, and Magrew wouldn't let us go to the movies, 'cause they flickered
so bad in them days. So we just set around, stewin' and frettin'.

One of the newspaper boys come over to take a pitture of Billy
Klinger and Whitey Cott shakin' hands—this reporter'd heard about the
fight—and whilst they was standin' there, toe to toe, shakin' hands, Billy
give a back lunge and a jerk, and throwed Whitey over his shoulder into
a corner of the room, like a sack a salt. Whitey come back at him with
a chair, and Bethlehem broke loose in that there room. The camera was
tromped to pieces like a berry basket. When we finely got 'em pulled
apart, I heard a laugh, and there was Magrew and the midget standin'
in the door and givin' us the iron eye.

"Wrasslers," says Magrew, cold-like, "that's what I got for a ball club,
Mr. du Monville, wrasslers—and not very good wrasslers at that, you ast
me."

"A man can't be good at everythin'," says Pearl, "but he oughta be
good at somethin'."

This sets Magrew guffawin' again, and away they go, the midget
taggin' along by his side like a hound dog and handin' him a fast line of
so-called comic cracks.

When we went out to face that battlin' St. Louis club in a double-
header the next afternoon, the boys was jumpy as tin toys with keys in
their back. We lose the first game, 7 to 2, and are trailin', 4 to 0, when
the second game ain't but ten minutes old. Magrew set there like a stone
statue, speakin' to nobody. Then, in their half a the fourth, somebody
singled to center and knocked in two more runs for St. Louis.

That made Magrew squawk. "I wisht one thing," he says. "I wisht I
was manager of a old ladies' sewin' circus 'stead of a ball club."

"You are, Junior, you are," says a familyer and disagreeable voice.
It was that Pearl du Monville again, poppin' up outa nowheres,

swingin' his bamboo cane and smokin' a cigar that's three sizes too big for his face. By this time we'd finely got the other side out, and Hank Metters slithered a bat acrost the ground, and the midget had to jump to keep both his ankles from bein' broke.

I thought Magrew'd bust a blood vessel. "You hurt Pearl and I'll break your neck!" he yelled.

Hank muttered somethin' and went on up to the plate and struck out.

We managed to get a couple runs acrost in our half a the sixth, but they come back with three more in their half a the seventh, and this was too much for Magrew.

"Come on, Pearl," he says. "We're gettin' outa here."

"Where you think you're goin'?" I ast him.

"To the lawyer's again," he says cryptly.

"I didn't know you'd been to the lawyer's once, yet," I says.

"Which that goes to show how much you don't know," he says.

With that, they was gone, and I didn't see 'em the rest of the day, nor know what they was up to which was a God's blessin'. We lose the nightcap, 9 to 3, and that puts us into second place plenty, and as low in our mind as a ball club can get.

The next day was a horrible day, like anybody that lived through it can tell you. Practice was just over and the St. Louis club was takin' the field, when I hears this strange sound from the stands. It sounds like the nervous whickerin' a horse gives when he smells somethin' funny on the wind. It was the fans ketchin' sight of Pearl du Monville, like you have prob'ly guessed. The midget had popped up onto the field all dressed up in a minacher club uniform, sox, cap, little letters sewed onto his chest, and all. He was swingin' a kid's bat and the only thing kept him from lookin' like a real ballplayer seen through the wrong end of a microscope was this cigar he was smokin'.

Bugs Courtney reached over and jerked it outa his mouth and throwed it away. "You're wearin' that suit on the playin' field," he says to him, severe as a judge. "You go insultin' it and I'll take you out to the zoo and feed you to the bears."

Pearl just blowed some smoke at him which he still has in his mouth.

Whilst Whitey was foulin' off four or five prior to strikin' out, I went on over to Magrew. "If I was as comic as you," I says, "I'd laugh myself to death," I says. "Is that any way to treat the uniform, makin' a mockery out of it?"

"It might surprise you to know I ain't makin' no mockery outa the uniform," says Magrew. "Pearl du Monville here has been made a bone-of-fida member of this so-called ball club. I fixed it up with the front office by long-distance phone."

"Yeh?" I says. "I can just hear Mr. Dillworth or Bart Jenkins agreein' to hire a midget for the ball club. I can just hear 'em." Mr. Dillworth was the owner of the club and Bart Jenkins was the secretary, and they never stood for no monkey business. "May I be so bold as to inquire," I says, "just what you told 'em?"

"I told 'em," he says, "I wanted to sign up a guy they ain't no pitcher in the league can strike him out."

"Uh-huh," I says, "and did you tell 'em what size of a man he is?"

"Never mind about that," he says. "I got papers on me, made out legal and proper, constitutin' one Pearl du Monville a bone-of-fida member of this former ball club. Maybe that'll shame them big babies into gettin' in there and swingin', knowin' I can replace any one of 'em with a midget, if I have a mind to. A St. Louis lawyer I seen twice tells me it's all legal and proper."

"A St. Louis lawyer would," I says, "seein' nothin' could make him happier than havin' you makin' a mockery outa this one-time baseball outfit," I says.

Well, sir, it'll all be there in the papers of thirty, thirty-one year ago, and you could look it up. The game went along without no scorin' for seven innings, and since they ain't nothin' much to watch but guys poppin' up or strikin' out, the fans pay most of their attention to the goin's-on of Pearl du Monville. He's out there in front a the dugout, turnin' handsprings, balancin' his bat on his chin, walkin' a imaginary line, and so on. The fans clapped and laughed at him, and he ate it up.

So it went up to the last a the eighth, nothin' to nothin', not more'n seven, eight hits all told, and no errors on neither side. Our pitcher gets the first two men out easy in the eighth. Then up come a fella name of Porter or Billings, or some such name, and he lammed one up against the tobacco sign for three bases. The next guy up slapped the first ball out into left for a base hit, and in come the fella from third for the only run of the ball game so far. The crowd yelled, the look a death come onto Magrew's face again, and even the midget quit his tomfoolin'. Their next man fouled out back a third, and we come up for our last bats like a bunch a schoolgirls steppin' into a pool of cold water. I was lower in my mind than I'd been since the day in nineteen-four when Chesbro throwed the wild pitch in the ninth inning with a man on third and lost the pennant for the Highlanders. I knowed something just as bad was goin' to happen, which shows I'm a clairvoyun, or was then.

When Gordy Mills hit out to second, I just closed my eyes. I opened 'em up again to see Dutch Muller standin' on second, dustin' off his pants, him havin' got his first hit in maybe twenty times to the plate. Next up was Harry Loesing, battin' for our pitcher, and he got a base on balls, walkin' on a fourth one you could 'a' combed your hair with.

Then up come Whitey Cott, our lead-off man. He crotches down in what was prob'ly the most fearsome stanch in organized ball, but all he can do is pop out to short. That brung up Billy Klinger, with two down and a man on first and second. Billy took a cut at one you could 'a' knocked a plug hat offa this here Carnera with it, but then he gets sense enough to wait 'em out, and finely he walks, too, fillin' the bases.

Yes, sir, there you are; the tyin' run on third and the winnin' run on second, first a the ninth, two men down, and Hank Metters comin' to the bat. Hank was built like a Pope-Hartford and he couldn't run no faster'n President Taft, but he had five home runs to his credit for the season, and that wasn't bad in them days. Hank was still hittin' better'n anybody else on the ball club, and it was mighty heartenin', seein' him stridin' up towards the plate. But he never got there.

"Wait a minute!" yells Magrew, jumpin' to his feet. "I'm sendin' in a pinch hitter!" he yells.

You could 'a' heard a bomb drop. When a ball-club manager says he's sendin' in a pinch hitter for the best batter on the club, you know and I know and everybody knows he's lost his holt.

"They're goin' to be sendin' the funny wagon for you, if you don't watch out," I says, grabbin' a holt of his arm.

But he pulled away and ran out towards the plate, yellin', "Du Monville battin' for Metters!"

All the fellas begun squawlin' at once, except Hank, and he just stood there starin' at Magrew like he'd gone crazy and was claimin' to be Ty Cobb's grandma or somethin'. Their pitcher stood out there with his hands on his hips and a disagreeable look on his face, and the plate umpire told Magrew to go on and get a batter up. Magrew told him again Du Monville was battin' for Metters, and the St. Louis manager finely got the idea. It brung him outa his dugout, howlin' and bawlin' like he'd lost a female dog and her seven pups.

Magrew pushed the midget towards the plate and he says to him, he says, "Just stand up there and hold that bat on your shoulder. They ain't a man in the world can throw three strikes in there 'fore he throws four balls!" he says.

"I get it, Junior!" says the midget. "He'll walk me and force in the tyin' run!" And he starts on up to the plate as cocky as if he was Willie Keeler.

"I don't need to tell you Bethlehem broke loose on that there ball field. The fans got onto their hind legs, yellin' and whistlin', and everybody on the field begun wavin' their arms and hollerin' and shovin'. The plate umpire stalked over to Magrew like a traffic cop, waggin' his jaw and pointin' his finger, and the St. Louis manager kept yellin' like his house was on fire. When Pearl got up to the plate and stood there, the pitcher slammed his glove down onto the ground and started stompin' on it, and they ain't nobody can blame him. He's just walked two normal-sized human bein's, and now here's a guy up to the plate they ain't more'n twenty inches between his knees and his shoulders.

The plate umpire called in the field umpire, and they talked a while, like a couple doctors seein' the bucolic plague or somethin' for the first time. Then the plate umpire come over to Magrew with his arms folded acrost his chest, and he told him to go on and get a batter up, or he'd forfeit the game to St. Louis. He pulled out his watch, but somebody batted it outa his hand in the scufflin', and I thought there'd be a free-for-all, with everybody yellin' and shovin' except Pearl du Monville, who stood up at the plate with his little bat on his shoulder, not movin' a muscle.

Then Magrew played his ace. I seen him pull some papers outa his pocket and show 'em to the plate umpire. The umpire begun lookin' at 'em like they was bills for somethin' he not only never bought it, he never even heard of it. The other umpire studied 'em like they was a death warren, and all this time the St. Louis manager and the fans and the players is yellin' and hollerin'.

Well, sir, they fought about him bein' a midget, and they fought about him usin' a kid's bat, and they fought about where'd he been all season. They was eight or nine rule books brung out and everybody was thumbin' through 'em, tryin' to find out what it says about midgets, but it don't say nothin' about midgets, 'cause this was somethin' never'd come up in the history of the game before, and nobody'd ever dreamed about it, even when they has nightmares. Maybe you can't send no midgets in to bat nowadays, 'cause the old game's changed a lot, mostly for the worst, but you could then, it turned out.

The plate umpire finely decided the contract papers was all legal and proper, like Magrew said, so he waved the St. Louis players back to their places and he pointed his finger at their manager and told him to quit hollerin' and get on back in the dugout. The manager says the game is percedin' under protest, and the umpire bawls, "Play ball!" over 'n' above the yellin' and booin', him havin' a voice like a hog-caller.

The St. Louis pitcher picked up his glove and beat at it with his fist six or eight times, and then got set on the mound and studied the situation. The fans realized he was really goin' to pitch to the midget, and they went crazy, hoopin' and hollerin' louder'n ever, and throwin' pop bottles and hats and cushions down onto the field. It took five, ten minutes to get the fans quieted down again, whilst our fellas that was on base set down on the bags and waited. And Pearl du Monville kept standin' up there with the bat on his shoulder, like he'd been told to.

So the pitcher starts studyin' the setup again, and you got to admit it was the strangest setup in a ball game since the players cut off their beards and begun wearin' gloves. I wisht I could call the pitcher's name —it wasn't old Barney Pelty nor Nig Jack Powell nor Harry Howell. He was a big right-hander, but I can't call his name. You could look it up. Even in a crotchin' position, the ketcher towers over the midget like the Washington Monument.

The plate umpire tries standin' on his tiptoes, then he tries crotchin' down, and he finely gets hisself into a stanch nobody'd ever seen on a ball field before, kinda squattin' down on his hanches.

Well, the pitcher is sore as a old buggy horse in fly time. He slams in the first pitch, hard and wild, and maybe two foot higher 'n the midget's head.

"Ball one!" hollers the umpire over 'n' above the racket, 'cause everybody is yellin' worsten ever.

The ketcher goes on out towards the mound and talks to the pitcher and hands him the ball. This time the big right-hander tries a undershoot, and it comes in a little closer, maybe no higher'n a foot, foot and a half above Pearl's head. It would 'a' been a strike with a human bein' in there, but the umpire's got to call it, and he does.

"Ball two!" he bellers.

The ketcher walks on out to the mound again, and the whole infield comes over and gives advice to the pitcher about what they'd do in a case like this, with two balls and no strikes on a batter that oughta be in a bottle of alcohol 'stead of up there at the plate in a big-league game between the teams that is fightin' for first place.

For the third pitch, the pitcher stands there flat-footed and tosses up the ball like he's playin' ketch with a little girl.

Pearl stands there motionless as a hitchin' post, and the ball comes in big and slow and high—high for Pearl, that is, it bein' about on a level with his eyes, or a little higher'n a grown man's knees.

They ain't nothin' else for the umpire to do, so he calls, "Ball three!"

Everybody is onto their feet, hoopin' and hollerin', as the pitcher sets to throw ball four. The St. Louis manager is makin' signs and faces like he was a contorturer, and the infield is givin' the pitcher some more advice about what to do this time. Our boys who was on base stick right onto the bag, runnin' no risk of bein' nipped for the last out.

Well, the pitcher decides to give him a toss again, seein' he come closer with that than with a fast ball. They ain't nobody ever seen a slower ball throwed. It come in big as a balloon and slower'n any ball ever throwed before in the major leagues. It come right in over the plate in front of Pearl's chest, lookin' prob'ly big as a full moon to Pearl. They ain't never been a minute like the minute that followed since the United States was founded by the Pilgrim grandfathers.

Pearl du Monville took a cut at that ball, and he hit it! Magrew give a groan like a poleaxed steer as the ball rolls out in front a the plate into fair territory.

"Fair ball!" yells the umpire, and the midget starts runnin' for first, still carryin' that little bat, and makin' maybe ninety foot an hour. Bethlehem breaks loose on that ball field and in them stands. They ain't never been nothin' like it since creation was begun.

The ball's rollin' slow, on down towards third, goin' maybe eight, ten foot. The infield comes in fast and our boys break from their bases like hares in a brush fire. Everybody is standin' up, yellin' and hollerin', and Magrew is tearin' his hair outa his head, and the midget is scamperin' for first with all the speed of one of them little dashhounds carryin' a satchel in his mouth.

The ketcher gets to the ball first, but he boots it on out past the pitcher's box, the pitcher fallin' on his face tryin' to stop it, the shortstop sprawlin' after it full length and zaggin' it on over towards the second baseman, whilst Muller is scorin' with the tyin' run and Loesing is roundin' third with the winnin' run. Ty Cobb could 'a' made a three-bagger outa that bunt, with everybody fallin' over theirself tryin' to pick the ball up. But Pearl is still maybe fifteen, twenty feet from the bag, toddlin' like a baby and yeepin' like a trapped rabbit, when the second baseman finely gets a holt of that ball and slams it over to first. The first baseman ketches it and stomps on the bag, the base umpire waves Pearl out, and there goes your old ball game, the craziest ball game ever played in the history of the organized world.

Their players start runnin' in, and then I see Magrew. He starts after Pearl, runnin' faster'n any man ever run before. Pearl sees him comin' and runs behind the base umpire's legs and gets a holt onto 'em. Magrew comes up, pantin' and roarin', and him and the midget plays ring-around-a-rosy with the umpire, who keeps shovin' at Magrew with one hand and tryin' to slap the midget loose from his legs with the other.

Finely Magrew ketches the midget, who is still yeepin' like a stuck sheep. He gets holt of that little guy by both his ankles and starts whirlin' him round and round his head like Magrew was a hammer thrower and Pearl was the hammer. Nobody can stop him without gettin' their head knocked off, so everybody just stands there and yells. Then Magrew lets the midget fly. He flies on out towards second, high and fast, like a human home run, headed for the soap sign in center field.

Their shortstop tries to get to him, but he can't make it, and I knowed the little fella was goin' to bust to pieces like a dollar watch on a asphalt street when he hit the ground. But it so happens their center fielder is just crossin' second, and he starts runnin' back, tryin' to get under the midget, who had took to spiralin' like a football 'stead of turnin' head over foot, which give him more speed and more distance.

I know you never seen a midget ketched, and you prob'ly never even seen one throwed. To ketch a midget that's been throwed by a heavy-muscled man and is flyin' through the air, you got to run under him and with him and pull your hands and arms back and down when you ketch him, to break the compact of his body, or you'll bust him in two like a matchstick. I seen Bill Lange and Willie Keeler and Tris Speaker make some wonderful ketches in my day, but I never seen nothin' like that center fielder. He goes back and back and still further back and he pulls that midget down outa the air like he was liftin' a sleepin' baby from a cradle. They wasn't a bruise onto him, only his face

was the color of cat's meat and he ain't got no air in his chest. In his
excitement, the base umpire, who was runnin' back with the center
fielder when he ketched Pearl, yells, "Out!" and that give hysteries to the
Bethlehem which was ragin' like Niagry on that ball field.

Everybody was hoopin' and hollerin' and yellin' and runnin', with
the fans swarmin' onto the field, and the cops tryin' to keep order, and
some guys laughin' and some of the women fans cryin', and six or eight
of us holdin' onto Magrew to keep him from gettin' at that midget and
finishin' him off. Some of the fans picks up the St. Louis pitcher and the
center fielder, and starts carryin' 'em around on their shoulders, and they
was the craziest goin's-on knowed to the history of organized ball on this
side of the 'Lantic Ocean.

I seen Pearl du Monville strugglin' in the arms of a lady fan with a
ample bosom, who was laughin' and cryin' at the same time, and him
beatin' at her with his little fists and bawlin' and yellin'. He clawed his
way loose finely and disappeared in the forest of legs which made that
ball field look like it was Coney Island on a hot summer's day.

That was the last I ever seen of Pearl du Monville. I never seen hide
nor hair of him from that day to this, and neither did nobody else. He
just vanished into the thin of the air, as the fella says. He was ketched for
the final out of the ball game and that was the end of him, just like it was
the end of the ball game, you might say, and also the end of our losin'
streak, like I'm goin' to tell you.

That night we piled onto a train for Chicago, but we wasn't snarlin'
and snappin' any more. No, sir, the ice was finely broke and a new spirit
come into that ball club. The old zip come back with the disappearance
of Pearl du Monville out back a second base. We got to laughin' and
talkin' and kiddin' together, and 'fore long Magrew was laughin' with us.
He got a human look onto his pan again, and he quit whinin' and complain-
in' and wishtin' he was in heaven with the angels.

Well, sir, we wiped up that Chicago series, winnin' all four games,
and makin' seventeen hits in one of 'em. Funny thing was, St. Louis was
so shook up by that last game with us, they never did hit their stride
again. Their center fielder took to misjudgin' everything that come his
way, and the rest a the fellas followed suit, the way a club'll do when one
guy blows up.

'Fore we left Chicago, I and some of the fellas went out and bought
a pair of them little baby shoes, which we had 'em golded over and give
'em to Magrew for a souvenir, and he took it all in good spirit. Whitey
Cott and Billy Klinger made up and was fast friends again, and we hit
our home lot like a ton of dynamite and they was nothin' could stop us
from then on.

I don't recollect things as clear as I did thirty, forty years ago. I can't
read no fine print no more, and the only person I got to check with on
the golden days of the national pastime, as the fella says, is my friend, old

Milt Kline, over in Springfield, and his mind ain't as strong as it once was.

He gets Rube Waddell mixed up with Rube Marquard, for one thing, and anybody does that oughta be put away where he won't bother nobody. So I can't tell you the exact margin we win the pennant by. Maybe it was two and a half games, or maybe it was three and a half. But it'll all be there in the newspapers and record books of thirty, thirty-one year ago and, like I was sayin', you could look it up.

FICTION

THIS SIXTH-CENTURY experiment, alas, never came off, for the various players were to become caught up in the devastating carnage wrought by Launcelot's love for Guinevere. More's the pity.

From *A Connecticut Yankee in King Arthur's Court*

MARK TWAIN

AT THE END of a month I sent the vessel home for fresh supplies, and for news. We expected her back in three or four days. She would bring me, along with other news, the result of a certain experiment which I had been starting. It was a project of mine to replace the tournament with something which might furnish an escape for the extra steam of the chivalry, keep those bucks entertained and out of mischief, and at the same time preserve the best thing in them, which was their hardy spirit of emulation. I had had a choice band of them in private training for some time, and the date was now arriving for their first public effort.

This experiment was baseball. In order to give the thing vogue from the start, and place it out of the reach of criticism, I chose my nines by rank, not capacity. There wasn't a knight in either team who wasn't a sceptered sovereign. As for material of this sort, there was a glut of it always around Arthur. You couldn't throw a brick in any direction and not cripple a king. Of course, I couldn't get these people to leave off their armor; they wouldn't do that when they bathed. They consented to differentiate the armor so that a body could tell one team from the other, but that was the most they would do. So, one of the teams wore chain-mail ulsters, and the other wore plate armor made of my new Bessemer steel. Their practice in the field was the most fantastic thing I ever saw. Being ball-proof, they never skipped out of the way, but stood still and took the result; when a Bessemer was at the bat and a ball hit him, it would bound a hundred and fifty yards sometimes. And when a man was running, and threw himself on his stomach to slide to his base, it was like an ironclad coming into port. At first I appointed men of no rank to act as umpires, but I had to discontinue that. These people were no easier to please than other nines. The umpire's first decision was usually his last; they broke him in two with a bat, and his friends toted him home on a shutter. When it was noticed that no umpire ever survived a game, umpiring got to be unpopular. So I was obliged to appoint somebody whose rank and lofty position under the government would protect him.

Here are the names of the nines:

BESSEMERS	ULSTERS
KING ARTHUR.	EMPEROR LUCIUS.
KING LOT OF LOTHIAN.	KING LOGRIS.
KING OF NORTHGALIS.	KING MARHALT OF IRELAND.
KING MARSIL.	KING MORGANORE.
KING OF LITTLE BRITAIN.	KING MARK OF CORNWALL.
KING LABOR.	KING NENTRES OF GARLOT.
KING PELLAM OF LISTENGESE.	KING MELIODAS OF LIONES.
KING BAGDEMAGUS.	KING OF THE LAKE.
KING TOLLEME LA FEINTES.	THE SOWDAN OF SYRIA.

Umpire—CLARENCE.

The first public game would certainly draw fifty thousand people; and for solid fun would be worth going around the world to see. Everything would be favorable; it was balmy and beautiful spring weather now, and Nature was all tailored out in her new clothes.

— ENTERTAINMENT —

"UNKNOWN" differs from "Anonymous," I guess, in that the latter doesn't know who wrote it, while the former doesn't know if it was ever written at all. And I don't believe "Who's on First?" ever existed in script form before the first *Fireside Book of Baseball.* Many vaudeville pairs used the routine; by all-time consensus, the best of them were Bud Abbott and Lou Costello. But even they would work it short or long, as the occasion invited. A short version is presented here. If you want the long version, watch your TV listings for the next rerun of the Abbott and Costello movie *The Gay Nineties.*

Who's on First?

UNKNOWN

COSTELLO: Hey, Abbott, tell me the names of the players on our baseball team so I can say hello to them.

ABBOTT: Sure, Now, Who's on first, What's on second, I-Don't-Know on third . . .

COSTELLO: Wait a minute.

ABBOTT: What's the matter?

COSTELLO: I want to know the names of the players.

ABBOTT: I'm telling you. Who's on first, What's on second, I-Don't-Know on third . . .

COSTELLO: Now, wait. What's the name of the first baseman?

ABBOTT: No, What's the name of the second baseman.

COSTELLO: I don't know.

ABBOTT: He's the third baseman.

COSTELLO: Let's start over.

ABBOTT: Okay. Who's on first . . .

COSTELLO: I'm asking *you* what's the name of the first baseman.

ABBOTT: What's the name of the second baseman.

COSTELLO: I don't know.

ABBOTT: He's on third.

COSTELLO: All I'm trying to find out is the name of the first baseman.

ABBOTT: I keep telling you. Who's on first.

COSTELLO: I'm asking YOU what's the name of the first baseman.

ABBOTT *(Rapidly):* What's the name of the second baseman.

COSTELLO *(More rapidly):* I don't know.

BOTH *(Most rapidly):* Third base!!

COSTELLO: All right. Okay. You won't tell what's the name of the first baseman.

ABBOTT: I've *been* telling you. What's the name of the second baseman.

COSTELLO: I'm asking *you* who's on second.

ABBOTT: *Who's* on *first.*

COSTELLO: I don't know.

ABBOTT: He's on third.

COSTELLO: Let's do it this way. You pay the players on this team?

ABBOTT: Absolutely.

COSTELLO: All right. Now, when you give the first baseman his paycheck, who gets the money?

ABBOTT: Every penny of it.

COSTELLO: *Who?*

ABBOTT: Naturally.

COSTELLO: *Naturally?*

ABBOTT: Of course.

COSTELLO: All right. Then Naturally's on first . . .

ABBOTT: No. Who's on first.

COSTELLO: *I'm asking you!* What's the name of the first baseman?

ABBOTT: And I'm telling you! What's the name of the second baseman.

COSTELLO: You say third base, I'll . . . *(Pause)* Wait a minute. You got a pitcher on this team?

ABBOTT: Did you ever hear of a team without a pitcher?

COSTELLO: All right. Tell me the pitcher's name.

ABBOTT: Tomorrow.

COSTELLO: You don't want to tell me now?

ABBOTT: I said I'd tell you. Tomorrow.

COSTELLO: What's wrong with today?

ABBOTT: Nothing. He's a pretty good catcher.

COSTELLO: Who's the catcher?

ABBOTT: No, Who's the first baseman.

COSTELLO: All right, tell me that. What's the first baseman's name?

ABBOTT: No, What's the second baseman's name.

COSTELLO: I-don't-know-third-base.

ABBOTT: Look, it's very simple.

COSTELLO: I know it's simple. You got a pitcher. Tomorrow. He throws the ball to Today. Today throws the ball to Who, he throws the ball to What, What throws the ball to I-Don't-Know, *he's* on third . . . and what's more, I-Don't-Give-A-Darn!

ABBOTT: What's that?

COSTELLO: I said, I-Don't-Give-A-Darn.

ABBOTT: Oh, he's our shortstop.

SPOT REPORTING

THIS SPLENDID ARTICLE was done by a truly fine writer, John Updike, in the pages of *The New Yorker* following the 1960 season. In the forenote to the Ed Linn piece earlier in this book, we suggested that you read this one by Updike before the one by Linn, and I think if you do it in that order, you will see why. Both pieces report the same event—Ted Williams' last game—and, speaking of the Updike, Herbert Warren Wind has written: "It is easy to picture Williams reading it with enormous pleasure—he read (and remembered) practically everything written about him—and saying to himself as he nodded his head, *'This* fellow has got it right.' " Mr. Linn confirms, in his article, that Williams *did* read—and remember—practically everything written about him. I do not want to guess at the Williams reaction to the Linn piece, and neither, I suspect, will Herbert Warren Wind. But I think the presence of these two stories in the same book gives an authentic added dimension to the event, and one that is rewarding and unique.

Note the agreement between Linn and Updike on the salient features (such as the cap-tipping)—an agreement by no means shared by others who were also there. I wasn't there. I'll have to go with Updike and Linn.

1960:
Hub Fans Bid Kid Adieu

JOHN UPDIKE

FENWAY PARK, in Boston, is a lyric little bandbox of a ballpark. Everything is painted green and seems in curiously sharp focus, like the inside of an old-fashioned peeping-type Easter egg. It was built in 1912 and rebuilt in 1934, and offers, as do most Boston artifacts, a compromise between Man's Euclidean determinations and Nature's beguiling irregularities. Its right field is one of the deepest in the American League, while its left field is the shortest; the high left-field wall, 315 feet from home plate along the foul line, virtually thrusts its surface at right-handed hitters. On the afternoon of Wednesday, September 28, as I took a seat behind third base, a uniformed groundkeeper was treading the top of this wall, picking batting-practice home runs out of the screen, like a mushroom gatherer seen in Wordsworthian perspective on the verge of a cliff. The day was overcast, chill, and uninspirational. The Boston team was the worst in twenty-seven seasons. A jangling medley of incompetent youth and aging competence, the Red Sox were finishing in seventh place only because the Kansas City Athletics had locked them out of the cellar. They were scheduled to play the Baltimore Orioles, a much nimbler blend of May and December, who had been dumped from pennant contention a week before by the insatiable Yankees. I, and 10,453 others, had shown up primarily because this was the Red Sox's last home game of the season, and therefore the last time in all eternity that their regular left fielder, known to the headlines as TED, KID, SPLINTER, THUMPER, TW, and, most cloyingly, MISTER WONDERFUL, would play in Boston. "WHAT WILL WE DO WITHOUT TED? HUB FANS ASK" ran the headline on a newspaper being read by a bulb-nosed cigar smoker a few rows away. Williams' retirement had been announced, doubted (he had been threatening retirement for years), confirmed by Tom Yawkey, the Red Sox owner, and at last widely accepted as the sad but probable truth. He was forty-two and had redeemed his abysmal season of 1959 with a—considering his advanced age—fine one. He had been giving away his gloves and bats and had grudgingly consented to a sentimental ceremony today.

This was not necessarily his last game; the Red Sox were scheduled to travel to New York and wind up the season with three games there.

I arrived early. The Orioles were hitting fungoes on the field. The day before, they had spitefully smothered the Red Sox, 17–4, and neither their faces nor their drab gray visiting-team uniforms seemed very gracious. I wondered who had invited them to the party. Between our heads and the lowering clouds a frenzied organ was thundering through, with an appositeness perhaps accidental, "You *maaaade* me love you, I didn't wanna do it, I didn't wanna do it . . ."

The affair between Boston and Ted Williams has been no mere summer romance; it has been a marriage, composed of spats, mutual disappointments, and, toward the end, a mellowing hoard of shared memories. It falls into three stages, which may be termed Youth, Maturity, and Age, or Thesis, Antithesis, and Synthesis; or Jason, Achilles, and Nestor.

First, there was the by now legendary epoch when the young bridegroom came out of the West, announced, "All I want out of life is that when I walk down the street folks will say, 'There goes the greatest hitter who ever lived.' " The dowagers of local journalism attempted to give elementary deportment lessons to this child who spake as a god, and to their horror were themselves rebuked. Thus began the long exchange of backbiting, bat-flipping, booing, and spitting that has distinguished Williams' public relations. The spitting incidents of 1957 and 1958 and the similar dockside courtesies that Williams has now and then extended to the grandstand should be judged against this background: the left-field stands at Fenway for twenty years have held a large number of customers who have bought their way in primarily for the privilege of showering abuse on Williams. Greatness necessarily attracts debunkers, but in Williams' case the hostility has been systematic and unappeasable. His basic offense against the fans has been to wish that they weren't there. Seeking a perfectionist's vacuum, he has quixotically desired to sever the game from the ground of paid spectatorship and publicity that supports it. Hence his refusal to tip his cap to the crowd or turn the other cheek to newsmen. It has been a costly theory—it has probably cost him, among other evidences of good will, two Most Valuable Player awards, which are voted by reporters—but he has held to it from his rookie year on. While his critics, oral and literary, remained beyond the reach of his discipline, the opposing pitchers were accessible, and he spanked them to the tune of .406 in 1941. He slumped to .356 in 1942 and went off to war.

In 1946 Williams returned from three years as a Marine pilot to the second of his baseball avatars, that of Achilles, the hero of incomparable prowess and beauty who nevertheless was to be found sulking in his tent while the Trojans (mostly Yankees) fought through to the ships. Yawkey, a timber and mining maharajah, had surrounded his central jewel with many gems of slightly lesser water, such as Bobby Doerr, Dom DiMaggio, Rudy York, Birdie Tebbetts, and Johnny Pesky. Throughout the late forties, the Red Sox were the best paper team in baseball, yet they had little three-dimensional to show for it, and if this was a tragedy, Williams was Hamlet. A succinct review of the indictment—and a fair sample of appreciative sports-page prose—appeared the very day of Williams' vale-dictory, in a column by Huck Finnegan in the Boston *American* (no sentimentalist, Huck):

Williams' career, in contrast [to Babe Ruth's], has been a series of failures except for his averages. He flopped in the only World Series he ever played in (1946) when he batted only .200. He flopped in the play-off game with Cleveland in 1948. He flopped in the final game of the 1949 season with the pennant hinging on the outcome (Yanks 5, Sox 3). He flopped in 1950 when he returned to the lineup after a two-month absence and ruined the morale of a club that seemed pennant-bound under Steve O'Neill. It has always been Williams' rec-ords first, the team second, and the Sox nonwinning record is proof enough of that.

There are answers to all this, of course. The fatal weakness of the great Sox slugging teams was not-quite-good-enough pitching rather than Williams' failure to hit a home run every time he came to bat. Again, Williams' depressing effect on his teammates has never been proved. Despite ample coaching to the contrary, most insisted that they *liked* him. He has been generous with advice to any player who asked for it. In an increasingly combative baseball atmosphere, he continued to duck beanballs docilely. With umpires he was gracious to a fault. This courtesy itself annoyed his critics, whom there was no pleasing. And against the ten crucial games (the seven World Series games with the St. Louis Cardinals, the 1948 play-off with the Cleveland Indians, and the two-game series with the Yankees at the end of the 1949 season, winning either one of which would have given the Red Sox the pennant) that make up the Achilles' heel of Williams' record, a mass of statistics can be set showing that day in and day out he was no slouch in the clutch. The correspondence columns of the Boston papers now and then suffer a sharp flurry of arithmetic on this score; indeed, for Williams to have distributed all his hits so they did nobody else any good would constitute a feat of placement unparalleled in the annals of selfishness.

Whatever residue of truth remains of the Finnegan charge those of us who love Williams must transmute as best we can, in our own personal crucibles. My personal memories of Williams begin when I was a boy in Pennsylvania, with two last-place teams in Philadelphia to keep me com-pany. For me, "W'ms, lf" was a figment of the box scores who always seemed to be going 3-for-5. He radiated, from afar, the hard blue glow of high purpose. I remember listening over the radio to the All-Star

Game of 1946, in which Williams hit two singles and two home runs, the second one off a Rip Sewell "blooper" pitch; it was like hitting a balloon out of the park. I remember watching one of his home runs from the bleachers of Shibe Park; it went over the first baseman's head and rose meticulously along a straight line and was still rising when it cleared the fence. The trajectory seemed qualitatively different from anything anyone else might hit. For me, Williams is the classic ballplayer of the game on a hot August weekday, before a small crowd, when the only thing at stake is the tissue-thin difference between a thing done well and a thing done ill. Baseball is a game of the long season, of relentless and gradual averaging-out. Irrelevance—since the reference point of most individual games is remote and statistical—always threatens its interest, which can be maintained not by the occasional heroics that sportswriters feed upon but by players who always *care;* who care, that is to say, about themselves and their art. Insofar as the clutch hitter is not a sportswriter's myth, he is a vulgarity, like a writer who writes only for money. It may be that, compared to managers' dreams such as Joe DiMaggio and the always helpful Stan Musial, Williams is an icy star. But of all team sports, baseball, with its graceful intermittences of action, its immense and tranquil field sparsely settled with poised men in white, its dispassionate mathematics, seems to be best suited to accommodate, and be ornamented by, a loner. It is an essentially lonely game. No other player visible to my generation has concentrated within himself so much of the sport's poignance, has so assiduously refined his natural skills, has so constantly brought to the plate that intensity of competence that crowds the throat with joy.

By the time I went to college, near Boston, the lesser stars Yawkey had assembled around Williams had faded, and his craftsmanship, his rigorous pride, had become itself a kind of heroism. This brittle and temperamental player developed an unexpected quality of persistence. He was always coming back—back from Korea, back from a broken collarbone, a shattered elbow, a bruised heel, back from drastic bouts of flu and ptomaine poisoning. Hardly a season went by without some enfeebling mishap, yet he always came back, and always looked like himself. The delicate mechanism of timing and power seemed locked, shockproof, in some case outside his body. In addition to injuries, there were a heavily publicized divorce, and the usual storms with the press, and the Williams Shift—the maneuver, custom-built by Lou Boudreau, of the Cleveland Indians, whereby three infielders were concentrated on the right side of the infield, where a left-handed pull hitter like Williams generally hits the ball. Williams could easily have learned to punch singles through the vacancy on his left and fattened his average hugely. This was what Ty Cobb, the Einstein of average, told him to do. But the game had changed since Cobb; Williams believed that his value to the club and to the game was as a slugger, so he went on pulling the ball, trying to blast it through three men, and paid the price of perhaps fifteen points of lifetime average. Like Ruth before him, he bought the occasional home run at the cost of many directed singles—a calculated sacrifice certainly not, in the case of a hitter as average-minded as Williams, entirely selfish.

After a prime so harassed and hobbled, Williams was granted by the relenting fates a golden twilight. He became at the end of his career perhaps the best *old* hitter of the century. The dividing line came between the 1956 and the 1957 seasons. In September of the first year, he and Mickey Mantle were contending for the batting championship. Both were hitting around .350, and there was no one else near them. The season ended with a three-game series between the Yankees and the Sox, and, living in New York then, I went up to the Stadium. Williams was slightly shy of the four hundred at-bats needed to qualify; the fear was expressed that the Yankee pitchers would walk him to protect Mantle. Instead, they pitched to him—a wise decision. He looked terrible at the plate, tired and discouraged and unconvincing. He never looked very good to me in the Stadium. (Last week, in *Life*, Williams, a sportswriter himself now, wrote gloomily of the Stadium, "There's the bigness of it. There are those high stands and all those people smoking—and, of course, the shadows. . . . It takes at least one Series to get accustomed to the Stadium and even then you're not sure.") The final outcome in 1956 was Mantle .353, Williams .345.

The next year, I moved from New York to New England, and it made all the difference. For in September of 1957, in the same situation, the story was reversed. Mantle finally hit .365; it was the best season of his career. But Williams, though sick and old, had run away from him. A bout of flu had laid him low in September. He emerged from his cave in the Hotel Somerset haggard but irresistible; he hit four successive pinch-hit home runs. "I feel terrible," he confessed, "but every time I take a swing at the ball it goes out of the park." He ended the season with thirty-eight home runs and an average of .388, the highest in either league since his own .406, and, coming from a decrepit man of thirty-nine, an even more supernal figure. With eight or so of the "leg hits" that a younger man would have beaten out, it would have been .400. And the next year, Williams, who in 1949 and 1953 had lost batting championships by decimal whiskers to George Kell and Mickey Vernon, sneaked in behind his teammate Pete Runnels and filched his sixth title, a bargain at .328.

In 1959, it seemed all over. The dinosaur thrashed around in the .200 swamp for the first half of the season, and was even benched ("rested," manager Mike Higgins tactfully said). Old foes like the late Bill Cunningham began to offer batting tips. Cunningham thought Williams was jiggling his elbows; in truth, Williams' neck was so stiff he could hardly turn his head to look at the pitcher. When he swung, it looked like a Calder mobile with one thread cut; it reminded you that since 1953 Williams' shoulders had been wired together. A solicitous pall settled over the sports pages. In the two decades since Williams had come to Boston, his status had imperceptibly shifted from that of a naughty prodigy to that of a municipal monument. As his shadow in the record books lengthened, the Red Sox teams around him declined, and the entire American League seemed to be losing life and color to the National. The inconsistency of the new superstars—Mantle, Colavito, and Kaline—served to make Williams appear all the more singular. And off the field, his private philanthropy—in particular, his zealous chairmanship of the Jimmy Fund, a charity for children with cancer—gave him a civic presence somewhat like that of Richard Cardinal Cushing. In religion, Williams appears to be a humanist, and a selective one at that, but he and the Cardinal, when their good works intersect and they appear in the public eye together, make a handsome and heartening pair.

Humiliated by his '59 season, Williams determined, once more, to come back. I, as a specimen Williams partisan, was both glad and fearful. All baseball fans believe in miracles; the question is, how *many* do you believe in? He looked like a ghost in spring training. Manager Jurges warned us ahead of time that if Williams didn't come through he would be benched, just like anybody else. As it turned out, it was Jurges who was benched. Williams entered the 1960 season needing eight home runs to have a lifetime total of 500; after one time at bat in Washington, he needed seven. For a stretch, he was hitting a home run every second game that he played. He passed Lou Gehrig's lifetime total, then the number 500, then Mel Ott's total, and finished with 521, thirteen behind Jimmy Foxx, who alone stands between Williams and Babe Ruth's unapproachable 714. The summer was a statistician's picnic. His two-thousandth walk came and went, his eighteen-hundredth run batted in, his sixteenth All-Star Game. At one point, he hit a home run off a pitcher, Don Lee, off whose father, Thornton Lee, he had hit a home run a generation before. The only comparable season for a forty-two-year-old man was Ty Cobb's in 1928. Cobb batted .323 and hit one homer. Williams batted .316 but hit twenty-nine homers.

In sum, though generally conceded to be the greatest hitter of his era, he did not establish himself as "the greatest hitter who ever lived." Cobb, for average, and Ruth, for power, remain supreme. Cobb, Rogers Hornsby, Joe Jackson, and Lefty O'Doul, among players since 1900, have higher lifetime averages than Williams' .344. Unlike Foxx, Gehrig, Hack Wilson, Hank Greenberg, and Ralph Kiner, Williams never came close to matching Babe Ruth's season home-run total of sixty. In the list of major-league batting records, not one is held by Williams. He is second in walks drawn, third in home runs, fifth in lifetime averages, sixth in runs batted in, eighth in runs scored and in total bases, fourteenth in doubles, and thirtieth in hits. But if we allow him merely average seasons for the four-plus seasons he lost to two wars, and add another season for the months he lost to injuries, we get a man who in all the power totals would be second, and not a very distant second, to Ruth. And if we further allow that these years would have been not merely average but prime years, if we allow for all the months when Williams was playing in sub-par condition, if we permit his early and later years in baseball to be some sort of index of what the middle years could have been, if we give him a right-field fence that is not, like Fenway's, one of the most distant in the league, and if—the least excusable "if"—we imagine him condescending to outsmart the Williams Shift, we can defensibly assemble, like a colossus induced from the sizable fragments that do remain, a statistical figure not incommensurate with his grandiose ambition. From the statistics that are on the books, a good case can be made that in the *combination* of power and average Williams is first; nobody else ranks so high in both categories. Finally, there is the witness of the eyes; men whose memories go back to Shoeless Joe Jackson—another unlucky natural— rank him and Williams together as the best-looking hitters they have seen. It was for our last look that ten thousand of us had come.

Two girls, one of them with pert buckteeth and eyes as black as vest buttons, the other with white skin and flesh-colored hair, like an underdeveloped photograph of a redhead, came and sat on my right. On my other side was one of those frowning, chestless young-old men who can frequently be seen, often wearing sailor hats, attending ball games alone. He did not once open his program but instead tapped it, rolled up, on his knee as he gave the game his disconsolate attention. A young lady, with freckles and a depressed, dainty nose that by an optical illusion seemed to thrust her lips forward for a kiss, sauntered down into the box seats and with striking aplomb took a seat right behind the roof of the Oriole dugout. She wore a blue coat with a Northeastern University emblem sewed to it. The girls beside me took it into their heads that this was Williams' daughter. She looked too old to me, and why would she be sitting behind the visitors' dugout? On the other hand, from the way she sat there, staring at the sky and French-inhaling, she clearly was *some* body. Other fans came and eclipsed her from view. The crowd looked less like a weekday ball-park crowd than like the folks you might find in Yellowstone National Park, or emerging from automobiles at the top of scenic Mount Mansfield. There were a lot of competitively well-dressed couples of tourist age, and not a few babes in arms. A row of five seats in front of me was abruptly filled with a woman and four children, the youngest of them two years old, if that. Someday, presumably, he could tell his grandchildren that he saw Williams play. Along with these tots and second-honeymooners, there were Harvard freshmen, giving off that peculiar nervous glow created when a quantity of insouciance is saturated with insecurity; thick-necked Army officers with brass on their shoulders and lead in their voices; pepperings of priests; perfumed bouquets of Roxbury Fabian fans; shiny salesmen from Albany and Fall River; and those gray, hoarse men—taxi drivers, slaughterers, and bartenders—who will continue to click through the turnstiles long after everyone else has deserted to television and tramporamas. Behind me, two young male voices blossomed, cracking a joke about God's five proofs that Thomas Aquinas exists—typical Boston College levity.

The batting cage was trundled away. The Orioles fluttered to the sidelines. Diagonally across the field, by the Red Sox dugout, a cluster of men in overcoats were festering like maggots. I could see a splinter of white uniform, and Williams' head, held at a self-deprecating and evasive tilt. Williams' conversational stance is that of a six-foot-three-inch man under a six-foot ceiling. He moved away to the patter of flash bulbs, and began playing catch with a young Negro outfielder named Willie Tasby. His arm, never very powerful, had grown lax with the years, and his throwing motion was a kind of muscular drawl. To catch the ball, he flicked his glove onto his left shoulder (he batted left but threw right, as every schoolboy ought to know) and let the ball plop into it comically. This catch session with Tasby was the only time all afternoon I saw him grin.

A tight little flock of human sparrows who, from the lambent and pampered pink of their faces, could only have been Boston politicians moved toward the plate. The loudspeakers mammothly coughed as someone huffed on the microphone. The ceremonies began. Curt Gowdy, the Red Sox radio and television announcer, who sounds like everybody's brother-in-law, delivered a brief sermon, taking the two words "pride" and "champion" as his text. It began, "Twenty-one years ago, a skinny kid from San Diego, California . . ." and ended, "I don't think we'll ever see another like him." Robert Tibolt, chairman of the board of the Greater Boston Chamber of Commerce, presented Williams with a big Paul Revere silver bowl. Harry Carlson, a member of the sports committee of the Boston Chamber, gave him a plaque, whose inscription he did not read in its entirety, out of deference to Williams' distaste for this sort of fuss. Mayor Collins presented the Jimmy Fund with a thousand-dollar check.

Then the occasion himself stooped to the microphone, and his voice sounded, after the others, very Californian; it seemed to be coming, excellently amplified, from a great distance, adolescently young and as smooth as a butternut. His thanks for the gifts had not died from our ears before he glided, as if helplessly, into "In spite of all the terrible things that have been said about me by the maestros of the keyboard up there . . ." He glanced up at the press rows suspended above home plate. (All the Boston reporters, incidentally, reported the phrase as "knights of the keyboard," but I heard it as "maestros" and prefer it that way.) The crowd tittered, appalled. A frightful vision flashed upon me, of the press gallery pelting Williams with erasers, of Williams clambering up the foul screen to slug journalists, of a riot, of Mayor Collins being crushed. ". . . And they *were* terrible things," Williams insisted, with level melancholy, into the mike. "I'd like to forget them, but I can't." He paused, swallowed his memories, and went on, "I want to say that my years in Boston have been the greatest thing in my life." The crowd, like an immense sail going limp in a change of wind, sighed with relief. Taking all the parts himself, Williams then acted out a vivacious little morality drama in which an imaginary tempter came to him at the beginning of his career and said, "Ted, you can play anywhere you like." Leaping nimbly into the role of his younger self (who in biographical actuality had yearned to be a Yankee), Williams gallantly chose Boston over all the other cities, and told us that Tom Yawkey was the greatest owner in baseball and we were the greatest fans. We applauded ourselves heartily. The umpire came out and dusted the plate. The voice of doom announced over the loudspeakers that after Williams' retirement his uniform number, 9, would be permanently retired—the first time the Red Sox had so honored a player. We cheered. The national anthem was played. We cheered. The game began.

Williams was third in the batting order, so he came up in the bottom of the first inning, and Steve Barber, a young pitcher who was not yet born when Williams began playing for the Red Sox, offered him four pitches, at all of which he disdained to swing, since none of them were within the strike zone. This demonstrated simultaneously that Williams' eyes were razor-sharp and that Barber's control wasn't. Shortly, the bases were full, with Williams on second. "Oh, I hope he gets held up at third! That would be wonderful," the girl beside me moaned, and, sure enough, the man at bat walked and Williams was delivered into our foreground. He struck the pose of Donatello's David, the third-base bag being Goliath's head. Fiddling with his cap, swapping small talk with the Oriole third baseman (who seemed delighted to have him drop in), swinging his arms with a sort of prancing nervousness, he looked fine—flexible, hard, and not unbecomingly substantial through the middle. The long neck, the small head, the knickers whose cuffs were worn down near his ankles —all these points, often observed by caricaturists, were visible in the flesh.

One of the collegiate voices behind me said, "He looks old, doesn't he, old; big deep wrinkles in his face . . ."

"Yeah," the other voice said, "but he looks like an old hawk, doesn't he?"

With each pitch, Williams danced down the base line, waving his arms and stirring dust, ponderous but menacing, like an attacking goose. It occurred to about a dozen humorists at once to shout, "Steal home! Go, go!" Williams' speed afoot was never legendary. Lou Clinton, a young Sox outfielder, hit a fairly deep fly to center field. Williams tagged up and ran home. As he slid across the plate, the ball, thrown with unusual heft by Jackie Brandt, the Oriole center fielder, hit him on the back.

"Boy, he was really loafing, wasn't he?" one of the boys behind me said.

"It's cold," the other explained. "He doesn't play well when it's cold. He likes heat. He's a hedonist."

The run that Williams scored was the second and last of the inning. Gus Triandos, of the Orioles, quickly evened the score by plunking a home run over the handy left-field wall. Williams, who had had this wall at his back for twenty years, played the ball flawlessly. He didn't budge. He just stood there, in the center of the little patch of grass that his patient footsteps had worn brown, and, limp with lack of interest, watched the ball pass overhead. It was not a very interesting game. Mike Higgins, the Red Sox manager, with nothing to lose, had restricted his major-league players to the left-field line—along with Williams, Frank Malzone, a first-rate third baseman, played the game—and had peopled the rest of the terrain with unpredictable youngsters fresh, or not so fresh, off the farms. Other than Williams' recurrent appearances at the plate, the *maladresse* of the Sox infield was the sole focus of suspense; the second baseman turned every grounder into a juggling act, while the shortstop did a breathtaking impersonation of an open window. With this sort of assistance, the Orioles wheedled their way into a 4-2 lead. They had early replaced Barber with another young pitcher, Jack Fisher. Fortunately (as it turned out), Fisher is no cutie; he is willing to burn the ball through the strike zone, and inning after inning this tactic punctured Higgins' string of test balloons.

Whenever Williams appeared at the plate—pounding the dirt from his cleats, gouging a pit in the batter's box with his left foot, wringing resin out of the bat handle with his vehement grip, switching the stick at the pitcher with an electric ferocity—it was like having a familiar Leonardo appear in a shuffle of *Saturday Evening Post* covers. This man, you realized—and here, perhaps, was the difference, greater than the difference in gifts—really intended to hit the ball. In the third inning, he hoisted a high fly to deep center. In the fifth, we thought he had it; he smacked the ball hard and high into the heart of his power zone, but the deep right field in Fenway and the heavy air and a casual east wind defeated him. The ball died. Al Pilarcik leaned his back against the big "380" painted on the right-field wall and caught it. On another day, in another park, it would have been gone. (After the game, Williams said, "I didn't think I could hit one any harder than that. The conditions weren't good.")

The afternoon grew so glowering that in the sixth inning the arc lights were turned on—always a wan sight in the daytime, like the burning headlights of a funeral procession. Aided by the gloom, Fisher was slicing through the Sox rookies, and Williams did not come to bat in the seventh. He was second up in the eighth. This was almost certainly his last time to come to the plate in Fenway Park, and instead of merely cheering, as we had at his three previous appearances, we stood, all of us—stood and applauded. Have you ever heard applause in a ball park? Just applause—no calling, no whistling, just an ocean of handclaps, minute after minute, burst after burst, crowding and running together in continuous succession like the pushes of surf at the edge of the sand. It was a somber and considered tumult. There was not a boo in it. It seemed to renew itself out of a shifting set of memories as the kid, the Marine, the veteran of feuds and failures and injuries, the friend of children, and the enduring old pro evolved down the bright tunnel of twenty-one summers toward this moment. At last, the umpire signaled for Fisher to pitch; with the other players, he had been frozen in position. Only Williams had moved during the ovation, switching his bat impatiently, ignoring everything except his cherished task. Fisher wound up, and the applause sank into a hush.

Understand that we were a crowd of rational people. We knew that a home run cannot be produced at will; the right pitch must be perfectly met and luck must ride with the ball. Three innings before, we had seen a brave effort fail. The air was soggy; the season was exhausted. Nevertheless, there will always lurk, around a corner in a pocket of our knowledge of the odds, an indefensible hope, and this was one of the times, which you now and then find in sports, when a density of expectation hangs in the air and plucks an event out of the future.

Fisher, after his unsettling wait, was wide with the first pitch. He put the second one over, and Williams swung mightily and missed. The crowd grunted, seeing that classic swing, so long and smooth and quick, exposed, naked in its failure. Fisher threw the third time, Williams swung again, and there it was. The ball climbed on a diagonal line into the vast volume of air over center field. From my angle, behind third base, the ball seemed less an object in flight than the tip of a towering, motionless construct, like the Eiffel Tower or the Tappan Zee Bridge. It was in the books while it was still in the sky. Brandt ran back to the deepest corner of the outfield grass; the ball descended beyond his reach and struck in the crotch where the bullpen met the wall, bounced chunkily, and, as far as I could see, vanished.

Like a feather caught in a vortex, Williams ran around the square of bases at the center of our beseeching screaming. He ran as he always ran out home runs—hurriedly, unsmiling, head down, as if our praise were a storm of rain to get out of. He didn't tip his cap. Though we thumped, wept, and chanted, "We want Ted," for minutes after he hid in the dugout, he did not come back. Our noise for some seconds passed beyond excitement into a kind of immense open anguish, a wailing, a cry to be saved. But immortality is nontransferable. The papers said that the other players, and even the umpires on the field, begged him to come out and acknowledge us in some way, but he never had and did not now. Gods do not answer letters.

Every true story has an anticlimax. The men on the field refused to disappear, as would have seemed decent, in the smoke of Williams' miracle. Fisher continued to pitch, and escaped further harm. At the end of the inning, Higgins sent Williams out to his left-field position, then instantly replaced him with Carrol Hardy, so we had a long last look at Williams as he ran out there and then back, his uniform jogging, his eyes steadfast on the ground. It was nice, and we were grateful, but it left a funny taste.

One of the scholasticists behind me said, "Let's go. We've seen everything. I don't want to spoil it." This seemed a sound aesthetic decision. Williams' last word had been so exquisitely chosen, such a perfect fusion of expectation, intention, and execution, that already it felt a little unreal in my head, and I wanted to get out before the castle collapsed. But the game, though played by clumsy midgets under the feeble glow of the arc lights, began to tug at my attention, and I loitered in the runway until it was over. Williams' homer had, quite incidentally, made the score 4-3. In the bottom of the ninth inning, with one out, Marlin Coughtry, the second-base juggler, singled. Vic Wertz, pinch-hitting, doubled off the left-field wall, Coughtry advancing to third. Pumpsie Green walked to load the bases. Willie Tasby hit a double-play ball to the third baseman, but in making the pivot throw Billy Klaus, an ex-Red Sox infielder, reverted to form and threw the ball past the first baseman and into the Red Sox dugout. The Sox won, 5-4. On the car radio as I drove home I heard that Williams had decided not to accompany the team to New York. So he knew how to do even that, the hardest thing. Quit.

─────────────── FICTION ───────────────

THIS is a splendid Wodehouse story, and I would love to see a box score with "Van Puyster, p" in it. But its best line, undimmed by the years that have passed since the story was written, has naught to do with baseball. "Hush!" the girl says, "we must be quiet. Daddy and Grandpa are busy in there cornering wheat."

The Pitcher and the Plutocrat

P. G. WODEHOUSE

THE MAIN DIFFICULTY in writing a story is to convey to the reader clearly yet tersely the natures and dispositions of one's leading characters. Brevity, brevity—that is the cry. Perhaps, after all, the playbill style is the best. In this drama of love, baseball, frenzied finance, and tainted millions, then, the principals are as follows, in their order of entry:

Isabel Rackstraw (a peach).
Clarence Van Puyster (a Greek god).
Old Man Van Puyster (a proud old aristocrat).
Old Man Rackstraw (a tainted millionaire).

More about Clarence later. For the moment let him go as a Greek God. There were other sides, too, to Old Man Rackstraw's character; but for the moment let him go as a Tainted Millionaire. Not that it is satisfactory. It is too mild. He was *the* Tainted Millionaire. The Tainted Millions of other Tainted Millionaires were as attar of roses compared with the Tainted Millions of Tainted Millionaire Rackstraw. He preferred his millions tainted. His attitude toward an untainted million was that of the sportsman toward the sitting bird. These things are purely a matter of taste. Some people like Limburger cheese.

It was at a charity bazaar that Isabel and Clarence first met. Isabel was presiding over the Billiken, Teddy Bear, and Fancy Goods stall. There she stood, that slim, radiant girl, buncoing the Younger Set out of its father's hard-earned with a smile that alone was nearly worth the money, when she observed, approaching, the handsomest man she had ever seen. It was —this is not one of those mystery stories—it was Clarence Van Puyster. Over the heads of the bevy of gilded youths who clustered round the stall their eyes met. A thrill ran through Isabel. She dropped her eyes. The next moment Clarence had bucked center; the Younger Set had shredded away like a mist; and he was leaning toward her, opening negotiations for the purchase of a yellow Teddy Bear at sixteen times its face value.

He returned at intervals during the afternoon. Over the second Teddy Bear they became friendly; over the third, intimate. He proposed as she was wrapping up the fourth Golliwog, and she gave him her heart and the parcel simultaneously. At six o'clock, carrying four Teddy Bears, seven photograph frames, five Golliwogs, and a Billiken, Clarence went home to tell the news to his father.

Clarence, when not at college, lived with his only surviving parent in an old red-brick house at the north end of Washington Square. The original Van Puyster had come over in Governor Stuyvesant's time in one of the then fashionable ninety-four-day boats. Those were the stirring days when they were giving away chunks of Manhattan Island in exchange for trading-stamps; for the bright brain which conceived the idea that the city might possibly at some remote date extend above Liberty Street had not come into existence. The original Van Puyster had acquired a square mile or so in the heart of things for ten dollars cash and a quarter interest in a peddler's outfit. The *Columbus Echo and Vespucci Intelligencer* gave him a column and a half under the heading: "Reckless Speculator. Prominent Citizen's Gamble in Land." On the proceeds of that deal his descendants had led quiet, peaceful lives ever since. If any of them ever did a day's work, the family records are silent on the point. Blood was their long suit, not Energy. They were plain, homely folk, with a refined distaste for wealth and vulgar hustle. They lived simply, without envy of their richer fellow citizens, on their three hundred thousand dollars a year. They asked no more. It enabled them to entertain on a modest scale; the boys could go to college, the girls buy an occasional new frock. They were satisfied.

Having dressed for dinner, Clarence proceeded to the library, where he found his father slowly pacing the room. Silver-haired old Vansuyther Van Puyster seemed wrapped in thought. And this was unusual, for he was not given to thinking. To be absolutely frank, the old man had just about enough brain to make a jay-bird fly crooked, and no more.

"Ah, my boy," he said, looking up as Clarence entered. "Let us go in to dinner. I have been awaiting you for some little time now. I was about to inquire as to your whereabouts. Let us be going."

Mr. Van Puyster always spoke like that. This was due to Blood.

Until the servants had left them to their coffee and cigarettes, the conversation was desultory and commonplace. But when the door had closed, Mr. Van Puyster leaned forward.

"My boy," he said quietly, "we are ruined."

Clarence looked at him inquiringly.

"Ruined much?" he asked.

"Paupers," said his father. "I doubt if when all is over, I shall have much more than a bare fifty or sixty thousand dollars a year."

A lesser man would have betrayed agitation, but Clarence was a Van Puyster. He lit a cigarette.

"Ah," he said calmly. "How's that?"

Mr. Van Puyster toyed with his coffee-spoon. "I was induced to speculate—rashly, I fear—on the advice of a man I chanced to meet at a public·dinner, in the shares of a certain mine. I did not thoroughly understand the matter, but my acquaintance appeared to be well versed in such operations, so I allowed him to—and, well, in fact, to cut a long story short. I am ruined."

"Who was the fellow?"

"A man of the name of Rackstraw. Daniel Rackstraw."

"Daniel Rackstraw!"

Not even Clarence's training and traditions could prevent a slight start as he heard the name.

"Daniel Rackstraw," repeated his father. "A man, I fear, not entirely honest. In fact, it seems that he has made a very large fortune by similar transactions. Friends of mine, acquainted with these matters, tell me his behavior toward me amounted practically to theft. However, for myself I care little. We can rough it, we of the old Van Puyster stock. If there is but fifty thousand a year left, well—I must make it serve. It is for your sake that I am troubled, my poor boy. I shall be compelled to stop your allowance. I fear you will be obliged to adopt some profession." He hesitated for a moment. "In fact, work," he added.

Clarence drew at his cigarette.

"Work?" he echoed thoughtfully. "Well, of course, mind you, fellows *do* work. I met a man at the club only yesterday who knew a fellow who had met a man whose cousin worked."

He reflected for a while.

"I shall pitch," he said suddenly.

"Pitch, my boy?"

"Sign on as a professional ballplayer."

His father's fine old eyebrows rose a little.

"But, my boy, er— The—ah—family name. Our—shall I say *noblesse oblige?* Can a Van Puyster pitch and not be defiled?"

"I shall take a new name," said Clarence. "I will call myself Brown." He lit another cigarette. "I can get signed on in a minute. McGraw will jump at me."

This was no idle boast. Clarence had had a good college education, and was now an exceedingly fine pitcher. It was a pleasing sight to see him, poised on one foot in the attitude of a Salome dancer, with one eye on the batter, the other gazing coldly at the man who was trying to steal third, uncurl abruptly like the mainspring of a watch and sneak over a swift one. Under Clarence's guidance a ball could do practically everything except talk. It could fly like a shot from a gun, hesitate, take the first turning to the left, go up two blocks, take the second to the right, bound in mid-air like a jack rabbit, and end by dropping as the gentle dew from heaven upon the plate beneath. Briefly, there was class to Clarence. He was the goods.

Scarcely had he uttered these momentous words when the butler entered with the announcement that he was wanted by a lady at the telephone.

It was Isabel.

Isabel was disturbed.

"Oh, Clarence," she cried, "my precious angel wonder-child, I don't know how to begin."

"Begin just like that," said Clarence approvingly. "It's fine. You can't beat it."

"Clarence, a terrible thing has happened. I told Papa of our engagement, and he wouldn't hear of it. He was furious. He c-called you a b-b-b—"

"A what?"

"A p-p-p—"

"That's a new one on me," said Clarence, wondering.

"A b-beggarly p-pauper. I knew you weren't well off, but I thought you had two or three millions. I told him so. But he said no, your father had lost all his money."

"It is too true, dearest," said Clarence. "I am a pauper. But I'm going to work. Something tells me I shall be rather good at work. I am going to work with all the accumulated energy of generations of ancestors who have never done a hand's turn. And some day when I—"

"Good-by," said Isabel hastily, "I hear Papa coming."

The season during which Clarence Van Puyster pitched for the Giants is destined to live long in the memory of followers of baseball. Probably never in the history of the game has there been such persistent and widespread mortality among the more distant relatives of office-boys and junior clerks. Statisticians have estimated that if all the grandmothers alone who perished between the months of April and October that year could have been placed end to end they would have reached considerably further than Minneapolis. And it was Clarence who was responsible for this holocaust. Previous to the opening of the season skeptics had shaken their heads over the Giants' chances for the pennant. It had been assumed that as little new blood would be forthcoming as in other years, and that the fate of Our City would rest, as usual, on the shoulders of the white-haired veterans who were boys with Lafayette.

And then, like a meteor, Clarence Van Puyster had flashed upon the world of fans, bugs, chewing gum, and nuts (pea and human). In the opening game he had done horrid things to nine men from Boston; and from then onward, except for an occasional check, the Giants had never looked back.

Among the spectators who thronged the bleachers to watch Clarence perform there appeared week after week a little, gray, dried-up man, insignificant except for a certain happy choice of language in moments of emotion and an enthusiasm far surpassing that of the ordinary spectator. To the trained eye there is a subtle but well marked difference between the fan, the bug, and—the last phase—the nut of the baseball world. This man was an undoubted nut. It was writ clear across his brow.

Fate had made Daniel Rackstraw—for it was he—a Tainted Millionaire, but at heart he was a baseball spectator. He never missed a game. His library of baseball literature was the finest in the country. His baseball museum had but one equal, that of Mr. Jacob Dodson of Detroit. Between them the two had cornered, at enormous expense, the curio market of the game. It was Rackstraw who had secured the glove worn by Neal Ball, the Cleveland shortstop, when he made the only unassisted triple play in the history of the game; but it was Dodson who possessed the bat which Hans Wagner used as a boy. The two men were friends, as far as rival connoisseurs can be friends; and Mr. Dodson, when at leisure, would frequently pay a visit to Mr. Rackstraw's country home, where he would spend hours gazing wistfully at the Neal Ball glove buoyed up only by the thought of the Wagner bat at home.

Isabel saw little of Clarence during the summer months, except from a distance. She contented herself with clipping photographs of him from the evening papers. Each was a little more unlike him than the last, and this lent variety to the collection. Her father marked her new-born enthusiasm for the national game with approval. It had been secretly a great grief to the old buccaneer that his only child did not know the difference between a bunt and a swat, and, more, did not seem to care to know. He felt himself drawn closer to her. An understanding, as pleasant as it was new and strange, began to spring up between parent and child.

As for Clarence, how easy it would be to cut loose to practically an unlimited extent on the subject of his emotions at this time. One can figure him, after the game is over and the gay throng has dispersed, creeping moodily—but what's the use? Brevity. That is the cry. Brevity. Let us on.

The months sped by. August came and went, and September; and soon it was plain to even the casual follower of the game that, unless something untoward should happen, the Giants must secure the National League pennant. Those were delirious days for Daniel Rackstraw. Long before the beginning of October his voice had dwindled to a husky whisper. Deep lines appeared on his forehead; for it is an awful thing for a baseball nut to be compelled to root, in the very crisis of the season, purely by means of facial expression. In this time of affliction he found Isabel an ever-increasing comfort to him. Side by side they would sit at the Polo Grounds, and the old man's face would lose its drawn look, and light up, as her clear young soprano pealed out above the din, urging this player to slide for second, that to knock the stitching off the ball; or describing the umpire in no uncertain voice as a reincarnation of the late Mr. Jesse James.

Meanwhile, in the American League, Detroit had been heading the list with equal pertinacity; and in far-off Michigan Mr. Jacob Dodson's enthusiasm had been every whit as great as Mr. Rackstraw's in New York. It was universally admitted that when the championship series came to be played, there would certainly be something doing.

But, alas! How truly does Epictetus observe: "We know not what awaiteth us around the corner, and the hand that counteth its chickens ere they be hatched ofttimes graspeth but a lemon." The prophets who anticipated a struggle closer than any one record were destined to be proved false.

It was not that their judgment of form was at fault. By every law of averages the Giants and the Tigers should have been the two most evenly matched nines in the history of the game. In fielding there was nothing to choose between them. At hitting the Tigers held a slight superiority; but this was balanced by the inspired pitching of Clarence Van Puyster. Even the keenest supporters of either side were not confident. They argued at length, figuring out the odds with the aid of stubs of pencils and the backs of envelopes, but they were not confident. Out of all those frenzied millions two men alone had no doubts. Mr. Daniel Rackstraw said that he did not desire to be unfair to Detroit. He wished it to be clearly understood that in their own class the Tigers might quite possibly show to considerable advantage. In some rural league down South, for instance, he did not deny that they might sweep all before them. But when it came to competing with the Giants—here words failed Mr. Rackstraw, and he had to rush to Wall Street and collect several tainted millions before he could recover his composure.

Mr. Jacob Dodson, interviewed by the Detroit *Weekly Rooter,* stated that his decision, arrived at after a close and careful study of the work of both teams, was that the Giants had rather less chance in the forthcoming tourney than a lone gumdrop at an Eskimo tea-party. It was his carefully considered opinion that in a contest with the Avenue B Juniors the Giants might, with an effort, scrape home. But when it was a question of meeting a live team like Detroit—here Mr. Dodson, shrugging his shoulders despairingly, sank back in his chair, and watchful secretaries brought him round with oxygen.

Throughout the whole country nothing but the approaching series was discussed. Wherever civilization reigned, and in Jersey City, one question alone was on every lip: Who would win? Octogenarians mumbled it. Infants lisped it. Tired businessmen, trampled underfoot in the rush for the West Farms express, asked it of the ambulance attendants who carried them to hospital.

And then, one bright, clear morning, when all Nature seemed to smile, Clarence Van Puyster developed mumps.

New York was in a ferment. I could have wished to go into details, to describe in crisp, burning sentences the panic that swept like a tornado through a million homes. A little encouragement, the slightest softening of the editorial austerity, and the thing would have been done. But no. Brevity. That was the cry. Brevity. Let us on.

The Tigers met the Giants at the Polo Grounds, and for five days the sweat of agony trickled unceasingly down the corrugated foreheads of the patriots who sat on the bleachers. The men from Detroit, freed from the fear of Clarence, smiled grim smiles and proceeded to knock holes through the fence. It was in vain that the home fielders skimmed like swallows around the diamond. They could not keep the score down. From start to finish the Giants were a beaten side.

Broadway during that black week was a desert. Gloom gripped Lobster Square. In distant Harlem red-eyed wives faced silently scowling husbands at the evening meal, and the children were sent early to bed. Newsboys called the extras in a whisper.

Few took the tragedy more nearly to heart than Daniel Rackstraw. Each afternoon found him more deeply plunged in sorrow. On the last day, leaving the ground with the air of a father mourning over some prodigal son, he encountered Mr. Jacob Dodson of Detroit.

Now, Mr. Dodson was perhaps the slightest bit shy on the finer feelings. He should have respected the grief of a fallen foe. He should have abstained from exulting. But he was in too exhilarated a condition to be magnanimous. Sighting Mr. Rackstraw, he addressed himself joyously to the task of rubbing the thing in. Mr. Rackstraw listened in silent anguish.

"If we had had Brown—" he said at length.

"That's what they all say," whooped Mr. Dodson. "Brown! Who's Brown?"

"If we had had Brown, we should have—" He paused. An idea had flashed upon his overwrought mind. "Dodson," he said, "listen here. Wait till Brown is well again, and let us play this thing off again for anything you like a side in my private park."

Mr. Dodson reflected.

"You're on," he said. "What side bet? A million? Two million? Three?"

Mr. Rackstraw shook his head scornfully.

"A million? Who wants a million? I'll put up my Neal Ball glove against your Hans Wagner bat. The best of three games. Does that go?"

"I should say it did," said Mr. Dodson joyfully. "I've been wanting that glove for years. It's like finding it in one's Christmas stocking."

"Very well," said Mr. Rackstraw. "Then let's get it fixed up."

Honestly, it is but a dog's life, that of the short-story writer. I particularly wished at this point to introduce a description of Mr. Rackstraw's country home and estate, featuring the private ball park with its fringe of noble trees. It would have served a double purpose, not only charming the lover of nature, but acting as a fine stimulus to the youth of the country, showing them the sort of home they would be able to buy some day if they worked hard and saved their money. But no. You shall have three guesses as to what was the cry. You give it up? It was "Brevity! Brevity!" Let us on.

The two teams arrived at the Rackstraw house in time for lunch. Clarence, his features once more reduced to their customary finely chiseled proportions, alighted from the automobile with a swelling heart. He could see nothing of Isabel, but that did not disturb him. Letters had passed between the two. Clarence had warned her not to embrace him in public, as McGraw would not like it; and Isabel accordingly had arranged a tryst among the noble trees which fringed the ball park.

I will pass lightly over the meeting of the two lovers. I will not describe the dewy softness of their eyes, the catching of their breath, their murmured endearments. I could, mind you. It is at just such descriptions that I am particularly happy. But I have grown discouraged. My spirit is broken. It is enough to say that Clarence had reached a level of emotional eloquence rarely met with among pitchers of the National League, when Isabel broke from him with a startled exclamation, and vanished behind a tree; and, looking over his shoulder, Clarence observed Mr. Daniel Rackstraw moving toward him.

It was evident from the millionaire's demeanor that he had seen nothing. The look on his face was anxious, but not wrathful. He sighted Clarence, and hurried up to him.

"Say, Brown," he said, "I've been looking for you. I want a word with you."

"A thousand, if you wish it," said Clarence courteously.

"Now, see here," said Mr. Rackstraw. "I want to explain to you just what this ball game means to me. Don't run away with the idea I've had you fellows down to play an exhibition game just to keep me merry and bright. If the Giants win today, it means that I shall be able to hold up my head again and look my fellow man in the face, instead of crawling around on my stomach and feeling like thirty cents. Do you get that?"

"I am hep," replied Clarence with simple dignity.

"And not only that," went on the millionaire. "There's more to it. I have put up my Neal Ball glove against Mr. Dodson's Wagner bat as a side bet. You understand what that means? It means that either you win or my life is soured for keeps. See?"

"I have got you," said Clarence.

"Good. Then what I wanted to say was this. Today is your day for pitching as you've never pitched before. Everything depends on whether you make good or not. With you pitching like mother used to make it, the Giants are some nine. Otherwise they are Nature's citrons. It's one thing or the other. It's all up to you. Win, and there's twenty thousand dollars waiting for you above what you share with the others."

Clarence waved his hand deprecatingly.

"Mr. Rackstraw," he said, "keep your dough. I care nothing for money."

"You don't?" cried the millionaire. "Then you ought to exhibit yourself in a dime museum."

"All I ask of you," proceeded Clarence, "is your consent to my engagement to your daughter."

Mr. Rackstraw looked sharply at him.

"Repeat that," he said. "I don't think I quite got it."

"All I ask is your consent to my engagement to your daughter."

"Young man," said Mr. Rackstraw, not without a touch of admiration, "you have gall."

"My friends have sometimes said so," said Clarence.

"And I admire gall. But there is a limit. That limit you have passed so far that you'd need to look for it with a telescope."

"You refuse your consent."

"I never said you weren't a clever guesser."

"Why?"

Mr. Rackstraw laughed. One of those nasty, sharp, metallic laughs that hit you like a bullet.

"How would you support my daughter?"

"I was thinking that you would help to some extent."

"You were, were you?"

"I was."

"Oh?"

Mr. Rackstraw emitted another of those laughs.

"Well," he said, "it's off. You can take that as coming from an authoritative source. No wedding bells for you."

Clarence drew himself up, fire flashing from his eyes and a bitter smile curving his expressive lips.

"And no Wagner bat for you!" he cried.

Mr. Rackstraw started as if some strong hand had plunged an auger into him.

"What!" he shouted.

Clarence shrugged his superbly modeled shoulders in silence.

"Say," said Mr. Rackstraw, "you wouldn't let a little private difference like that influence you any in a really important thing like this ball game, would you?"

"I would."

"You would hold up the father of the girl you love?"

"Every time."

"Her white haired old father?"

"The color of his hair would not affect me."

"Nothing would move you?"

"Nothing."

"Then, by George, you're just the son-in-law I want. You shall marry Isabel; and I'll take you into partnership this very day. I've been looking for a good, husky bandit like you for years. You make Dick Turpin look like a preliminary three-round bout. My boy, we'll be the greatest team, you and I, that ever hit Wall Street."

"Papa!" cried Isabel, bounding happily from behind her tree.

Mr. Rackstraw joined their hands, deeply moved, and spoke in low, vibrant tones:

"Play ball!"

Little remains to be said, but I am going to say it, if it snows. I am at my best in these tender scenes of idyllic domesticity.

Four years have passed. Once more we are in the Rackstraw home. A lady is coming down the stairs, leading by the hand her little son. It is Isabel. The years have dealt lightly with her. She is still the same stately, beautiful creature whom I would have described in detail long ago if I had been given half a chance. At the foot of the stairs the child stops and points at a small, wooden object in a glass case.

"Wah?" he says.

"That?" says Isabel. "That is the bat Mr. Wagner used to use when he was a little boy."

She looks at a door on the left of the hall, and puts a finger to her lip.

"Hush!" she says. "We must be quiet. Daddy and Grandpa are busy in there cornering wheat."

And softly mother and child go out into the sunlit garden.

——————————— FICTION ———————————

LEE ALLEN wrote, "It is said that when Thomas Wolfe died, a ticket to the Baseball Writers' dinner in New York was found in the suit he was wearing. One of Wolfe's greatest characters, Nebraska Crane, was a big-league player, although a completely fictional one. It is thought that he represented Wolfe's childish ambition to become a player."

From *You Can't Go Home Again*

THOMAS WOLFE

AT THE FAR END of the car a man stood up and started back down the aisle toward the washroom. He walked with a slight limp and leaned upon a cane, and with his free hand he held onto the backs of the seats to brace himself against the lurching of the train. As he came abreast of George, who sat there gazing out the window, the man stopped abruptly. A strong, good-natured voice, warm, easy, bantering, unafraid, unchanged—exactly as it was when it was fourteen years of age—broke like a flood of living light upon his consciousness:

"Well I'll be dogged! Hi, there, Monkus! Where you goin'?"

At the sound of the old jesting nickname George looked up quickly. It was Nebraska Crane. The square, freckled, sunburned visage had the same humorous friendliness it had always had, and the tar-black Cherokee eyes looked out with the same straight, deadly fearlessness. The big brown paw came out and they clasped each other firmly. And, instantly, it was like coming home to a strong and friendly place. In another moment they were seated together, talking with the familiarity of people whom no gulf of years and distance could alter or separate.

George had seen Nebraska Crane only once in all the years since he himself had first left Libya Hill and gone away to college. But he had not lost sight of him. Nobody had lost sight of Nebraska Crane. That wiry, fearless little figure of the Cherokee boy who used to come down the hill on Locust Street with the bat slung over his shoulder and the well-oiled fielder's mitt protruding from his hip pocket had been prophetic of a greater destiny, for Nebraska had become a professional baseball player, he had crashed into the big leagues, and his name had been emblazoned in the papers every day.

The newspapers had had a lot to do with his seeing Nebraska that other time. It was in August 1925, just after George had returned to New York from his first trip abroad. That very night, in fact, a little before midnight, as he was seated in a Childs Restaurant with smoking wheatcakes, coffee, and an ink-fresh copy of next morning's *Herald-Tribune* before him, the headline jumped out at him: "Crane Slams Another Homer." He read the account of the game eagerly, and felt a strong desire to see Nebraska again and to get back in his blood once more the honest tang of America. Acting on a sudden impulse, he decided to call him up. Sure enough, his name was in the book, with an address way up in the Bronx. He gave the number and waited. A man's voice answered the phone, but at first he didn't recognize it.

"Hello! . . . Hello! . . . Is Mr. Crane there? . . . Is that you, Bras?"

"Hello." Nebraska's voice was hesitant, slow, a little hostile, touched with the caution and suspicion of mountain people when speaking to a stranger. "Who is that? . . . Who? . . . Is that *you*, Monk?"—suddenly and quickly, as he recognized who it was. "Well I'll be dogged!" he cried. His tone was delighted, astounded, warm with friendly greeting now, and had the somewhat high and faintly howling quality that mountain people's voices often have when they are talking to someone over the telephone: the tone was full, sonorous, countrified, and a little puzzled, as if he were yelling to someone on an adjoining mountain peak on a gusty day in autumn when the wind was thrashing through the trees. "Where'd you come from? How the hell are you, boy?" he yelled before George could answer. "Where you been all this time, anyway?"

"I've been in Europe. I just got back this morning."

"Well I'll be dogged!"—still astounded, delighted, full of howling friendliness. "When am I gonna see you? How about comin' to the game tomorrow? I'll fix you up. And say," he went on rapidly, "if you can stick aroun' after the game, I'll take you home to meet the wife and kid. How about it?"

So it was agreed. George went to the game and saw Nebraska knock another home run, but he remembered best what happened afterwards. When the player had had his shower and had dressed, the two friends left the ball park, and as they went out a crowd of young boys who had been waiting at the gate rushed upon them. They were those dark-faced, dark-eyed, dark-haired little urchins who spring up like dragon seed from the grim pavements of New York, but in whose tough little faces and raucous voices there still remains, curiously, the innocence and faith of children everywhere.

"It's Bras!" the children cried. "Hi, Bras! Hey, Bras!" In a moment they were pressing round him in a swarming horde, deafening the ears with their shrill cries, begging, shouting, tugging at his sleeves, doing everything they could to attract his attention, holding dirty little scraps of paper toward him, stubs of pencils, battered little notebooks, asking him to sign his autograph.

He behaved with the spontaneous warmth and kindliness of his character. He scrawled his name out rapidly on a dozen grimy bits of paper, skillfully working his way along through the yelling, pushing, jumping group, and all the time keeping up a rapid fire of banter, badinage, and good-natured reproof:

"All right—give it here, then! . . . Why don't you fellahs pick on somebody else once in a while? . . . Say, boy!" he said suddenly, turning to look down at one unfortunate child, and pointing an accusing finger at him—"what you doin' aroun' here again today? I signed my name fer you at least a dozen times!"

"No, sir. Misteh Crane!" the urchin earnestly replied. "Honest—not me!"

"Ain't that right?" Nebraska said, appealing to the other children. "Don't this boy keep comin' back here every day?"

They grinned, delighted at the chagrin of their fellow petitioner. "Dat's right, Misteh Crane! Dat guy's got a whole book wit' nuttin' but yoeh name in it!"

"Ah-h!" the victim cried, and turned upon his betrayers bitterly. "What youse guys tryin' to do—get wise or somep'n? Honest, Misteh Crane!—" he looked up earnestly again at Nebraska—"Don't believe 'em! I jest want yoeh ottygraph! Please, Misteh Crane, it'll only take a minute!"

For a moment more Nebraska stood looking down at the child with an expression of mock sternness; at last he took the outstretched notebook, rapidly scratched his name across a page, and handed it back. And as he did so, he put his big paw on the urchin's head and gave it a clumsy pat; then, gently and playfully, he shoved it from him and walked off down the street.

The apartment where Nebraska lived was like a hundred thousand others in the Bronx. The ugly yellow brick building had a false front, with meaningless little turrets at the corners of the roof, and a general air of spurious luxury about it. The rooms were rather small and cramped, and were made even more so by the heavy, overstuffed Grand Rapids furniture. The walls of the living room, painted a mottled, rusty cream, were bare except for a couple of sentimental colored prints, while the place of honor over the mantel was reserved for an enlarged and garishly tinted photograph of Nebraska's little son at the age of two, looking straight and solemnly out at all comers from a gilded oval frame.

Myrtle, Nebraska's wife, was small and plump, and pretty in a doll-like way. Her cornsilk hair was frizzled in a halo about her face, and her chubby features were heavily accented by rouge and lipstick. But she was simple and natural in her talk and bearing, and George liked her at once. She welcomed him with a warm and friendly smile and said she had heard a lot about him.

They all sat down. The child, who was three or four years old by this time, and who had been shy, holding onto his mother's dress and peeping out from behind her, now ran across the room to his father and began climbing all over him. Nebraska and Myrtle asked George a lot of questions about himself, what he had been doing, where he had been, and especially what countries he had visited in Europe. They seemed to think of Europe as a place so far away that anyone who had actually been there was touched with an unbelievable aura of strangeness and romance.

"Whereall did you go over there, anyway?" asked Nebraska.

"Oh, everywhere, Bras," George said—"France, England, Holland, Germany, Denmark, Sweden, Italy—all over the place."

"Well I'll be dogged!"—in frank astonishment. "You sure do git aroun', don't you?"

"Not the way *you* do, Bras. You're traveling most of the time."

"Who—*me?* Oh, hell, I don't get anywhere—just the same ole places. Chicago, St. Looie, Philly—I seen 'em all so often I could find my way blindfolded!" He waved them aside with a gesture of his hand. Then, suddenly, he looked at George as though he were just seeing him for the first time, and he reached over and slapped him on the knee and exclaimed: "Well I'll be dogged! How you doin', anyway, Monkus?"

"Oh, can't complain. How about you? But I don't need to ask that. I've been reading all about you in the papers."

"Yes, Monkus," he said. "I been havin' a good year. But, boy!—" he shook his head suddenly and grinned—"do the ole dogs feel it!"

He was silent a moment, then he went on quietly:

"I been up here since 1919—that's seven years, and it's a long time in this game. Not many of 'em stay much longer. When you been shaggin' flies as long as that you may lose count, but you don't need to count— your legs'll tell you."

"But, good Lord, Bras, *you're* all right! Why, the way you got around out there today you looked like a colt!"

"Yeah," Nebraska said, "maybe I *looked* like a colt, but I felt like a plow horse." He fell silent again, then he tapped his friend gently on the knee with his brown hand and said abruptly, "No, Monkus. When you been in this business as long as I have, you know it."

"Oh, come on, Bras, quit your kidding!" said George, remembering that the player was only two years older than himself. "You're still a young man. Why, you're only twenty-seven!"

"Sure, sure," Nebraska answered quietly. "But it's like I say. You cain't stay in this business much longer than I have. Of course, Cobb an' Speaker an' a few like that—they was up here a long time. But eight years is about the average, an' I been here seven already. So if I can hang on a few years more, I won't have no kick to make. . . . Hell!" he said in a moment, with the old hearty ring in his voice, "I ain't got no kick to make, no way. If I got my release tomorrow, I'd still feel I done all right . . . Ain't that so, Buzz?" he cried genially to the child, who had settled down on his knee, at the same time seizing the boy and cradling him comfortably in his strong arm. "Ole Bras has done all right, ain't he?"

"That's the way me an' Bras feel about it," remarked Myrtle, who during this conversation had been rocking back and forth, placidly ruminating on a wad of gum. "Along there last year it looked once or twice as if Bras might git traded. He said to me one day before the game, "Well, ole lady, if I don't get some hits today somethin' tells me you an' me is goin' to take a trip.' So I says, 'Trip where?' An' he says, 'I don't know, but they're goin' to sell me down the river if I don't git goin', an' somethin' tells me it's now or never!' So I just looks at him," continued Myrtle placidly, "an' I says, 'Well, what do you want me to do? Do you want me to come today or not?' You know, gener'ly, Bras won't let me come when he ain't hittin'—he says it's bad luck. But he just looks at me a minute, an' I can see him sort of studyin' it over, an' all of a sudden he makes up his mind an' says, 'Yes, come on if you want to; I couldn't have no more bad luck than I been havin', noway, an' maybe it's come time fer things to change, so you come on.' Well, I went—an' I don't know whether I brought him luck or not, but somethin' did," said Myrtle, rocking in her chair complacently.

"Dogged if she didn't!" Nebraska chuckled. "I got three hits out of four times up that day, an' two of 'em was home runs!"

"Yeah," Myrtle agreed, "an' that Philadelphia fast-ball thrower was throwin' 'em, too."

"He sure was!" said Nebraska.

"I know," went on Myrtle, chewing placidly, "because I heard some of the boys say later that it was like he was throwin' 'em up there from out of the bleachers, with all them men in shirt-sleeves right behind him, an' the boys said half the time they couldn't even see the ball. But Bras must of saw it—or been lucky—because he hit two home runs off of him, an' that pitcher didn't like it, either. The second one Bras got, he went stompin' an' tearin' around out there like a wild bull. He sure did look mad," said Myrtle in her customary placid tone.

"Maddest man I ever seen!" Nebraska cried delightedly. "I thought he was goin' to dig a hole plumb through to China. . . . But that's the way it was. She's right about it. That was the day I got goin'. I know one of the boys said to me later, 'Bras,' he says, 'we all thought you was goin' to take a ride, but you sure dug in, didn't you?' That's the way it is in this game. I seen Babe Ruth go fer weeks when he couldn't hit a balloon, an' all of a sudden he lams into it. Seems like he just cain't miss from then on."

All this had happened four years ago. Now the two friends had met again, and were seated side by side in the speeding train, talking and catching up on one another. When George explained the reason for his going home, Nebraska turned to him with open-mouthed astonishment, genuine concern written in the frown upon his brown and homely face.

"Well, what d'you know about that!" he said. "I sure am sorry, Monk." He was silent while he thought about it, and embarrassed, not knowing what to say. Then, after a moment: "Gee!—" he shook his head—"your aunt was one swell cook! I never will fergit it! Remember how she used to feed us kids—every danged one of us in the whole neighborhood?" He paused, then grinned up shyly at his friend: "I sure wish I had a fistful of them good ole cookies of hers right this minute!"

Nebraska's right ankle was taped and bandaged; a heavy cane rested between his knees. George asked him what had happened.

"I pulled a tendon," Nebraska said, "an' got laid off. So I thought I might as well run down an' see the folks. Myrtle, she couldn't come—the kid's got to git ready for school."

"How are they?" George asked.

"Oh, fine, fine. All wool an' a yard wide, both of 'em!" He was silent for a moment, then he looked at his friend with a tolerant Cherokee grin and said, "But I'm crackin' up, Monkus. Guess I cain't stan' the gaff much more."

Nebraska was only thirty-one now, and George was incredulous. Nebraska smiled good-naturedly again.

"That's an ole man in baseball, Monk. I went up when I was twenty-one. I been aroun' a long time."

The quiet resignation of the player touched his friend with sadness. It was hard and painful for him to face the fact that this strong and fearless creature, who had stood in his life always for courage and for victory, should now be speaking with such ready acceptance of defeat.

"But, Bras," he protested, "you've been hitting just as well this season as you ever did! I've read about you in the papers, and the reporters have all said the same thing."

"Oh, I can still hit 'em," Nebraska quietly agreed. "It ain't the hittin' that bothers me. That's the last thing you lose, anyway. Leastways, it's goin' to be that way with me, an' I talked to other fellahs who said it was that way with them." After a pause he went on in a low tone: "If this ole leg heals up in time, I'll go on back an' git in the game again an' finish out the season. An' if I'm lucky, maybe they'll keep me on a couple more years, because they know I can still hit. But, hell," he added quietly, "they know I'm through. They already got me all tied up with string."

As Nebraska talked, George saw that the Cherokee in him was the same now as it had been when he was a boy. His cheerful fatalism had always been the source of his great strength and courage. That was why he had never been afraid of anything, not even death. But, seeing the look of regret on George's face, Nebraska smiled again and went on lightly:

"That's the way it is, Monk. You're good up there as long as you're good. After that they sell you down the river. Hell, I ain't kickin'. I been lucky. I had ten years of it already, an' that's more than most. An' I been in three World's Serious. If I can hold on fer another year or two—if they don't let me go or trade me—I think maybe we'll be in again. Me an' Myrtle has figgered it all out. I had to help her people some, an' I bought a farm fer Mama an' the Ole Man—that's where they always wanted to be. An' I got three hundred acres of my own in Zebulon—all paid fer, too!—an' if I git a good price this year fer my tobacco, I stan' to clear two thousand dollars. So if I can git two years more in the League an' one more good World's Serious, why—" he turned his square face toward his friend and grinned his brown and freckled grin, just as he used to as a boy—"we'll be all set."

"And—you mean you'll be satisfied?"

"Huh? Satisfied?" Nebraska turned to him with a puzzled look. "How do you mean?"

"I mean after all you've seen and done, Bras—the big cities and the crowds, and all the people shouting—and the newspapers, and the headlines, and the World Series—and—and—the first of March, and St. Petersburg, and meeting all the fellows again, and spring training—"

Nebraska groaned.

"Why, what's the matter?"

"Spring trainin'."

"You mean you don't like it?"

"Like it! Them first three weeks is just plain hell. It ain't bad when you're a kid. You don't put on much weight durin' the winter, an' when you come down in the spring it only takes a few days to loosen up an' git the kinks out. In two weeks' time you're loose as ashes. But wait till you been aroun' as long as I have!" He laughed loudly and shook his head.

"Boy! The first time you go after a grounder you can hear your joints creak. After a while you begin to limber up—you work into it an' git the soreness out of your muscles. By the time the season starts, along in April, you feel pretty good. By May you're goin' like a house afire, an' you tell yourself you're good as you ever was. You're still goin' strong along in June. An' then you hit July, an' you get them double-headers in St. Looie! Boy, oh, boy!" Again he shook his head and laughed, baring big square teeth. "Monkus," he said quietly, turning to his companion, and now his face was serious and he had his black Indian look—"you ever been in St. Looie in July?"

"No."

"All right, then," he said very softly and scornfully. "An' you ain't played *ball* there in July. You come up to bat with sweat bustin' from your ears. You step up an' look out there to where the pitcher ought to be, an' you see four of him. The crowd in the bleachers is out there roastin' in their shirt-sleeves, an' when the pitcher throws the ball it just comes from nowheres—it comes right out of all them shirt-sleeves in the bleachers. It's on top of you before you know it. Well, anyway, you dig in an' git a toe-hold, take your cut, an' maybe you connect. You straighten out a fast one. It's good fer two bases if you hustle. In the old days you could've made it standin' up. But now—boy!" He shook his head slowly. "You cain't tell me nothin' about that ball park in St. Looie in July! They got it all growed out in grass in April, but after July first—" he gave a short laugh—"hell!—it's paved with concrete! An' when you git to first, them dogs is sayin', 'Boy, let's stay here!' But you gotta keep on goin'—you know the manager is watchin' you—you're gonna ketch hell if you don't take that extra base, it may mean the game. An' the boys up in the press box, they got their eyes glued on you, too—they've begun to say old Crane is playin' on a dime—an' you're thinkin' about next year an' maybe gittin' in another Serious—an' you hope to God you don't git traded to St. Looie. So you take it on the lam, you slide into second like the Twentieth Century comin' into the Chicago yards—an' when you git up an' feel yourself all over to see if any of your parts is missin', you gotta listen to one of that second baseman's wisecracks: 'What's the hurry, Bras? Afraid you'll be late fer the Veterans' Reunion?' "

"I begin to see what you mean, all right," said George.

"See what I mean? Why, say! One day this season I ast one of the boys what month it was, an' when he told me it was just the middle of July, I says to him: 'July, hell! If it ain't September I'll eat your hat!' 'Go ahead, then,' he says, 'an' eat it, because it ain't September, Bras—it's July.' 'Well,' I says, 'they must be havin' sixty days a month this year—it's the longest damn July *I* ever felt!' An' lemme tell you, I didn't miss it fer, either—I'll be dogged if I did! When you git old in this business, it may be only July, but you think it's September." He was silent for a moment.

"But they'll keep you in there, gener'ly, as long as you can hit. If you can smack that ole apple, they'll send you out there if they've got to use glue to keep you from fallin' apart. So maybe I'll git in another year or two if I'm lucky. So long's I can hit 'em, maybe they'll keep sendin' me out there till all the other players has to grunt every time ole Bras goes after a ground ball!" He laughed. "I ain't that bad yet, but soon's I am, I'm through."

"You won't mind it, then, when you have to quit?"

He didn't answer at once. He sat there looking out the window at the factory-blighted landscape of New Jersey. Then he laughed a little wearily:

"Boy, this may be a ride on the train to you, but to *me*—say!—I covered this stretch so often that I can tell you what telephone post we're passin' without even lookin' out the window. Why, hell yes!—" he laughed loudly now, in the old infectious way—"I used to have 'em numbered—now I got 'em *named!*"

"And you think you can get used to spending all your time out on the farm in Zebulon?"

"Git used to it?" In Nebraska's voice there was now the same note of scornful protest that it had when he was a boy, and for a moment he turned and looked at his friend with an expression of astonished disgust. "Why, what are you talkin' about? That's the greatest life in the world!"

AUTOBIOGRAPHY

"A LETTER TO MY SON" appeared in *Sport* magazine, the result of a series of interviews which Furman Bisher, sports editor of the *Atlanta Constitution* and a fine baseball writer, held with Rudy York. The letter was addressed to York's teen-age son, who wanted to become a professional ballplayer.

A Letter to My Son

RUDY YORK *as told to* FURMAN BISHER

DEAR SON:

You were only twelve years old and it couldn't have made much of an impression on you when the mailman delivered my release from the Philadelphia Athletics in January 1949. I wasn't surprised. I knew it was coming, for after you've played in only 31 games and hit .157, you know you're not scaring the pitchers any more and you know you're over the hill. Still, it's like death and taxes, and releases. You know they're bound to come, but you don't think about them until they hit you between the eyes.

The release was unconditional. No other club in the major leagues wanted to sign me. So there I was, washed up at 35. Then I began the longest spring I ever spent. You were too young to realize it. All it meant to you was that I wouldn't be going off anywhere and that I'd be there at night when you came home from school. Nobody can know what it's like, unless you're one of the lucky guys who has been going off to a training camp ever since you were in your teens. And baseball players are lucky—lucky to have the ability to play the game, like you have. And lucky in a lot of other ways, if they use their heads. That's why I'm writing this to you. I want to help you use your head like I didn't use mine.

I made something like $250,000 in thirteen years in the majors, but when I was through I had nothing to show for it but the brick bungalow where we live, you and your mother, and your sister, Blanche Fay, and Mary Jane, before she got married. That's a mistake you can't take back, but there's a story that goes with it and I'll get around to that later.

That long spring gave me plenty of time to think, and I've been thinking ever since, for me and for you. The first thing I thought was that I hadn't used my head for anything but a place to hang my cap. Then I got to thinking about what I'd have done different if I had a chance to do it all over again, and that's where you come in. I made my mistakes, plenty of them, but I didn't have what you've got. I didn't have anybody going ahead for me telling me what it was like, and what to do and what not to do. I was on my own from the start.

You never have known much about my young days, so I'll tell you. I was born in a little mountain mill town, Ragland, Alabama, and then we moved to another mill town, Aragon, Georgia, and then to another mill town, Atco, Georgia, right over here where you've played ball yourself. That's where I grew up, right in the shadow of the mill here on the edge of Cartersville.

Our family was poor. We lived from hand to mouth, and from pay day to pay day, and the pay days were nothing like the major-league pay days later on. There were five of us kids, and when my parents were separated I had to quit the third grade and go to work in the mill to help feed all those mouths. That was the last time I saw the inside of a schoolroom. At the same age when you're going to school and getting an education, I was sweating in a mill.

I'm not going to say that you should have had it as hard as I did. I wouldn't wish that on anybody. But in the long run, it turned out just as well for me, I guess. I was thirteen years old and I could play baseball for the mill team. From that time on, all I ever knew was baseball, and I'm thankful for it, for baseball was my ticket out of the mill. I pitched, played the outfield or infield, and caught—anywhere they put me, just like you've been doing in high school and on the American Legion team. We're a lot alike in some ways. I just wanted to play, and so do you, and I could give the ball a long ride, and so can you. Somebody told Colonel Bob Allen in Knoxville about me. Knoxville was in the Southern Association in those days, and Allen asked me to meet the club in Atlanta for a tryout. That's how I got my start.

Knoxville signed me and kept me on the bench for about a month. Now, you'll run into all sorts of people in baseball, and you'll find them all, even the smart ones, making mistakes now and then. This Colonel Allen made one, and he was known as a smart baseball man. I could spit over the left-field fence in Knoxville. It was built for a right-handed power hitter like me. In fact, five years later Hank Greenberg and I hit eight over it in two days when Detroit stopped there on an exhibition tour.

But Colonel Allen made a mistake. He released me. If he had held onto me another year, he could have sold me for $50,000 or more.

I was playing semipro ball down in southern Georgia when Eddie Goosetree came through and signed me for Detroit later that year. That was the best break I ever got, because there never have been better people to play baseball for than the Briggs family.

There I was, just a kid nineteen years old, on my way to the big leagues. It sounds easy, but, son, that's where the hard knocks begin to set in, and you've got to find out if you can take it or not. There's a lot more to it than just stepping up to bat and knocking your way into the majors. You've got to remember to be patient. I went through enough to discourage most any kid, but baseball was all I knew and I stayed with it.

Here's what I mean. At Knoxville I was an outfielder. At Shreveport, where they sent me after Goosetree signed me, I was a second baseman. At Beaumont I was a catcher, pitcher, first baseman, third baseman and outfielder. At Fort Worth I was a catcher and outfielder. At Detroit I was a catcher, outfielder and third baseman before they finally put me on first base to stay.

I didn't ask any questions. I played where they told me and did the best I could. But I think the best thing for a young fellow like you is to find his position as soon as he can and stick to it. You've been playing all over, third base, outfield, first base and pitching. You're still young, but it's getting about time we figured out what is your best position.

You've got good footwork. That's awfully important in playing third, good foot action. If you're a good judge of a fly ball, maybe you ought to settle in the outfield, because you've got a good arm and you can hit. Anybody that hits around .500 for the Legion team, like you did a couple of years ago, hits enough to play the outfield, and hitting does come first out there. Your arm is good enough for pitching, too. We'll just have to see how that works out this year. There's no rush about it yet, but pretty soon it will be time to settle down to one position, before you start into pro ball, anyway.

It was a long time coming for me, but finally, in 1940, Del Baker, who managed the Tigers then, sent Greenberg to the outfield and me to first base. A lot of these big-league sports writers would try to make you believe I wasn't much of a fielder. I guess you've read that famous line in my scrapbooks that described me as "part Indian, part first baseman." Well, I can read you another line that said I was the best first baseman the Red Sox had during the Tom Yawkey regime, and there was a guy by the name of Jimmy Foxx there before me. The fielding averages show that your old man was a pretty good first baseman. I never was under .980 in the majors, and in 1947 I led the American League with .995. Because of the pivot he's got to make, it's difficult for a right handed first baseman to make the double play at second. Still, in 1943 I set a league record for assists by a first baseman, and the next year I set a major-league record for double plays by a first baseman.

But don't pay too much attention to averages of any kind. I'll confess that fielding averages don't always tell the whole truth. There was 1939, for instance, when I led the American League catchers in fielding. I'd be the last man in the world to claim that I was a good catcher. I threw sinkers to second; I was so big I had trouble shifting behind the plate— and that's mighty important—and I never was a bear on pop fouls. I never was a good outfielder, either. I always did insist they should have let me wear the mask out there. But just to show you how deceiving those averages are—in 1947, when I was traded from the Red Sox to the White Sox, my batting average was only .233, but I hit 21 homers and drove in 91 runs.

I never was much of a hitter for an average, but a fellow who winds up with .275, 277 homers, drives in 1,152 runs and plays in three World Series and five All-Star games in the majors shouldn't feel too badly about his career. My best season was 1943, when I led the league in total bases, home runs and runs batted in.

When you do settle down to that one position, son, work at it, slave at it, if necessary. I guess I didn't do as well at all the positions as I did at first base because I didn't work as hard at them. There was one stretch, though, when I gave third base everything I had. Mickey Cochrane was managing the Tigers in 1936 and he decided I was a third baseman. For a month during spring training, I and Del Baker—he was a coach then —and twenty baseballs played third base. Del wore out the fungo bat hitting ground balls to me before and after exhibition games. During the games I played first base, for Greenberg was holding out, and Marv Owen, a pretty fair country ballplayer, was at third. But they were going to make a third baseman out of me and put me in the infield with Billy Rogell at short, Charley Gehringer at second and Greenberg at first.

When Greenberg signed, though, they decided I wasn't a third baseman, either. They sent me to Milwaukee, and when the American Association opened, I was a first baseman again. I had my greatest season, was voted the most valuable player, and went back to Detroit to stay. But I was still a man without a position.

This had been going on since the time I reported to Beaumont, Texas, in 1934. Beaumont had two fine catchers, Mike Tresh and Dutch Lorbeer, but Jack Zeller, the Detroit farm director, said I was a catcher. I worked five weeks taking lessons in catching, and on opening day Zeller called me in.

"Did you ever play first base?" he asked me.

"I've fooled around with it some," I told him.

"Well, you're our first baseman," he said. Just like that.

I didn't even have a first baseman's mitt, and George Archie, who had been playing first, wouldn't let me use his. I played the bag with a finger glove until Greenberg sent me a mitt from Detroit. That was the first thing he ever did for me, but he's done a lot for me since, especially in the last few years when I've needed help. He's the best friend a guy ever had.

When I got to Detroit, it was more of the same. I reported on my birthday, August 17, 1934, and that No. 24 that I put on my back was the first major-league uniform I ever saw. First thing when I arrived, Mickey Cochrane said to me: "You're a catcher, aren't you?"

I told him I had caught some, so they gave me a mitt and sent me to the bull pen.

As I said, that sort of thing went on for years. The newspapermen always wrote that they couldn't find a position for me. They had the position, but Hank Greenberg was playing it. Nobody was moving Greenberg off first—not until they saw that I had to play there or no place at all. That's why I say, find your position and stick to it and work at it every minute. Become so good at it that nobody can move you.

It's a good business, too, in these days of the bonus. I'm not one of these fellows, son, who thinks "bonus" is a nasty word. If a boy is worth it, I think he should collect when he signs. There are always stories about bonuses ruining young ballplayers. I don't believe it—that money can ruin a boy who's got the ability and the character. If he's got it, he's going to make it. A bonus won't hinder the right kind of kid. I hope you're going to be good enough to get a bonus when you sign, because it's nice to have a bank account to start out with. A lot of lucky things have happened to ballplayers since I was a kid. Once you get to the big leagues you'll get in on this pension plan, a great thing for the player. I'm looking forward to becoming eligible for my pension. It's almost ten years away, but when I reach fifty I start drawing $100 a month. That's an advantage you've got to build on, and it's another reason you should put everything you've got into reaching the big leagues.

Since hitting runs in the family, I guess it comes natural with you. I like to think you're a chip off the old block, a hitting fool. But don't go power crazy. Use good judgment as you go along. You're just seventeen and you shouldn't be using a heavy bat just because it has a star's name on it. Get a bat you can master, about 28 or 30 ounces now, and increase the weight as you go. As the season goes on and the days get hotter you'll find the bat getting heavier and heavier, anyway.

Still, the best hitting streak I ever had was in August, the hottest month of them all. That was in 1937, when I hit eighteen homers in one month and broke Babe Ruth's record of seventeen. Incidentally, that happened while I was catching. Mickey Cochrane had been beaned and I took his place. I went into the last day of the month needing two homers for the record. I honestly never gave it much thought. You just don't think about things like that; they either happen or they don't. We played Washington and I got my two, both off Pete Appleton. It's a strange thing, but August always was my month. I could hit anything they threw at me, golf ball, tennis ball or Ping-pong ball.

Son, there are some things about my baseball career I'm proud of, and some I'm not so proud of. They gave me a reputation for boozing, but you can take any story about ballplayers and drinking with several grains of salt. Sure, I had my drink when I wanted it. So did a lot of other fellows. But remember this—I'm an Indian, so that means you're part Indian, too. All an Indian's got to do is be seen drinking a beer and he's drunk. Any time an Indian puts on a baseball uniform he becomes about six times as much of a character as any other player.

We're Cherokee and I'm proud of it. I've run into some pretty good Indian ballplayers in my time, like Bob and Roy Johnson, Ben Tincup, Chief Bender and Elon Hogsett, who was my roommate at Detroit for a while. I'd like to add the name of Joe Wilburn York to that list.

You've noticed that scar on my left cheek. I got it when I was nine years old. I ran into an axe my brother was swinging while he chopped wood. It makes me look tough, I guess, so I didn't have to do much to be called a bad boy.

But son, leave that liquor alone. I can tell you it never helped anybody, and if I had to do it over again that's one thing I'd use a lot less. I'd have had a couple more years of baseball left in me if I'd stayed away from it.

I guess you've read in the scrapbooks that I led the major leagues in arson. I've gone to sleep with a cigarette in my hand and smoked up a hotel room a little, but by the time the stories went the rounds, I was supposed to have set fire to every hotel in the country. When I was with the White Sox in '47, I was two blocks down the street buying a shirt when fire engines pulled up at the Stevens Hotel, where I lived. When

I got to the lobby I heard there was a fire on my floor, and on my floor I heard it was in my room. But a cigar started that one, and I never did smoke cigars.

What all this means is that ballplayers have to be twice as careful of their behavior away from their work as anybody else. On the field I never had any trouble, and I hope you get along with umpires as well as I did. I never "got on" them because I figured they had a job to do, too, and that they were going to make some mistakes, same as me. I have no raps against umpires and I think they have none against me.

Don't be a clubhouse lawyer, either. That has ruined as many good ballplayers as booze has. Go about your job and keep your mouth shut, except to kid with the fellows. Leave the lawyering to somebody else. The only time I ever really raised my voice in the clubhouse was in 1946, when I was with the Red Sox and we were battling for the pennant. It was a close race and one day it seemed to some of us that Ted Williams was slow playing a hit out in left field. A run scored on it and we lost the game. When we got to the clubhouse I had a few things to say to him. "We're about to win this pennant," I told him, "and everybody's in it together. All we got to do is play our best and we've got it in the bag. Anybody who loafs on this ball club has got to answer to me. I'm about washed up and you've got a long way to go. I'm not aiming to let a pennant slip away from me now, and I'm not aiming to see you let it slip away, either."

Williams was a good friend of mine and he took it in the right spirit. I always did say he's the greatest hitter I ever saw step in the box. He's one of those rare fellows with so much natural talent that he didn't have to work at it much.

Be sure not to forget the folks back home. Make friends here in Cartersville, for this is where you're going to live. I don't think I left an enemy behind in baseball, and I can't think of a man I played with or against that I don't like. That's a pretty good record, when you consider the jealousies and the competition in the game. I never was much for emotion; it isn't part of my nature. But I always tried to be friendly. Newspapermen were nice to me, too, in spite of some of the things they wrote about me. I've even got a lot of respect for Dave Egan, a Boston writer that most of the guys hated. I've got to give him credit for being smart. But I never did put much into making friends back home. I don't think it was all my fault, though, even if I was a little stand-offish. I never was one for standing on the street corner or in the drugstore shooting the breeze. I like to hunt, and you know yourself how much time we've spent together out with the bird dogs.

Not many folks around Cartersville paid me much attention, except when I was in trouble. I can understand some of it now, though, for to them I was an Indian from the mill village. They were glad to claim me and brag about me when I was hitting home runs, but when the shouting was over they weren't breaking their backs to socialize with me.

I said I wasn't much of a hitter for an average. The reason I wasn't was I learned to hit just one way—overpower the ball. I want you to learn how to hit with the pitch. In other words, if it's an outside pitch, punch it into right field. If that ball was outside to me, I was willing to take a strike. Those pitchers will have more respect for you if you're able to meet the ball where it is instead of trying to pull everything. Del Baker was one reason I hit as well as I did. The guy is the greatest sign-stealer who ever lived, and he used to call the pitches for me. When I knew what was coming I could usually hit it a mile.

You'll find that players have funny hitting habits, anyway, as you go along. Charley Gehringer was the best second baseman who ever lived, and Charley had a habit of taking the first pitch. We roomed together some when I was with the Tigers and I asked him once why he did it.

"So the pitcher can start off even with me," he said.

That Charley was a card. He didn't say much, but when he did, he was a card. I hope you're lucky enough to have some good friends like him and Greenberg.

I said earlier there's a story that explains why I'm broke and fighting fires for the Georgia Forestry Commission for $150 a month. Like I wrote, I made a lot of money, around $250,000, maybe more. But I never saved any. When I started making money it burned a hole in my pocket. I'd never had anything when I was a kid, and I wanted to spend it for things I'd always wanted, and for you and Viola and the rest of the family. You can imagine what happens to a poor mill-town boy who makes $40,000 a year, which I did in '41. I bought new cars every year. I'd take long hunting trips, like that time when I packed all of us off to South Dakota. I bought everything in sight. But the best buy I ever made was our house. I'd be in bad shape if I didn't have it now.

When you start making money, son, get an adviser, somebody to help you invest it. I never did know who I could trust, and the only place I ever put mine was in a checking account, and that made it too easy to get at. Get your money to work for you, because I don't want you to finish up with nothing to show for it but your clippings. You never think it's going to end while you're riding high. I lived from game to game and for each time I went to bat. I was always happy with a bat in my hand.

Don't be shortsighted. Remember there's a future after you're through playing ball. If you make a good name and a good reputation for yourself, you can always stay in baseball. There'll always be a good job as a manager, or a coach, or in some end of the game, for a fellow who conducts himself wisely while he's a player. If I do say so myself, you're smart, you've got a good head on your shoulders, and I want to see you use it. Go ahead and play your football and basketball now, but when you get out of high school, put everything else away but baseball.

I had it pretty rough trying to stay with baseball after the Athletics released me. Me and the minor leagues didn't get along too well. In June 1949, I got a call to manage Griffin, Georgia, in the Georgia-Alabama League, Class D.

"We've got a team," the man told me over the telephone. "All we need is a manager."

Buck Etchison, who played some first base for the Braves, had been the manager, and when I got there I could see why he had left. They had two ballplayers. The rest were a bunch of kids who couldn't tie their shoelaces. They were in last place when I got there and they finished last. That's where they belonged. You remember when I came back home and Greenberg called me to finish out the season managing Union City, Tennessee, in the Kitty League.

Then, in 1951, Greenberg came for me again, to play for Youngstown, Ohio, in the Middle Atlantic League. Now, there was an experience. By June 1, we had drawn 1,912 attendance, believe it or not. They moved the franchise to Oil City, Pennsylvania, and after Mike Garbark, the old Yankee catcher, quit as manager, I took over. I had a great season as a player, hit 34 homers, drove in 107 runs and had an average of .291. But we won just 24 games before the club disbanded in August.

That was the end of my playing days. Now it's either managing or scouting or coaching for me, or I'm out of baseball, and I hate to think of having to give it up. After all, it's the only life I ever knew, and it was good to me. That's why I'm warning you not to abuse your opportunity and to profit by the mistakes your old man made.

I saw sights I'd never seen before, rode in Pullman cars, stayed in fancy hotels and ate high-priced food. I'll never forget the first time I saw Yankee Stadium. "They don't play baseball here, do they?" I asked Gehringer. "It's too big."

You can imagine what it was like the first time I saw a subway in New York. I was afraid they'd run so fast they'd never come out from under the ground. Everything was pretty exciting in those days.

I've had my picture on breakfast cereal signs as big as the side of a house. I've had kids mob me for my autograph. I've heard thousands cheer for me, like the time when I hit the home run that beat the Cardinals in the first game of the 1946 World Series. I've been rich. It was a great life and I miss it.

That's the reason I'm writing this to you. I want to save you the heartaches I've had. I want to tell you about the mistakes you might make before you make them. I want you to have everything I had, plus the advantage of an assured future after you're through playing. There's nothing that would make me happier than to see you play in the major leagues, and some day you'll get there. When you do, make the most of it. Live a little, but plan a lot. Look around you. You can learn something every day. Listen. There's always somebody willing to give you a helping hand, if you'll take it. And when you're through, there'll be somebody there with a job for you. You won't have to give it up and come back home to fight fires for $150 a month.

I made enough mistakes for both of us. Let it stay that way. Sure, I lived, but I'd be living a lot better now. I want to be sure that you do when it comes time for you to put your glove and bat away. I don't want you to have to write a letter to your son about the mistakes you've made.

Your Dad,
RUDY YORK

─────────── SPOT REPORTING ───────────

COVERING BASEBALL, as opposed to other sports, is often easier from the pressure standpoint, because the more that happens, the more time you have to work with in the press box—a big rally will lead to the changing of pitchers, which takes time, and so forth. The exception is the last-minute stroke that changes everything—Thomson's home run, for example, and certainly this game, which had the most unforgettable ending in the history of the World Series. Dick Young of the *New York Daily News*, with a deadline and a totally unforeseen climax thrown in his lap, wrote an unforgettable story.

1947:
Brooklyn Dodgers 3,
New York Yankees 2

DICK YOUNG

OUT OF THE MOCKERY and ridicule of "the worst World Series in history," the greatest baseball game ever played was born yesterday. They'll talk about it forever, those 33,443 fans who saw it. They'll say: "I was there. I saw Bill Bevens come within one out of the only series no-hitter; I saw the winning run purposely put on base by the Yankees; I saw Cookie Lavagetto send that winning run across a moment later with a pinch-hit double off the right-field wall—the only hit, but big enough to give the Brooks the 3-2 victory that put them even-up at two games apiece."

And maybe they'll talk about the mad minute that followed—the most frenzied scene ever erupted in this legendary spot called Ebbets

Field: How some of the Faithful hugged each other in the stands; how others ran out to the center of the diamond and buried Lavagetto in their caresses; how Cookie's mates pushed the public off because they themselves wanted the right to swarm all over him; how Cookie, the man who had to plead for his job this spring, finally fought his way down the dugout steps—laughing and crying at the same time in the first stages of joyous hysteria.

Elsewhere in the park, another man was so emotionally shaken he sought solitude. That was Branch Rickey, the supposedly cold, calloused businessman, the man who has seen thousands and thousands of ball games and should therefore be expected to take anything in stride. But Rickey had to be alone. He left his family, sat down in a quiet little room just off the press box, and posted a guard outside the door.

After ten minutes of nerve-soothing ceiling-staring, Rickey was asked if he'd see a writer. He would. Now he was calm and wanted to talk. He wanted to talk about the ninth-inning finish—but he started a little earlier than that.

He flashed back to the top half of the frame, when Hughie Casey had come in with the bases loaded and one out, and got Tommy Henrich to hit a DP ball right back at him on the first serve. "Just one pitch, and he's the winning pitcher of a World Series game," Branch chuckled. "That's wonderful."

Rickey then turned to his favorite subject. "It was speed that won it," he said. This tickled Rickey because it had been the speed of Al Gionfriddo which saved the game. They had laughed at Gionfriddo when he came to the Brooks back in June in that $300,000 deal with the Pirates. They had said: "What did Rickey get that little squirt for; to carry the money in a satchel from Pittsburgh?" And they had added, "He'll be in Montreal in a couple of weeks."

But, here it was World Series time, and "little Gi" was still around. Suddenly he was useful. Furillo was on first with two out. Carl had got there just as eight Brooks before him had—by walking. For a prospective no-hit pitcher, Bevens had been under constant pressure because of control trouble. A couple of these passes had led to the Brooks' run in the fifth, and had cut New York's lead down to 2-1.

That's the way it still was when Gionfriddo went in to run for Furillo, and Pete Reiser was sent up to swing for Casey. Only now Bevens was just one out away from having his bronze image placed among the all-time greats in Cooperstown. Already, at the conclusion of the eighth frame, the chubby Yank righty had pitched the longest string of no-hit ball in series history—topping Red Ruffing's 7 innings against the Cards in '42.

Now Bill was out for the jackpot. He got the first out in the ninth on a gasp provoker, a long drive by Edwards which forced Lindell up against the left wall for the stretching grab. Furillo walked and Jorgensen fouled meekly to McQuinn, who was white as a sheet as he made the catch.

One out to go—and then came the first of several switches that were destined to make a genius of Burt Shotton and an eternal second-guess target of Bucky Harris.

"Reiser batting for Casey," boomed the loudspeaker, "and Gionfriddo running for Furillo."

Soon the count was 2-1 on Pete. Down came the next pitch—and up went a feverish screech. Gionfriddo had broken for second. Berra's peg flew down to second—high, just high enough to enable Gi to slide head first under Rizzuto's descending tag. For the briefest moment, all mouths snapped shut and all eyes stared at umpire Babe Pinelli. Down went the umpire's plams, signaling that the Brooks had stolen base No. 7 on the weak-winged Yankee backstop corps.

The pitch on which Gionfriddo went down had been high, making the count on Reiser 3-and-1. Then came the maneuver that makes Bucky Harris the most second-guessed man in baseball. The Yankee pilot signaled Berra to step out and take an intentional fourth ball from Bevens.

The cardinal principle of baseball had been disdained by Harris. The "winning run" had been put on—and Miksis replaced the sore-ankled Reiser on first.

It was possible for Reiser to hurt more than Stanky in such a situation —and the Brooks had run out of lefty pinch hitters. But a good right-side swinger, a clutch money player like Lavagetto, who batted for Muggsy, didn't get to be a fourteen-year man by being able to hit only one kind of chucking.

On the first pitch, Harris' guess still looked like a good one. Cookie swung at a fast ball and missed. Then another fast one, slightly high and toward the outside. Again Lavagetto swung. The ball soared toward the right corner—a territory seldom patronized by Cookie.

Because of that, Tommy Henrich had been swung over toward right-center. Frantically, Tommy took off after the drive, racing toward the line. He got there and leaped, but it was a hopeless leap. The ball flew some six feet over his glove and banged against the wooden wall. Gionfriddo was tearing around third and over with the tying run.

The ball caromed under Henrich's legs as Tommy struggled to put the brakes on his dash. On the second grab, Henrich clutched it and, still off balance, hurried a peg to McQuinn at the edge of the infield. The first-sacker whirled desperately and heaved home—but even as he loosed the ball, speedy young Miksis was plowing over the plate with a sitting slide. A big grin on his puss, Eddie, just turned 21 last week, sat right on home plate like an elated kid. He was home with the winning run, and he didn't want to get up. For what seemed like much more than the actual three or four seconds, Miksis just sat there, looked up at his mates gathered around the plate and laughed insanely.

That's when God's Little Green Acre became a bedlam. The clock read 3:51, Brooklyn Standard Time—the most emotional minute in the lives of thousands of Faithful. There was Lavagetto being mobbed—and off to the side, there was Bevens, head bowed low, walking dejectedly through the swarming crowd, and completely ignored by it. Just a few seconds earlier, he was the one everybody was planning to pat on the back. He was the one who would have been carried off the field—the only pitcher ever to toss a no-hitter in a series.

Now he was just another loser. It didn't matter that his one-hitter had matched the other classic performances of two Cub pitchers—Ed Reulbach against the Chisox in '06 and Passeau against Detroit in '45. The third one-hitter in series annals—but Bevens was still nothing more than a loser.

Bev felt bluer than Harry Taylor had at the start of this memorable struggle. In the first five minutes, Taylor had been a momentous failure. Unable to get his sore-elbowed arm to do what his mind demanded of it, the rookie righty had thrown his team into a seemingly hopeless hole before a Yankee had been retired.

Stirnweiss had singled. So had Henrich. And then Reese had dropped Robinson's peg of Berra's bouncer, loading the bases. Then Harry walked DiMaggio on four straight serves, forcing in a run. Still nobody out, still bases full. Taylor was through; he had been a losing gamble. In one inning, the Yanks were about to blow the game wide open and clamp a 3-1 lock on the series.

But, just as has happened so often this year, the shabby Brook pitching staff delivered a clutch performer. This time it was Hal Gregg, who had looked so mediocre in relief against the Yanks two days before. Gregg got McQuinn to pop up and then made Johnson bang a DP ball right at Reese.

Only one run out of all that mess. The Faithful regained hope. This optimism grew as DiMag was cut down at the plate attempting to score from first when Edwards threw McQuinn's dumpy third-frame single into short right. But, in the next stanza, as the Yanks did their only real teeing off on Gregg, the Brook hopes drooped. Johnson poled a tremendous triple to the center-field gate and Lindell followed with a booming two-bagger high off the scoreboard in right.

There was some hope, based on Bevens' own wildness. The Brooks couldn't buy a hit, but they had men aboard in almost every inning, sometime two. Altogether, Bev was to go on to issue ten passes, just topping the undesirable series record set by Jack Coombs of the A's in the 1910 grapple with the Cubs.

Finally, in the fifth, Bill's wildness cost him a run. He walked Jorgensen and Gregg to open the stanza. Stanky bunted them along, and Jorgy scored while Gregg was being nailed at third on Reese's grounder to Rizzuto. Pee Wee then stole second for his third swipe of the series, and continued on to third as Berra's peg flew into center. But Robinson left him there with a whiff.

Thus, before they had a hit, the Brooks had a run. And right about now, the crowd was starting to grow no-hit conscious. A fine catch by DiMaggio, on which Joe twisted his left ankle slightly, had deprived Hermanski of a long hit in the fourth, and Henrich's leaping stab of another Hermanski clout in front of the scoreboard for the final out in the eighth again saved Bill's blossoming epic.

Then the Yanks threatened to sew up the decision in the ninth. Behrman had taken over the chucking an inning earlier as a result of Gregg's being lifted for a pinch swinger and Hank got into a bases-bulging jam that wasn't exactly his responsibility. Lindell's lead-off hit through the left side was legit enough, but after Rizzuto forced Johnny, Bevens' bunt was heaved tardily to second by Bruce Edwards. Stirnweiss then looped a fist-hit into right center. Hugh Casey was rushed in.

Hugh threw one pitch, his million-dollar serve which had forced DiMag to hit into a key DP the day before. This time the low-and-away curve was jammed into the dirt by Henrich. Casey's glove flew out for a quick stab . . . the throw home . . . the relay to first . . . and Hughie was set up to become the first pitcher credited with World Series victories on successive days.

Tough luck cost Hughie two series defeats against these same Yanks in '41. Things are evened up a bit now.